The Ghost of One's Self

ALSO BY PAUL MEEHAN
AND FROM MCFARLAND

*Tech-Noir: The Fusion of Science Fiction
and Film Noir* (2008; softcover 2017)

The Vampire in Science Fiction Film and Literature (2014)

Horror Noir: Where Cinema's Dark Sisters Meet (2011)

*Cinema of the Psychic Realm:
A Critical Survey* (2009)

The Ghost of One's Self

Doppelgangers in Mystery, Horror and Science Fiction Films

PAUL MEEHAN

McFarland & Company, Inc., Publishers
Jefferson, North Carolina

LIBRARY OF CONGRESS CATALOGUING-IN-PUBLICATION DATA

Names: Meehan, Paul, 1948– author.
Title: The ghost of one's self : doppelgangers in mystery, horror and science fiction films / Paul Meehan.
Description: Jefferson, North Carolina : McFarland & Company, Inc., Publishers, 2017 | Includes bibliographical references and index. | Includes filmography.
Identifiers: LCCN 2017036256 | ISBN 9781476665665 (softcover : acid free paper) ∞
Subjects: LCSH: Doubles in motion pictures. | Identity (Psychology) in motion pictures. | Doppelgängers. | Motion pictures—Plots, themes, etc.
Classification: LCC PN1995.9.D635 M44 2017 | DDC 791.43/675—dc23
LC record available at https://lccn.loc.gov/2017036256

BRITISH LIBRARY CATALOGUING DATA ARE AVAILABLE

ISBN (print) 978-1-4766-6566-5
ISBN (ebook) 978-1-4766-3025-0

© 2017 Paul Meehan. All rights reserved

No part of this book may be reproduced or transmitted in any form or by any means, electronic or mechanical, including photocopying or recording, or by any information storage and retrieval system, without permission in writing from the publisher.

On the cover: Hugo Weaving as Agent Smith in *The Matrix Reloaded*, 2003 (Warner Bros./Photofest)

Printed in the United States of America

*McFarland & Company, Inc., Publishers
Box 611, Jefferson, North Carolina 28640
www.mcfarlandpub.com*

Table of Contents

Preface	1
One. The Ghost of One's Self	3
Two. Double, Double, Toil and Trouble: Literature	11
Three. Double Jeopardy: Crime, Mystery and Film Noir	30
Four. Twins of Evil: Horror Films	84
Five. Human Duplicators: Science Fiction Films	135
Six. Conclusion: Double Impact	211
Filmography	215
Chapter Notes	223
Bibliography	224
Index	225

Preface

This book grew out of a chapter of my 2011 book *Horror Noir* entitled "Hitchcock's Psychological Ghosts and Doppelgangers." The chapter explored director Alfred Hitchcock's fascination with the doppelganger theme in many of his key works. In writing this chapter I was informed and inspired by Donald Spoto's exhaustive biography of Hitch, *The Dark Side of Genius*, which explicated the famous director's obsession with the theme not only in the plots of a number of his films but also in their very structures. I am deeply indebted to the author's seminal treatment of the many "doublings" that characterize some of the greatest works by one of the most acclaimed artists in cinema history.

Seeing how prevalent the theme was in Hitchcock's works, I became curious about other films on the topic and discovered that there were numerous examples from a wide variety of genres, including adaptations of historical dramas such as *The Man in the Iron Mask*, *The Corsican Brothers* and *The Prince and the Pauper* as well as comedies like *The Nutty Professor* and *On the Double*. It soon became apparent, however, that the doppelganger was most apparent in the dark genres of mystery, horror and science fiction. These genres explored the theme within realms of the uncanny that best exemplified the fantastic nature of the concept. The scope of the book was therefore narrowed to only include films in these three categories.

While most previous studies of the doppelganger theme treat the idea as a purely psychological concept, I decided to explore the double as a real world phenomenon. As described in the first chapter of this book, the double can be perceived due to a variety of organic illnesses and psychiatric conditions. In addition, the doppelganger is also associated with psychic phenomena such as out of body experiences, bilocation, so-called "apparitions of the living" and shamanic dream states, and it therefore transcends a strictly psychological/literary model of the concept.

The doppelganger has been part of human existence since time immemorial and will no doubt continue to be part of our cinematic culture in the future.

CHAPTER ONE

The Ghost of One's Self

It looks just like you, down to the last detail.

It's you but it's not you. It's an inverse mirror image, a double, an alter ego, a simulacrum, a clone. It's your shadow self, your evil twin, your most significant other, your dark half.

It's your doppelganger.

For thousands of years, across many cultures, mankind has held folk beliefs about the existence of the doppelganger, a German word that translates as "double-walker." It is the exact twin of a living person that co-exists in some uncanny relationship with the original persona. The doppelganger, or "double," is generally thought to be a product of the Gothic and Victorian literary imagination and appears in famous works by Edgar Allan Poe, Guy de Maupassant, Robert Louis Stevenson, Fyodor Dostoyevsky, Oscar Wilde and others, but the idea of the doppelganger derives from folkloric beliefs found in many different cultures throughout the world and across many historical eras.

According to these beliefs, everyone is thought to have a double, an identical second self that is often the antithesis of one's original identity. Folklore beliefs are curiously consistent on one point: it is dangerous, or even fatal, to be in the same place at the same time as one's double, and seeing one's doppelganger is usually considered an omen of death or misfortune. In Celtic folklore, for instance, the double is referred to as the *fetch*, an identical twin that is said to appear at the moment of one's death, a kind of psychopomp that escorts the soul to the afterlife. In Norse mythology these beings were sometimes known as *vardogers*, ghostly doubles that mimic the doings of their living counterparts. The equivalent word in English is "wraith."

An episode involving the *fetch* occurs in *The Saga of Eirik the Red*, a medieval Norse book dating back to the 13th century. One passage relates how an illness caused the deaths of several workers on a farm in Greenland. "It was not long until the inhabitants caught the sickness, one after the other and died, until Thorstein Eiriksson and Sigrid, the farmer's wife, fell ill, too." One night Sigrid and Gudrid, Thorstein's wife, look out of the door of the farmhouse and Sigrid has a vision. "'All of those who are dead are standing there before the door; among them I recognize your husband Thorstein and myself as well. How horrible to see it!' Before morning came she was dead and a coffin made for her body.... Thorstein Eiriksson died near sundown."[1] Sigrid saw a vision of her *fetch*, a doppelganger that was a portent of her death.

The notion of the doppelganger usually engenders feelings of the uncanny that are associated with the loss of one's identity and uniqueness. It is psychologically disturbing to think that there is an alternate you lurking out there somewhere like a ghost of one's self. The German ghost story writer E.T.A. Hoffman wrote: "I imagine my ego being viewed through a lens: all the forms that move about me are egos; and whatever they do, or leave undone, vexes me."[2] In her doppelganger novel *Strangers on a Train*, mystery writer Patricia Highsmith eloquently expresses the concept thusly: "All things have opposites close by, every decision a reason against it, every animal an animal that destroys it.... Nothing could be without its opposite that was bound up with it.... Each was what the other had chosen not to be, the cast-off self, what he thought he hated but perhaps in reality loved ... there was that duality permeating nature.... Two people in every person. There's also a person exactly the opposite of you. Like the unseen part of you, somewhere in the world and he waits in ambush."[3]

Freud analyzed the psychological aspects of the doppelganger in his 1919 essay entitled "The Uncanny," in which he notes that the double is an object of terror, a harbinger of death that is associated with mirror-images, shadows, guardian spirits, the doctrine of the soul and the fear of death in primitive cultures. In the modern world, the doppelganger emerges from the narcissism of the child as a projection of multiple selves that serve to insure its immortality, but when it is encountered later in life, after the child has passed through its narcissistic state into adulthood, it is experienced as an aspect of the uncanny. According to Freud, the double is an externalized manifestation of the ego's repressed drives and desires, that is, everything that is unacceptable to it. He links the double to the formation of the superego, which projects these primitive repressions onto the uncanny double in a manner similar to the way that the gods of antiquity were transformed into demons after the demise of the pagan world. In his analysis, Freud cites German fantasy writer E.T.A. Hoffmann's novel *The Devil's Elixir* as exemplifying the doppelganger in literature (see Chapter Two).

Modern psychological theory may account for the doppelganger as an aspect of schizophrenia, organic disease or multiple personality disorder, but in pre–20th-century societies the double was thought to be a real being. A number of famous historical personages reportedly encountered their doubles. Perhaps the most well-known of these was President Abraham Lincoln in a mysterious incident that Lincoln himself reported to friends. On Election Day in 1860, Lincoln had become fatigued while waiting for election results to come in, and decided to go home to rest. Throwing himself down upon a couch in his chamber, he observed a double image of his face in a mirror on a bureau opposite him. This second visage was paler than his own, and Lincoln took this as an omen to mean that he would be elected twice, but would not survive his second term. While this double image may have been due to an illusion, a fault in the mirror or a defect in the President's vision, Lincoln was elected twice and was assassinated before completing his second term.

Catherine the Great, the Empress of Russia also reportedly encountered her doppelganger. The Tsarina was awakened in her bed one night by servants who were surprised to see her there because she had just been spotted in the throne room. In disbelief, Catherine hastened to the throne room, where she observed a double of herself sitting on the throne, whereupon she immediately ordered her guards to open fire on the apparition. While the fusillade did not seem to have an effect on the doppelganger, Catherine died of a stroke just a few weeks after the incident.

In his autobiography the great German poet Johann Wolfgang von Goethe relates the visionary experience of meeting his double while traveling on the road to the town of

Drusehneim. Goethe observed a figure on horseback coming toward him that he recognized as his doppelganger. The apparition was wearing a gray-colored garment edged with gold that stuck in his memory. This strange figure abruptly vanished, but eight years later Goethe found himself riding down the same road in the opposite direction wearing the same outfit he had seen in his vision years earlier.

The English poet Percy Bysshe Shelley reportedly encountered his double while staying at Pisa, Italy, with his wife, Mary, on June 23, 1822. Shelley told her that the figure addressed him with the words, "How long do you mean to be content?" Other people also reported seeing Shelley's double around this time. On July 8 the poet drowned in a boating accident in the Bay of Spezia, near Lerici. Mary Shelley had authored the seminal doppelganger novel *Frankenstein* (1818), while Shelley's poem *Prometheus Unbound* (1820) contains the following passage: "Ere Babylon was dust,/ The Magus Zoroaster, my dead child,/ Met his own image walking in the garden./ That apparition, sole of men, he saw./ For know that there are two worlds of life and death:/ One that which thou beholdest; but the other/ Is underneath the grave, where do inhabit/ The shadows of all forms that think and live/ Till death unite them and they part no more."[4]

The Swedish playwright and novelist August Strindberg, writing in his autobiographical novel *Inferno*, related how he found himself confronting an "unknown man" a duplicate self who copied his every movement and mannerism. Strindberg was more irritated than mystified by the doppelganger's antics. In a similar fashion, his fellow Swede Carl Linnaeus, the naturalist who invented the taxonomic classification system still in use today to classify plants and animals, would often observe his "other self," a double who would copy his every movement and even occupy his own seat at his library desk.

While these encounters with the doppelganger may appear uncanny, some of them may be explained by modern medicine. In his book *Hallucinations*, the late clinical neurologist Dr. Oliver Sacks (author of *Awakenings*, which was made into an Oscar-nominated film starring Robert De Niro and Robin Williams and the popular book *The Man Who Mistook His Wife for a Hat*) details how various neurological conditions can produce the hallucination of the double, including migraine, epilepsy, encephalitis and schizophrenia. In medical parlance, the apparition of the double is called "autoscopy." Sacks writes, "The autoscopic double is literally a mirror image of oneself, with right transposed to left and vice versa, mirroring one's positions and actions. The double is a purely physical phenomenon, with no identity or intentionality of its own. It has no desires and takes no initiatives; it is passive and neutral."[5]

Sacks relates how a young man being treated for temporal lobe seizures following a head injury was sitting in a café when he became aware of his double staring at him through the café window. The image did not speak, and vanished after a minute or so. Another patient, a young woman recovering from a coma and partial paralysis, started seeing an image of herself reflected as if in a mirror about a meter away. As the patient's condition improved, the mirror image of the double gradually faded away.

There is a more complex and extreme form of autoscopy called "heautoscopy," in which the apparition of the double is not merely passive but interacts with the person, usually in a hostile way. Unlike the autoscopic double, which only imitates the person's actions, the heautoscopic entity appears to have independent volition and freedom of action. Sacks writes: "Moreover, there may be deep bewilderment as to who is the 'original' and who the 'double,' for consciousness and sense of self tend to shift from one to the other. One may see the world first with one's own eyes, then through the double's eyes, and this can provoke the thought that he—the other—is the real person.... But the heautoscopic double, mocking or stealing one's identity, may arouse feelings of fear and horror and provoke impulsive and desperate acts."[6]

Dr. Sacks cites a case in which a young man suffering from temporal lobe epilepsy woke up one morning to find a double of himself still lying in bed asleep. Confused, he tried to wake the body in the bed by shouting at it and beating it, but the double remained asleep. Strangely, his point of view would sometimes switch to that of the double, where he lay paralyzed and helpless on the bed while his alter ego assaulted him. Becoming more and more agitated by the shifting perspectives of his consciousness, he decided to jump out of his third floor window to end the intolerable feeling of being divided. Fortunately, his fall was broken by a large bush underneath the window, and he woke up in the hospital, in pain but one person once more.[7]

A more tragic case from the 19th century involved a man who was haunted by a double who constantly argued with him and humiliated him with its superior powers of logical argument. Becoming more and more weary of the double's constant vitriolic tirades, he decided to end his life. He paid all his debts and put his affairs in order before shooting himself in the mouth with a pistol on the stroke of midnight on New Year's Eve.[8]

These two cases of heautoscopy have an uncanny quality despite their medical explanations. It is difficult, for instance, to conceive of an organic, neurological mechanism that has the capacity to shift a person's subjective viewpoint back and forth from that of the original person to their double, or to create a double that is intellectually superior to the original person. It's easy to see how these complex hallucinations could lead to a belief in the supernatural doppelganger. The 19th-century French writer Guy de Maupassant penned a story about a man who is plagued by an invisible and malignant doppelganger entitled "The Horla." At the time he wrote the story he was suffering from neurosyphilis that caused him to see hallucinations of his double on an almost daily basis.

The opposite of autoscopy and heautoscopy is a medical condition known as Capgras Syndrome or Capgras Delusion, in which the patient believes that the people around him have been replaced by doppelgangers. The syndrome is named for the French physician Joseph Capgras, who first diagnosed the condition in a patient he referred to as Madame M., who thought that her family and friends were not themselves but clever lookalikes. The delusion can even extend to the sufferer's pets or inanimate objects like articles of clothing. In one horribly tragic case, a man believed that his father had been replaced by a robot double and decapitated him in order to examine his insides.

Capgras Syndrome was originally thought to be purely psychological in nature, but more recent studies have linked it to head trauma and brain lesions, along with a number of diseases such as migraine, dementia and hypothyroidism. It surely provided inspiration for Jack Finney's seminal science fiction doppelganger novel *The Body Snatchers* (1955), in which the protagonist is a small town doctor who is faced with a mass outbreak of the delusion in a rural community that is in actuality a covert alien invasion.

So-called "out of body experiences" (or OBEs for short) can also produce the perception that one can view one's own body from a different vantage point. OBEs can occur during drug-induced altered states, self-induced trances, migraine attacks, or when the brain is not receiving enough oxygen due to cardiac arrest, massive loss of blood, or shock. Usually the percipients feel themselves floating upward toward the ceiling and look down to observe their bodies lying below. This is similar to the phenomenon of "bilocation" sometimes reported by psychics, in which one's viewpoint can appear to be in two places simultaneously. Sleep disorders such as sleep paralysis and associated hypnogogic and hypnopompic visions seen while falling asleep or waking up can also lead to the double perception of oneself while sleeping.

Some doppelganger experiences, however, seem to transcend materialist science. In 1886 the parapsychologists Edmund Gurney, Fredric W.H. Myers and Frank Podmore published their study entitled *Phantasms of the Living*, a book that chronicled many cases of so-called "crisis apparitions," in which the double of a person on their deathbed can appear to others in a different location. One famous example occurred on June 22, 1893, in which the doppelganger of British Vice-Admiral Sir George Tryon was seen walking through his drawing room in London by several guests at a party being given by his wife. The apparition of Sir George was observed looking straight ahead, and did not exchange a word with anyone. It was later learned that at that very moment the Admiral was going down with his ship, the *HMS Victoria* after a freak collision with the *HMS Camperdown* as the ships were maneuvering off the coast of Syria with the Mediterranean Squadron. Note that Sir George's double was collectively perceived by several different people at the party, a circumstance that makes it hard to explain away as a mere hallucination.

UCLA anthropologist Carlos Castaneda wrote a number of best-selling books during the 1960s and 70s about his purported experiences as a "sorcerer's apprentice" with Yaqui Indian shamans in Mexico who reportedly initiated him into mystical supernatural realms. In his 1974 book *Tales of Power*, Castaneda's teachers, the sorcerers Don Juan and Don Genaro, introduce him to their magical concept of the double. According to Don Juan, sorcerers possess a double that is a sort of augmented self that is developed through the magical process called *dreaming*, a process of gaining power that is accomplished through the controlled use of dreams. The double begins in a sorcerer's *dreaming*, and, once developed, is capable of unimaginable feats of power. The self and the double co-exist in two places at the same time, but have a completely separate awareness from each other. "A sorcerer has no notion that he is in two places at once," Don Juan explains to his apprentice. "To be aware of that would be the equivalent of facing his double, and the sorcerer that finds himself face to face with himself is a dead sorcerer. That is the rule."[9] He further elaborates, "You yourself are a dream and … your double is dreaming you."[10]

Castaneda's other mentor, Don Genaro, tells him about one of his first experiences with the double. He relates how he had fallen into a deep sleep one afternoon in his house in Central Mexico and was suddenly awakened by rain leaking through the roof. He went up on the roof and fixed the leak, but oddly, did not get wet. Going back in the house, he tried to have something to eat but found he was unable to swallow any food. When he tried to get back to sleep he was shocked to find himself still lying in his bed sound asleep. Panicked, he ran outside into the pouring rainstorm and walked about aimlessly until an intense burst of lightning and thunder suddenly woke him. He did not awaken in his bed at home, however, but in the hills in the rain.[11]

During their training, Don Juan and Don Genaro attempted to make Castaneda experience the double, with mixed results. While the magical stories in *Tales of Power* are dramatic and seem to ring true, the majority of anthropologists tend to regard Castaneda's books as works of novelistic fiction rather than objective anthropological fieldwork. There are some, however, who think that he may have had informants who were knowledgeable about Native American traditions. Whether they are fact or fiction, his tales of the double remain magical and strangely compelling.

An association between the double and dreaming states has become a theme in a number of recent science fiction films. In *The Matrix* (1999), the characters can project their consciousness into the alternate subjective reality of the matrix, where their digital doppelgangers have fantastic powers while their real bodies lie in a sleep-like torpor. Similarly, in *Avatar* (2009) the hero is enclosed in a hi-tech coffin that allows him to occupy the artificial body of an alien creature while in a dreaming state of REM sleep. *Surrogates* (2009) posits a future society in which everyone possesses an android double, a more youthful version of themselves that is remotely controlled via a mind-meld apparatus.

In many works of fiction, identical twins constitute another variation of the doppelganger theme. Throughout the centuries twins have held a special fascination in the human imagination and have been thought to possess special powers and abilities. In Roman mythology, for instance, Romulus and Remus were feral twins raised by wolves who were believed to have founded the city of Rome. Similarly, the Mayan book *Popul Vuh* chronicles the exploits of the magical twin culture heroes Xbalanque and Hunahpu.

Identical (monozygotic) twins are formed when a single fertilized egg cell, or zygote, splits into two separate embryos. The embryos then develop into two offspring that are genetically identical. Twins are said to share a special dual consciousness, a sort of telepathic link that creates a bond that is deeper than any other type of human relationship. Twins have a saying that if they stand back to back they can see the world from a 360-degree perspective. Scientists who study twins that have been separated at birth have found that they share the same traits even when they have never met each other. As children they sometimes create their own invented language (a process called *idioglossia*) that is intelligible only between themselves, or can communicate via a subtle form of mental telepathy as if they share a single personality.

Fictional treatments of twins in the dark genres of mystery and horror usually involve the concept of "evil twins," in which one or both of the twins are evil personalities. Unfortunately, there are real-life examples of this phenomenon. In his book *Evil Twins*, true crime writer John Glatt chronicles a number of cases that fall into this category. Glatt writes, "When twins kill together—using their bond in such a diabolical way—an unparalleled instrument of evil is unleashed.... Although cases of evil twins are very rare in the annals of criminology they do occur and are usually far more mysterious and complex than other cases of routine homicide."[12] One famous case was that of Stewart and Cyril Marcus, twin gynecologists who descended from brilliant medical careers to a shared hell of madness, drug addiction and suicide. This case provided the inspiration for director David Cronenberg's medical horror film *Dead Ringers* (1988). Another infamous example is that of the Kray brothers, twins who controlled the criminal underworld in London during the 1960s, and whose homicidal exploits were chronicled in the films *The Krays* (1990) and *Legend* (2015).

The connection between twins and the doppelganger is more apparent in plots in which one twin is on the side of the angels and the other embraces the depths of hell. The good vs. evil twin motif creates a dramaturgic situation that is fraught with tension and moral ambiguity. This dynamic of the struggle between good and evil identical twins appears in mystery films like *Among the Living* (1941), *The Dark Mirror* (1946) and *Dead Ringer* (1964) and horror movies such as *The Black Room* (1935), *Twins of Evil* (1971), *The Other* (1972) and *Sisters* (1973). In all of these films the dark half of the equation seeks to supplant or destroy their moral opposite.

Good and evil twins who are in diametric conflict exist in real life. This situation can arise because of an intense rivalry between the identical siblings. One well-publicized case was that of Sunny and Gina Han, South Korean-born twins who emigrated to Southern California. Gina, who had problems making a living, became insanely jealous of her sister's financial success, and plotted to murder her and assume her twin's identity. She hired a couple of would-be assassins to help her kill Sunny, but their harebrained scheme was foiled before they could commit the homicide. Gina was charged with attempted murder and the sensationalized trial was covered on tabloid television shows like *Hard Copy* and the proceedings televised on Court TV. In a bizarre twist Sunny became her twin sister's biggest supporter and advocate, but despite her efforts Gina was found guilty of conspiracy to murder her sibling and sentenced to 26 years in prison on November 20, 1997.

Some identical twins are "mirror image" twins that are formed when there is a delay in the splitting of the blastocyst and the formation of dual embryos in the womb. In this case the embryos will develop as symmetrical mirror images of each other. One mirror image twin will have body organs on the opposite side to the other. One will be right-handed and the other left-handed. Even their personality traits will be 180 degrees out of phase with each other. This mirror image effect may provide a biological basis for the mental and emotional dichotomy between good and evil twins.

Another aspect of the doppelganger concept is the *alter ego*, a Latin phrase meaning "the other I" coined by the Roman philosopher Cicero, who described it as being "a second self." In this case, it is an individual who possesses a secondary identity, an alternative self, and therefore embodies their own doppelganger. The seminal example is found in Robert Louis Stevenson's classic novella *The Strange Case of Dr. Jekyll and Mr. Hyde*, in which a straight-laced Victorian physician concocts a formula that transforms him into his opposite number, the Id-dominated psychopath Mr. Hyde. Stevenson's work has been filmed countless times, and the alter ego concept has been examined in films as diverse as *The Haunted Strangler* (1958), *Psycho* (1960), *The Tenant* (1976), *The Dark Half* (1993) and *Fight Club* (1999). Super hero characters usually have "secret identity" alter egos that mask their existence. Superman's secret identity is the mild-mannered Clark Kent, while Batman's is millionaire playboy Bruce Wayne.

A literary variation on the alter ego refers to two characters that become connected to each other by chance or fate and whose destinies are inextricably linked. This theme was explored brilliantly in many of the films of Alfred Hitchcock, including *Shadow of a Doubt* (1943), *Strangers on a Train* (1951), *The Wrong Man* (1957), *North by Northwest* (1959) and *Frenzy* (1972). In these films the protagonists and their alter egos have personalities that are diametrically opposite to each other, much like good and evil twins.

Dr. Jekyll and Mr. Hyde was written in the late 19th century, when the psychological condition known as Multiple Personality Disorder was first diagnosed. Referred to in today's medical parlance as Dissociative Identity Disorder (DID), it is an affliction in which an individual's core personality has become fragmented, usually through some early childhood trauma, and other personas inhabit the same mind and body. These alternate personalities, or "alters," are quite separate and distinct from the original person and can exhibit different physical characteristics. For instance, an alter can have different eye-sightedness than that of the core person, have different allergies or even different brainwave patterns. The alters shift personalities in a manner similar to the process that transformed Dr. Jekyll into Mr. Hyde, albeit without recourse to pharmaceuticals.

As incredible as it may seem, there are instances in which people come face to face with their real-world doppelgangers. On June 11, 2015, the ABC news site ran an item on a 27-year-old woman named Niamh Geaney, who had traveled to Genoa, Italy to meet her double, Luisa Guizzardi, who was also 27. Ms. Geaney had contacted Ms. Guizzardi via a website she maintains called "Twin Strangers" that links people who have similar facial features. Once the two young ladies were together, even Ms. Guizzardi's mother reportedly couldn't tell them apart. Side-by-side photos of the two women posted on the ABC website show a remarkable resemblance, demonstrating that it's possible for two individuals to resemble each other to the point of being identical twins and not be genetically related.[13]

So the doppelganger is not entirely a creature of the imagination. It exists within the shadow worlds of mental illness, hallucination, organic disease and multiple personality. It also exists in the mysteries of twinship, in folklore and legend and in the realm of psychic and mystical experiences of bilocation, apparitions of the living, out of body ramblings and magical dream states. It's therefore no wonder that this uncanny phenomenon should hold such inspiration for the human imagination.

CHAPTER TWO

Double, Double, Toil and Trouble
Literature

Although the theme of the doppelganger had existed in myth and folklore throughout history, the literary history of the double is generally traced back to the Gothic/Romantic period of the 19th century. It provided inspiration for some of the most popular and enduring works of imagination by a number of important authors, a list that includes Mary Shelley, Edgar Allan Poe, Fyodor Dostoyevsky, Robert Louis Stevenson, Oscar Wilde and others. But the doppelganger theme goes much farther back in time, to the very beginnings of written literature.

The art of writing was first invented by the ancient Sumerian people in what is now Iraq in the third millennium B.C.E. Writing in cuneiform script upon tablets of wet clay, the Sumerian scribes wrote down an epic poem that has come to be known as *The Epic of Gilgamesh*. It chronicles the myths and legends of Gilgamesh, king of the Mesopotamian city-state of Uruk, who is thought to have been a real historical personage.

The story is told in two symmetrical halves. The first half opens in the city of Uruk, where Gilgamesh the demigod is king but is oppressing his people by satisfying his wants and lusts at their expense. Because of his enormous strength and godlike power, however, none can oppose him. The priests of Uruk pray to their gods for deliverance, and in response the deities create a special being, a wild man named Enkidu, who can match Gilgamesh in strength.

Enkidu leads a feral existence among the animals of the forest until he is seduced by a temple harlot, and upon losing his innocence he also loses his kinship with the wild. The harlot convinces him to travel to Uruk, where he soon encounters his opposite, Gilgamesh. A momentous physical struggle between the pair ensues, with Gilgamesh eventually coming out on top, but after the fight the two heroes become best friends forever.

The influence of Enkidu takes the edge off of Gilgamesh and serves to make the king's behavior more temperate. The two become inseparable companions who slay monsters and perform feats of might and valor until, falling prey to hubris, they offend the gods. In retaliation the gods decree that one of the twin heroes must die for these offenses, and they decide that it will be Enkidu. They send a wasting illness to afflict him, and when he dies at the height of his great power Gilgamesh is inconsolable.

In the second half of the epic Gilgamesh's grief and fear of death cause him to leave Uruk and embark on a quest to obtain eternal life. He becomes the double of Enkidu, dressing in animal skins and roaming through the wilderness. He meets several fantastic creatures on his odyssey before reaching the distant land of a man named Uta-Napishtam, a mortal who has been granted eternal life by the gods in return for having saved mankind and animal life in a gigantic ship during a worldwide flood.

Uta-Napishtam reveals that the secret of immortality lies in a certain plant that grows under the sea. Tying rocks to his feet, Gilgamesh ventures into the ocean and obtains the plant, intending to take it back to civilization so that he can bestow the gift of eternal life upon all mankind. Unfortunately, a snake steals the plant away from him while he sleeps. Despondent after the failure of his quest, Gilgamesh returns to Uruk empty-handed and resigned to his mortality.

The story's narrative structure is clearly divided into symmetrical halves that reflect the duality of Gilgamesh and Enkidu. In the first half Enkidu leaves the wild and travels to Uruk, where he becomes a civilized man and a double of Gilgamesh. In the second half Gilgamesh assumes Enkidu's persona after his death, leaving the city to become a wild man. The two heroes become virtual twins even though their origins are entirely different: Gilgamesh is a demigod while Enkidu is a unique creation of the gods. Each is a magical being, larger than life and more than human. Their fates are tightly intertwined as if they share a single soul, and when Enkidu dies Gilgamesh is diminished.

The *Epic of Gilgamesh* is the first treatment of the doppelganger theme in the history of literature. It was widely disseminated around the ancient world and some of its plot elements would later become incorporated into Greek legends about Odysseus and Heracles, while the stories of the flood and the Ark and the serpent stealing eternal life away from mankind would find their way into the Book of Genesis.

Classical Greek myths recorded by the writers Homer, Pindar and Lucian tell stories about the divine hero twins Castor and Pollux. Zeus, king of the gods, visited the mortal woman Leda in the form of a swan, and as a result of their union she gave birth to an egg, from which the twins were hatched. According to one version of the story Castor was born a mortal while his brother Pollux was an immortal, but in other versions they are referred to as the *Diosocuri*, which means "the sons of Zeus." They grew up into a pair of splendid young men; Castor was renowned for his skill with horses, while Pollux became an expert boxer. The two heroes accompanied Jason and the Argonauts on the Quest for the Golden Fleece, and after this epic sea voyage became the patron deities of mariners. They later became associated with the phenomenon known today as St. Elmo's Fire, ghostly-looking static electricity charges that sometimes appear on the masts of ships under certain weather conditions.

After the voyage of the Argo, the twins journeyed to a far land where they became involved in a dispute over some cattle with a couple of shady characters named Idas and Lynceus. During the argument Idas stabbed and killed Castor, whereupon Pollux dispatched Lynceus with his sword and Zeus struck Idas dead with a thunderbolt. Inconsolable over the death of Castor, Pollux begged his father to let him share his brother's fate, but instead Zeus united the two inseparable twins for eternity by placing them among the stars where they became the Gemini twins of the modern Zodiac.

A parallel myth of hero twins emerged during the Roman era in stories by writers Livy, Plutarch and others about Romulus and Remus, the founders of the Roman state. According to the legend Amulius, the king of Alba Longa had deposed his brother, Numitor, and forced Numitor's daughter, Rhea Silvia, into lifelong chastity as a Vestal Virgin. Despite this, Mars, the god of war, seduced and impregnated her. When the twins were born Amulis ordered that they be drowned in the Tiber river, but a servant interceded by placing them in a basket on the bank of the Tiber.

Tibernius, the river god, guided the basket safely to shore downstream where the twins were found and suckled by the she-wolf Lupa. The feral children were later discovered by the shepherd Faustulus and taken to his hut, where they were raised to manhood by Faustulus and his wife. When the brothers discover their true origin, they lead a revolt to overthrow Amulius and restore Numitor to the throne. Going forth to found their own city, the twins quarreled over where it should be built, leading Romulus to kill Remus. Romulus founded the city of Rome on the Palantine Hill and was worshipped as the divine progenitor of the Roman people. In some versions of the myth Romulus ascends into heaven to be deified.

Being the sons of Mars, Romulus and Remus are classed as demigods like Castor and Pollux, and like the Greek hero twins one of them is killed while the other survives. In another similarity with the Greek myth, Romulus is taken up into the heavens to become immortal. The motif of placing the children in a boat set adrift upon a river and rescued to become great leaders also appears in legends about ancient figures such as the Assyrian conqueror Sargon the Great and Moses in the Book of Exodus.

Another ancient mythic cycle involving a pair of magical hero twins can be found in the Mayan book *Popul Vuh*. The legends of the Quiche Maya tribe were written down in the Mayan language shortly after the conquest of Mexico by the Spaniards in the mid–16th century, and were transcribed into Spanish 150 years later by the priest Father Francisco Ximenez. The mythological narratives in *Popul Vuh* are thought to date back to the Classic period of Mayan civilization circa 300–900 A.D.

The central characters in *Popul Vuh* are the hero twins Hunahpu and Xbalanque, whose mission is to avenge the deaths of their father and uncle at the hands of the lords of the underworld, One Death and Seven Death, who dwell in the netherworld of Xibalba. They deliberately provoke the Death Lords by playing the ritual ball game above their heads and disturbing them with the noise (this was the Mesoamerican ritual ball game played with a hard rubber ball on a court shaped like a letter I). Annoyed, the Lords of Xibalba summoned the twins to the underworld to play ball on their court and to undergo a series of grueling trials.

Hunahpu and Xbalanque are forced to endure various ordeals whenever they lose a game against the Xibalbans. These include being placed in the pitch black Dark House, the Razor House full of moving knives, the icy Cold House and the Bat House inhabited by deadly vampire bats. The twins survive these tests, but finally the Death Lords seek to lure them into a gigantic oven and roast them to death. Hunahpu and Xbalanque, however, following their own master plan, deliberately allow themselves to be incinerated and have their bones ground into dust, whereupon the exultant Xibalbans cast their remains into a river.

The two heroes regenerate their bodies in the river and re-emerge as a pair of magicians who roam around Xibalba performing miraculous feats. When One Death and Seven Death hear about their performances, they summon the magicians to entertain them at their court not realizing their true identities. They watch in amazement as the brothers perform their act. First they take a dog, sacrifice it, then bring it back to life. Then they perform the same feat on a man, sacrificing him and bringing him back to life. In the *piece de resistance*, Xbalanque sacrifices Hunahpu and resurrects him from the dead.

Delighted with these tricks, the Lords of Death demanded that the miracle be performed upon them. Obligingly, the twins sacrifice them, but do not bring them back to life. Their vendetta to avenge the death of their father and uncle having been accomplished and the netherworld of Xibalba defeated, the twins climb back to the surface of the earth, then ascend into the heavens, where one became the sun and the other the moon, heralding the beginning of a new age.

In his introduction to *Popul Vuh*, translator Ralph Nelson notes, "The notion of polarity is often said to be a key to understanding Mayan religion."[1] The hero twins Xbalanque and Hunahpu are a representation of this duality: one represents the fire of the sun and the other the coldness of the moon. Mayan scholars have noted that in the scenes that take place in the upperworld, Hunahpu has the dominant role, while Xbalanque dominates when they enter the underworld. As such, they are mirror-image opposites of each other. The divine hero twins were worshipped as deities, and their cult may have spread as far as the Mound Builder cultures of North America centuries later.

The literary doppelganger did not begin to flourish, however, until the late 18th and early 19th centuries during the heyday of the Gothic novel. Beginning with works such as Horace Walpole's *The Castle of Otranto* (1764), William Beckford's *Vathek* (1786), Anne Radcliffe's *The Mysteries of Udolpho* (1794) and Mathew Gregory Lewis's *The Monk* (1796), Gothic novelists offered up lurid tales of haunted castles, debauched clergy, mysterious plots, insanity, death and decay that achieved great popularity with the reading public. These novels would have a profound influence on the works of later writers of fantasy, horror and mystery fiction such as Edgar Allan Poe, Guy de Maupassant, Wilkie Collins and Bram Stoker.

The word doppelganger was first coined during this period in the German writer Jean Paul Richter's novel *Siebenkas* (1796), the full title of which is *Flower, Fruit and Thorn Pieces: or the Wedded Life, Death and Marriage of Firman Stanislaus Siebenkas, Parish Advocate in the Burgh of Kuhschnappel, a Genuine Thorn Piece*. A satiric commentary on married life, the novel is told in a comedic style as the unhappily married protagonist Firman Stanislaus Siebenkas consults his close friend and alter ego Leibgeber about a solution to his predicament. His doppelganger Leibgeber convinces him to fake his own death in order to escape the confines of his unhappy marriage. Siebenkas accomplishes this, assumes another identity and soon falls in love with the beautiful Natalie and weds her, which is the "wedding after death" referred to in the title. *Siebenkas* portrays the double in a comedic rather than horrific fashion in a novel which is basically a critique of the strictures of marriage rather than an exercise in the uncanny. The neologism "doppelganger" is explained in a footnote as referring to people who have the ability to see themselves.

One writer of the period who seemed to be obsessed with the doppelganger theme was the German fantasist Ernst Theodor Amadeus (or E.T.A.) Hoffmann. He is remembered today primarily as the author of the novella *Nutcracker and the King of Mice* (1816) which was the basis for Tchaikovsky's classic ballet *The Nutcracker*, and Jacques Offenbach's opera *Tales of Hoffmann*, which was derived from several of the author's shorter works. Expanding on Richter's concept of the doppelganger, Hoffmann would bring the double into the realm of the supernatural and would put a distinctly German flavor to the theme.

Hoffmann's first treatment of the doppelganger theme appeared in his novel *The Devil's Elixir* (1815), a gothic work clearly inspired by Lewis's *The Monk*. The novel's protagonist is a Capuchin monk named Medardus, an orphan raised in a secluded monastery who has no knowledge of his parents or lineage. A holy relic, the Elixir of St. Anthony, has been entrusted to the care of the pious monk, but Medardus rebels and, succumbing to temptation, partakes of the forbidden potion and undergoes a personality transformation. He becomes more charismatic and lustful, causing the prior of the monastery to send him on an important mission to Rome.

While traveling through a high mountain pass Medardus encounters his doppelganger asleep on the edge of a cliff, but when he attempts to awaken him the double is startled and falls over the edge of the precipice, presumably to his death. Dressing himself in the double's clothes and assuming his identity, he continues on his journey until he reaches a castle, where he is mistaken for his twin brother, Count Viktorin. The newly-minted Count is soon involved in a love affair with his half-sister Euphemie and a conspiracy to murder his half-brother, Hermogen. He winds up poisoning Euphemie and killing Hermogen in a duel, but his real desire is for Euphemie's sister, (and his own half sister), the princess Aurelie.

After the fratricides, Medardus is spooked when he encounters the double once more in one of the halls of the castle. It seems that Viktorin had not died in the fall off the cliff after all and has returned from the abyss as a madman and avenging conscience to plague Medardus for his sins. Medardus flees the castle pursued by the doppelganger but is aided by an eccentric barber with the dual personalities Peter Schoenfeld and Pietro Belcampo. After many wanderings he is convicted of killing Euphemie and Hermogen and imprisoned, but is acquitted when Viktorin appears and is blamed for the crimes. Medardus, however, manages to free Viktorin on the day of his execution and eventually wends his way back to his monastery with the help of Peter/Pietro. Re-assuming his original identity, he learns that Aurelie is going to take her final vows to become a nun, but during the ceremony the doppelganger suddenly appears and stabs her to death. As penance for his sins, Medardus is compelled to write the manuscript that details his perfidy.

Hoffman's bizarre tale of lust, murder and perverse religiosity was the first serious treatment of the doppelganger theme in the Gothic novel. Here the double acquires the aura of the uncanny, even the satanic, and is associated with insanity, homicide, and multiple personality. As the narrative unfolds Medardus becomes less grounded in his own identity and confounded by the mysterious and antisocial actions of his double. An identity exchange occurs when Medardus first encounters the double: he becomes the Count while Viktorin, deprived by madness of his own identity, assumes the role of monk. In the end, Medardus exorcises his doppelganger and regains his true self.

Critics have long noted that Hoffmann's concept of the double has a psychological dimension. In an introduction to Hoffman's work, E.F. Bleiler writes: "For Hoffmann, the doppelganger had a special significance. It was not simply a mysterious, supernatural double; instead it was associated with the strange phenomena of the mind, with personality fragments, with multiple personalities ... and with the emergence of an unconscious mind. In story technique this meant that ... two persons who were physically nearly identical might fuse, to form a single personality, or to create an impermanent, rotating personality which shifts from pole to pole of identity. This is the case in *The Devil's Elixir*, where two persons in a doppelganger relationship contaminate each other."[2] Note that the Medardus/Viktorin duality is mirrored in the parallel relationship between the split personalities of the Peter Schoenfeld/Pietro Belcampo double entity.

The Devil's Exilir placed the doppelganger squarely into the literature of the uncanny, and the novel would influence treatments of the theme in later works by Poe, Dostoyevsky and others. But its most profound influence may have been on Stevenson's *Dr. Jekyll and Mr. Hyde*. Both works feature a fantastic potion that transforms the protagonist from a pious individual into a lustful sociopathic doppelganger, and the Freudian superego is pitted against the Id, which ultimately triumphs. In both cases the double acts out the protagonist's forbidden impulses, a motif that would become a standard feature in later doppelganger tales.

The theme of the double appears in a number of Hoffmann's other works. In his short story "The Sandman" (1816–1817), for instance, the villain of the piece, the lawyer/alchemist Coppelius has a dual identity as the Piedmontese optician Guissepe Coppola. In "Signor Formica" (1819), a stage actor becomes the exact double of a man he is trying to humiliate and manipulate. Bleiler notes that in this story, "Hoffmann makes use of the doppelganger motive in a novel way. The idea is now completely secularized and stripped of its supernatural associations, and as stage imposture it serves to resolve the story."[3] He returned to the theme in "The Doppelgangers" (1821), in which two babies born to two different women are exactly alike, down to a small, moon-shaped mole on the left temple of both children. Moreover, both babies bear a resemblance to a man that only one of the women has made love to. The innocent woman and her child are banished by the woman's husband, causing her to believe she committed adultery in the confines of her own mind.

In terms of cinema history, however, Hoffmann's story entitled "A New Year's Eve Adventure" (1816) would have the most influence. The story concerns a German named Erasmus Spikher, a married gent who embarks on a solo vacation to Italy, where he is beguiled by a beautiful Italian woman named Guiletta. Unfortunately, she turns out to be a witchy femme fatale who is in league with a flamboyant and mysterious individual named Doctor Dappertutto, who is in reality the Devil. Completely bewitched by Guiletta, Erasmus kills a man in a jealous rage over her and must leave Italy at once, but before they must part Guiletta implores him to leave his mirror image behind so that she will always possess a part of him.

He consents and "she released him and stretched out her arms longingly to the mirror. Erasmus saw his image step forward independent of his movements, glide into Guiletta's arms, and disappear with her in a strange vapor."[4] Deprived of his mirror reflection, Erasmus becomes a marked man who inspires a superstitious dread in others and falls under the influence of the diabolic Doctor Dappertutto until he manages to free himself from the Devil's bargain. Hoffman's tale provided inspiration for a later work by another German master of the macabre, Hanns Heinz Ewers. Ewers's screenplay for *The Student of Prague* (1913) concerned a poor student who sold his mirror image to the Devil in order to woo a rich girl he is in love with. Unfortunately, his mirror image doppelganger takes on an evil life of its own. *The Student of Prague* was the first of the fantastic German "shudder films" (and the first feature-length horror film), predating even the Expressionist classic *The Cabinet of Dr. Caligari* (1919) by several years, and was remade in Germany during the Weimar period in 1928 and 1935.

While Hoffman's writing has fallen into relative obscurity, Mary Shelley's gothic novel *Frankenstein* (1818) has endured through the centuries, thanks in part to seemingly innumerable stage and cinematic adaptations that have continued into the 21st century. These dramatic interpretations, however, have blurred Shelley's original plot almost beyond recognition. In the novel Victor Frankenstein, a maverick student of the "natural sciences" at the University of Ingolstadt, discovers a technique for imparting life to inanimate matter. He assembles a humanoid creature from various charnel house and dissecting room leftovers and imbues it with the spark of life. The creature is eight feet tall with yellow skin, yellow eyes and a hideous countenance. The scientist flees in terror from his creation and the Monster disappears, much to Frankenstein's relief. But in the aftermath he suffers from a "nervous fever" that leaves him incapacitated for several months while he is nursed back to health by his family friend Henry Clerval. He keeps the existence of the Monster a secret, fearing that no one will believe him and hoping that the situation will somehow resolve itself.

Two years pass as Frankenstein continues his studies at the university, but one day he receives a letter from his father informing him that his seven-year-old brother William has been murdered. He departs Ingolstadt to return home to Geneva at once, and on the way he arrives late and is obliged to spend the evening in a village near the city's environs. That night he resolves to visit the site of William's murder and encounters the Monster, whose grotesque form is revealed in a sudden flash of lightning. The creature escapes by clambering up the face of a cliff like an ape as his creator realizes in a flash of insight that it is the murderer.

Returning home, he comforts his father, his surviving brother Ernest and his cousin Elizabeth, whom he is hoping to marry. But his sorrows deepen when William's nanny, Justine Moritz, is convicted of the homicide when some jewels belonging to the murdered boy turn up in her possession, and she is sentenced to death. Knowing intuitively that the Monster is responsible for planting this evidence, yet fearing once more that he will be judged insane if he reveals the true murderer, Frankenstein lets Justine go to the gallows and now has two deaths on his conscience after realizing, "I, not in deed but in effect, was the true murderer."[5]

Smitten with grief, he goes roaming across the Swiss glacial valleys, where he encounters the Monster once more, but now the creature has acquired the power of speech by observing humans. The monster regales his creator with its tale of woe about being rejected by humankind because of its monstrous nature and of his murdering William in revenge. It demands that Frankenstein create a female creature to be its mate, swearing to leave civilization and trouble him no more if he does so. Frankenstein accepts the bargain and departs for the British Isles accompanied by Clerval. The scientist travels alone to a remote island off the coast of Scotland to resume his grisly work, but fearing that he will create an even more fiendish creature, destroys the half-finished artificial woman before he can imbue it with life. At this point the Monster appears and vows revenge for Frankenstein's treachery, promising, "I will be with you on your wedding night."

Quitting the island in a small boat, he is blown out to sea and, by a freak twist of fate, comes ashore in Ireland where he finds himself accused of the murder of Clerval, who has become the Monster's latest victim. Once again he remains silent concerning the true identity of the killer, but is finally exonerated by the court and returns to Geneva. On his father's insistence he is persuaded to marry Elizabeth and does so, but the Monster makes good on his threat by murdering Elizabeth on the night of their wedding. Vowing revenge, the scientist stalks his creation throughout Europe to the northern polar regions where they both perish in their struggle with each other.

In this tragic tale Frankenstein creates his own doppelganger, who he frequently refers to as his "daemon," a word that in today's usage is a variant of "demon," but is actually the Latinized form of the classical Greek term *daimon*. In ancient Greek culture the *daimon* was thought to be a tutelary deity or guardian spirit, similar to the Christian concept of the guardian angel, although one's *daimon* could sometimes have negative qualities. The Greek philosopher Socrates famously claimed to be guided by his *daimon* in his everyday affairs. The Monster and its creator are bound together by a similar fateful connection and are inextricably linked to one another as if they are matching halves of a single entity. His creation becomes an external projection of Frankenstein's divided and conflicted personality. Their actions mimic each other: the Monster swears vengeance on his creator until Frankenstein destroys his mate, and when the Monster kills his bride, Frankenstein vows revenge and pursues the creature. When Frankenstein dies, the Monster kills himself.

Despite its gross physicality, the Monster is curiously insubstantial and seems to pop in and out of nowhere like a wraith or apparition. For the most part, it appears only to Frankenstein and to its victims just before they are about to be killed. His ghostly double commits homicidal acts for which Frankenstein must suffer the guilt, even as he must conceal them from the world.

According to most literary critics, *Frankenstein* constitutes the first true science fiction work in the history of literature. Breaking with Gothic traditions, its Monster was not a creature of the supernatural realm but a creation of science, and as such constitutes the first in a long line of sci-fi doppelgangers. There are many affinities between *Frankenstein* and Stevenson's *Dr. Jekyll and Mr. Hyde*. Both works feature an upright man of science who makes a breakthrough discovery that leads to the creation of a monstrous double whose homicidal acts are kept secret. While Shelley's classic has been the subject of many film adaptations, the only one that has any fidelity to the original novel is Kenneth Branagh's 1994 version, *Mary Shelley's Frankenstein*.

Scottish novelist James Hogg offered a diabolical take on the doppelganger theme in his Gothic masterwork *The Private Memoirs and Confessions of a Justified Sinner* (1824). Like *Gilgamesh*, the story is structured in two symmetrical halves. The first half, entitled "The Editor's Narrative," is written in the third person and described as "a detail of curious traditionary facts, and other evidence, by the editor," relates a series of uncanny and mysterious events taking place in 18th-century Edinburgh. The second part, "The Private Memoirs and Confessions of a Sinner," tells the same story in the first person from the viewpoint of the eponymous Sinner.

In "The Editor's Narrative" a Scottish nobleman, the laird (lord) of Dalcastle marries a willful, overly devout woman who rejects him due to his lack of religiosity, but before they separate she bears him a son, George Colwan. After the separation Lady Dalcastle takes up with a local parson and gives birth to a second child, Robert Wringhim. George, brought up as the laird's heir by his father and his father's mistress, Miss Logan, is a good-natured lad while Robert is raised under the strict religious tutelage of the Reverend

Wringhim to have a sour disposition. The two half brothers grow up entirely independent of each other until they meet as adults in Edinburgh.

Motivated by spite, jealousy and religious bigotry, Robert commences to torment George, berating him at every turn and seeking to humiliate him in front of his friends on every occasion. In a manner that appears uncanny, Robert seems to pop up everywhere to torment the hapless George. Matters come to a head when George is killed in a duel under mysterious circumstances and his father dies of grief, leaving Robert to inherit the Dalcastle estate, but Miss Logan, George's foster mother, suspects foul play. She unearths evidence proving that Robert murdered George with the aid of an unknown accomplice and presents the facts to the authorities, but when they come to arrest Robert no trace of the new laird can be found.

While the "Editor's Narrative" unfolds as a mystery story with supernatural overtones, the "Confessions" descends into pure horror as told in Robert Wringhim's "Private Memoirs." His foster father, the pious Reverend Wringhim has instilled him with the Calvinist doctrine that he is one of the "elect" or "justified," a soul who is pre-destined to attain salvation and is therefore incapable of committing sin regardless of his actions. One day while walking in the countryside Robert comes face to face with a remarkable individual. "What was my astonishment, on perceiving that he was the same being as myself!" he marvels. "The clothes were the same to the smallest item. The form was the same; the apparent age; the color of the hair; the eyes ... the features too were the very same."[6]

Mystified by this doppelganger, Robert soon comes under the sway of this being, who gives his name as Mr. Gil-Martin. Possessing seemingly preternatural powers, Gil-Martin beguiles Robert with his intellectual prowess and sophisticated insights into Calvinist dogma. It soon becomes obvious to the reader (but not to Robert), that Gil-Martin is in reality the Devil, who is leading young Wringhim down the primrose path to damnation. The evil one possesses the chameleon-like ability to change his appearance to look like anyone he chooses. He explains to Robert, "by looking at a person attentively, I by degrees assume his likeness, and by assuming his likeness I attain the possession of his most secret thoughts."[7] In other words, he can become both the inner and outer double of any individual.

The diabolical Gil-Martin plays upon Robert's resentments toward his brother and convinces him to murder George. Becoming the doppelganger of one of George's friends, Thomas Drummond, with whom he has just quarreled, Gil-Martin and Robert lure George into a dark alley one night, where Robert stabs his brother in the back. Drummond flees the country and is convicted of the murder *in absentia*, while Wringhim becomes the new laird of Dalcastle. After moving into the Dalcastle manor, however, Robert begins to suffer from amnesiac blackouts and commits a number of acts he has no memory of, although it is not clear whether Gil-Martin has possessed him or done these deeds while disguised as his doppelganger. In the end he is convicted of having murdered his mother and a local girl who he has compromised, but manages to escape punishment. He becomes a ragged fugitive who winds up taking his own life in a most pathetic manner.

Hogg's intricately constructed novel is one of the most intriguing treatments of the doppelganger theme in 19th-century literature. While much of Hogg's intent is to satirize and critique Calvinist doctrine, which he paints as a satanic delusion, he also exhibits a fascination with the supernatural that is evident in his earlier novels, *The Brownie of Bods-*

beck (1818) and *The Three Perils of Man* (1822). Contemporary readers would surely have believed in the reality of the Devil and in the book's fantastic premise. *The Confessions of a Justified Sinner* contains a number of doublings: the two halves of the plot conveyed in two different voices, the two brothers and Gil-Martin's numerous doppelgangers. As in Hoffmann's "A New Year's Eve Adventure," the doppelganger is connected with a satanic agency. In copying a person's appearance, the Devil also establishes a telepathic link with their mind as well, becoming both a physical and mental simulacrum of the original.

Like Hoffman's supernatural tales of the doppelganger, Hogg's work has also faded into an undeserved obscurity. The Gothic locale of 18th-century Edinburgh, with its dark, twisty streets, provides a brooding backdrop for the supernatural proceedings, and the novel ends on a ghastly note of morbidity and melancholy. *Confessions* was filmed as *Memoirs of a Sinner* in 1985 by Polish director Wojciech Jerzy Has.

The doppelganger motif migrated from Europe to America in Edgar Allan Poe's short story "William Wilson" (1839), in which the narrator and titular character is haunted throughout his life by a being who is his nemesis, double and namesake. From the time he is a schoolboy, Wilson is forced to contend with a second William Wilson who acts as a rival and competitor for his identity. Although they are not related, Wilson learns that he and his twin were born on the same day. The weird similarity leads to Wilson having feelings of hatred and loathing toward his double. Oddly, Wilson's double always speaks to him in a strange whispering voice.

Leaving the academy, Wilson resumes his studies at Eton, where he descends into a life of drunkenness, gambling and debauchery, but when the doppelganger pursues him there he departs for Oxford. He continues his bad behavior at the university, where he devises a plot to cheat a young English nobleman, Lord Glendinning, out of a large sum during a crooked card game. His devious scheme is on the point of succeeding when the doppelganger makes a dramatic entrance and, in a stage whisper, reveals Wilson's treachery to the other gamers.

Wilson is obliged to leave Oxford in the wake of the scandal and vows to resolve the situation if their paths ever cross again. He travels to Rome where he attempts to seduce a duke's wife but is confronted by his double once more. Enraged, he compels the double to duel with him, whereupon Wilson skewers his enemy with his sword. His triumph is short-lived, however, as he perceives his own bloodied image standing before him as if he is gazing into a mirror. "You have conquered me, and I yield," announces the doppelganger, no longer speaking in a whisper. "Yet, henceforward art thou also dead—dead to the World, to Heaven and to Hope! In me didst thou exist—and, in my death, see by this image, which is thine own, how utterly thou hast murdered thyself."[8]

In this story the doppelganger clearly symbolizes Wilson's conscience, a kind of guardian angel that appears at critical junctures in his life to guide him back onto a moral path. Wilson observes that his double appears in order "to frustrate those schemes, or to disturb those actions, which, if fully carried out, might have resulted in bitter mischief."[9] The narrator/protagonist exhibits the behavior of a sociopath, showing no remorse for his actions and only outrage toward his avenging conscience for thwarting his nefarious schemes. Note that the doppelganger speaks in a whisper, like the still, small voice of a guardian angel urging him toward the good. While the double appears here in a symbolic role, Poe also imbues the ghostly apparition with all the trappings of the uncanny and the supernatural. As in folklore beliefs, to confront one's double leads to the destruction of the self.

Although Poe denied having been influenced by the German Gothic writers, many critics believe that he may have cribbed the doppelganger theme from the works of E.T.A. Hoffmann. "William Wilson" was filmed as part of the European horror omnibus feature *Spirits of the Dead* (1968) by the French director Louis Malle, with Euro-heartthrob Alain Delon playing both the title character and his double.

The acclaimed Russian novelist Fyodor Dostoyevsky offered his take on the doppelganger in his novel *The Double: A Petersburg Poem* (1846). Its protagonist is one Yakov Petrovich Golyadkin, a minor civil servant in the city of St. Petersburg, who frets that his lack of guile in dealing with office politics has ruined his chances for career advancement. In spite of his perceived moral uprightness, Golyadkin is not liked by his co-workers. After being ejected from a birthday party thrown by one of his superiors because of his gauche behavior, he wanders through the snowbound streets of the city in a funk until he comes to rest at the Izmaylovsky Bridge at midnight. While he is contemplating suicide a figure emerges out of the snowstorm that he recognizes as his double. Trembling with fright, Golyadkin watches as the mysterious doppelganger vanishes into the darkness.

When he goes to work the next day he is astonished to find his double working as a clerk in the same bureau. Over the course of the novel the doppelganger, who he refers to as "Golyadkin Junior," advances his position in the bureaucracy at the expense of "Golyadkin Senior" because the double possesses the social skills that the original Golyadkin sorely lacks. Subjected to a series of humiliating ordeals at the hands of Golyadkin Junior, he begins to lose his sanity as he loses the basis of his very identity. In the finale he is remanded into a doctor's care and, with his double and co-workers cheering, is carted off to an insane asylum.

Except for the initial meeting between Golyadkin and his double, Dostoyevsky strips the doppelganger of the trappings of the supernatural in favor of social satire. The two identical beings are thought to be the work of "divine Providence" instead of diabolical agency. The protagonist is doomed precisely because he lacks his double's ability to use gossip and double-dealing to advance his position within the rigid bureaucracy. His moral uprightness causes his humiliation at the hands of the unscrupulous Golyadkin Junior, while his society, acting without any pity, condemns him to madness and ostracism. Here the notion of doppelganger represents a fear of the loss of one's identity and uniqueness.

The Double was Dostoyevsky's second work of published fiction and most critics do not consider it one of the novelist's finer works. Its florid style and repetitious scenes would later lead the author to critique the form, but not the theme, of his book, which he rewrote and republished in 1866. The protagonist's unrelenting suffering, humiliation and descent into insanity make for unpleasant reading. *The Double* was the basis for a 2013 film of the same name written and directed by Richard Ayoade and starring Jesse Eisenberg.

As discussed in the previous chapter, the great French short story writer Guy de Maupassant suffered from syphilis, a condition that caused him to hallucinate visions of his double. Paranoia and a fear of madness inform much of the writer's later works as he struggled with the ravages of this dread disease, which would kill him at the age of 42. One example is de Maupassant's short story "The Horla," first published in 1887.

Set in the provincial city of Rouen, the story unfolds as a series of diary entries as the narrator describes his nightmarish experiences with a hostile invisible being he calls the "Horla." The Horla attacks him in his sleep and seems to follow him with invisible footsteps. It appears to drink water from a bottle he leaves out at night, causing him to think that he may be a somnambulist. "I lived," he laments, "without knowing it, that mysterious double life which makes us doubt whether there are not two beings in us."[10]

The narrator continues to descend into his private hell, observing the Horla moving objects around in a poltergeist-like fashion. He learns that his tormentor is not an insubstantial spook, but has a material existence that even obscures his image in a mirror at one point. Finally, in desperation, he contrives to trap the Horla inside his house and incinerate it into oblivion, but only succeeds in immolating the servants trapped inside, leaving the Horla free to continue plaguing him.

De Maupassant's eerie tale reeks of madness and obsession as its unfortunate protagonist descends into his private hell of murder and insanity. It is never clear whether the dreaded Horla is a disembodied spirit or poltergeist, a product of the diarist's paranoid dementia or even an alien being from outer space, as all these possibilities are presented to the reader as explanations by the narrator. The Horla represents the first use of what may be called the "unseen doppelganger," an invisible but not intangible double that attaches itself to an individual. Another example of this concept is the invisible "monster from the Id" a being that is the alter ego of a scientist on an alien world in the sci-fi classic *Forbidden Planet* (1956). "The Horla" was loosely adapted for the screen in the 1967 horror film *Diary of a Madman*, starring Vincent Price.

Suffering from syphilis, for which there was no cure at the time, made de Maupassant hallucinate his doppelganger, and the stricken writer was known to fire a pistol at unseen enemies. "The Horla" also contains a classic description of an experience of a sleep disorder known today as sleep paralysis. During this experience the subject believes they have just awakened from sleep, but in reality they are still dreaming. In a paralyzed state, they will perceive that a being, who is frequently invisible, will crawl on top of them and exert a smothering pressure on the subject's chest. The dreamer then emerges into full wakefulness to find themselves alone in their bedroom with the feeling of having been attacked by a ghostly assailant.

In light of this phenomenon, consider the following passage from the story: "I feel that I am in bed and asleep.... I feel it and I know it ... and I feel also that somebody is coming close to me, is looking at me, touching me, is getting on to my bed, is kneeling on my chest, is taking my neck between his hands and squeezing it ... squeezing with all his might in order to strangle me. I struggle, bound by that terrible sense of powerlessness which paralyzes us in our dreams.... I want to move—I cannot do so.... And then, suddenly, I wake up trembling and bathed in perspiration; I light a candle and find that I am alone."[11] Surely this nightmarish experience must have provided the inspiration for de Maupassant's invisible Horla.

Like *Frankenstein*, Robert Louis Stevenson's 1888 novella *The Strange Case of Dr. Jekyll and Mr. Hyde* has undergone a seemingly infinite number of stage and screen iterations that have obscured the story's original narrative. The novel's viewpoint character is a London barrister named Mr. Utterson, who is confronted with a series of enigmatic events centering around his friend and client, the utterly respectable Victorian physician, Dr. Henry Jeykll and the mysterious Mr. Edward Hyde, a brutish person of questionable, possibly criminal character. Jekyll has recently had Utterson draw up a will naming Hyde as his heir in the event of his death. Mystified by the strange relationship between the two, the lawyer decides to investigate, fearing that Hyde is blackmailing Jekyll over some past indiscretion.

Utterson notes that Hyde has a key to a dingy backdoor entrance to Jekyll's townhouse and stakes out the location in the hope of contriving a meeting. His patience is rewarded one evening when he meets Hyde face to face. "Mr. Hyde was pale and dwarfish," he observes, "he gave the impression of deformity without any nameable malformation.... God bless me, the man seems hardly human! Something troglodytic, shall we say?... Or is it the mere radiance of a foul soul that thus transpires through, and transfigures, its clay containment?"[12]

Having taken the measure of the man, Utterson introduces himself as Jekyll's lawyer and obtains Hyde's address in the rundown neighborhood of Soho. Nearly a year later a Member of Parliament, Sir Danvers Carew, is brutally murdered on the streets of London one night and a witness fingers Hyde as the killer. Utterson leads the police to Hyde's apartment in Soho, where they find the murder weapon, a walking stick, but no trace of the suspect. The lawyer then confronts Jekyll about the case, hoping that his client is not shielding the murderer. He fears that Jekyll might be Hyde's next victim, but the doctor assures him that Hyde has made a perfect escape and will never return.

With Hyde out of the picture, Jekyll appears to resume his normal life but gradually begins to retreat into solitude due to a mysterious illness. One evening Jekyll's manservant, Poole, calls on Utterson begging for help, fearing that Hyde has murdered his master. They go back to the doctor's house and force their way into the laboratory area, where they discover Hyde has committed suicide, but can find no trace of Jekyll. The mystery is resolved when Utterson reads a posthumous letter from the doctor revealing that Jekyll had invented a chemical formula that physically transformed him into the brutish Edward Hyde, and that the Hyde identity eventually came to dominate the personality of Henry Jekyll.

Stevenson's parable of the good versus evil sides of human nature produced a novel take on the doppelganger concept. Instead of being the exact duplicate of another person, the double is the person himself transmogrified into an alternative self. Henry Jekyll in no way resembles his counterpart, Mr. Hyde: Jekyll is described as "a large, well-made, smooth-faced man of fifty, with something of a slyish cast perhaps, but every mark of capacity and kindness,"[13] while Hyde is physically smaller, hairier, younger and more vital, but who "must be deformed somewhere; he gives a strong feeling of deformity, although I couldn't specify the point."[14] Stevenson consistently describes Hyde as being "troglodytic" or "ape-like," as if he is a throwback to a more primitive form of humanity.

Like Shelley's *Frankenstein*, the novel posits a monstrous double that is a product of science rather than sorcery and therefore represents a second example of the science fiction doppelganger. Jekyll comes to the scientific realization "that man is not truly one, but truly two.... It was the curse of mankind that ... in the agonized womb of consciousness these polar twins should be continuously struggling. How, then, were they dissociated?"[15] Like his fellow Scot James Hogg, Stevenson's Calvinist upbringing fueled his interest in the nature of evil. By means of the transforming draught, the Hyde persona can indulge in any sociopathic behavior, including murder, and escape the consequences by reverting back to the staid, imminently respectable Jekyll. Consequently, the temptation of Hyde's youth and wild abandon eventually overwhelms the doctor's moral compass and ultimately leads to his permanent transformation into his evil alter ego. As in *Frankenstein*, the scientist creates a diabolical double whose evil deeds are kept secret, even in the face of murder.

Stevenson's original story reads like a mystery involving murder and blackmail. It is not until the novella's final chapters that the reader learns that Jekyll and Hyde are in fact a single person. This narrative structure has been dispensed with in all subsequent stage and screen adaptations in favor of showing Jekyll's dramatic transformation into Hyde early on in order to remove all ambiguity. Most of the later theatrical and film versions also feature additional characters such as an upper-class fiancé for Jekyll and a lower class love interest for Hyde that do not appear in the novel. Some of Hollywood's most acclaimed actors have starred in the dual role, including John Barrymore in the 1920 silent version, Fredric March in the 1931 early talkie, and Spencer Tracy in MGM's 1941 remake.

Jekyll and Hyde was written three decades before Sigmund Freud published his theories on the nature of human personality, but the novella clearly illustrates the contrast and conflict between what Freud called the superego, the logical, reasoning part of the persona, represented by Jekyll, and the irrational, immoral, pleasure-seeking component termed the Id, represented by Hyde. The two sides of their living quarters illustrate this contrast: the respectable Dr. Jekyll enters his dwelling through the grand façade of the building's front, while Hyde comes and goes through the building's squalid back door. Stevenson was also reportedly inspired by a real-life psychiatric case of "split personality" involving the Frenchman Louis Vivet reported in the medical literature of the time. Vivet, who may have had as many as ten personalities, was one of the first individuals diagnosed with multiple personality disorder (MPD) in 1885.

Oscar Wilde's novel *The Picture of Dorian Gray* (1891) is the other great Victorian essay on the doppelganger and its relationship to the dark regions of the self. The novel's antihero, Dorian Gray, an innocent young nobleman of exquisite good looks, inspires the artist Basil Hallward to paint a vividly lifelike portrait of the youthful Gray. The painting is such a perfect likeness that Dorian impulsively wishes that he would give away his soul if the picture would age while his features would remain forever young. Having a foreshadowing of future dire events connected with the painting, Hallward is on the point of destroying it when he is restrained by Gray, to whom he makes a gift of the portrait instead.

Dorian's angelic innocence is perverted when Hallward introduces him to the cynical Lord Henry Wotton, whose eloquent discourse on the delights of hedonism soon lead the young lad astray. Gray enters into a love affair with a beautiful lower class actress named Sybil Vane, but callously rejects her after she turns in a lackluster performance in a Shakespeare play. The poor girl is devastated and commits suicide after losing her "Prince Charming," but Gray shows no remorse for having caused her death. Soon afterward he notices that the expression on the portrait's face has miraculously been altered from a pleasant smile to a cruel sneer. Realizing that his strange wish has somehow come true, he hides the painting away in a secret room, where the magic portrait slowly assumes the ugly countenance of his many sins while Dorian's features remain eternally youthful.

Under the baleful influence of the charming but amoral Lord Henry, Dorian is led down the primrose path of wickedness. "That curiosity about life which Lord Henry had first stirred in him ... seemed to increase with gratification. The more he knew, the more he desired to know. He had mad hungers that grew more ravenous as he fed them."[16] As the years pass, Gray's immoral deeds tarnish his reputation in London society in spite of his pleasant appearance. One night he runs into Hallward by chance and the painter confronts him with rumors he has heard concerning Dorian's moral lapses and begs him to seek repentance. Dorian responds by sharing the secret of the portrait with its creator, then stabbing him to death in a sudden fit of murderous rage. Afterwards, he enlists the help of Alan Campbell, a chemist who is one of the men he has compromised, to help him dispose of Hallward's body by using the threat of blackmail.

Dorian Gray has gotten away with murder, but the hands of the portrait become stained blood-red. As the newspapers puzzle over Hallward's mysterious disappearance, Campbell commits suicide and Gray sinks deeper into his life of debauchery. One night, while visiting an opium den on the London docks, he is recognized by Sybil Vane's brother James, who has returned from overseas and is seeking the gentleman who drove his sister to suicide 18 years earlier. At first he is bewildered by Gray's apparent youth, but when the identity of Sybil's "Prince Charming" is confirmed, Vane begins stalking him with a pistol. Before he can exact his revenge, however, Vane is accidently shot and killed in a hunting accident, leaving Gray in the clear once more.

Even though he has escaped punishment for his misdeeds, the deaths begin to weigh on Dorian's mind, and he begins to experience bouts of irrational terror and fainting spells. He even makes a half-hearted attempt to repent and change his life, and comes to believe that the painting itself is responsible for everything. "There was only one bit of evidence left against him. The picture itself—that was the evidence. He would destroy it.... It had been like conscience to him." He seizes the knife he had used to kill Basil Hallward and stands before the horrible portrait. "As it had killed the painter, so it would kill the painter's work, and all that meant.... It would kill this monstrous soul-life, and, without its hideous warnings, he would be at peace."[17] He plunges the blade into the picture and cries out in horrible agony at the death blow. The frightened servants break into the secret room to find the painting restored to its former glory and Dorian Gray's loathsome corpse lying on the floor with the knife in its heart.

Dorian Gray's picture represents a novel take on the doppelganger concept. Although the basic premise of the tale relies on a supernatural agency, the novel is a parable as much as it is a horror story. As in "William Wilson," the double is clearly an externalization of Gray's conscience, and as in Poe's story the protagonist destroys himself in a climactic struggle in which his mirror image is pierced by a blade. And while the Devil makes no appearance in the text, his presence is implied in Gray's unholy bargain in "giving his soul" to achieve his heart's desire. To whom, after all, is he offering his soul? The figure of Lord Henry, who tempts Dorian into a life of iniquity, becomes a secularized version of the Evil One.

There are a number of similarities between *Dorian Gray* and *Jekyll and Hyde*. Both works feature an immoral sociopath who conceals himself behind a mask of Victorian respectability, and both stories culminate with the protagonist dying and being transformed into their evil doppelganger whose secret sins are finally revealed to the world. In both stories the double enables the protagonist to regain his youth in a kind of Faustian bargain.

In addition to the duality of Gray and his painting, there are other doppelganger relationships in the novel. One is between the artist, Basil Hallward, and his creation. He confides to Lord Henry that "every portrait that is painted with feeling is a portrait of the artist, not of the sitter. The sitter is merely the accident, the occasion. It is not he who is revealed by the painter; it is rather the painter who, on the coloured canvas, reveals himself. The reason I will not exhibit this picture is that I am afraid that I have shown in it the secret of my own soul."[18] Hallward is in love with Dorian, who has transformed his art, and has rendered the purity and innocence of his love onto the canvas in transcendent fashion. The painting is therefore his double as well. During the course of the novel Hallward strives to restore Dorian's lost innocence, and when the corruption of his work is revealed he is likewise destroyed.

Similarly, Lord Henry also uses Dorian as a blank canvas onto which he can re-create Gray psychologically in his own image. "To project one's soul into some gracious form," he muses about his influence over Dorian, "to convey one's temperament into another as though it were a subtle fluid or a strange perfume.... He was a marvelous type, too, this lad ... or could be fashioned into a marvelous type, at any rate.... There was nothing that one could not do with him. He could be made a Titan or a toy.... He would seek to dominate him.... He would make that wonderful spirit his own."[19] As Hallward creates a spiritual mirror of Dorian's physical image, Lord Henry fashions him into a mental simulacrum of his own perverse psyche in a doppelganger relationship between the polar opposites of the Jekyll-like Dorian Gray and the Hyde-like Lord Henry. Thus, both Lord Henry and Basil Hallward seek to transform Dorian into their own inner likenesses.

While *Jekyll and Hyde* has been the subject of numerous screen adaptations, the similarly-themed *Dorian Gray* has had only one significant cinema version. Hurd Hatfield starred as the title character in MGM's lavish 1945 production, along with Angela Lansbury in an Oscar-nominated performance as Sybil Vane and George Sanders perfectly cast as the cynical Lord Henry. Writer/director Albert Lewin fashioned one of the most faithful screen versions of a novel in screen history, incorporating large swathes of Wilde's brilliant, epigrammatic dialogue into the exquisitely literate screenplay.

After its flowering in the 19th-century literature of the uncanny where it had been associated with ghosts, sorcery, psychopathology and diabolism, the doppelganger concept began to move away from the realm of the supernatural into the newly-formed idiom of science fiction. In the realm of sci-fi, the double would mutate into new forms: shape-shifting extraterrestrials, android simulacra and bio-engineered clones. One early example is John W. Campbell, Jr.'s classic novella *Who Goes There?*, first published in *Astounding Stories* magazine in 1938.

A scientific expedition to Antarctica discovers an alien spaceship that has crashed near the South Pole and been buried in the ice for 20 million years, along with the body of a frozen alien being. The creature is carefully chipped out of the ice and transported back to their base, where the expedition's leaders, Commander Garry and his Second-in-Command McReady opt to thaw the alien out of its block of ice for scientific study. Big mistake. The extraterrestrial, described as being blue-colored, four feet-tall with three red eyes and snake-like tendrils on top of its head, de-ices and rampages through the camp. It exhibits intelligence, but shows nothing but hostility toward the human species.

The scientists soon learn that the alien has telepathic powers and is able to alter its cellular structure to mimic the form of any living thing. They also find it can duplicate its original mass and assume the likeness, personality and memories of any of the men by absorbing their bodies. Before long several of the crew members have been duplicated, and the men fear that if the creature is allowed to reach civilization it will multiply itself until it is the only organism left on the planet. McReady eventually comes up with a test that will separate the human beings from the alien doppelgangers. Realizing that even small parts of the creature exhibit an independent life, he orders each man to draw a blood sample into a test tube, into which a heated wire is passed. If the blood recoils from the wire, the alien double is immediately killed via electrocution. Fourteen of the 37 members of the expedition, including Commander Garry, are found to be doppelgangers and eliminated, saving the Earth from an invasion.

Campbell's novella is classic 1930s pulp fiction, with no clear protagonist and no attempt at characterization. The scientists spout technical jargon and treat the dire situation of an alien takeover of the planet chiefly as a scientific puzzle to be solved. It is as much a horror story as it is science fiction. The setting in the hostile remoteness of the Antarctic wasteland inspires claustrophobia, while the alien "thing" is a typical "bug-eyed monster" of the period, but it is the paranoia engendered by the presence of the doppelgangers and the effort to detect them that provides the story's main tension. The creature copies the men cell by cell, forming a double that is indistinguishable from the original person and whose alien identity can only be ascertained by means of an ingenious test.

Who Goes There? provided inspiration for a number of screen iterations, the first of which was Howard Hawks's 1951 version entitled *The Thing from Another World*. Campbell's story was updated into the atomic 1950s, but the screenplay dispensed with the notion of an alien shape-shifter in favor of a vampiric extraterrestrial who resembled Frankenstein's monster in a space suit. By contrast, John Carpenter's 1982 remake, *The Thing*, stuck close to Campbell's original plot and depicted the xenomorphic creature using gory special effects. A third version, also titled *The Thing* (2011) was a prequel to the Carpenter film and likewise featured the doppelganger theme and updated digital effects.

Jack Finney's famous novel *The Body Snatchers* (1954) offered a more sophisticated science fiction treatment of the theme. The novel is set in the Northern California locale of Mill Valley, an actual township in Marin County just north of San Francisco. Dr. Miles Bennell is the town's general practitioner who suddenly faces an outbreak of a mass paranoia in sleepy Mill Valley. His patients are all laboring under the eerie delusion that their close relatives have been replaced by imposters. Puzzled by the unusual phenomenon, he is drawn deeper into the mystery when his good friend Jack Bellicec shows him the simulacrum of a human body he has discovered in his home. The naked "body," laid out on a billiard table for Miles's inspection, resembles a partly-formed replica of Jack. Upon examining the body, Miles learns that it is not a corpse, but a "blank" organism that has never lived. Later that night Miles discovers a second blank hidden in the basement of his girlfriend Becky Driscoll, but both of the blanks vanish under mysterious circumstances.

Little by little Miles discovers the horrifying truth. The good citizens of Mill Valley are being replaced one by one with alien doppelgangers. Parasitic organisms resembling huge seed pods have reached Earth after traveling through the vastness of outer space and are in the process of duplicating its life forms. The process takes place during sleep; when a pod is placed next to a living human it pops open and a blank of the person begins to form. The alien plant then absorbs the electromagnetic signature of the individual atom by atom until a perfect duplicate is created. Once this happens the person's original atoms are reduced to inertness and form a gray fluff which then blows away. In this way most of the town's inhabitants have been transformed into pod people who are perfect doubles of the originals but have no human emotions.

Trapped in a town full of inhuman doppelgangers, Miles and Becky can only watch helplessly as the pod people round up and replicate the few remaining humans and begin to spread the infection throughout Marin County. They get captured by the aliens but manage to avoid being duplicated and escape into the surrounding countryside. Evading capture, they chance upon a farm facility where the seed pods are being cultivated and set it afire. This act of defiance makes the aliens realize that human hostility will make the planet uninhabitable for them, whereupon the pods all float back into outer space looking for a more hospitable piece of real estate to invade. The remaining pod people, who only have a five-year life span, are left to slowly vegetate into non-existence.

Finney's novel has been interpreted as a parable of 50s-era anti–Communist paranoia, although the author insists he was just spinning a good sci-fi horror yarn about the loss of individuality, a classic genre theme. The novel's small town setting provides a prosaic background for the fantastic premise of an alien invasion. As in *Who Goes There?*, an extraterrestrial organism has the ability to re-create and reproduce itself by copying human beings with the goal of eventually replacing humankind altogether. The notion of human doppelgangers hatching out of giant seed pods is particularly macabre.

The pod people look just like us but are devoid of all emotion and motivation. Being as alike as "peas in a pod" they exist within a hive mind of common thought that is foreign to normal human experience. The doubles copy individuals down to the smallest detail and imperfection while absorbing their memory and personality at the same time. These doppelgangers are inferior to their originals, however, as they only live for five years. The duplication process obliterates the original template by reducing it to "inert atoms" in a manner that is vaguely described and less than satisfying to the reader. Finney later admitted, "I was never satisfied with my own explanation of how these dry leaflike objects came to resemble the people they imitated; it seemed, and it seems weak, but it was the best I could do."[20]

As mentioned in the previous chapter, the plot of *The Body Snatchers* seems to have been informed by the psychological condition known as Capgras Syndrome or Capgras Delusion, a mental aberration in which the sufferer is under the delusion that everyone close to him has been replaced by duplicates. While the Capgras Syndrome is not specifically mentioned in the text, it is obliquely referenced by one of the characters named Mannie Kaufmann, the town psychiatrist. "Down there in Mill Valley a week or ten days ago," he explains, "someone formed a delusion; a member of his family was not what he seemed, but an imposter. It's not a common delusion precisely, but it happens occasionally, and every psychiatrist encounters it sooner or later."[21]

The Body Snatchers was adapted for the screen four times, most notably by Don Siegel as *Invasion of the Body Snatchers* in 1956, which follows the plot of Finney's novel closely and is considered a landmark of classic science fiction cinema. Philip Kaufman's 1978 remake preserves the basic framework of the book, but moves the action across the Bay to urban San Francisco. The other versions, *Body Snatchers* (1993) and *The Invasion* (2011), are radically different from the original work.

In later decades the doppelganger theme migrated into the realm of pop fiction in a series of novels by well-known writers. Chief among these was Ira Levin, best known for his supernatural thriller *Rosemary's Baby*, which also became a hit movie. In his novel *The Stepford Wives* a scientist is replacing human wives with android doubles in the bucolic town of Stepford, Connecticut in a conspiracy with their husbands in order to transform them into automated love machines. The book was the basis for a 1975 screen adaptation scripted by William Goldman and starring Katherine Ross, as well as three made-for-TV sequels and a 2004 remake. Levin's novel *The Boys from Brazil* (1976) posited another conspiracy, this one perpetrated by the notorious Nazi scientist Dr. Mengele, to clone Adolf Hitler's DNA into a whole slew of evil teenage doppelgangers. The 1978 film version of Levin's bestseller starred Gregory Peck as Mengele and Sir Laurence Olivier as a Jewish Nazi hunter trying to unravel the mystery.

Actor turned author Thomas Tryon's debut novel, *The Other* (1971) was another bestselling treatment of the theme. Set in the rural community of Pequot Landing, Connecticut, in 1935, the story revolves around a pair of twin adolescent boys, one good, the other pure evil, one who is living and one who is dead, who share a preternatural bond. The question is, who is who? Tryon's American Gothic gem was lensed by director Robert Mulligan in 1972. A mysterious doppelganger was the subject of Tryon's 1976 novella *Fedora*, the tale of an enigmatic Dorian Gray–like actress who seemingly possesses eternal youth. *Fedora* was brought to the screen by the acclaimed writer/director Billy Wilder in a 1978 adaptation starring William Holden.

Horrormeister Stephen King's thriller *The Dark Half* (1989) concerns a staid New England novelist who writes popular books about a nasty serial killer character. Seeking to exorcize the literary demon from his life, he stages a mock funeral for his evil alter ego, whereupon the fictional killer promptly comes to life and perpetrates a number of real-life murders for which the writer is blamed. King's bestseller was filmed by horror director George Romero in 1991.

Thus, the doppelganger has had a long and illustrious presence in the literature of mystery, horror and science fiction, from Sumerian epic to pop novel. This enduring theme, which came to full flower in the works of 19th-century literary giants like Shelley, Poe, Dostoyevsky, Stevenson and Wilde, continues to have resonance in the 21st. The notion of the mysterious double seems to strike an uncanny chord within the human psyche.

With the exception of the ancient literature, most of the literary works cited have been translated into film. The following chapters will examine the treatment of the doppelganger theme in the dark and fantastic realms of mystery, horror and science fiction cinema.

CHAPTER THREE

Double Jeopardy
Crime, Mystery and Film Noir

Within the realistic milieu of the crime film, the doppelganger loses its overt connection with the fantastic, yet still retains an aura of mystery and the uncanny. The theme translates seamlessly into the world of criminality, where identities are fluid, good and evil twins strive against each other and diseased egos seek out their hidden selves. In this underworld the double is linked to larceny, deceit and murder as detectives seek to unravel the truth about their dual identities.

Pairs of innocent and homicidal twins confound the efforts of sleuths in the mystery films *Among the Living* (1941), *The Dark Mirror* (1946) and *Dead Ringer* (1964). Another variant of this idea are films that feature mother/daughter doppelgangers in *Obsession* (1976) and *Fedora* (1978). Mysterious doubles that defy explanation appear in *The Man Who Haunted Himself* (1970), *The Double* (2013) and *Enemy* (2013). Plastic surgery is another method used by criminals to imitate others in *Strange Impersonation* (1946), *The Double Man* (1967) and *Face/Off* (1997).

Individuals who are fatefully linked with their criminal opposite numbers appear in many of Alfred Hitchcock's crime melodramas, including *Shadow of a Doubt* (1943), *Strangers on a Train* (1951), *The Wrong Man* (1957), *Frenzy* (1972) and *Family Plot* (1976). Psychological doppelgangers also feature in a number of Hitchcock's other films, including *Rebecca* (1940), *Vertigo* (1958) and *Psycho* (1960).

Perhaps the most outré variations on the theme are films in which the protagonists pursue a shadowy or even invisible double that is in reality a hidden aspect of their own selves. This proves to be the case in *The Big Clock* (1948), *Angel Heart* (1987) and *Fight Club* (1999). Consistent with folklore beliefs, it is dangerous or even fatal to exist in the same place and the same timeframe as one's doppelganger.

The mystery film underwent a thematic and stylistic metamorphosis during the early 1940s into what came to be known as film noir. Derived from a French term that translates as "black film," the new genre incorporated the dark stylistics of the German expressionist "shudder films" of the 1920s and 30s. Using low-key lighting setups, extreme camera angles and other visual conventions derived from the horror movie, film noir created a dark universe of night and fear populated by grotesque criminals, sociopathic femmes fatales, crooked cops, pathetic losers and other denizens of the criminal demimonde.

Cinema historians generally trace the genesis of film noir to the year 1941, which saw the release of unusual crime melodramas such as *I Wake Up Screaming*, *The Shanghai Gesture* and the Humphrey Bogart vehicles *High Sierra* and *The Maltese Falcon*. This dark milieu also brought forth a number of films that embodied the doppelganger theme. The seminal year of 1941 produced the first of these in noir director Stuart Heisler's unusual thriller *Among the Living*.

The film stars Albert Dekker as John Raden, the son of wealthy textile magnate Maxen Raden, who is returning home to the southern mill town of Radentown after 25 years to attend his father's funeral. Accompanying him to the graveside are his wife, Elaine (Frances Farmer), the family physician Dr. Ben Saunders (Harey Carey) and the Raden estate's chief retainer, Pompey (Ernest Whitman). After the ceremony Dr. Saunders tells John that his twin brother Paul, who was thought to be dead, is still alive and living in Maxen Raden's abandoned mansion, Raden House. Paul (Dekker) is hopelessly insane as a result of enduring physical and mental abuse at the hands of his father. Unwilling to face the scandal of having Paul committed to an asylum, Maxem bribed Dr. Saunders to fake Paul's death. The unfortunate twin has been cared for in secret at Raden House by Pompey for the last quarter century.

John and Dr. Saunders pay a visit to the spooky southern mansion to find that Paul has strangled Pompey and escaped from his confinement with some cash stolen from the estate. While they frantically search for the demented twin, the childlike Paul wanders into Radentown, where he takes up residence in a boarding house and is befriended by Millie Pickens (Susan Hayward), the landlady's daughter. Millie is a bit of a femme fatale who manipulates the naïve Paul into giving her money and buying her expensive gifts.

Deciding to confront his brother, Paul pays a visit to John in his room at the town's hotel. Although they are identical, the twins are a study in contrast. John stands upright, is clean-shaved and wears a tailored suit, while the grizzled Paul slouches forward, dresses in rumpled old clothes and has a perpetual five o'clock shadow. The Raden brothers fail to reconcile their differences, causing Paul to flee out into the streets of Radentown.

Having been kept in seclusion for his entire adult life, Paul is bewildered by the world around him. He later visits a juke joint filled with loud music and gyrating dancers, where bar girl Peggy Nolan (Jean Phillips) flirts with him when he buys her drinks, then scornfully laughs at his naiveté. Stung, he waits for her to leave work then chases her into a dark alley where he brutally strangles her.

When her body is discovered the next day the town is outraged by the killing, but Dr. Saunders compels John to keep quiet by threatening to have him declared insane. Instead, John offers a reward of $5,000 for the capture of the murderer. In the meantime, Millie convinces Paul to purchase a suit and a razor, and is thus transformed into a dead ringer for his twin. As the denizens of Radentown go into a frenzy as they round up the usual suspects hoping to collect the reward, Millie thinks the killer is hiding out at the old mansion and drags Paul out there with her. Paul is upset by returning to the place of his confinement and menaces Millie, but she is saved when some of the townsfolk arrive and Paul is wounded during the melee.

The secret of the Raden twins is still unknown to the townsfolk when John arrives at Raden House and is mistaken for his brother in the confusion. The enraged townspeople hold a mock trial where they propose to lynch him on the spot, but John manages to escape from the mob and discovers Paul's corpse lying over their mother's grave. Soon afterward, Dr. Saunders arrives to reveal the truth to the crowd and declare John's innocence.

Director Heisler's early essay in film noir contains an element of Southern Gothic a la William Faulkner, with its creepy old manse festooned with Spanish moss that contains a secret room inhabited by a demented relative. The early scenes depicting the discovery of Pompey's murder at Raden House and the climactic episodes in the cemetery have the eerie atmospherics of a horror movie due to the cinematography of Theodor Sparkuhl, who had photographed many of the German expressionist classics of the 1920s. Critic Robert Porfirio notes that "Sparkuhl's work is one indication of the American film noir's debt to German expressionism…. The jazz sequence in a bar and the shot of Paul killing the B-girl in the alley (an extreme example of depth staging), are particularly important and set a stylistic precedent for expressing confusion and violence."[1] Director Stuart Heisler lensed another feature that combined elements of horror and film noir, *The Monster and the Girl*, in the same year. Thus, the long shadows of the German haunted screen enveloped this early incarnation of the doppelganger in an American noir film.

Scripted by Garrett Fort, who had written the screenplays for classic Universal horror movies like *Frankenstein* and *Dracula*, *Among the Living* contains elements of *Dr. Jekyll and Mr. Hyde* in its bipolar protagonists, and Shelley's *Frankenstein* in its portrayal of Paul as a sympathetic social outcast whose rejection by human society compels him to murder the innocent. While the Jekyll-like character of John Raden is largely inactive and impotent, his evil twin drives the action of the plot. Albert Dekker, whose forté was oddball character parts, shines in his dual role as the Raden twins, especially in his portrayal of the childlike but misguided murderer Paul. Susan Hayward also delivers a memorable performance as the cynical femme fatale Millie, who befriends Paul when he is her sugar daddy and then throws him to the wolves during the mock trial. As in many doppelganger stories, an innocent man suffers for the transgressions committed by his double.

The German émigré director Robert Siodmak, who produced some of the most expressionistic thrillers in the noir canon such as *Phantom Lady* (1944) and *Criss Cross* (1949), offered another take on the film noir doppelganger in *The Dark Mirror* (1946). The film begins with the murder of a prominent physician who is found stabbed to death in his town house. Two witnesses identify Ruth Collins (Olivia de Havilland) as having been seen leaving the scene of the crime, but homicide detective Lt. Stevenson (Thomas Mitchell), who is investigating the case, learns that Ruth has a solid alibi for being in another place that evening, and that she lives with her identical twin sister, Terry.

Unable to bring charges under these circumstances, Stevenson calls upon the expertise of psychiatrist Dr. Scott Elliott (Lew Ayres), an expert on the psychology of twins, to determine which of the Collins siblings is the murderess. Dr. Elliott subjects Ruth and Terry to a battery of psychological exams, including Rorschach ink blot and lie detector tests. He soon discovers that the twins are polar opposites. Ruth is sweet-natured and passive, while Terry is aggressive and manipulative. As the investigation progresses Dr. Elliott becomes convinced that Terry is the killer, as Ruth begins to form a romantic attraction to him. Terry, who is insanely jealous of her sibling and seeking to avoid the murder rap, plans to do away with her sister and assume her identity. In order to catch the killer, the detective and the psychiatrist devise a ruse that causes Terry to incriminate herself.

Siodmak is in fine form directing this shadow play of good and evil doppelgangers. Using his signature chiaroscuro, he conjures the fear-drenched mood of German Expressionist cinema ably assisted by cameraman Milton Krassner. The optical effects by J. Devereaux Jennings and Paul Lerpae that render the double images onscreen in the same frame are flawless. But it is the performances of Olivia de Havilland in the dual roles of the good and evil twins that ultimately carries the film. In her only film noir outing, it is Ms. De Havilland's portrayal of the psychotic femme fatale Terry Collins that captures the essence of the dark universe of noir. The film's greatest flaw is the screenplay by Nunnally Johnson, which occasionally veers into maudlin romantic sentiment.

Like *Among the Living*, *The Dark Mirror* exploits the theme of good and evil twins. Terry the bad twin is frequently clothed in black and shot in shadow, while her wholesome counterpart Ruth wears bright-colored outfits and is photographed in light. Sometimes the filmmakers resort to using necklaces spelling out the names of the twins or monogrammed brooches to signify the identities of the sisters. The film utilizes symmetrical Rorschach ink blots and mirror images to convey the concept of the twin's duality. Siodmak's Expressionistic visuals impart an air of the uncanny to the doppelganger twins in what is otherwise a straightforward murder mystery narrative.

Noir director Anthony Mann moved away from the good vs. evil twin motif in his B-movie thriller *Strange Impersonation* (1946). The film stars Brenda Marshall as lady scientist Dr. Nora Goodrich, a brilliant chemist who has created an innovative new anesthetic that she hopes to market. Seeking to avoid the red tape that she will be burdened with while conducting standard clinical trials, she decides to test the substance on herself at her residence and enlists the aid of research assistant Arline Cole (Hillary Brooke) to assist her. While driving home that evening Nora accidentally backs her car into inebriated pedestrian Jane Karaski (Ruth Ford), and although the young woman is not seriously injured Jane is approached by the ambulance-chasing shyster lawyer Jeremiah Rinse (George Chandler), who tells her she has a case and gives her his business card.

That night Nora's fellow researcher and fiancé Dr. Stephen Lindstrom (William Gargan) drops by to inform her that he is leaving that very night to accept a new job in France and proposes matrimony. Nora, however, is too intent on pursuing her new discovery and rebuffs him, whereupon he departs. Later that evening, Nora and Arline conduct the experiment as Nora injects herself with the anesthetic and falls into a deep torpor. What she doesn't know is that Arline wants Dr. Lindstrom to herself and is not above committing murder in order to eliminate her rival. She mixes up a batch of volatile chemicals that catch fire, hoping to burn Nora to death, but Stephen returns unexpectedly and rescues her from the flames. In the aftermath

Olivia de Havilland is pictured as a pair of good and evil twins in this poster for Robert Siodmak's film noir *The Dark Mirror* (1946).

Nora is horribly burned and her face disfigured in the fire, while Arline insists the conflagration was an accident. Arline wastes no time moving in on her rival and steals Dr. Lindstrom's affections away from his scarred fiancé.

To make matters worse, when Nora is discharged from the hospital she is visited by Jane Karaski, who is looking to extort money from her in connection with the accident. Jane pulls a gun on Nora and proceeds to appropriate Nora's money and possessions, including her engagement ring, but the two women get into a tussle that causes the gun to go off and Jane to fall out the window to her death. As Jane's features were smashed beyond recognition in the fall and she was found with Nora's engagement ring, she is mistaken for Nora by the authorities. At this point Nora conceives the idea of trading identities with the dead woman so she can start life anew.

Nora goes to a plastic surgeon, Dr. Mansfield (H.B. Warner), for some facial reconstruction surgery to make her facial features resemble Jane's. She learns that Arline has married Dr. Lindstrom and goes back to work at the same institute as a research assistant under her assumed identity. Lindstrom falls for her all over again and plans to leave his wife, but just as the pair are about to embark on a plane to France, "Jane Karaski" is arrested for the murder of Nora Goodrich and detective inspector Malloy (Lyle Talbot) is assigned to unravel the mystery of their shared identity. Unfortunately, the film concludes with a lame ending in which Nora wakes up to find that "it was all a dream."

One of director Mann's early efforts, *Strange Impersonation* was shot at low rent Republic Pictures rather than one of the major studios, but the director nonetheless manages to craft this neat little B-thriller with a number of unusual and startling images, such as Nora lecturing in front of a bizarre anatomical manikin, Nora's cyclopean eye staring out of a head completely swathed in bandages, and the female scientist's scarred, disfigured face partly hidden behind a veil. The film's laboratory settings, female scientists and plastic surgery transformations give it a visual ambience of science fiction, and these themes seem to anticipate the sci-fi horror flicks to come in the 1950s. The screenplay by pulp fiction and radio mystery writer Mindret Lord takes several unexpected and improbable turns but is marred by a ridiculous denouement. Fortunately, Mann keeps the pacing tight during the film's brisk 68 minute running time. Brenda Marshall acquits herself well playing the unusual role of cold fish lady scientist Nora Goodrich, and the film's typically noir menagerie of oddball characters as portrayed by Hillary Brooke, Ruth Ford and silent film star H.B. Warner add spice to the mix.

Plastic surgery was featured in a number of classic films noir such as *Dark Passage* (1948) and *Man in the Dark* (1953) as a plot device used to change the protagonist's identity into an alter ego. *Strange Impersonation* carried this notion a step further with the idea of using facial reconstruction techniques to create the doppelganger of a dead person. Once again the double is stylistically linked to a nightmare world of dread amid the cinematic trappings of the uncanny. While Nora believes that her physical makeover will transform her into another person, before she has the operation Dr. Mansfield tells her that, "You can change your face—with clever surgery you can change your face completely—but you cannot change yourself. You cannot change the person you are." Ironically, her assumption of another's identity leads her to be charged with her own murder in a bizarre twist of fate. Doppelgangers created via plastic surgery would later feature prominently in the crime melodramas *The Man with My Face* (1951) and *Face/Off* (1997).

A pair of homicidal evil twins appeared in the obscure British noir *Dual Alibi* (1947). English actor Herbert Lom is cast in a dual role as the twin French trapeze artists Jules and Georges de Lisle, who work their act in a modest circus run by the avuncular Vincent Barney (Ronald Frankau). The de Lisle twins are so identical, "like peas in a pod," that no one can tell them apart. While the circus is touring in France the brothers buy a ticket in the French lottery on a whim, which Georges, the more conservative of the two brothers, hangs on to for safekeeping.

When the circus returns to Blackpool, England, the circus's sleazy publicity man Mike Bergen (Terence de Marney) intercepts a letter giving advance notice that the de Lisles have won one million francs in the lottery. Bergen hatches a plot to have his girlfriend Penny (Phyllis Dixey) work on Jules in order to get the winning ticket away from Georges. Jules soon becomes enamored with the comely lass, and when the results of the lottery are published in the newspaper, Jules insists on receiving his portion of the cash immediately so he can marry Penny. Georges, however, wants to use the money to buy a place so that the brothers can retire from the circus. The twins get into a fist fight over what to do with their newfound wealth in which Jules injures his hands, so they agree to let Barney hold the ticket to prevent any further arguments. Unfortunately for the de Lisles, Bergen is able to briefly get his hands on the ticket and makes a counterfeit copy. He and Penny then hurry to France to cash it in before the twins know what has happened.

Suspecting nothing, the twins visit the lottery bureau to cash out the ticket and are shocked to learn that the money has already been paid out. They consult a lawyer, who tells them that their case would have jurisdictional problems in British and French courts, and that the case could take years to settle. Figuring out that Bergen and Penny have swindled them out of the winnings, they manage to track them down, only to find that Bergen has hired out some rent-a-thugs for protection. Their only recourse is a revenge that they plan meticulously. While one of them performs a solo on the high wire, the other guns down Bergen in a nearby café and returns to the circus before the trapeze act finishes. When they are arrested and tried for murder, neither the police nor the witnesses can determine whether it was Jules or Georges who committed the homicide. The twins may have committed the perfect murder, but the film ultimately proceeds to a tragic denouement.

This neat little British noir, directed by Alfred Travers for the English poverty row studio British National Films, is an effective, well-paced thriller despite its modest budget. It is squarely in the tradition of quirky British films noir such as *Night and the City* (1950), while the circus setting recalls similar carnivals in noirs like *Ministry of Fear* (1944) and *Nightmare Alley* (1947). British thesp Herbert Lom conveys an ethereal screen presence in his dual role as the brooding de Lisle siblings, but unlike the polar opposite twins in *Among the Living* and *The Dark Mirror*, the two brothers are virtually the same person. Lom went on to a long career playing heavies in movies like the Hammer iteration of *The Phantom of the Opera* (1962) and *Asylum* (1972). Phyllis Dixey, the notorious "peekaboo girl" who posed for many World War II pinups, uses her feminine charms well as the film's obligatory femme fatale.

The de Lisle twins are an odd couple of doppelgangers. While they are performing their high wire act they dress identically in top hat, white tie and tails and sport dark eye makeup and empty facial expressions that make them seem more like dolls than living people, a trait that lends them an aura of the uncanny. The film's circus backdrop also creates an atmosphere of illusion and unreality that is typical of many horror films. Like some real-life evil twins such as the Krays, they plan and execute their crime in perfect unison. Once again the double is associated with death, tragedy, criminality and misfortune as the twins cannot escape their terrible fate.

Another quirky noir angle on the double appears in John Farrow's mystery thriller *The Big Clock* (1948). Ray Milland stars as George Stroud, editor-in-chief of the popular true crime magazine *Crimeways*. The secret of Stroud's success lies in his system of creating psychological profiles of the perpetrators so that he can anticipate their actions and his use of a crack team of reporters to aid the police in catching the criminals. George is scheduled to take a well deserved vacation from the editor's desk with his wife Georgette (Maureen O'Sullivan), but as he is about to leave his dictatorial boss, publishing magnate Earl Janoth (Charles Laughton) insists he stay on to complete an important article. Disgusted, George tenders his resignation on the spot and stalks off to the nearest tavern to drown his sorrows.

While George is tying one on he happens to meet Janoth's mistress Pauline York (Rita Johnson) at the bar, and the two go on a bender together that winds up with a drunken George passed out on a couch in Pauline's apartment. Around 1:30 in the morning Pauline sees Janoth's car arrive at her building for an unexpected visit and hustles George out, but Janoth observes a male figure leaving the apartment and confronts Pauline, demanding to know the identity of his rival. She identifies him only by the pseudonym "Jefferson Randolph," and a heated argument ensues that climaxes with Janoth killing her in a fit of jealous rage with an antique sundial.

Fleeing the premises without being seen, Janoth confesses the murder to his chief assistant Steve Hagen (George McReady) who returns to Pauline's apartment and removes all incriminating evidence in order to frame the unknown Jefferson Randolph for the murder. George, meanwhile, has joined his wife on vacation after telling her a phony story about having missed the train the previous evening. His getaway proves to be short-lived, however, when an apologetic Janoth convinces him to return to *Crimeways* and use his detective skills to locate Jefferson Randolph and George, realizing that Janoth is the real killer and that he could be implicated in Pauline's murder, returns to throw Janoth off the scent.

Using his sophisticated profiling techniques and deploying his team of reporters, George begins hunting his fictional alter ego while at the same time trying to deflect suspicion away from himself. As the investigation progresses his assistants locate a number of eyewitnesses who saw a man out carousing with the victim on the night of the murder. The witnesses are brought to the Janoth Building, where one of them spies George and proclaims that the suspect is in the building. What follows is a game of cat and mouse as George strives to stay one step ahead of the reporters and witnesses while pretending to lead the hunt for his non-existent doppelganger Jefferson Randolph. As the plot unfolds the true killer's identity is finally revealed and Janoth winds up paying for his crime.

Director Farrow was best known for his quirky, offbeat noirs such as the psychic thriller *Night has a Thousand Eyes* (1948) and the modern-day retelling of the Faust legend, *Alias Nick Beal* (1949). *The Big Clock,* with most of the action taking place against the surrealistic backdrop of the Janoth Building, is in a similar vein. The big clock of the title is a baroque cylindrical device containing a map of the world that tracks the time in all the zones around the Earth. Farrow's fluid camera smoothly tracks the characters as they move through this confined and dreamlike space. The principal actors, including Milland as the resourceful George Stroud, turn in fine performances, but it is Charles Laughton's portrayal of the obsessive/compulsive killer Earl Janoth that dominates the film. Laughton is frequently shot in wide-angled close-ups that subtly distort his features into an inhuman mask. The screenplay by John Latimer offers an intriguing and original premise, unusual characters and pithy noir dialogue.

George Stroud's doppelganger is of the invisible variety, an alter ego who is nothing but a fiction and yet, like many doubles in literature and film, assumes the mantle of guilt for an innocent man. As in folklore beliefs, it is fatal to be in the same place at the same time as one's double, as George chases his phantom self Jefferson Randolph through the dark caverns of his enemy's fortress in a desperate race against time as the minutes tick away on the big clock. A similar transference of identity occurs in Hitchcock's espionage thriller *North by Northwest*, in which the protagonist, Roger Thornhill (Cary Grant) takes on the identity of a non-existent spy named George Kaplan. Hitch also used the idea of an innocent man wrongfully accused of a crime perpetrated by a doppelganger in *The Wrong Man* (1957) and *Frenzy* (1972). *The Big Clock* was remade in 1987 as *No Way Out*, with Kevin Costner in the lead role as a naval officer framed for murder. While the film updates the story into the world of computers and espionage, it bears little resemblance to the original source material.

In *Hollow Triumph* (a.k.a. *The Scar*, 1948), Paul Henreid plays petty

Ray Milland is menaced by killer Charles Laughton in this poster for John Farrow's *The Big Clock* (1948).

criminal John Muller, who has just been released from jail after doing time for stock fraud and practicing psychiatry without a license. Because Muller has studied medicine, the parole board sets him up with a low-level job in a medical supply company in Los Angeles. Muller, however, has more grandiose plans to knock over a gambling casino owned by vicious mobster Rocky Stansyck (Thomas Brown Henry). Muller and his gang pull off the heist to the tune of 60g's, but the vengeful Rocky has a rep for getting even. "Get him," he tells his hoods, "if it takes twenty years, get him."

Trying to escape retribution from Rocky's gang, Muller flees to L.A. and takes the menial job at the medical outfit. One day while running an errand a man on the street mistakes him for a psychiatrist named Dr. Victor Bartok. Intrigued, Muller locates the doctor and finds that he has, "a real double, down to the last detail," except that Bartok has a prominent scar running down one cheek. Aiming to replace Bartok, Muller seduces his attractive young secretary Evelyn Nash (Joan Bennett), who gives him access to the psychiatrist's case files and specimens of his signature, which Muller assiduously learns to forge. In the meantime, Rocky's thugs have followed him to L.A., where Muller narrowly escapes with his life after the gangsters attack him on the famous Angel's Flight on Bunker Hill.

One final touch will transform Muller into Bartok's doppelganger. Using a close-up photo he has surreptitiously taken of the doctor, he uses a surgical scalpel to replicate the scar on the doctor's cheek. Unfortunately, he is unaware that the photo he is using is a reverse negative print and he has scarred himself on the opposite cheek. He eventually learns of his error, but decides to go through with his plan anyway, murdering Bartok on a bridge and disposing of his body in the river. Oddly, when he replaces the psychiatrist no one notices that the scar has changed position as he smoothly slips into Bartok's identity, including his psychiatric practice and his wife, Virginia (Leslie Brooks). As Bartok he lives the high life in the doctor's swanky townhouse, eating in fancy restaurants and gaming at Maxwell's upscale casino.

One day Muller's brother Fredrick (Eduard Franz) comes looking for his brother, having deduced some connection between Muller and the doctor. Fredrick tells him that Rocky has been arrested and deported, so that he no longer has to fear being hunted down and killed by the gang. Rather than return to his old life, however, Muller decides to leave town with Evelyn, with whom he has fallen in love. Hurrying down to the docks to join Evelyn on a ship sailing to Honolulu, he is cornered by two thugs, who inform him that Dr. Bartok has a 90g tab at Maxwell's casino and the boss is not pleased that he tried to skip town without paying his gambling debt. As he protests that he is Muller and not Bartok, the hoods brutally gun him down as he watches the ship depart for Hawaii with a heartbroken Evelyn on board.

This tightly-paced crime thriller has faded into an undeserved obscurity within the noir cannon. The screenplay by Daniel Fuchs, adapted from a novel by Murray Forbes, employs the unusual narrative technique of painting a vicious criminal as the sympathetic protagonist. The execution by director Steve Sekely makes excellent use of photogenic Los Angeles landmarks like the Angel's Flight funicular railway, the Third Street Tunnel, the Barclay Hotel and the Olympic Theater. The visuals are greatly enhanced by the beautifully evocative lighting and camerawork of ace cinematographer John Alton, who was best known for his work with Anthony Mann on noirs like *T-Men* (1947), *Raw Deal* (1948) and *He*

Walked by Night (1948). Austrian actor Paul Henreid, who played the role of Victor Laszlo in *Casablanca* (1942), delivers a powerful, if understated portrayal of a criminal struggling to survive by any means necessary in an underworld of betrayal and violence, and also worked as producer on the film. His co-star Joan Bennett, who had graced the memorable Fritz Lang noirs *Woman in the Window* (1944) and *Scarlet Street* (1945) shines in her role as the cynical working girl Evelyn Nash.

Once again, via John Alton's expressionistic cinematography, the film noir doppelganger is visually associated with a shadow world of night and fear. The protagonist's double is not a biological twin or a surgical simulacrum, but their identical resemblance is simply an "act of divine providence" as in Dostoyevsky's *The Double*. Scarring himself on the opposite cheek as a result of a reversed negative photograph makes Muller into a mirror image copy of Bartok. Muller assumes not only the appearance but the very identity of the doctor as well, taking over his medical practice, his wife, and, unknowingly, his gambling debts. Ironically, the identity switch does not alter Muller's ultimate fate.

British writer Wilkie Collins's mid–19th-century mystery novel *The Woman in White* was brought to the big screen by the Warner Brothers studio in a lavish, big budget adaptation of the author's work. The movie is set in 1850s England, where painter Walter Hartright (Gig Young) has been hired as an art tutor for the wealthy Fairlie family. Walking through a wooded area enroute to the Fairlie residence at rural Limmeridge House, he encounters a mysterious young woman (Eleanor Parker) who speaks to him incoherently before disappearing back into the woods.

At Limmeridge House, Walter is introduced to its inhabitants, including eccentric uncle Fredrick Fairlie (John Abbott), pretty young cousin Marian (Alexis Smith) and the menacing Count Fosco (Sydney Greenstreet). The next day he sees a woman in the estate's garden dressed entirely in white that bears a striking resemblance to the woman he met the previous night. She is Laura Fairlie (also played by Alexis Smith), the heir to the family fortune and the pupil he has been hired to tutor. He is startled by Laura's likeness to the Woman in White, but no answers are immediately forthcoming concerning the mysterious lady's identity.

Walter takes an immediate dislike to Count Fosco, who seems to have an inordinate interest in his meeting with the mystery woman. Some light is shed on the doppelganger enigma when Marian discovers a letter written by Laura's mother concerning a Fairlie cousin named Anne Catherick, who visited the estate many years ago and looked a lot like Laura. Several days later, Walter has a second encounter with the double, who reveals that she is indeed Anne, and that she has recently escaped from a nearby insane asylum where she was kept imprisoned by Fosco. She also tells him that the Count is scheming to get his hands on Laura's fortune before vanishing into the scenery once more. Walter confronts Fosco and Laura's fiancé, Sir Percival Glyde (John Emery) about the accusations, but as a result is forced to leave Limmeridge House.

Laura marries Sir Percival, and Fosco and his wife, the Countess (Agnes Morehead), move into the Fairlie mansion. It transpires that the Count is using drugs and hypnotism to brainwash Laura and is plotting with Sir Percy to swindle the heiress out of her fortune. One day Anne suddenly appears at Laura's bedside to warn her about the conspirator's dire intentions before disappearing once more. Unbeknownst to anyone, the Countess has been keeping Anne concealed inside a secret room in the cellar of the mansion. But the next time she slips into Laura's bedroom via a hidden passageway, she is apprehended by Fosco and Percival, and the shock causes Anne to die of a heart attack The conspirators quickly use this to their advantage by substituting Anne in place of Laura in order for Sir Percy to inherit the estate, while Laura is placed in Newberry asylum and hypnotized into believing she is Anne Catherick.

Their plan starts to go awry when Walter attends "Laura's" funeral and is able to tell the difference between the cousins with his artist's eye, "to whom every plane and facet of feature has a special meaning." They surmise that Laura has been ensconced in the asylum in Anne's place, where she will eventually suffer a mental breakdown and assume Anne's identity. Walter and Marian hatch their own plot against the conspirators, but while Walter goes off to Newberry to rescue Laura, Marian returns to Limmeridge House to try and strike a deal with Fosco. She proposes to become his mistress if he will release Laura and leave England with her. During their negotiations, however, the Count reveals that his wife, the Countess, is Fredrick Fairlie's sister, who bore Anne out of wedlock, whereupon the child was sent to Italy to avoid any hint of scandal.

Unfortunately for him, Fosco's wife has been listening in on this exchange and becomes infuriated, stabbing the Count to death with a dagger. In the meantime, Laura has come to her senses and manages to escape from the asylum. Intercepted by Sir Percy during the rescue attempt, Walter tangles with the nobleman, who is accidentally killed during the struggle. Linking up with Laura, they return to Limmeridge House with the police just as Fosco expires. In the aftermath, Walter marries Marian and the Countess is remanded to Newberry Asylum.

Stephen Morehouse Avery's screenplay hews closely to the plot of Wilkie Collins's seminal 1859 mystery novel, while director Peter Godfrey imbues the proceedings with gobs of murky atmosphere that are appropriate to this Gothic mystery. Period set design by George Sotham and fluid camerawork and evocative lighting by cinematographer Carl B. Guthrie contribute greatly to the film's total effect. Veteran film composer Max Steiner contributed a rousing orchestral score that serves to enhance the film's mysterious mood. With its cast of bizarre characters and dark ambience, the film resembles other films noir set during the 19th century such as George Cukor's *Gaslight* (1944) and Edward G. Ulmer's *Bluebeard* (1944), which also featured dastardly plots directed at unassuming women. A distinguished cast, including Alexis Smith, Gig Young and Agnes Morehead deliver dignified dramatic performances, while John Abbott provides comic relief as the hypochondriac Fairlie uncle. Eleanor Parker, playing a dual role, is sweet and innocent as Laura and mysterious and remote as her doppelganger, Anne. It is perennial film noir heavy Sydney Greenstreet, however, who delivers the film's most memorable performance as the grotesquely villainous Count Fosco, his vast bulk and scowling face projecting a brooding air of menace that recalls his roles in classic noirs like *The Maltese Falcon*.

Laura Fairlie's double Anne Catherick roams through the narrative as an enigma who appears and disappears mysteriously like a Gothic ghost. Once again the doppelganger is associated with insanity and the otherworldly in the person of the spectral Woman in White. The plotting must avoid Anne being Laura's twin or sibling, and so resorts to the notion that, in Fosco's words, "the family strain was strong enough like her to be a twin." The idea of "identical cousins" may have been cribbed for the central premise of the doppelgangers appearing in the TV sitcom *The Patty Duke Show*. Note that Laura is subjected to mind altering techniques administered by an unscrupulous medico in an effort to brainwash her into believing she is another person in a manner similar to the procedures used to exchange personalities in Billy Wilder's *Fedora* (1978) to be discussed later in this chapter. Walter being able to discern the difference between Laura and Anne using his painterly eye for detail is an interesting twist.

"This guy was my double," reads the tag line on the poster for *The Man with My Face* (1951). Here's the setup: Charles "Chick" Graham (Barry Nelson), who operates a small insurance business in Puerto Rico, comes home from work one night to find that his wife Cora (Lynn Ainley) and brother-in-law and business partner Buster (John Harvey) do not recognize him. Even his faithful dog attacks him as if he is a total stranger. The mystery deepens when his doppelganger (also played by Nelson) enters the room claiming to be the real Chick Graham. A policeman is called in, but when the original Chick's signature and fingerprints do not match those on his identity card, he is taken into custody for false impersonation. As he is being escorted to the local jail, however, Chick and the officer are attacked by a trained Doberman and Chick escapes in the melee.

As a bewildered Chick wanders the streets of San Juan trying to unravel the mystery, the local papers are running a story about a man named Albert Rand who has stolen half a million dollars in bonds from a bank in Miami. A reward is offered for the felon's capture, and photos of Rand's features in the paper look exactly like Chick's. Chick takes refuge with an old flame, Mary Davis (Carole Mathews) and tries to stay one step ahead of the cops, but finds himself shadowed by a mysterious man named Meadows (Jim Boles) and his deadly Doberman.

When Rand and his gang manage to capture Chick, the criminal reveals a complex scheme to steal Chick's identity and frame him for the heist that Rand had been planning for years. Rand had plastic surgery to make his face resemble Chick's, then co-opted his wife, Cora, who replaced Chick's I.D. with a bogus card bearing Rand's fingerprints and signature. Dog trainer Meadows got rid of Chick's pet and substituted a pooch that was trained to attack him. Chick is confined to a remote beach house while the gang plots to murder Chick by arranging a "car accident" that will leave Rand in the clear in his new identity.

The crooks leave Chick locked inside the house guarded by the Doberman, but Chick traps the dog inside one of the rooms and escapes. Running down a nearby beach, he is pursued by Rand as Meadows frees the dog, who also takes off after him. In the meantime, Mary arrives with the police to arrest Meadows and the cops chase Rand down the beach. Relentlessly pursued by the vicious Doberman, Chick hides inside the crumbling ruins of Fort San Cristobal, where the dog chases him through a maze of darkened stone passageways. Rand arrives at the fort and pretends to be Chick as the police drive up, but the Doberman also mistakes him for Chick and attacks, causing Rand to fall to his death on the rocks below.

Based on the novel *The Man with My Face* by Samuel W. Taylor, the film version relocates the action from California to the more exotic locale of Puerto Rico, where director Edward Montagne uses the San Juan locations to great effect in this low-budget thriller. Star Barry Nelson carries the film in his dual role as the hapless Chick and his sinister double, Rand, and Jim Boles cuts a menacing figure as the crooked dog trainer, Meadows. The menacing Doberman presents an economical yet effective threat, and the murderous canine was featured prominently in poster art for the film.

As in *Among the Living* and *The Big Clock*, an innocent man is made to assume the guilt for crimes committed by his doppelganger in this take on the "wrong man" theme. The film exploits fears of loss of one's identity and individuality, as an evil double takes over the protagonist's entire life and even makes him doubt his own sanity. At times *The Man with My Face* has the ambience of an episode of the classic TV series *The Twilight Zone,* in which an ordinary man is suddenly thrust out of his comfortable world and into a fantastic situation. However, Rand's complex scheme to replace Chick, which includes undergoing plastic surgery, seducing his victim's wife, forging his identity documents and even substituting a bogus pet in place of his dog tends to strain credulity.

British director Alfred Hitchcock was one of the most celebrated and well-known filmmakers in the history of the cinema. Over his long career he directed a plethora of screen thrillers, including *The Man Who Knew Too Much, The Lady Vanishes, The 39 Steps, Suspicion, Spellbound, Dial M for Murder, Rear Window* and *The Birds,* among others, that earned him the sobriquet of "The Master of Suspense." Hitchcock began making movies at Germany's UFA studios in the 1920s, where he absorbed elements of the Weimar Expressionist style from the work of directors like Fritz Lang and F.W. Murnau. He returned to his native England during the late 20s, where he found his niche with the Jack the Ripper crime melodrama *The Lodger* (1927). During the 1940s he emigrated to Hollywood where he hit his stride making a series of acclaimed and popular suspense films beginning with the Academy Award–winning *Rebecca* (1940). More than any other filmmaker before or since, Hitchcock was fascinated with the theme of the doppelganger and used it as a motif that enlivens some of his greatest and most influential works.

In his seminal biography of Hitchcock, *The Dark Side of Genius,* author Donald Spoto notes, "The theme of the double was available to Hitchcock from the literary traditions that were available to him. From E.T.A. Hoffmann's first novel *The Devil's Elixirs* and his tale 'The Doubles,' he took the device of the doppelganger.... Hitchcock knew the dramatic value of describing two persons drawn together by fate, by love and by murderous impulses. From 'William Wilson' by Edgar Allan Poe, he had taken the same motif, as he had from Dostoyevsky's tale *The Double.* Stevenson's *The Strange Case of Dr. Jekyll and Mr. Hyde* he knew well.... Intimate with these sources, Hitchcock could make the double—in *Shadow of a Doubt* and *Strangers on a Train,* as later in *Psycho* and *Frenzy*—the messenger of death."[2]

Working within the realistic genre of the crime melodrama, Hitchcock dispenses with the preternatural doppelganger in favor of the psychological variety, creating pairs of characters who represent the good and evil polarities of the human psyche. In her noir novel *Strangers on a Train,* (filmed by Hitchcock in 1951), author Patricia Highsmith expresses this concept thusly: "But love and hate, he thought now, good and evil, lived side by side in the human heart, and not merely in differing proportions in one man and the next, but all good and all evil. One merely had to look for a little of either to find it all, and one merely had to scratch the surface."[3]

Hitchcock's initial exploration of the doppelganger theme occurs in his first American film, *Rebecca* (1940). The story, adapted from a popular neo-Gothic novel by Daphne du Maurier, centers around a submissive young working-class woman (who has no name in the book or the movie), played by Joan Fontaine. She marries Maxim de Winter (Laurence Olivier), a wealthy but enigmatic older man who is consumed with grief after the death of his wife, Rebecca, in a boating accident. After a whirlwind courtship the couple returns to Max's ancestral home of Manderley, an imposing mansion poised on the edge of the rugged

Cornish coast. The heroine must cope with adjusting to her new station in life as the mistress of Manderley, and with the palatial home's forbidding housekeeper, Mrs. Danvers (Judith Anderson).

Before long the second Mrs. De Winter begins to perceive that the ghostly presence of Rebecca still permeates the house. She is surrounded by the dead woman's clothes, furniture, bric-a-brac and monogrammed items that are markers of Rebecca's persona. Moreover, Max has ensconced his new wife in Manderley's humble guest quarters, while Rebecca's room, "the most beautiful room in the house," remains locked, as if her disembodied spirit is still in residence there. Rebecca's ghost is being kept alive by Max's brooding about the past and by Mrs. Danvers's necrophiliac longing for her dead mistress. The housekeeper has maintained Rebecca's quarters exactly as they were on the day of her death, and when the second Mrs. de Winter gains access to the rooms, Danvers displays the dead woman's exquisite clothes, furs, lingerie and feminine accoutrements in order to intimate that Max's second wife can never measure up to Rebecca's exalted standard of womanhood.

Trying to assert her own identity, the new wife proposes to Max that they throw a costume ball at Manderley, whereupon Danvers suggests that she copy the elaborate outfit worn by Max's ancestor Lady Caroline in a family portrait. On the night of the ball, however, Max is horrified to see her thus attired because Rebecca had worn the same costume to a previous ball. Confronting Mrs. Danvers about her treachery, the housekeeper responds by telling her that Max can never love her because he is still obsessed with Rebecca. "She's too strong, you can't fight her," says Danvers about the ghost, sending the new Mrs. De Winter into a fit of suicidal despair.

Soon afterward Rebecca's sunken sailboat is discovered off the coast with the dead woman's corpse still inside and evidence that the craft had been deliberately scuttled. Max confesses to his wife that Rebecca was really a venal, promiscuous woman who he never loved. One night she taunted him about being pregnant by another man and Rebecca was accidentally killed during the quarrel. It was Max who placed her body in the boat and deliberately sank it, and now that this evidence has come to light he will stand trial for her murder. During the trial, however, Max is exonerated when it is revealed that Rebecca was terminally ill and apparently committed suicide. Rather than let the new Mrs. De Winter become the mistress of Manderly in Rebecca's place, Mrs. Danvers sets fire to the great house and perishes inside.

Rebecca deftly translates the 19th-century Gothic tale, replete with tropes like a brooding wealthy man with a terrible secret, a haunted mansion and a secret room that harbors a phantom, into a modern idiom. It has been called "a ghost story without a ghost," as Rebecca's specter is a psychological construct kept alive by Mrs. Danvers's necro-erotic longings, Max's guilty obsession and the solidity of Manderley itself. The screenplay by Joan Harrison and Robert Sherwood sticks closely to the plot of the du Maurier novel to capture the nameless heroine's haunting dilemma, while the lush production values provided by the acclaimed producer David O. Selznick adds the gloss of the celebrated "Selznick touch" to the proceedings. Hitchcock is in fine form directing this unusual material, his camera eerily gliding through the magnificent Manderley sets created by art director Lyle Wheeler. A seasoned cast of British thespians deliver fine performances, most notably Laurence Olivier as the tormented Max, Joan Fontaine as the nameless "second Mrs. De Winter" and Judith Anderson as her sadistic nemesis Mrs. Danvers.

The second Mrs. De Winter (Joan Fontaine) confronts her husband Maxim (Laurence Olivier) in Alfred Hitchcock's *Rebecca* (1940).

The film's chief dramatic conflict is between the two Mrs. De Winters, one a living woman and the other a ghostly doppelganger, for the affections of their mutual husband and the possession of Manderley. Unbeknownst to the film's protagonist, Max chooses her to be his new wife because her innocent and modest personality is the polar opposite to Rebecca's flamboyant decadence. The heroine is a nameless person whose identity is overshadowed by that of her dead rival, an unseen doppelganger whose presence is projected through material objects. Rebecca's rooms are the finest in the house, with enormous windows and lavish furnishings, while the new Mrs. De Winter is confined to Manderley's humble guest quarters. Using contrasting spaces to illustrate the difference between paired opposites harks back to Stevenson's *Jekyll and Hyde* (see Chapter Two), and would later be used in Hitchcock's *Psycho*.

Hitch's next essay in the double came a few years later in his film noir *Shadow of a Doubt* (1943). Charles Oakley (Joseph Cotten) is a psychotic serial murderer dubbed the "Merry Widow Killer" because he preys on elderly women. Escaping from two detectives who are tailing him on the East Coast, Charlie heads west, hoping to lay low for a while by visiting his sister Emma Newton (Patricia Collinge) and her family in sleepy Santa Rosa,

California. Emma's daughter Charlie (Teresa Wright) is named after her uncle and seems to have a telepathic link with him.

Arriving in Santa Rosa, Uncle Charlie quickly charms his relatives and the locals with his charismatic personality and hefty bank account. His niece, however, is compelled by curiosity to probe deeper into Uncle Charlie's psyche. Charlie's mental link with her uncle eventually makes her suspect that he may be the serial killer. Her suspicions are confirmed when Uncle Charlie gives her a ring bearing the initials of one of the Merry Widow Killer's victims, and when she receives a visit from two detectives who are on the murderer's trail. Fearing that she has uncovered his secret, her uncle makes several attempts to murder her and nearly succeeds.

Joseph Cotten's chilling portrayal of the psycho-killer Uncle Charlie dominates the film and was the first in a line of homicidal psychopaths that would populate Hitch's later thrillers, while Teresa Wright provides the perfect foil for his villainy as the virginal ingénue Charlie. The murderer's perverse inner world is revealed through the use of the sparkling dialogue in *Our Town* playwright Thornton Wilder's screenplay. Hitchcock builds suspense around the notion of an amoral sociopath concealing himself among a group of normal small-town people who are unwilling to perceive his true nature. The film builds to one of Hitchcock's typically exciting climaxes as the two main characters become locked in a life and death battle in the final scenes.

Psychopathic murderer Uncle Charlie (Joseph Cotten) has a telepathic link with his niece Charlie (Teresa Wright) in Hitchcock's *Shadow of a Doubt* (1943).

The two Charlies represent the good and evil aspects of human nature, Jekyll and Hyde doppelgangers who are linked by fate and inexorably thrown into conflict with each other. Unaware of the homicidal deeds of her uncle, Charlie muses to him about the peculiarities of their relationship thus: "I'm glad that mother named me after you and that she thinks we're both alike. I think we are too.... We're not just an uncle and a niece. It's something else. I know you.... We're sort of like twins, don't you see? We have to know." Their telepathic link lends them a unique closeness that imperils both of them.

Donald Spoto notes that the doppelganger concept is further reinforced by the very structure of the film. "The structural element at work in *Shadow of a Doubt*," he writes, "is the almost infinite accumulation of doubles: the two Charlies; two detectives in the East pursuing Uncle Charlie, then two in the West; two criminals sought; two women with eyeglasses; two dinner sequences; ... two double brandies served at the 'Till Two' bar by a waitress who has worked there for two weeks; two attempts to kill the girl before the final scene ... and so on, almost past counting."[4] These structural doublings would recur in some of Hitchcock's later films that embody the doppelganger theme.

Hitchcock's obsession with the double continued in his film noir *Strangers on a Train* (1951). As the film begins, two strangers, tennis pro Guy Haines (Farley Granger) and wealthy playboy Bruno Anthony (Robert Walker) meet by chance on a train and strike up a conversation. Bruno is a tennis fan who knows about Guy's marital problems with trying to obtain a divorce from his first wife and marry his present sweetheart, senator's daughter Anne Morton (Ruth Roman). The smooth-talking Bruno casually remarks that he should murder Guy's wife in exchange for Guy murdering Bruno's father so he can get his hands on the family estate. Guy jokingly agrees to the arrangement, not realizing that Bruno is a psychotic who intends to carry out the bizarre plan.

Soon after their meeting, Bruno brutally murders Guy's wife Miriam (Laura Elliott) in an amusement park, then contacts Guy and demands he fulfill his part of the bargain. Guy is hesitant about going to the police, who suspect him of the murder but have no proof. Trying to clear his name, Guy stalls for time but is shadowed through the streets of Washington, D.C., by the figure of Bruno, who seems to haunt him everywhere like a guilty conscience. Finally tiring of the charade, Bruno intends to plant incriminating evidence at the murder scene, but Guy follows him to the amusement park, where Bruno is killed in a mishap on an out of control merry go round and dies with the evidence still in his possession, thereby exonerating Guy.

Strangers on a Train, adapted from a novel by the acclaimed mystery writer Patricia Highsmith by noir icon Raymond Chandler, is one of Hitchcock's most finely crafted thrillers. The director uses familiar Washington, D.C., landmarks to great effect as Bruno stalks Guy through the marble monuments of the nation's capital in several nightmarish sequences. The most unusual scene in the film is the strangulation murder of Guy's wife Laura by Bruno, which is shown as a distorted image reflected in a lens of Laura's eyeglasses. To achieve this hallucinatory effect Hitchcock had an enormous distorting camera lens constructed and filmed the actors at a 90-degree angle. The climactic sequence on the merry go round involved complex low-angle rear projection shots combined with miniature work. Farley Granger carries much of the film in his role as the guileless protagonist Guy, but Robert Walker, a comic actor cast against type as a psychopath, delivers a knockout performance as the demented Bruno.

Tennis pro Guy Hanies (Farley Granger, left) has a chance encounter with psychopathic playboy Bruno Anthony (Robert Walker) that leads to murder in *Strangers on a Train* (1951).

As in *Shadow of a Doubt*, the two main characters are doppelgangers representing the forces of good and evil in the human psyche. They are total strangers who are drawn together by the capricious forces of fate. Like the two Charlies in the earlier film, Guy and Bruno are paired opposites. Guy is a clean-cut professional athlete, while Bruno is depicted as an effete mother's boy of uncertain sexuality. Guy wears crisp white tennis outfits and light-colored sports clothes, while Bruno dresses in contrasting dark formal attire. Guy is a regular joe trying to move up in the world, while Bruno is a wealthy, cultured socialite. Spoto notes, "The controlling idea of *Shadow of a Doubt* had been the motif of the double.... As in the earlier film, the form of the film is in its meaning: doubles and pairs, accumulated and intercut in an almost endless series, mediate the theme.... There are, at the outset, two pairs of feet and two sets of train rails that cross twice ... two respectable and influential fathers, two women with eyeglasses.... All this doubling—which has no precedent in the novel—was quite deliberately added by Hitchcock, and is the key element in the film's structure."[5]

On January 14, 1953, Christopher Emmanuel Balestero, a musician who worked a night gig at New York's swanky Stork Club, was arrested and charged with a robbery he did not commit. He was eventually exonerated when the real criminal, who bore a striking resemblance to Balestero, confessed to the crime, but not before he had endured imprisonment and the mental deterioration of his wife. *Life* magazine ran a feature on this incident entitled "A Case of Identity" that became the basis for Hitchcock's film noir *The Wrong Man* (1956).

In the film Balestero, nicknamed "Manny" (Henry Fonda) tries to draw some money out of an insurance policy to pay for his wife's dental work when he is mistaken for a thief who has held up the office twice. Arrested for the crimes, he is picked out of a police lineup by the insurance company's employees, and when he misspells a word in the same manner as the crook did in a note, he is arraigned for grand larceny and thrown into jail. Manny hires a lawyer to defend him at his upcoming trial, which puts a severe strain on the household's finances and causes his wife Rose (Vera Miles) to descend into a private mental hell.

The case goes to trial but a mistrial is declared on a technicality, which prolongs the couple's legal and financial woes to the breaking point. One night in the solitude of his jail cell a dejected Manny prays for deliverance and his prayers are answered. In the film's most remarkable sequence, the director uses a slow, lingering dissolve on a tight close-up of Manny's face as the features of his criminal double are superimposed over his own. The perspective shifts to that of the hoodlum, Daniell, (Richard Robbins) as he attempts an armed robbery of a neighborhood grocery store and gets nabbed. Daniell confesses to robbing the insurance company while in police custody and Manny is freed, but the ordeal has taken its toll on Rose, who has experienced a mental breakdown. In real life, Mrs. Ballestero was institutionalized in a mental hospital but later recovered.

The Wrong Man was a gritty, realistic film noir that proved to be a departure from the slick Technicolor thrillers shot in exotic locales that Hitchcock had made in the mid–1950s such as *Dial M for Murder* (1954), *To Catch a Thief* (1955) and *The Man who Knew Too Much* (1956). *The Wrong Man* was filmed on the streets of Jackson Heights and Ridgewood in the borough of Queens where the actual events had taken place, lending the film a documentary verisimilitude typical of late 50s films noir such as *Naked City*, *Call Northside 777* and *Kiss of Death*. Henry Fonda delivers a fine, understated performance as the wrongly accused Manny, but Vera Miles shines in her vivid portrayal of Rose's pathetic descent into mental illness. Ms. Miles was reportedly subjected to grueling, hours-long private coaching sessions with Hitchcock for the role. The director's frequent musical collaborator Bernard Herrmann contributed a moody jazz score for the soundtrack.

Once again the narrative's protagonist is linked to their doppelganger by some quirk of fate and suffers for the evil deeds committed by their double. Once again the folk motif of being in the same place and time as one's doppelganger is in evidence in the dramatic scene in which the hoodlum Daniell appears to walk right into Manny's image in a slow dissolve. Manny briefly confronts Daniell in a scene that takes place in a police station after the thief has been apprehended, and even though it is shot in a realistic manner there is something uncanny about their close resemblance. Hitchcock suggests that an act of God is responsible for the resolution of the problem of their dual identities.

Most critics agree that Hitchcock's next three films, *Vertigo* (1958), *North by Northwest* (1959) and *Psycho* (1960) represent the master's greatest works, and in all of them the doppelganger is a major theme. In *Vertigo*, San Francisco detective Scottie Ferguson (James Stewart) has developed a severe fear of heights after a police accident and has been obliged to resign from the force. He is approached by an old school chum, Gavin Elster (Tom Helmore), who has read about his predicament in the newspapers, to perform a little private detective work. Elster explains that he wants Scottie to keep tabs on his wealthy wife, Madeleine, who is having mental problems and believes herself to be possessed by the spirit of her dead ancestor, a woman named Carlotta Valdes.

On a whim, Scottie accepts the unusual assignment and is soon tailing Mrs. Elster (Kim Novak) as she rides around the city until they are brought face to face when she attempts suicide by jumping into San Francisco Bay. Before long, Scottie becomes obsessed with this mysterious, beautiful woman and the two become lovers. One day they take a trip to the old Spanish mission of San Juan Batista and Madeleine goes into one of her fits, running to the top of a church tower where Scottie cannot follow her because of his vertigo. Unable to prevent a second suicide attempt, Scottie watches helplessly as Madeleine plunges to her death from the bell tower.

Feeling responsible for her death, Scottie suffers a mental breakdown, but wandering around the streets one day he sees a woman who bears a striking resemblance to Madeleine, although her clothes and mannerisms are completely different. Intrigued, he follows her to her hotel and interrogates her, learning that she is a department store clerk named Judy Barton. He wants to take her out on a date and she accepts, but it is revealed to the audience that Judy impersonated Madeleine in a plot to murder Elster's wife for her fortune. Elster gambled that Scottie's vertigo would prevent him from climbing to the top of the bell tower while he hurled the real Madeleine to her death.

Scottie takes Judy out a few times, but something is missing. He insists that she change her hair color, hair style, makeup and wardrobe to make her look like Madeleine. Judy resists at first, but finally gives in, allowing him to transform her into the image of his lost love, and Judy goes along because she has fallen in love with him. Once she has been made over into Madeleine Elster for a second time, Scottie is ecstatic, but his joy is short-

Henry Fonda and Vera Miles, along with a procession of Fonda doubles, are presided over by the bland visage of director Hitchcock in this poster for his fact-based crime melodrama *The Wrong Man* (1957).

lived when he notices Judy wearing Madeleine's necklace and perceives the truth. In an attempt to exorcise his inner demons, he drives her back to the Mission San Juan Bautista and confronts her about her role in the murder plot as he drags her to the top of the bell tower. Judy admits to everything, and when they are interrupted by a nun walking out of the shadows, Madeleine is startled and falls to her death.

Many critics consider *Vertigo* Hitchcock's ultimate masterpiece, and a number of books have been written about this classic film in which mystery, romance and suspense are seamlessly blended. While the subject matter involving murder, obsession, bogus supernaturalism and haunted love might call for claustrophobic locales and expressionist shadows,

Kim Novak poses as her alter egos Madeleine Elster (left) and Judy Barton in this publicity still for *Vertigo* (1958).

Hitchcock instead employs bright, pastel colors and uses the airy, open spaces and picturesque monuments of San Francisco to tell this unusual story. The director also utilizes experimental film techniques such as a simultaneous dolly out and zoom in shot of the bell tower stairs to depict Scottie's vertiginous fear as the ground comes rushing toward him, the construction of a circular set to shoot a 360-degree shot of the lovers kissing in Judy's hotel room, and the use of an animated cartoon to simulate a nightmare.

Based on the novel *D'Entre des Morts* (*From Among the Dead*) by French suspense writers Pierre Boileau and Thomas Narcejac, the complex plot devised by screenwriters Alec Coppel and Samuel Taylor sometimes strains credulity but hangs together in the end. James Stewart delivers one of the most memorable performances of his career as the erotically obsessed Scottie and Kim Novak matches his intensity in her dual role as the ethereal Madeleine and the seemingly naive Judy. Bernard Hermann's magnificent score conveys both romantic longing and haunted mystery, and is widely considered some of the finest screen music in cinema history.

In *Vertigo* the doppelganger takes the form of an ideal woman who does not exist. Scottie cannot love her for herself and must re-create her in the form of Madeleine's double, but in reality the ghost-haunted "Madeleine" that Scottie is obsessed with is merely a construct of Gavin Elster's imagination. Judy's real double, Mrs. Elster, is only shown briefly as a corpse dressed in the same outfit as her impersonator during her "suicide" scene. She presumably provides a template for Judy to copy, at least sartorially, but she is a non-entity and her persona is a cipher in the narrative. Judy, who is really a gauche farm girl from Kansas, is the stylistic opposite of her prim, upper-class lookalike. Hitchcock utilizes mirrors in several key scenes as a means of calling attention to the many doublings represented by Judy and the false Madeleine, a motif he would return to in *Psycho*. While the plot of *Vertigo* eventually unravels into a mundane murder mystery, most of the film is presented through the lens of Scottie's imaginative vision in which the doppelganger is associated with portents of the uncanny such as identity transference and spirit possession by the dead.

The film noir cycle had burned itself out by the late 1950s, a victim of changing tastes and the coming of the color film that superseded the black and white B-movie milieu of noir. Hitchcok's next film was the lavish MGM production *North by Northwest* (1958), a breezy, fast-paced spy thriller that anticipated the James Bond series of films by several years. Cary Grant stars as New York advertising man Roger O. Thornhill (read: ROT), a milquetoast mama's boy who accidentally gets caught up in a spy game when he assumes the identity of a non-existent secret agent.

During a business meeting at NYC's swanky Plaza Hotel, Thornhill wants to send a telegram and flags down a pageboy who is calling for a man named George Kaplan. This draws the attention of two thugs who think he's Kaplan and force him into a waiting car at gunpoint. They drive him out to a mansion in Long Island, where he is interrogated by a distinguished man (James Mason) who gives his name as "Lester Townsend." When Thornhill attempts to assert his identity, "Townsend" proceeds to list items in "Kaplan's" travel itinerary, including his occupancy of room 796 at the Plaza and planned stops in Chicago and Rapid City, South Dakota. The men attempt to get information out of Thornhill by forcing him to drink a large amount of liquor, and when this fails they try to dispose of him by arranging a car accident, but he manages to escape from their clutches even in his inebriated state. He returns to the estate with the police the next day and is informed that

Townsend is not at home and is due to deliver an address at the United Nations later that afternoon.

Puzzled by these strange events, Thornhill and his mother (Jessie Royce Landis) go back to the Plaza and manage to gain access to Kaplan's room where they find luggage, a closetful of clothes and other personal belongings, but no Kaplan. Thornhill heads to the UN to confront Townsend (Philip Ober), but upon meeting Townsend finds that he is not the same person he had met on Long Island. Just then one of the thugs hurls a knife into Townsend's back and when Thornhill instinctively pulls it out, someone takes a picture of him standing over the corpse with a knife in his hand and he is instantly framed for the murder. Pictured as the "UN murderer" on the front page of every newspaper in the country, Thornhill becomes a wanted man on the run.

In the meantime, at a meeting of U.S. government agents in Washington chaired by a veteran spy known only as "The Professor" (Leo G. Carroll), it is revealed that "George Kaplan" is a non-existent person created to flush out a nest of spies headed up by an agent named Philip Vandamm (Mason). The Professor and his counterspies have carefully crafted the bogus Kaplan identity by creating hotel reservations in his name and having agents move his "belongings" in and out of the hotel rooms. Now that Thornhill has assumed the identity of Kaplan, the agency is obliged to keep an eye on him in the hope he will lead them to Vandamm.

Learning that Kaplan has a reservation at the Regency Hotel in Chicago, Thornhill boards the next train to Chi-town, where he meets a young woman named Eve Kendall (Eva Marie Saint) seemingly by accident. Eve knows he is a murder suspect wanted by the police but enables him to evade the authorities by hiding him in her sleeping compartment. The two strike up a budding relationship during the trip, but it soon becomes apparent that she is working for Vandamm.

The rest of the film is a rollicking road trip as Thornhill/Kaplan tries to keep one step ahead of the law and Vandamm's spies while navigating through Eve's shifting allegiances. Memorable scenes include Thornhill being menaced by a crop dusting plane in the middle of a wide-open prairie and a rousing climax atop the monumental sculptured heads on Mount Rushmore. It turns out that Eve is a double agent working with the Professor to retrieve some valuable microfilm hidden inside a figurine and capture Vandamm and his spies before they can leave the country with the government secrets coded on the microfilm.

The theme of a man wrongly accused of murder and pursued by both police and spies constituted the essential narrative device for Hitchcock's earlier thrillers *The 39 Steps* (1935) and *Saboteur* (1942), but he perfected the formula in *North by Northwest*. Sequences such as the murder at the UN, the airplane attack in the middle of a featureless prairie and the pursuit over the giant presidential heads on Rushmore lend the film a disturbing, dreamlike ambience. At the same time, Hitch crafts his spy melodrama with a light touch that includes a number of comic interludes, such as Thornhill's drunken escape from the speeding car and a serious art auction played for laughs. Ernest Lehman's screenplay is engaging and original and leads the viewer in many unexpected directions. Cary Grant is at the top of his comic form, yet also satisfies as an action hero playing the pre–Bond secret agent man Thornhill, while Eva Marie Saint provides the glamour as the lady spy Eve and James Mason exudes continental menace as the sinister enemy agent Vandamm. Bernard Hermann contributed a lively and romantic musical score that provided a stirring counterpoint to the fast-paced action onscreen.

Like *The Big Clock*, *North by Northwest* combines the "wrong man" theme with that of the invisible doppelganger. Its protagonist, the mild-mannered Roger O. Thornhill begins the narrative as a virtual non-entity. The hollowness, or ROT, at the center of his being is indicated by his middle initial. When Eve asks him what the "O" stands for, he replies, "nothing." It is only when he assumes the identity of a non-existent person that he is thrust into a world of danger, excitement and romance. As in *Vertigo*, the protagonist chooses to trade their identity for that of a fictitious, fantastical double that slowly subsumes their original persona. As is frequently the case, the individual is made to suffer for the deeds committed by their doppelganger.

Hitchcock's next foray into the uncanny realm of the doppelganger was *Psycho* (1960), widely considered to be his most famous and influential movie. The film opens in Phoenix, Arizona, where secretary Marion Crane (Janet Leigh) is having an affair with divorced storekeeper Sam Loomis (John Gavin). Marion wants to marry Sam but this is financially impossible because of alimony payments he must make to his former spouse. On an impulse, Marion steals $40,000 in cash from one of her boss's clients and skips town with the money and with no destination in mind. After several days on the road she seeks refuge from a rainstorm at the rundown Bates Motel in a rural area of Northern California.

The motel is operated by the boyishly charming Norman Bates (Anthony Perkins), who gives her a warm welcome. On a rise overlooking the motel is Norman's abode, a spooky old gingerbread house that is also inhabited by Norman's elderly but domineering mother. That night Marion is brutally stabbed to death while taking a shower by Norman's mother, and Norman covers up the crime by removing all the evidence and sinking Marion's corpse, along with her car and the money into a nearby bog.

In the wake of Marion's disappearance, her sister, Lila (Vera Miles), contacts Sam to see if he has any info, but he is equally perplexed. They soon learn that a private detective named Arbogast (Martin Balsam) is also looking for Marion and the missing $40,000, and promises to keep them in the loop if he digs up anything. Arbogast burns up a lot of gasoline and shoe leather before hitting paydirt at the Bates Motel, where he discovers that Marion had spent a night. He phones Sam and Lila to tell them he thinks Marion may still be at the motel, but when he tries to explore the Bates house he is knifed to death by Ma Bates. In the aftermath of the killing, Norman is seen in an extreme high shot carrying his protesting mother downstairs to be confined in the fruit cellar.

When Arbogast disappears Sam and Lila decide to investigate for themselves. Traveling to a town near the motel, they learn from the local sheriff that Norman's mother has been dead for many years. Pretending to be husband and wife, they register at the motel and find clues that indicate that Marion had indeed been there. Lila starts snooping through the Bates house, where she finds that the mother's bedroom is a grand affair, complete with a large bed, full-length mirrors, ornate bric-a-brac and other feminine accoutrements, while Norman's room is a small, cramped alcove filled with toys and other childish objects. She finds her way into the fruit cellar, where she discovers the mummified corpse of Mrs. Bates as Norman charges into the room dressed in his mother's clothes, a wig, and brandishing a knife, but the psycho is quickly overcome by Sam.

In the aftermath a psychiatrist (Simon Oakland) explains to Sam, Lila and the authorities that Norman and his mother are two halves of a split personality. "Norman Bates no longer exists," he elucidates. "He only half existed to begin with, and now, the other half has taken over, probably for all time." Norman's incestuous desire for his mother led him to poison her when she took a lover, but guilt over the matricide obsessed him and compelled him to dig up her corpse and preserve it using his skills at taxidermy. But even this wasn't enough, so he had to create the illusion that his mother was alive by wearing her clothes and speaking in her voice. "He was never all Norman," the psychiatrist explains, "but he was often only mother, and now the dominant personality has won." A chilling final scene shows Norman alone, speaking in his mother's voice, totally dominated by his maternal persona.

Hitchcock's twisted tale of a mother-obsessed serial killer was a monster hit that was destined to become a classic of American cinema despite its lurid subject matter. *Psycho* shows the Master of Suspense at the apex of his cinematic powers as he plays the audience like a Stradivarius with his morbid imagery, fluid camerawork and shock cutting. Joseph Stefano's screenplay, adapted from Robert Bloch's novel, keeps the viewer off balance with its surprise twists and doesn't resolve the mystery surrounding Norman and his mother

Sam Loomis (John Gavin, left) and Lila Crane (Vera Miles) check into the Bates Motel in *Psycho* (1960). Note the resemblance between Gavin and Norman Bates (Anthony Perkins).

until the final reels. Principals Janet Leigh and Tony Perkins turn in riveting performances and are ably assisted by supporting actors Vera Miles, John Gavin and Martin Balsam. Other talents who contributed to the film's success include cameraman John L. Russell, editor George Tomasini, titler and storyboarder Saul Bass and, most especially, the brooding, eerie musical score composed by Bernard Herrmann.

Psycho was Hitchcock's only essay in the horror film, and although it begins in the realm of the crime melodrama, it soon transforms into an American Gothic ghost story

Norman Bates (Anthony Perkins) poses in front of the Bates house from *Psycho* (1960).

with all the cinematic trappings of the supernatural. Norman Bates's mother is the most terrifying doppelganger in any of his films, an elusive, spectral presence who nonetheless presents a real homicidal menace. As in *Vertigo*, the double is associated with necrophilia and the possession of a living person by a ghost, only in this case it is literally true as Norman's personality is overwhelmed by the persona of his dead mother. This unbalanced relationship is illustrated by the contrast between their rooms: Mrs. Bates's room is grand and lavish, while Norman's is small and cramped and appears to be seldom used. The dynamic contrast between the boyish, seemingly innocent Norman and his murderous, domineering mother drives much of the dramatic conflict in the film. Another doppelganger relationship lies in the resemblance between Tony Perkins and John Gavin in their roles as Norman and Sam. Their features and hairstyles are similar, but Sam is a more robust, more "masculine" version of the skinny and sexually repressed Norman.

Critics have pointed to the use of mirrors in *Vertigo* and *Psycho* to suggest the idea of the double. Spoto notes that "from the famous film *The Student of Prague*, which had so impressed him in his teenage years, he had first learned the enormous emotional power of the mirror to convey schizophrenia in a dramatic narrative."[6] Mirrors appear everywhere in *Psycho*, but they figure most importantly as props in the scenes in Mother Bates's bedroom, where full-length mirrors generate multiple images.

Hitchcock returned to England after a long hiatus in Hollywood to film another violent story of a serial killer and his doppelganger in *Frenzy* (1972). Set in London's wholesale produce district of Covent Garden, the narrative centers around fruit merchant Robert Rusk (Barry Foster), who is responsible for a string of rapes and strangulation murders of women in the district, and his buddy Dick Blaney (Jon Finch). Blaney is a hothead who is seen arguing in public with his ex-wife Brenda (Barbara Leigh-Hunt), who runs a dating service. Rusk shows up at her flat one day, ostensibly to use her service, but instead attempts to rape her, and when he proves to be impotent, he strangles her with his necktie in what is perhaps the most brutal murder scene in any of Hitchcock's films. For his next trick, Rusk murders Blarney's girl friend, Barbara Milligan (Anna Massey) and disposes of the body late that night by stuffing it in a potato sack and loading it onto the back of a vegetable truck. He soon learns, however, that he is missing a monogrammed tie clip held in his victim's grasp, and must return to the truck in order to pry the incriminating evidence from Barbara's cold, dead fingers.

All the evidence points to Blaney as the killer, and Scotland Yard detective Inspector Oxford (Alec McCowen) arrests him and charges him with the crimes, but while Blaney is in jail awaiting trial the inspector begins to suspect that he has arrested the wrong man and that Rusk is the real murderer who has set Blaney up. When Blaney manages to escape from jail, Oxford reasons he will head for Rusk's place to exact his revenge and follows him there. Once inside Rusk's apartment, Blaney sees what he thinks is Rusk's form asleep in bed and attacks it, only to find it is really the body of the serial killer's latest female victim. Oxford arrives to find Blaney standing over the corpse and protesting his innocence, but just then they hear the sound of someone dragging something heavy up the stairs. They watch as Rusk enters the room dragging a large trunk, which he intends to use to dispose of the body. "Mr. Rusk," Inspector Oxford wryly observes, "you're not wearing your tie."

After opening the Pandora's Box of explicit screen violence in *Psycho* back in 1960, Hitchcock felt he had to up the ante by devising the horrific rape/murder scene in *Frenzy*

Wronged man Richard Blaney (John Finch, left) confers with psycho-killer Bob Rusk (Barry Foster) in *Frenzy* **(1972).**

that also included some nudity. The result is a less artful and more gratuitously violent sequence compared to the shower murder in *Psycho*. Hitch's template for the film was the equally disturbing novel *Goodbye Piccadilly, Farewell Leicester Square* by Arthur La Bern as adapted for the screen by *Sleuth* playwright Anthony Shaffer, who kept all of the book's morbidity intact. Despite these flaws, *Frenzy* was a commercial success and is widely considered the best film of the director's late period because of its skilled film-making technique and earnest performances by a cast of relatively unknown British actors struggling through the disturbing material.

This was another treatment of the "wrong man" theme so prevalent in Hitchcock's works. The dapper, aristocratic psychopath Rusk is the opposite of the working class antihero Blaney. Ironically, the homicidal Rusk is outwardly controlled and charming, while Blaney, in contrast, is painted as an abrasive personality with anger management problems. As in *Strangers on a Train*, two men whose fates are linked by murder become doppelgangers, and the one who is innocent of the crime is made to suffer for the misdeeds of the guilty party.

Hitchcock's final feature was *Family Plot* (1976), a comic thriller involving psychic mediumship, jewel thievery, kidnapping and murder. The film opens during a séance conducted by bogus medium "Madame" Blanche Tyler (Barbara Harris), who is attempting to locate the nephew of wealthy dowager Julia Rainbird (Cathleen Nesbitt). Mrs. Rainbird is obsessed with finding her sister's lost son and sole surviving relative, and commissions Madame Blanche to find the lost heir using her ESP for a reward of $10,000.

In reality Blanche has no psychic powers but instead relies on the investigative skills of her boyfriend, cab driver and con man George Lumley (Bruce Dern). Going through the county adoption records, George begins to trace the identity of the missing heir, but what he and Blanche don't know is that the nephew faked his own death years ago and has assumed the identity of a prominent San Francisco jeweler named Arthur Adamson (William Devane). Adamson and his girlfriend Fran (Karen Black) are a notorious pair of serial kidnappers who prey upon the rich and famous and have just received a valuable diamond as a ransom payment that they have hidden in a chandelier.

Adamson soon becomes aware that George and Blanche are looking for him, but can't figure out why the couple is prying into his affairs. Things come to a head when Blanche strikes out on her own and traces Adamson to his home address, intending to tell him about the inheritance. Unfortunately, she interrupts the two kidnappers as they are abducting their latest victim, a Catholic bishop (William Prince). Fran and Adamson trap Blanche, drug her and imprison her in a secret room in their basement, intending to murder her after they have completed their latest caper. The resourceful George, however, follows her to Adamson's house, and sneaks in through a basement window and hides out until the kidnappers return with their loot. As the couple plan to dispose of Blanche, George manages to rescue her and lock them inside their own secret room. In a surprise finish, Blanche somehow manifests genuine ESP and discerns the true diamond amid the faux gems of the chandelier.

The director was in ill health during the shooting of *Family Plot*, and as a consequence the film lacks some of the verve of Hitchcock's earlier works. It would prove to be Hitch's swan song, and the Master of Suspense moved on to that big studio in the sky in 1980. His career ended on a whimsical note, as *Family Plot* was scripted by Ernest Lehman, who had written the equally breezy *North by Northwest*, and this comic thriller moved away from the violence and morbidity of his previous effort, *Frenzy*, but is considered one of Hitch's minor works by critics. Bruce Dern delivers a typically quirky performance as the taxi driver turned con man George Lumley, while William Devane exudes oily menace as the cold-blooded Arthur Adamson.

The plot of *Family Plot* centers around two pairs of male/female doppelgangers who become connected to each other through some odd whim of fate. Hitchcock frequently intercuts between the two couples, who are a study in contrasts. George and Blanche are harmless, pleasant small-time crooks, while Arthur and Fran are deadly thieves, kidnappers and murderers. In a sense, Arthur and Fran are the kind of successful criminals that George and Blanche might fantasize about being, and can be considered their fully realized doubles. As in many mystery treatments of the theme, the doppelganger is associated with elements of the uncanny, including a psychic séance and an extended scene filmed in a graveyard.

In addition to his feature films that embody the theme of the double, Hitchcock also devoted an episode of his CBS series, *Alfred Hitchcock Presents*, to a doppelganger story. "The Case of Mr. Pelham" was one of a small number of half-hour telefilms that Hitchcock himself directed, and was broadcast as the tenth installment of the series on December 4, 1955. Comic actor Tom Ewell plays the titular Mr. Albert Pelham, the head of a small New York investment firm, who confides to his psychiatrist friend Doctor Harley (Raymond Bailey) that he is deeply troubled about a recent series of incidents in which an unknown person has been impersonating him. People have reported seeing him in places he hasn't been and doing things his mild-mannered self would never do. Dr. Harley tries to reassure him that his fears are nothing more than a case of mistaken identity.

At first Pelham thinks someone is playing an elaborate joke on him, but things get more serious when his double starts showing up at his home when he's not there and taking over his job functions whenever he's away from his desk. These baffling events are so disturbing that he begins to suspect that there is "more than a purely human agency involved in this." In order to differentiate himself from his imposter, Pelham buys a unique but outlandishly loud tie to replace his usually conservative neckwear. When he returns to the office he calls his home and the double answers the phone speaking in his own voice. Realizing that "he's there now," Pelham hurries home to confront the doppelganger, who he meets in the flesh for the first time, but because he is wearing the unusual tie, he is taken to be the imposter. In an epilogue one year later, it is revealed that the double has completely replaced the original Mr. Pelham, who has been remanded to an insane asylum.

"The Case of Mr. Pelham" is widely considered the most eerie episode in the history of the Hitchcock TV show, a series that usually dealt with more mundane tales of real-world criminality and murder. With its quasi-supernatural overtones, it is more reminiscent of an episode of the fantasy oriented TV show *The Twilight Zone*. Hitchcock deftly weaves a mood of mystery and psychological horror around the enigmatic plight of the hapless Mr. Pelham in the show's 23 minute running time. Tom Ewell, best known for his comic roles in frothy comedies like *The Seven Year Itch* (1955) and *The Girl Can't Help It* (1956), plays it completely straight and delivers a riveting performance as the haunted everyman Mr. Pelham. The teleplay was adapted by Francis Cockrell from a short story by Anthony Armstrong, who later expanded the story into a novel entitled *The Strange Case of Mr. Pelham* (1957) which in turn was lensed as the feature film *The Man Who Haunted Himself* (1970).

The narrative elements of "The Case of Mr. Pelham" also show affinities with the plot of Dostoyevsky's novella *The Double*. In both stories a man is confronted by a mysterious doppelganger who invades his life, replaces him at his job, takes over his identity and sends him to the crazy house, but while Dostoyevsky's tale is played for satire, "Mr. Pelham" is firmly in the realm of the uncanny. No explanation is provided for the existence of the doppelganger other than Pelham's suggestion that there is "more than a purely human agency involved in this." Donald Spoto notes that the telefilm "fuses the established Hitchcock theme of the double with the terror of madness and enclosure."[7]

After completing the episode Hitchcock reportedly slipped into a period of exhaustion and depression despite the fact that his TV show had become an instant hit and he was at an artistic and economic high point of his career. Perhaps he was spooked by the doppelganger theme in "Mr. Pelham," one of a very few Hitchcock's films containing a supernatural element. The theme of the double seemed to fascinate him as he obsessively returned to it over the decades in some of his most memorable films. Hitch's doppelgangers take many forms: innocent individuals connected by fate to their criminal doubles in *Strangers on a Train*, *The Wrong Man*, *Frenzy* and *Family Plot*; relatives with a telepathic link in *Shadow of a Doubt*; an invisible, non-existent double in *North by Northwest*; ghosts and identity transference in *Rebecca*, *Vertigo* and *Psycho*. Biographer Spoto theorizes that the double represents the flip side of Hitch's highly controlled and well-mannered personality, that devil within all of us, or what he calls "the dark side of genius."

"If you meet your double, you should kill him," read the tag line for Johan Grimonpetz's quasi-documentary film *Double Take* (2009), in which Hitchcock himself is confronted by his own doppelganger. This Belgian-Dutch-German co-production features Hitchcock lookalike Ron Burrage as Hitch, who, while filming *The Birds* on the Universal lot in 1962, has a series of enigmatic encounters with an older self from decades in the future (the director died in April of 1980). The two Hitchcocks have a number of meetings in elegant settings where they trade homicidal innuendos in the jocular manner Hitch affected on his TV show, but the doubles soon descend into a miasma of fear and loathing for each other. As in folklore, it can be fatal to have a close encounter with one's doppelganger.

Along the way, director Grimonpetz manages to touch on the banality of television commercials, the "words from our sponsor" that Hitch perennially loathed on his TV show, as well as the Cold War anxieties of the 1960s. The film was based on the short story "August 25, 1983," by Jose Luis Borges which in turn derives from Dostoyevsky's novella *The Double*, and catches the uncanny mood of the doppelganger concept as expressed in these works. The unusual screenplay by Grimonpetz and Tom McCarthy, transforms Hitchcock from a historical personage to a fictional character who is forced to deal with one of the obsessive themes in many of his works, and contains short clips from *North By Northwest* and *The Birds*.

Hitchcock lookalike Ron Burrage poses as Hitch in this poster for Johan Grimonprez's satirical film *Double Take* (2009).

In 1962, Robert Aldrich's exercise in Hollywood gothic *What Ever Happened to Baby Jane?* was a hit movie that spawned a number of oddball thrillers starring the middle-aged drama queen Bette Davis in a series of highly unusual parts. *Dead Ringer* (1964) starred Ms. Davis in a dual role as good and evil twins and was directed by Paul Henreid, who had produced and starred in the doppelganger noir *Hollow Triumph* in 1948. The film was luridly advertised as being "for *Baby Jane* people."

Davis plays a pair of identical twin sisters, Edith "Edie" Phillips and Margaret "Maggie" DeLorca who have been estranged from each other for 18 years and reunite for the funeral of Maggie's husband, Frank. Edie is a frumpy, down on her luck dowager whose sole asset is a failing, low rent cocktail lounge, while Maggie enjoys a lavish lifestyle that she has inherited from her wealthy husband. On her way from Frank's funeral to Maggie's mansion after the ceremony, Edie learns from Maggie's chauffeur (George Chandler) that Frank, who had once been Edie's beau, had been tricked into marrying Maggie by pretending to be pregnant. Edie's resentment deepens when she sees Maggie's opulent surroundings for the first time and confronts her sister about her subterfuge in marrying Frank. Her jealousy leads Edie to conceive a daring homicidal scheme to murder her twin and obtain her wealth by impersonating her, and arranges for Maggie to visit her in the evening.

The day of the funeral also happens to be the sister's shared birthday, and that evening Edie's boyfriend, homicide detective Jim Hobson (Karl Malden), visits Edie in her ratty little flat above the bar and presents her with an expensive wristwatch as a present. After Jim leaves, Maggie shows up and the twins get into an argument, whereupon Edie shoots her in the head and arranges the corpse to make the murder look like a suicide. She then exchanges clothes with her dead twin and reluctantly puts Jim's watch on Maggie's wrist and alters her hairstyle to make the impersonation complete.

Returning to the DeLorca mansion as Maggie, Edie fools the servants at first but they slowly begin to notice uncharacteristic behaviors that threaten to reveal her true identity. Unlike her twin, Edie smokes cigarettes and gets along with the mansion's watchdog, a Great Dane. Her signature also differs from her sister's, and she doesn't know the combination to the safe where Maggie's expensive jewelry is stored. On several occasions Jim visits her to question "Maggie" about "Edie's" death, but although the visits are poignant, Jim suspects nothing. Edie's plan seems to be succeeding until one day suave golf pro Tony Collins (Peter Lawford), who had been Maggie's secret lover, shows up at the mansion and immediately sees through her ruse. Threatening to expose her identity theft to the police, he proceeds to blackmail her out of some expensive items of jewelry.

Tony eventually reveals that he and Maggie had poisoned Frank with arsenic to get their hands on his fortune. When Tony and Edie get into an argument, Tony threatens her and is attacked and killed by the mansion's Great Dane. In the meantime, the police have become suspicious about Frank's death and Jim has been put in charge of the investigation. Frank's body is exhumed, traces of arsenic are found and Edie, as Maggie, is charged with his murder. When Jim shows up at the mansion with her arrest warrant, Edie confesses the truth to him, but he responds in disbelief that, "Edie would never hurt a fly." Edie is convicted and sentenced to death for the homicide, and as she is being escorted to prison, Jim asks her once again if she is Edie. To spare his feelings, she simply answers that, "Edie would never hurt a fly."

Dead Ringer was based on a 1946 Mexican film entitled *La Otra* (*The Other*, a.k.a. *Dead Pigeon*), which was adapted from a story by Rian James and starred Dolores Del Rio. Actor turned director Paul Henreid delivers a tightly paced, well-acted crime thriller, with visuals that are augmented by veteran cinematographer Ernest Haller. Shot in crisp, black and white neo-noir style, the film makes elegant use of Los Angeles and Beverly Hills locations such as the Greystone Mansion and Rosedale Cemetery. Ms. Davis, who had previously played a set of twins in the drama *A Stolen Life* (1946), dominates the film in her dual role as Edie/Maggie. As Maggie, she is an arrogant rich bitch, while Edie is a sympathetic loser who the audience hopes will get away with the crime even though she is a murderess herself.

Edith Phillips (Bette Davis) prepares to murder her identical twin sister Margaret (also Bette Davis) and assume her identity in *Dead Ringer* **(1964).**

Like the classic films noir *Among the Living* and *The Dark Mirror*, *Dead Ringer*'s narrative centers around the notion of a pair of twins in which one is good and one is evil, but in this case it's not clear which is which because both of the twins have committed cold-blooded acts of premeditated murder. As with many mystery genre treatments of the doppelganger theme, the film associates the double with death. In the movie's most macabre scene, Edie must strip her sister's corpse naked in order to exchange clothes with her while creating the pretense that the twins are making small talk so that no one will suspect what is going on. Like many of Hitchcock's films, *Dead Ringer* deals with the plot device of identity transference as Edie strives to falsely emulate the personality of her dead twin.

Espionage-themed entertainment came into its own during the Cold War years of the 1960s as the James Bond films and TV shows such as *The Man from U.N.C.L.E.* and *The Avengers* achieved mass popularity. Many of these spy vs. spy melodramas featured the concept of the "double agent," a rogue operative who pretended to be on one side while covertly working for the other. In *The Double Man* (1967), however, the double agent was another spy's doppelganger. The film begins at a meeting of Communist officials in East Berlin where senior operative Berthold (Anton Diffring) discusses plans for placing double agents inside the intelligence apparatus of the United States. Berthold assures the panel that he has put a daring plan into motion that will allow the Reds to infiltrate a spy inside a major U.S. intelligence agency.

Cut to the ski slopes high above the Austrian village of St. Anton, where a 16-year-old boy named Richard Slater is killed in a skiing accident. The boy was a student at an international school at St. Anton run by ex-spy Frank Wheatley (Clive Revill), who sends an urgent telegram to the boy's father back in the States informing him of the death. The father, Dan Slater (Yul Brynner), a high-echelon CIA spook, flies to Austria to attend the funeral, but as he is packing up Richard's belongings, he notices two holes in his son's jacket that are evidence of foul play. Slater decides to stay on at St. Anton to determine whether the death was an accident or homicide. He takes up with local ski bunny Gina (Britt Ekland), who tells him she went up on the lift that day with Richard and a mysterious man wearing a facemask.

It turns out that Gina and the masked man are all part of Berthold's master plan to replace Slater with a doppelganger named Kalmar (also Brynner) who has been turned into Slater's exact double via plastic surgery. Richard has been killed merely to lure Slater to St. Anton, where he will be disposed of and replaced by Kalmar, who was the mysterious masked man who pushed Richard to his death. Slater pursues his son's murderer with a special ruthlessness up and down the Alpine slopes while he is in turn pursued by Berthold's thugs in a deadly game of cat and mouse. By the final reels neither the viewer nor the characters can distinguish Slater from Kalmar, but the Communist double agent's identity is finally revealed because of scratches on his face made by Gina after Kalmar manhandles her, and the nefarious plot is thwarted.

This exercise in Cold War paranoia was directed by Franklin J. Schaffner, who would go on to better things with *Planet of the Apes* (1968), *Patton* (1970) and the sci-fi doppelganger thriller *The Boys from Brazil* (1978). Schaffner's pacing is tight, with some decent action scenes set amid the breathtaking landscapes of the Tyrolean Alps. Adapted from the well-regarded espionage novel *The Legacy of a Spy* by Harry Maxfield by screenwriters Frank Tarloff and Alfred Hayes, the film paints an unsympathetic portrait of the duplicities of the spy game. As the ostensible CIA good guy Slater, Yul Brynner comes off as a cold fish who displays little in the way of human emotion, and that goes double for his alter ego, Kalmar. Nonetheless, Brynner's strong performance in the dual roles carries the film, and he is aided by the dramatic talents of veteran thesps Clive Revill, Lloyd Nolan and Anton Diffring and the sex appeal of future Bond girl Britt Ekland.

As in *Strange Impersonation* and *The Man with my Face*, plastic surgery is used as a plot device to create a doppelganger, and like *Hollow Triumph*, the double is distinguished from the original person by means of a scratch on one side of his face. The dual Yuls aren't seen together onscreen until the last 30 minutes of the movie, and critics have noted that there's not much difference in character between the protagonist Slater and his antagonist Kalmar, as both are portrayed as being equally ruthless.

Future James Bond Roger Moore starred as a man who encounters an enigmatic doppelganger in *The Man Who Haunted Himself* (1970). As previously noted, the film was based on the same source material as the 1955 *Hitchcock Presents* telefilm "The Case of Mr. Pelham," a story (and later novel) entitled *The Strange Case of Mr. Pelham* by Anthony Armstrong. Moore plays Harold Pelham (or Pel to his friends), a staid executive at a London engineering firm who seems to enjoy an occasional walk on the wild side. One afternoon as he is driving home from work he begins to drive recklessly and gets into a serious car accident. Pelham is rushed to a hospital where he momentarily dies of his injuries, but when he revives the doctors notice a mysterious double heartbeat on the patient's ECG machine that is immediately dismissed as a mechanical glitch.

Pelham and his wife Eve (Hildegard Neil) travel to Spain to recuperate, but when Pel returns to London his life is assaulted by a series of baffling events. His friends insist they have seen and interacted with him while he was still in Spain. Worse yet, attractive photographer Julie Anderson (Olga Georges-Picot) claims that she has been having an affair with him. He soon begins to realize that he has a mysterious imposter that threatens to subsume his identity when the double shows up in his office and begins performing his work tasks at the company. Oddly, Pel always seems to be one step behind his doppelganger, as if the two of them are out of phase in the space-time continuum.

Fearing for his sanity, Pelham checks himself into a mental hospital, where he is treated by oddball psychiatrist Dr. Harris (Freddie Jones). After a number of therapy sessions, however, Dr. Jones's analysis is that Pelham's many social repressions have led to a case of split personality. He urges his patient to loosen up, and when Pel is discharged he takes the doctor's advice and buys some uncharacteristically flamboyant clothing. When he returns home, however, he finally encounters his doppelganger, who is dressed in his usual conservative attire, and Pel's own family does not recognize him as the real Mr. Pelham.

Confronting his doppelganger one-on-one for the first time, the ringer explains that he has always been part of him, but that Pelham's near death experience has allowed him to physically manifest as a separate being. Pelham was supposed to die on the operating table, but when he managed to pull through his alternate self was split off from the original, and the only way that the situation can be resolved is for one of them to die. The hapless Pel then rushes to his car, intending to go to the police station to resolve his identity problem, but the double follows and a second car crash ensues, from which only one of the two Mr. Pelhams will emerge alive.

This was the last film directed by veteran British director Basil Dearden, whose film career went back to the 1930s. Dearden infuses *The Man Who Haunted Himself* with a mood of brooding tension and subtle terror as the unfortunate Pelham pursues his shadow self through the maze of his own personality. The director uses photogenic 70s-era London locations to great effect, while the screenplay by Dearden and co-scripter Michael Relph keeps the viewer guessing whether Pelham is having a mental breakdown, being subjected to some kind of industrial espionage operation in connection with his job, or is the victim of a preternatural menace. Fans of Roger Moore, best known for his roles as the ultra cool secret agent James Bond and the suave TV sleuth *The Saint*, consider this his best performance, and it was reportedly one of the actor's favorite roles as well. Departing from his usually smooth screen persona, Moore paints a credible and sympathetic portrait of a repressed, conservative individual stressed to the breaking point by forces beyond his comprehension. A fine British cast provides worthy dramatic support, especially character actor Freddie Jones in a scenery-chewing role as the quirky psychiatrist Dr. Harris.

As the film's title suggests, *The Man Who Haunted Himself* is both a doppelganger tale and a ghost story and is reminiscent of Hitchcock's *Vertigo* and *Psycho* in its melding of these two motifs. The film exploits the powerful themes of madness and loss of identity, and once again the double becomes a harbinger of death. As in folklore, one must never be in the same time and place as one's doppelganger, as the meeting of the twain ultimately leads to the annihilation of the self. The double is explained as being Pelham's repressed, hidden persona, perhaps existing in a parallel universe, who escapes into reality during his near-death experience. Few films depict the uncanny nature of the doppelganger as vividly.

A man is deeply in love with a beautiful woman who dies tragically. He becomes obsessed with guilt over her death, but later finds another woman who is her dead ringer. He makes her over into the exact image of his dead lover without knowing that she is part of a criminal plot. If this narrative sounds suspiciously like the plot of Hitchcock's *Vertigo*, it's because director Brian de Palma appropriated story elements of Hitch's classic thriller as an homage (some might say rip-off) to the Master's work in his psychological mystery *Obsession* (1976).

The film begins in New Orleans in 1959, where successful real estate developer Michael Courtland (Cliff Robertson) is hosting a party for the ten-year anniversary of his marriage to his wife Elizabeth (Genevieve Bujold). During the party a band of criminals kidnaps Elizabeth and their daughter Amy (Wanda Blackman) and hold them for ransom. The police devise a complex scheme to catch the kidnappers that involves a briefcase full of phony money and a radio transmitter, but their plan goes horribly wrong. As the cops are chasing the gang their car collides with an oil truck, causing an explosion in which Amy and Elizabeth are killed along with the crooks, their bodies lost in the Mississippi River.

Fifteen years after the accident, Courtland is still obsessed with the death of his wife and builds an elaborate mausoleum to her memory that is a scale replica of the Basilica di San Miniato, the church in Florence where he first met Elizabeth. His business partner, Robert LaSalle (John Lithgow), keeps urging him to sell the tract of land upon which the monument rests, but even though the land has become quite valuable, Courtland is adamant about keeping it. When LaSalle plans to take a business trip to Florence to confer on a construction project, he convinces Courtland to accompany him.

One day Courtland decides to visit the Basilica where he first met Elizabeth and encounters a young Italian woman working on an art restoration project who bears a striking resemblance to his dead wife. Intrigued, he becomes increasingly obsessed with the woman, whose name is Sandra Portinari (Bujold), and begins to insinuate himself into her life. After making subtle changes to her appearance to make her into an exact mirror image of Elizabeth, he is hopelessly in love and proposes marriage, and she accepts.

The couple returns to the Big Easy for the wedding where the bride-to-be begins acting strangely. She roams through Courtland's mansion until she penetrates into Elizabeth's bedroom, where she puts on the dead woman's jewelry and reads from her diary. In the meantime, Courtland's psychiatrist Dr. Ellman (Stocker Fontlieu) is worried about his patient's obsession and urges him to resume therapy and delay the wedding, but Courtland will have none of it. On their wedding night Sandra is abducted and a note is left behind demanding ransom, and seeking to avoid a repeat of his first wife's kidnapping tragedy, he decides to pay the ransom of $500,000 as instructed.

In order to obtain the necessary cash, Courtland must transfer all of his property and company shares, including the site of Elizabeth's mausoleum, to LaSalle, but in the process he discovers that the kidnapping was an elaborate ruse to get Courtland to sign over all his assets to his partner. Enraged by this treachery, the deranged Courtland stabs LaSalle to death, takes the briefcase full of ransom money, and goes looking for Sandra, who he suspects is part of the plot. She is at the airport about to board a plane back to Florence where it is revealed in flashback that she is in actuality Courtland's daughter, Amy, who has grown up to become Elizabeth's double. She had survived the kidnapping and explosion only to be secreted away by LaSalle to live in Italy. For the next 15 years LaSalle has filled her head with lies about her father, telling her that Courtland had refused to pay the ransom money, so that she will go along with his plans to defraud her father.

Feeling deep remorse, Sandra slits her wrists in the jetliner's bathroom while the airplane is waiting for takeoff, and is escorted off the plane in a wheelchair. Courtland sees her and races forward with his gun drawn, but during a tussle with a security guard the briefcase breaks open and the money flies out. When she sees the bills she exclaims, "Daddy, you brought the money," and Courtland, realizing Sandra's true identity, embraces her as father and daughter are reconciled.

De Palma's directorial hand is sure in building the film's dark mood with spooky lighting setups, fluid camera movements and brooding interiors and exteriors shot on location in New Orleans and Florence by the acclaimed cinematographer Vilmos Zsigmond. Cliff Robertson gives a standout performance as the obsessive Courtland, his staring eyes beautifully expressing the character's guilt and longing, while Genevieve Bujold plays Sandra with the requisite air of distance and mystery. Hitchcock's musical collaborator Bernard Herrmann contributed a moody, romantic, *Vertigo*-like score that tends to overpower the visuals. The main problem with *Obsession*, however, is Paul Schrader's screenplay, which is overly derivative and frequently strains credulity in constructing the film's unusual plotline. For instance, the notion that LaSalle would devise a scheme that would take 15 years to come to fruition is not believable.

The film's heavy atmospherics and mysterious plot lend emphasis to the ghostly aspects of the doppelganger theme as the narrative unfolds through the viewpoint of the film's guilt-obsessed protagonist. His morbid fascination with his wife's death, and frequent visits to her monumental tomb and obsession with his wife's double constitute the film's primary narrative. Because there is no supernatural agency involved, however, the film must rely on an overly elaborate explanation for the dead woman's double that is too clever by half and spoils the uncanny mood of the film. Studio executives were reportedly concerned about the father-daughter incest plotline, and a scene in which Courtland and Sandra consummate their marriage had to be re-edited as a dream sequence in order to avoid controversy. De Palma had previously dealt with the doppelganger theme in his 1973 Hitchcock homage *Sisters*, while Genevieve Bujold would appear in David Cronenberg's 1988 evil twin thriller *Dead Ringers* (see Chapter Four).

In 1950 the acclaimed writer/director Billy Wilder lensed the film noir classic *Sunset Boulevard*, a Hollywood Gothic tale of an aging movie queen that starred William Holden. Nearly three decades later, Wilder and Holden once again collaborated on a similarly-themed story of a reclusive female star in *Fedora* (1978). The title character is a European mega-star, a veteran of 41 movie roles who is 67 years old but still has the appearance of a woman in her 20s. As the film opens, Fedora inexplicably jumps in front of a moving train in Paris and commits suicide. Washed-up film producer Barry "Dutch" Detweiler (Holden) is one of the mourners at her funeral who recalls the events leading up to her death in flashback.

Two weeks earlier Detweiler traveled to Corfu, where Fedora was living in seclusion on an island villa. His aim is to convince her to star in a new screen version of Tolstoy's *Anna Karenina*, but he finds that the forever young movie star is being held in virtual captivity by her entourage, a motley crew that includes the aged Polish Countess Sobryanski

(Hildegaard Knef), her stern assistant Miss Balfour (Frances Sternhagen), the brutal chauffeur Kritos (Gottfried John) and the eccentric Dr. Vando (Jose Ferrer). The brilliant plastic surgeon Vando has reportedly maintained Fedora's youth through the use of exotic regeneration techniques that include deep freeze, blood replacement therapy, hormone injections, laser surgery and tissue transplants administered at his famous Paris clinic over the years.

When Detweiler gets to meet Fedora in person he is amazed at her youthful appearance, but Vando points out that she must always wear gloves because he cannot disguise the age of her hands. Detweiler is puzzled, however, when he finds she has no memory of a brief affair he had with her in Hollywood (shown in flashback) decades earlier. After pitching his script to Fedora it becomes obvious that the actress is suffering from mental illness and drug addiction and believes she is being imprisoned by the Countess and Vando. One day he goes to the villa with the intent of getting her off the island, but he finds the estate strangely deserted. Roaming through the house at will, he finds puzzling items such as a drawer filled with white gloves and notebooks with the words "I am Fedora" written over and over on every page. While he is pondering these enigmas Kritos appears and knocks him unconscious, and he awakens a week later in his hotel in Corfu to find that Fedora has killed herself.

At the funeral, Detweiler accuses Vando and the Countess of driving Fedora to suicide with their cruelty, whereupon the Countess reveals the truth to him. In reality, she is Fedora and the woman lying in the coffin is her daughter, Antonia. Back in 1967, one of Vando's experimental treatments had gone terribly wrong and left her permanently disfigured. In order to continue her film career, Vando performed subtle surgery to make Antonia into the double of her mother, while Fedora assumed the identity of the Countess. All went well until Antonia fell in love with the actor Michael York (playing himself in a cameo) during a film shoot and decided to tell him the truth, whereupon her mother and the doctor spirited her away to Corfu and the production was abruptly canceled. A week before her death Antonia had been returned to Vando's clinic for psychiatric treatments, but after realizing that she could not regain her identity committed suicide in the same manner as the heroine of Tolstoy's novel. As proof, Fedora has Detweiler examine the hands of the corpse, which are the hands of a young woman. End titles inform the audience that the real Fedora died six weeks after the funeral.

A West German–French co-production, *Fedora* was shot on location in Europe and received a limited release in the United States, playing mostly in art house theaters to mixed reviews. Many critics found it to be hopelessly old fashioned in style with a dull, campy and predictable plot. Taking a fresh look, however, reveals that the film is underrated, with a finely constructed script by Wilder and I.A.L. Diamond that, like *Sunset Boulevard*, is at once a paean to the glories of old Hollywood and an offbeat mystery story. Much of the film takes place at "Fedora's" elaborate funeral, causing critic Janet Maslin to refer to it as being Wilder's "epitaph." Indeed, the director imbues the film with an overpowering mood of melancholy that is appropriate to the film's morbid subject matter. German actresses Marthe Keller and Hildegaard Knef both give strong performances portraying the linked character trio of Fedora, Antonia and the Countess, while the venerable William Holden holds the film together with his portrayal of the world weary yet mystified protagonist Dutch Detweiler.

Fedora was adapted from a novella by Tom Tryon that was part of his omnibus collection entitled *Crowned Heads*. Tryon, a former movie actor whose screen credits included the 1958 sci-fi doppelganger sleeper *I Married a Monster from Outer Space* (see Chapter Five), was also the author of the evil twin supernatural thriller *The Other*, which was filmed in 1973 (see Chapter Four). *Fedora* also references Oscar Wilde's *The Picture of Dorian Gray* in its depiction of an individual with seemingly eternal youth, a theme that Tryon as an actor must have found appealing. Once again plastic surgery, along with more arcane medical procedures, is utilized as a plot device to create the double. Like *Obsession*, the film featured a pair of mother/daughter doppelgangers who are part of an elaborate deception. *Fedora* plays upon the horror of loss of identity as Antonia is fashioned into her mother's perfect likeness and kills herself when she cannot regain her original persona. Although there is no supernatural element in the plot, the idea of the double is associated with morbidity and death.

Plastic surgeons were kept busy cranking out doppelgangers during the following decade in the film noir satire *The Man with Bogart's Face* (1980). The man in question is a retired Los Angeles detective who spends his entire life savings on a facial reconstruction job to make him into a ringer for his idol and role model, noir icon Humphrey Bogart The newly-minted Bogie lookalike, played by Robert Sacchi, changes his name to Sam Marlowe, a combination of the names of the classic film noir sleuths Sam Spade and Phillip Marlowe, buys himself a 1940s-era trench coat and fedora, and hangs out his shingle as a private eye.

Business is slow at first, with little for Marlowe and his loyal secretary Duchess (Misty Rowe) to do, until one day a mysterious fat man, Commodore Anastas (Victor Buono), arrives at the office and hires the detective to find a pair of priceless blue stones called the Eyes of Alexander that were pilfered from a statue of Alexander the Great in antiquity. While working to recover the gems, Marlowe is beset by a gaggle of sinister characters, including Mr. Zebra (Herbert Lom), Hakim (Franco Nero) and femme fatale Gena (Michelle Phillips). The film is basically a send-up of Dashiell Hammett's classic mystery novel *The Maltese Falcon* and the 1941 film version that made Bogart a mega-star. Other actors who appeared in classic films noir make cameo appearances, including Yvonne de Carlo, Mike Mazurki and George Raft in his final screen appearance.

As the film begins with Marlowe's surgical bandages being unwrapped after the surgery, the audience is not afforded a notion of his identity prior to the face change. The movie references the film noir *Dark Passage* (1947) in which Bogie plays an escaped convict who hires a plastic surgeon to change his features into Bogart's face. Another Bogie doppelganger had previously appeared in Woody Allen's 1972 comedy *Play It Again, Sam*, in which a ghostly Bogart gives Woody tips on how to conduct his love life. *The Bogie Man*, a 1992 telefilm based on a comic book, also featured a man obsessed with Humphrey Bogart, although not to the extent of having plastic surgery and becoming Bogie's double.

Writer/director Alan Parker's *Angel Heart* (1987) also referenced film noir, but in a very different way. The film opens in New York City in 1955, where perennially down-on-his-luck private eye Harry Angel (Mickey Rourke) is hired by enigmatic Frenchman Louis Cyphre (Robert De Niro) to find a missing person. The bearded, devilish-looking Cyphre is looking for a 1940s-era crooner named Johnny Favorite, with whom he had a contract. Johnny had a mental breakdown while serving in World War II and has been confined to an upstate mental asylum for treatment, and as a result Cyphre's contract was never honored.

It seems that Johnny has gone missing from the hospital and Cyphre wants Harry to find out if he has died or been released and to discover his current whereabouts, alive or dead.

Harry pays a visit to the nuthouse where he strong-arms Johnny's physician, the drug addicted Dr. Fowler (Michael Higgins) into revealing that his patient had checked out of the hospital back in 1943 with a man named Edward Kelly and an unidentified woman, and that he was paid to falsify Johnny's presence at the hospital by the mysterious couple ever since. Harry also learns that Johnny suffered from amnesia and has had his face altered with plastic surgery so that no one knows what he looks like. Soon after the interview Dr. Fowler is found dead, an apparent suicide, while Harry traces Kelly to New Orleans and follows the trail there.

Private eye Harry Angel (Mickey Rourke) searches for his lost self in Alan Parker's genre meld *Angel Heart* (1987).

Following clues through the Big Easy, Harry contacts Johnny's associates, fortune teller Margaret Crusemark (Charlotte Rampling) and musician Toots Sweet (Brownie McGhee), but hits dead ends in his search. Following another clue, Harry locates the daughter of Johnny's old flame Evangeline Proudfoot, Epiphany (Lisa Bonet), who is a priestess in a voodoo cult and claims that Johnny was her father. Not long after these contacts Toots comes up dead and Margaret is found murdered with her heart cut out and the N.O.P.D. considers Harry the prime suspect in the homicides. After Epiphany and Harry become lovers, the voodoo priestess is also found dead and Harry begins to suspect that Cyphre is setting him up to take the fall for the series of murders.

The final revelations come when Harry locates Edward Kelly, a.k.a. Ethan Crusemark (Stocker Fontelieu), the man who took Johnny out of the asylum. Favorite, he learns, was a Satanist who sold his soul to Louis Cyphre (a.k.a. Lucifer) for fame and fortune but later attempted to renege on the deal by murdering a soldier in a ritual killing and assuming his identity back in 1943. Harry is in reality Johnny, the man he was hired to find, and is responsible for the murders of everyone he has come in contact with during his quest. His damnation complete, Harry finds himself on an express elevator to Hell, going down.

Louis Cyphre (Robert De Niro) cuts a devilish figure in *Angel Heart* (1987).

Composed of equal parts detective story and supernatural diabolism, *Angel Heart* deftly walks the line between neo-noir and the horror film and succeeds admirably in both genres. Parker's screenplay, faithfully adapted from the novel *Falling Angel* by William Hjortsberg, re-locates the action in the second half of the film to New Orleans, a move that potentiates the voodoo angle of the story. As director, Parker makes use of timeless locations in New York and New Orleans to evoke the period detail of the late 1950s. Aided by cinematographer Michael Seresin, Parker creates exquisite landscapes of beauty and dread in the streets and back alleys of these shadow-haunted cities. Composer Trevor Jones utilizes a diverse sound palette that includes music from the genres of gospel, blues and Caribbean percussion that add an eerie counterpoint to the action.

The quirky Mickey Rourke, who is best known for playing a succession of unusual roles in movies like *Barfly* (1987), *The Wrestler* (2007) and *Iron Man 2* (2010), gives a bravura performance as the doomed, damned Harry Angel. Early in the film, Harry comes off as a violent, mean-spirited loser on a low road to nowhere, but is basically a sympathetic character. His transformation into a satanic homicidal maniac at the film's ending doesn't ring true. De Niro, as the enigmatic Cyphre, is a cool, understated Lucifer who nonetheless oozes otherworldly menace. Former "Cosby kid" Lisa Bonet shocked fans of the TV show in the grisly voodoo sequences and in her R-rated sex scene with Rourke.

Drawing on themes from both the film noir and horror genres, *Angel Heart*'s Harry Angel/Johnny Favorite duality combines the noir motifs of amnesia and plastic surgery with the diabolism of the horror film in its explication of the doppelganger. As in many mystery treatments of the theme, Harry is made to suffer for the evil deeds committed by his double. Like "Jefferson Randolph" in *The Big Clock* and "George Kaplan" in *North by Northwest*, "Johnny Favorite" is a non-person, a shadow self, that the protagonist is in hot pursuit of. The association of a devil's bargain with the doppelganger goes back to the works of E.T.A. Hoffmann and first appeared on the screen in the seminal German expressionist film *The Student of Prague* (1913).

The most notorious case of evil twins in the annals of crime is surely the story of the Kray brothers, Ronnie and Reggie, who ruled the criminal underworld in London during the 1960s. Born into poverty and a fatherless household in London's rough and tumble East End, the siblings would eventually rise to become the heads of "The Firm," the most feared criminal syndicate in the city and would ascend to celebrity status as the operators of a number of gangster chic nightclubs and gambling establishments where they rubbed shoulders with the likes of Frank Sinatra, Judy Garland, the Beatles, Roger Moore, George Raft and several members of Parliament. In 1968 the Krays were convicted of committing a couple of brutal murders and spent the remainder of their lives in prisons and psychiatric hospitals.

Oddly, these homicidal siblings were reportedly very close to their mother, Violet, causing some cultural observers to compare them to the similarly mother-obsessed killer Cody, played by James Cagney, in Raoul Walsh's classic gangster flick *White Heat* (1948). As with many sets of twins, Ronnie, the more psychotic of the two, dominated his brother Reggie. They also exhibited the often observed telepathy between identical twins. In his book *Evil Twins*, author John Glatt notes, "Even as babies there was an uncanny telepathic link between the twins. One always knew what the other was thinking."[8] The strange and terrible saga of the grim brothers Kray has been chronicled in two very different biopics, *The Krays* (1990) and *Legend* (2015).

Peter Medak's *The Krays* follows this dynamic duo from birth to adulthood as they mature from violent children into violent adults in London's impoverished East End under the tutelage of their doting mother, Violet (Billie Whitelaw). As young adults, bad seeds Ronnie (Gary Kemp) and Reggie (Martin Kemp) begin to grow their criminal enterprise when they become extortionists hitting up shops and small business for protection money. They quickly rise through the city's criminal hierarchy to head the most feared gang in the East End by virtue of their propensity for ruthless violence and their brotherly solidarity. The openly gay Ronnie has an abusive relationship with his lover, Steve (Gary Love), while the heterosexual Reggie courts and marries his working class sweetheart Frances Shea (Kate Hardie), who eventually has a mental breakdown and commits suicide trying to deal with Reggie's violent lifestyle.

Reggie has his own breakdown in the aftermath of his wife's suicide, causing both brothers to spiral out of control. When rival gang leader George Cornell (Steven Berkoff), publically insults Ronnie by calling him "a big fat poof" (a derogatory term for homosexual), Ronnie retaliates by shooting him to death in front of a slew of witnesses at a pub knowing that no one will dare finger him for the crime. Not to be outdone, Reggie goes after one of their gang, Jack McVitie (Tom Bell), who has been stealing from them, and brutally murders him with a knife when his pistol misfires. This time the brothers have gone too far, however, and Scotland Yard finally brings them to justice. The last scene in the film takes place years later at their mother's funeral, where the Krays are allowed to attend wearing handcuffs.

Although the film is ostensibly about the Kray twins, Philip Ridley's screenplay inexplicably spends an inordinate amount of screen time chronicling the doings of their mother, Violet, and the gaggle of eccentric female members of their extended family. These matriarchal stalwarts are fond of mouthing lines of dialogue like "Men are born children and they stay children," "It was the women who had the war," and "Housework is a lethal business," that imply that these domestic conflicts somehow inspired the Kray's dastardly deeds. The exploits of these tough mamas run in counterpoint to the main thrust of the gangster movie narrative, and frequently slow down the action.

Gary (left) and Martin Kemp appear as the real-life British gangster twins Ronnie and Reggie in the fact-based biopic *The Krays* (1990).

The venerable British actress Billie Whitelaw steals every scene she's in with her strong performance as the charismatic Violet Kray, while the twins, portrayed by brothers (but not identical twins) Gary and Martin Kemp of the rock group Spandau Ballet, are by turns cool and sadistically psychotic. Of the two, Martin has a juicier role playing the more sensitive Reggie Kray, while Gary's portrait of nuts boy Ronnie is colder and more distant. Director Medak shoots in a semi-documentary style using East End interior and exterior locations, which tends to give the visuals a dreary, washed out look, and the film's modest budget does not allow for the depiction of the Kray's opulent nightclub schmoozing with the rich and famous. The overall mood is one of morbidity and brooding melancholy, with many scenes taking place in cemeteries. Medak had also directed the 1980 ghost/doppelganger thriller *The Changeling* (see Chapter Four).

The film begins with Violet having a dream about a swan who lays two eggs, from which her twins hatch. This

Twin gangsters Ronnie (Gary Kemp, left) and Reggie Kray (Martin Kemp) draw swords together in *The Krays* (1990).

is a reference to the story of Leda and the swan from Greek mythology, whose hatchlings were the hero twins Castor and Pollux, an allusion that indicates the unusual nature of the Kray twins. As they mature, Ronnie and Reggie sometimes speak in unison, share the same dreams and anticipate each other's actions in a display of their telepathic linkage. The film's doppelganger imagery includes a two-headed baby in a jar on display in a freak show and a double headed snake sculpture presented to Ronnie by a Mafia liaison. Ronnie Kray died in 1995 and Reggie in 2000, and since then a number of British psychics have tried to contact them in the afterlife.

Writer/director Brian Helgeland offered an alternative take on the Kray saga in *Legend* (2015), in which both Ronnie and Reggie are played by Tom Hardy, who is rendered into filmic twins via 21st-century digital technology. Based on the biography *The Profession of Violence* by John Pearson, the film dispenses with their early years and chronicles their criminal exploits as adults. *Legend* depicts many of the same events in *The Krays*, including the brutal killings of Charlie Richardson (Paul Bettany) and Jack McVitie (Sam Spruell), their meetings with the Mafia, Ronnie's homosexuality and Reggie's abusive marriage to Frances Shea (Emily Browning) and her subsequent suicide. Frances provides an off-screen narration in the manner of many classic films noir that offers an ironic commentary on the sordid action.

In Helegeland's iteration the Krays are de-mythologized from being uncanny psychic twins into nothing more than a pair of unusual and charismatic hoodlums. The film's budget allowed for more extravagant depictions of the lavish nightclubs where they held court and were patronized by London's high society. Helegeland, who won an Oscar for his screenplay for the acclaimed neo-noir *L.A. Confidential* (1997), seems to be emulating director Martin Scorsese, and *Legend* frequently comes off as resembling Scorsese's gangster pic *Goodfellas* (1990) with a cockney accent.

Actor Tom Hardy's performance in the dual role of both Krays is at the heart of the film. Instead of stressing their identical resemblance, Hardy accentuates their differences. The twins have completely different hair styles, facial expressions and speech patterns. Reggie looks younger and more normal than his sibling, while Ronnie appears to be older, wears glasses, smokes cigars and frequently sports an almost inhuman, psychotic expression. An eerie touch is provided by Fran's narration, which continues after she is dead in an homage to a similar technique in Billy Wilder's classic film noir *Sunset Boulevard* (1950).

Another pair of unusual twins was involved in mystery and murder in London in *Double Vision* (1992). The twins involved are estranged sisters Lisa and Caroline Booth (both played by *Sex and the City*'s Kim Cattrall). Caroline is a staid medical student living with her father in Massachusetts, while Lisa is an aspiring actress, part-time waitress and high-priced call girl in London. Disturbed by a series of vivid nightmares and frightening visions in which she sees Lisa drowning, Caroline flies to the U.K. to check up on her sibling.

Meanwhile, in London, Lisa is torn between two lovers, her South Asian cab driver boyfriend Jimmy (Naveen Andrews) and her client, the wealthy, middle-aged Mr. Bernard (Christopher Lee). After they have sex in a hotel room, Lisa begs Bernard to leave his wife and marry her, but he is determined to keep his present marriage together. As Caroline's plane lands in London, Lisa makes a last ditch effort to persuade Bernard to divorce his spouse by making a scene at a party for the christening of his grandson. Trying to salvage the event, Bernard suggests she meet him at an abandoned boathouse near a river, but when she goes there she is strangled and drowned by an unseen assailant. During the murder Caroline, who has taken up residence in her sister's flat, telepathically experiences Lisa's death agonies.

Summoned by the police to identify her sister's body at the morgue the next day, she hears the dead Lisa tell her, "Don't run away this time" in her mind and resolves to stay in London until she can suss out her twin's killer. Donning her sister's sexy clothing, changing her hairstyle and assuming her mannerisms, Caroline assumes Lisa's identity and investigates the murder as her doppelganger. Her walk on the wild side as Lisa begins to change Caroline's personality from conservative to libidinous as the impersonation eventually uncovers her sister's murderer.

Loosely adapted from a short story by the "Modern Mistress of Suspense" Mary Higgins Clark by scenarist Tony Grisoni, the film's rambling narrative suggests that the meager source material was stretched out to accommodate a feature length film. Director Robert Knights fails to generate much in the way of suspense or horror given the film's uncanny premise. Glamour star Kim Cattrall brings some of her signature sexiness to the role of Lisa, but the screenplay never explores the individual personalities of the Booth twins. Co-star Christopher Lee, best known for playing Count Dracula and other horror roles in British films of the period, has a throwaway part as the object of a May/December romance with Lisa that strains credulity. This tepid preternatural mystery thriller did not run in theaters but was a direct to video release.

The notion of twins who share a telepathic mind meld has been observed by psychic researchers and also appears as a theme in numerous works of literature dating back to Dumas's *The Corsican Brothers*. Caroline is tormented by her dire dreams and visions into becoming her sister's double, and the film has a few eerie touches when Lisa speaks to her from beyond the grave. Identity transference between identical twins occurs in a number of murder mystery films, including *Among the Living*, *The Dark Mirror* and *Dead Ringer*.

In the same year and half a world away, another set of twins with a telepathic link struggled against the forces of crime. *Twin Dragons* (1992) featured action/comedy star Jackie Chan as a pair of mismatched identical twins who are separated at birth and have a fateful meeting as adults. The film begins in Hong Kong in 1965, where one of a pair of newborn twins is taken hostage by gang leader Crazy Kung (Kirk Wong), who has been taken to the hospital to have his wounds treated. The kidnapped twin is accidentally thrown into a wheelchair during the melee and goes careening off into the city, where it is found by a lower-class woman named Tsao (Lai-Ying Chow), who raises the child as her own. The parents take their remaining son back to New York and out of harm's way.

Twenty-six years later the Hong Kong twin who is named Boomer (Jackie Chan) is a martial artist, garage mechanic and speed racer on the city's mean streets, while his twin, John Ma (Chan), has been given a musical upbringing and is now a renowned concert pianist and orchestra conductor. The fun starts as Boomer and his goofball sidekick Tyson (Teddy Robin Kwan) run afoul of Boss Wing (Alfred Cheung) and are on the run from his gang as Ma arrives from the States to give a concert. As soon as the twins are in proximity they begin to telepathically sense each other's experiences, but are oblivious to each other's existence.

By chance the two brothers visit the same restaurant and are seated in adjacent booths with their girlfriends Barbara (Maggie Cheung) and Tammy (Nina Li Chi) when a fracas breaks out in the eatery and the twins wind up leaving with each other's partners. The rest of the film is a series of comic misadventures enlivened by Chan's signature kung-fu stunts and sight gags as the twins are mistaken for each other by the crooks, their girlfriends and musical fans alike. After the requisite number of car chases, boat chases, shoot-outs, explosions and *mano a mano* martial arts encounters Boomer and Ma defeat the hoodlums and put everything right.

This chop-sockey comedy of errors was lensed by Hong Kong action directors Ringo Lam and Tsui Hark as a typical Jackie Chan vehicle, but it's not generally considered one of the martial arts star's better efforts. The complex plot, devised by no less than five screenwriters, is a succession of vehicle chases, explosions, hand-to-hand brawls and scenes of general mayhem that seem formulaic and uninspired. Chan's signature comedy also falls flat, especially in a scene in which Boomer, mistaken for Ma, conducts a symphony orchestra using kung fu moves. On the plus side, the film's climax, filmed on location on the Hong Kong docks and at a Mitsubishi vehicle testing center, is exciting and original.

Exploiting the twin angle for laughs makes the film into a one-joke comedy, but there are also echoes of the uncanny. Once Ma and Boomer are in the same city they begin to experience each other's thoughts and perceptions: when Boomer is involved in a high-speed boat chase, Ma gets seasick; while Ma is playing a piano concerto, Boomer's fingers start to move over a phantom keyboard; when Boomer makes love to his girlfriend, Ma gets aroused. In the final scene Boomer, who is trapped inside a cage in the factory, must telepathically transfer his martial arts skills to Ma so he can beat the bad guy. In one running gag, when people see the doppelganger twins together they faint from the shock. Like the telepathic siblings in *The Krays* and *Double Vision*, the twins share a biological mind meld that forces them into a psychological unity with each other.

Another Hong Kong action director, John Woo, came to the United States to make films. His first Hollywood effort was an $80 million actioner entitled *Face/Off* (1997) that featured American mega-stars John Travolta and Nicolas Cage as opposite numbers who trade faces and identities. Travolta plays Los Angeles FBI agent Sean Archer, who has a personal vendetta against homicidal terrorist Castor Troy (Cage), who had killed his son six years earlier. Getting wind of a terrorist plot about to be perpetrated by Castor and his brother Pollux (Allesandro Nivola), Archer and his FBI team corner the brothers at a small airport, but during the ambush Pollux is captured and Castor reveals that he has planted a bomb set to go off somewhere in L.A. in the next few days before getting severely wounded and slipping into a coma.

Desperate to find the bomb, Archer's FBI colleague Tito Biondi (Robert Wisdom) comes up with a bold plan to transform Archer into Castor's double using advanced surgical techniques in skin grafting developed by Dr. Malcolm Walsh (Colm Feore). Archer undergoes these radical procedures at the Walsh Institute involving the removal of his features and the transplantation of Castor's face onto his own, surgery to alter his body and the implantation of a microchip that will allow him to speak in Castor's voice.

Archer (now played by Cage) is inserted into the maximum-security Erehwon prison where Pollux is incarcerated to try to gain information about the bomb. In the meantime, Castor comes out of his coma and realizes that his face has been stolen. Spying Archer's face mask floating in a jar, he has his gang kidnap Dr. Walsh and Tito and forces the surgeon to graft Archer's features over his bloody non-face. Once he has been transformed into the

FBI agent Sean Archer (Nicolas Cage, left) faces off against arch-criminal Castor Troy (John Travolta) in John Woo's action thriller *Face/Off* (1997).

likeness of his nemesis, Castor (now played by Travolta) kills Walsh and Tito and torches the Institute to obliterate any trace of the double operation. He assumes Archer's identity at the FBI and moves into his home and his wife's bed, while the real Archer is confined in the brutal Erehwon prison.

His newfound position causes Castor to change his plans. He pretends to have located the bomb and, knowing the code, disarms it, making him into an instant media celebrity. Soon the president is calling to congratulate him and he appears on the cover of Time Magazine as "the top cop in the country." His aim is to take over the FBI terrorist unit and use it to further his nefarious schemes. Visiting the prison, he taunts Archer with the knowledge that he has taken away his life while setting Pollux free. Instead of languishing in Jail, however, Archer engineers a prison riot, manages to escape and, impersonating Castor, takes control of his criminal gang. The two mortal enemies have now completely exchanged identities. "If you're Sean Archer," he muses, "I guess I'm Castor Troy."

Unfortunately, Castor gets wind of this arrangement and leads an FBI raid on his own gang during which many agents and most of the gang, including Pollux, are killed. Archer escapes once more and pays a visit to his wife, Dr. Eve Archer (Joan Allen) and shows her he is really her husband by proving he has the correct blood type. In the meantime, Archer's FBI mentor and supervisor Victor Lazaro (Harve Presnell) has become suspicious of Castor, but the gangster kills him and makes the death look like a heart attack and is promoted to acting director of the terrorism unit. When Archer visits Eve once more, she suggests that he go after Castor at Lazaro's funeral, when he will be vulnerable. Archer takes her advice, and a massive shootout takes place at the funeral chapel after the mourners have left that leaves both of them badly wounded. A high-speed boat chase ensues, which ends in Castor being killed by Archer with a spear gun. In the happy ending, Archer's features and identity are completely restored via corrective surgery.

Woo's stylish action thriller showcased the Hong Kong director's skills in utilizing balletic slow motion, artistic composition, special effects and beautifully choreographed scenes of violence and mayhem, with the director paying homage to his fellow master filmmakers Alfred Hitchcock, Sergio Leone and John Frankenheimer along the way. Mike Werb and Michael Colleary's screenplay caroms through gunfights, explosions, murders and high-speed chases like a runaway train, although some plot points definitely strain credulity. Hollywood icons John Travolta and Nicolas Cage turn in some of the most memorable performances of their careers in the film's unique, identity-bending dual roles. Cage in particular delivers a standout performance playing both the psychotic Castor Troy and the altruistic Sean Archer. The film was nominated for Best Sound Effects Editing at the 70th Academy Awards, but lost out to *Titanic*. *Face/Off*'s slick entertainment package proved to be highly successful at the box office and with critics alike.

While it is primarily a crime thriller, *Face/Off* strays into the realm of science fiction in order to create the film's doppelgangers via a hi-tech process that goes far beyond mere plastic surgery. Screenwriters Werb and Colleary have cited John Frankenheimer's 1966 sci-fi doppelganger film *Seconds* (see Chapter Five) as inspiration for the plot, while the film's gruesome full facial grafts recall George Franju's science fiction horror movie *Eyes Without a Face* (1956). Archer and Castor exchange identities along with their faces, as Castor adopts a paternal attitude toward Archer's teenage daughter Jamie (Dominique Swain), while Archer savors the forbidden delights of Castor's underworld milieu. Like

Francis Ford Coppola's *Godfather* movies, some of the film's most memorable scenes contain vivid Roman Catholic iconography. In one scene, for instance, Cage, as Castor Troy, is disguised as a priest who disrupts a performance of Handel's *Messiah*, while the climactic shoot out takes place in a funeral chapel complete with blood-spattered crucifixes and slow-motion flights of white doves. The names Castor and Pollux are a reference to the hero twins from Greek mythology.

One of the most bizarre treatments of the doppelganger theme in film occurs in David Fincher's *Fight Club* (1999). As in *Rebecca*, the film's narrator is an unnamed individual whose identity slowly becomes subsumed by a dominant but shadowy persona. The protagonist is an everyman (played by Edward Norton) who works in a dull job as an insurance claims adjuster and automobile recall specialist and leads a dreary, consumerist lifestyle. He suffers from insomnia and amnesiac bouts of narcolepsy until he starts to attend support groups for people with various serious illnesses that give him the emotional release of catharsis. These sessions cure his insomnia, but he soon notices another imposter, Goth chick Marla Singer (Helena Bonham Carter) at the meetings, and the two exchange phone numbers and agree to avoid each other by attending different sessions.

Flying home from a business trip he encounters Tyler Durden (Brad Pitt), an enigmatic, charismatic individual who makes his living selling a line of hand-made soap. Durden gives him his phone number and the two-part company at the airport, but when he returns home he finds that a mysterious explosion has destroyed his luxury condo. With nowhere to go, he calls Durden and the two meet in a bar where they become friends, but outside the tavern Durden provokes him into a fistfight as some sort of male bonding ritual. After beating each other black and blue, he moves into Durden's digs in a dilapidated mansion in a deserted area of the city.

Entranced by Durden's forceful personality and nihilist philosophy, he begins to rebel against his empty, consumerist lifestyle and is drawn into Durden's antisocial, hypermasculine orbit. They engage in a series of malicious but harmless pranks and steal bags of human fat from liposuction clinics that Durden uses to make into soap. More disturbingly, they organize a brutal "fight club" in the bar's basement, rowdy get-togethers in which men beat each other to bloody pulps. One day, out of the blue, Marla calls the narrator to tell him she is attempting to commit suicide by taking pills, but when he fluffs her off, Durden rescues her and starts a sexual relationship with Marla, much to the narrator's chagrin.

Fight clubs begin to sprout up all over the country like mushrooms, and Durden becomes revered as the head of this all-male sadomasochistic cult. Motivated by his anarchistic philosophy, the fight clubs metamorphose into a secret paramilitary organization called "Project Mayhem" that seems to have its tentacles everywhere. At first Durden commands them to merely commit simple pranks and property crimes, but soon his soap-making expertise is employed in the production of homemade explosives as he plans more serious actions. When Durden unexpectedly disappears, the narrator fears that he has hatched some truly insidious plan and goes looking for him, but in city after city he is puzzled when Project Mayhem members greet him as "Tyler Durden." Unfortunately, they are all tight-lipped about the impending operation that is about to be launched.

One night Durden seems to appear out of nowhere in his hotel room and reveals the bizarre truth. "We're the same person," Durden informs him, "all the ways you wish you could be is me." The narrator has created the Durden personality as a fantasy character, an alter ego, an imaginary friend that represents the yearnings of his own rebellious spirit. Still in the dark about the impending plot, he goes to the police, but finds that they, too, have been co-opted by Project Mayhem. He finally corners Durden in an office building at night and the two have one last fight, which the narrator loses, but when Durden pulls a gun on him he snatches it and shoots himself through the cheek, which somehow causes Durden's death from a head wound. At that moment some Project Mayhem members arrive, bringing Marla with them, and the couple witness the culmination of Durden's plan as skyscrapers housing banks and financial institutions explode to herald the coming of a new age.

It's difficult to assign *Fight Club* to any specific genre, but it combines elements of social satire, black comedy and the psychological thriller. Faithfully adapted from the "novel of transgression" of the same name by Chuck Palahniuk by screenwriter Jim Uhls, the complex narrative is by turns violent, outrageous, funny and mysterious, with the unbelievable plot twist saved for the end. Director David Fincher shot many scenes at night and used a silver retention process during post production to accentuate the contrast and darken the film's blacks, a technique that he had previously used in his serial killer thriller *Se7en* (1995). The result is a dirty, "stepped-on" look consisting of washed-out greens, blues and grays that conjure a gritty urban netherworld composed in sickly, bilious colors. This visual style can make *Fight Club* an unpleasant viewing experience, along with the curiously fascistic elements of the plot. The rendering of human fat into soap recalls the similar acts of Nazis in World War II concentration camps, while the film's Project Mayhem thugs have similarities with Hitler's private army of Brown Shirts, a group that enabled the dictator's rise to power during the 1930s. Finally, the demolition of skyscrapers housing financial institutions at the film's climax seems like an eerie premonition of the terrorist attacks on the World Trade Center on September 11, 2001. Because of its unusual subject matter the film did lukewarm business at the box office upon its original release, but has since attained the status of a cult film.

The doppelganger concept in *Fight Club* is confusing and seems unnecessary to the main thrust of the narrative. The psychological mechanism through which the Tyler Durden alter ego is created is ambiguous and remains unexplained. There are hints, however, that the narrator suffers from multiple personality disorder when he describes episodes of persistent insomnia, sleepwalking and amnesia. "I often wake up in strange places," he confides to his doctor, "with no idea how I got there." He later describes how Durden does things while he's asleep that he has no memory of, and how sometimes "Tyler's words come out of my mouth." As previously mentioned, the unnamed narrator (referred to as "Jack" in the screenplay) has affinities with the nameless heroine of Hitchcock's *Rebecca*, another submissive character who is haunted by a dominating presence.

The scenes in which Durden and "Jack" appear together were carefully staged so that they were not shown in two-shots with other actors in order to preserve the illusion of their duality. Ed Norton reportedly starved himself as the filming progressed, while Brad Pitt bulked up to make it appear that the narrator was wasting away while Durden became more solid. The relationship between the two personalities has an uncanny side that goes beyond a purely psychological explanation. In one brief scene, for instance, the presumably objective view from a surveillance camera shows the narrator being pulled along the ground by his hair by the unseen hand of Durden during their final dustup. A similar surveillance scene shows the narrator being attacked by an invisible assailant in a manner that suggests there is actually another person there.

Fyodor Dostoyevsky's novella *The Double* was the basis for director Richard Ayoade's film of the same name. Jesse Eisenberg stars as Simon James, a shy office worker toiling away at a dull office job in an unnamed Eastern European country. Poor Simon is so obscure that a colleague tells him, "you're a bit of a non-person." Looking out of the window of his drab apartment, he longingly watches the actions of his co-worker Hannah (Mia Wasikowska) through her window in the apartment building opposite his with a telescope. One night, however, he is startled to see a man commit suicide by jumping to his death from the floor above Hannah's.

Not long after the suicide, Simon sees the shadowy figure of a man entering his apartment building. He tries to follow the man, who quickly disappears into the gloom. The next day his boss, Mr. Papadoupoulos (Wallace Shawn) announces the arrival of a new hire, James Simon (Eisenberg), and Simon faints when he first sets eyes on his double. James is everything Simon is not. His personality is assertive and aggressive, and he is well liked by his co-workers, especially the women. At first James cozies up to Simon, giving him pointers on how to seduce Hannah, but when Simon goes out on a date with her James switches places with him and goes home with her. To make Simon's humiliation complete, James also carries on an affair with the boss's Goth/punk daughter Melanie (Yasmin Paige).

At work, James's star continues to rise at the expense of Simon's. James asserts total control over his double by threatening to show Mr. Papadoupoulos compromising erotic photos he has taken with Hannah, knowing that their boss will think Simon has seduced her. He forces Simon to give him the keys to Simon's apartment in order to carry out his dalliances with various women. Pushed to his limit, Simon causes a scene in his workplace and finally asserts himself, but James reacts by showing the incriminating pictures to

Simon James (Jesse Eisenberg) is beside himself in Joseph Ayoade's screen adaptation of Dostoyevsky's novel *The Double* (2013).

Papadoupoulos, who fires Simon on the spot. Humiliated beyond all endurance, Simon returns home intending to commit suicide that night, but when he takes a last look at Hannah's apartment he sees her laid out as if for burial and calls the police. Her life is saved, but the doctor informs him that she was pregnant with James's child and has miscarried. When she regains consciousness she is still lost in despair and suggests that he take his own life.

Taking her advice to heart, Simon returns to his apartment to find James asleep on his bed after a bout of lovemaking. He handcuffs the unconscious James to his bed and goes to the same perch across the courtyard, the place where he had observed the other man's suicide. James awakens and watches Simon's suicidal plunge through the telescope, then lies down on the floor as if he, too, is mortally wounded. On the way to the hospital inside the ambulance, the dying Simon blurts out, "I like to think I'm pretty unique" before expiring from his injuries.

Director Ayoade and co-scripter Avi Korine have taken the basic framework of Dostoyevsky's original plot and updated it into the 21st century, with mixed results. The sex lives and petty cruelties of the various characters are emphasized, while the protagonist is driven to suicide rather than madness. The action takes place almost entirely inside dingy interiors within some dark netherworld where the sun never shines. The work environment where many scenes take place has a retro sci-fi look that recalls Terry Gilliam's *Brazil* (1985). Jessie Eisenberg brings intelligence and wit to his dual performances as the polar opposites Simon James and James Simon that is the film's greatest asset. Some critics maintained that *The Double* was a black comedy, but it's hard to see any comedy or satire in this bleak study of a man humiliated into despair and suicide by an uncaring society. The film has affinities with another tale of an individual oppressed by an uncaring bureaucratic society, Orson Welles's screen adaptation of Franz Kafka's *The Trial* (1962).

As in Dostoyevsky's novella, the phenomenon of the protagonist's double is left unexplained, and the main dramatic irony is that no one recognizes the doppelganger as being his identical twin. In the film's final act there appears to be some strange affinity between Simon and his double; when Simon lays dying on the pavement after his suicide plunge, James lies prone on the floor of his apartment, looking as if he is also mortally wounded and apparently sharing Simon's fate. There are affinities with Fincher's *Fight Club* in the dynamic wherein a weak, recessive character is drawn to and dominated by a more aggressive, charismatic one. Simon characterizes himself as being, "lost, lonely, invisible," and "permanently outside myself," whose persona is overwhelmed by that of the aggressive, assertive James. The dramatic tension between the personalities of the main character and his double exploits the psychological fear of loss of identity in a manner similar to *The Man Who Haunted Himself*.

The similarly-themed Canadian/Spanish psychological thriller *Enemy* (2013) was released in the same year. The film begins at an underground sex show where a group of sweaty males are transfixed by the sight of a naked dancer in the act of crushing a tarantula under her high-heeled pumps. Cut to the dismal cityscape of Toronto, where history professor Adam Bell (Jake Gyllenhaal) suffers through a boring existence teaching and going through the motions of a tepid relationship with his girlfriend, Mary (Melanie Laurent). One day a faculty colleague (Joshua Peace) suggests that he lighten up by watching a comedy film entitled *Where There's a Will, There's a Way*. On a whim, Adam rents the film and notices an actor in a bit part who bears a strange resemblance to him. He becomes obsessed with his lookalike and learns that the actor's name is Anthony Claire (also played by Gyllenhaal).

Some internet research quickly reveals key information about Anthony and he begins to stalk his doppelganger by visiting his office, casing his apartment complex and calling his home, much to the confusion of Anthony's pregnant wife Helen (Sarah Gadon). Adam finally gets through to Anthony and explains the situation, whereupon Anthony suggests that they meet in a cheap motel on the outskirts of the city. When they are face to face they discover that they are completely identical, down to a similar scar they both have in the same place on their abdomen. After their meeting, Anthony turns the tables on Adam by obtaining his vital info and stalking Mary. In the meantime, Anthony's wife Helen begins to suspect that her husband has been having affairs with other women.

Her fears are justified as Anthony conceives a plan that will get him into bed with Mary. He makes a false accusation that Adam has been having an affair with his wife, and demands that he be allowed to have a one night stand with Mary in return, after which he will go away and never bother Adam again. Adam agrees to this proposition and lends Anthony his car keys for the tryst, but while Anthony is transporting Mary to the same motel where the doubles first met, Adam goes to Anthony's apartment, appropriates his clothes, and impersonates him. At the motel, Mary notices a mark on Anthony's finger where his wedding ring has been removed and realizes he is an imposter. Infuriated, she demands to be taken home, and on the way back to the city Anthony and Mary get into a heated argument that leads to a car crash in which they are both killed. In the meantime, Helen realizes that Adam is impersonating Anthony, but she accepts this and the two make love. In the aftermath, it appears that Adam is poised to assume Anthony's identity.

This moody psychological thriller takes place in the dreary urban environment of Toronto, a setting that is accentuated by director Denis Villeneuve's use of optical filters to produce a landscape of drab yellow tones that serves to exteriorize the social alienation of the characters. Surrealistic images of spiders occasionally intrude upon the narrative, including shots of a gigantic arachnid striding over the city's skyline, a spider-headed naked woman walking down a corridor, and, at the very end of the film, Adam's inexplicable encounter with an enormous tarantula inside Anthony's apartment. What these nightmarish arachnophobic motifs might symbolize is anyone's guess. Still, Villeneuve's direction is tight and he uses Toronto's monumental architecture to create an artificial, oppressive dreamscape as a backdrop for the action. Jake Gyllenhaal's deft performance as Adam/Anthony dominates the film, particularly his sensitive portrayal of Adam, who is the film's protagonist. He is aided and abetted by a fine cast, most notably Sarah Gadon's performance as Helen Claire and a cameo by cult fave Isabella Rossellini as Adam's mother.

Based on Jose Saramago's 2002 novel entitled *The Double*, the influence of Dostoyevsky's famous novella can be detected. Once again the protagonist is a shy, retiring type who is thrust into a conflict with a more aggressive version of himself. As in Dostoyevsky's work, no explanation is given for the existence of the doppelgangers who are identical down to the last detail. In this case, however, it is Adam, the more likeable and morally upright of the pair, who triumphs over his unscrupulous doppelganger in the end, and it is implied that Adam will assume his double's identity and his relationship with his wife. The hellish-looking metropolis and the spider imagery lend a feeling of the uncanny to the proceedings.

While good and evil twins, surgically created doubles, criminal schemers and psychological doppelgangers predominate in the mystery genre, in the horror film they have an even darker pedigree in the realm of ghosts, vampires, witches and the devil himself.

CHAPTER FOUR

Twins of Evil
Horror Films

Doppelganger is a German word. The term was coined by the German novelist Paul Richter in 1796 and the concept was further developed in the fantastic works of E.T.A. Hoffmann in the early 19th century. It is perhaps ironic that the first significant film in the history of German cinema was a horror movie on the doppelganger theme. This was years before the expressionist classic *The Cabinet of Dr. Caligari* (1919) ushered in the genre of the *Schauerfilme*, or "shudder films," the works of fantasy and imagination of the German silent cinema.

One of the luminaries of the German cinema of the period was Paul Wegener, an actor who had performed in Max Reinhardt's famed Deutsches Theatre. Wegener's stocky physique and craggy features were perfect for the screen, a medium that the young actor was eager to explore. In her study of German film *The Haunted Screen*, film historian Lotte Eisner relates how Wegener conceived the idea of making a film about the double. "In his public lecture in April, 1916 on the artistic possibilities of the cinema.... Wegener told the following anecdote. In 1913 a series of comic photographs of a man fencing and playing cards with himself had made him realize that the cinema was better equipped than any other art-form to capture the fantastic world of E.T.A. Hoffmann—above all, the famous theme of the Doppelganger."[1]

Wegener's collaborator on the film was one of Germany's masters of macabre literature, the infamous Hanns Heinz Ewers. Virtually forgotten today, Ewers was best known at the time for his horror stories and novels such as *The Sorcerer's Apprentice* (1907), a thriller involving witchcraft and Satanism, and *Vampire* (1921), a bizarre tale of psychological vampirism. His most famous work was *Alraune* (1911), a decadent novel about an artificial woman with no soul that was filmed several times during the silent and early sound period. Ewers would associate himself with the Nazi movement during the 1930s but his books would later be banned and his property seized by the Nazi regime because of their depravity. The author died in poverty in Berlin in 1943 and his works fell into an obscurity that continues to this day.

The script he wrote for Wegener, titled *The Student of Prague* (1913), drew its main inspiration from Hoffmann's 1816 short story "A New Year's Eve Adventure," in which the protagonist cedes his mirror reflection to the Devil for the love of a beautiful woman. In both stories the Evil One appears as an eccentric individual with an Italian name. In addition, Ewers utilized plot elements from Poe's 1839 story "William Wilson," about a man's fatal encounter with his doppelganger (see Chapter Two).

Lensed by Danish director Stellan Rye, *The Student of Prague* stars Wegener as Baldwin, a poor student in 1820 Prague who is tempted into signing away his mirror image to a mysterious individual named Scapinelli (John Gottowt), who is in reality the Devil, for riches and an advantageous marriage. Once the Faustian contract is signed, Baldwin's reflection emerges from a mirror and walks out of the room with Scapinelli. Having obtained his newfound wealth, Baldwin courts the pretty Countess Margit (Grete Berger), but she is already engaged to aristocrat Count Waldis von Schwarzenberg (Lothar Korner). The Count is incensed by Baldwin's advances and demands they fight a duel for the hand of his betrothed. Knowing that Baldwin is the best swordsman in Prague, the Count's father (Fritz Weidemann) begs him to spare his son's life, and Baldwin agrees. On the day of the duel, however, Baldwin is horrified to find that his doppelganger has slain the Count in his stead.

The double begins to haunt Baldwin, materializing like an apparition while he is conducting his affairs. Baldwin pays a visit to the Countess and tries to convince her to marry him but she is horrified to observe that he casts no reflection in her dressing-room mirror, and when the ghostly doppelganger materializes in front of her, she faints. Plagued by his demonic mirror image, Baldwin is driven near to madness until he devises a way to resolve the situation. He retreats to his room, takes out a pistol, and when the double appears he shoots it and it vanishes. Unfortunately, he has only succeeded in shooting himself and falls down dead, whereupon the Devil enters the room, tears the contract into small pieces, and gleefully showers them over Baldwin's corpse.

Besides being the first substantive film to come out of Germany, *The Student of Prague* has the distinction of being the first feature length horror film in the history of the cinema, beating D.W. Griffith's Poe adaptation *The Avenging Conscience* into release by a year. Shot on location in Prague, the film uses naturalistic outdoor settings shot in the monuments and narrow back streets of the old city to visually invoke the supernatural forces that surround the characters, including one scene that takes place amid the stately ornamental columns of the Lobkowitz Palace. Another scene in which Baldwin and the Countess ramble through the tombstones of the town's famous Jewish Cemetery (the setting of a recent novel by Umberto Eco) had to be shot on a reconstructed set when Prague's religious leaders refused to give the filmmakers permission to shoot there.

The narrative unfolds entirely in long shots that emphasize the characters within a haunted landscape. While the film's archaic techniques seem creaky by today's standards, its eerie mood still shines through. Double exposures, optical dissolves and other camera tricks are used to render Baldwin and his doppelganger in the same frame, techniques that are used, for the first time, to inspire dread rather than for mere cinematic novelty. Paul Wegener's restrained performance as Baldwin contrasts with his portrayal of his demonic mirror image, a creature who assumes the ghostly aura of the inhuman. Also noteworthy is John Gottowt's portrayal of the devilish Scapinelli, a rakish figure attired entirely in black with a tall, black hat, a wispy white beard and an evil, twisted smile. Ewers's melding of plot elements derived from Hoffmann, Poe and Goethe form a terse, compelling storyline that is perfectly realized by director Stellan Rye.

As in many works on the doppelganger theme, from *The Private Memoirs and Confessions of a Justified Sinner* to *Angel Heart*, the double is associated with black magic and a deal with the Devil. The film's bizarre events are clearly depicted as being in the realm of the supernatural, but have a psychological dimension as well. In his book on early German cinema *From Caligari to Hitler*, film historian Siegfried Kracauer notes, "Obviously the double is nothing more than the projection of one of the two souls inhabiting Baldwin. The greedy self that makes him succumb to devilish temptations assumes a life of its own and sets out to destroy the other and better self he has betrayed."[2] On the other hand, while Baldwin's double sometimes seems to be solid, at other times it appears and disappears like an insubstantial wraith.

Eisner writes, "When *The Student of Prague* came out, it was immediately realized that the cinema could become the perfect medium for Romantic anguish, dream-states, and those hazy imaginings which shade so easily into the infinite depths of that fragment of space-outside-time, the screen."[3] This approach struck a chord in the mystical, mythopoetic soul of the Germans, but it wasn't until after World War I, with the international success of *Caligari*, that these visions could be realized in their cinema. *Caligari*, with its highly stylized painted sets designed to visualize the inner world of madness, ushered in the shadow-haunted Expressionist style that enlivened horror films of the German silent period such as *The Golem* (1920), *Nosferatu* (1922), *The Hands of Orlac* (1924), *Waxworks* (1924) *The Chronicle of the Gray House* (1925), *Faust* (1926) and *Alraune* (1928), among others.

The Student of Prague was remade in 1926 by Henrik Galeen, who cast the two stars of *Caligari* in the lead roles. Werner Krauss, who had played the sinister hypnotist Dr. Caligari, portrayed the diabolical Scapinelli, while Conrad Veidt, who was the vampire-like somnambulist, played the role of Baldwin. The plot of the second version is identical to that of the first, but Galeen, who also scripted, expanded the original's 41 minute running time to 91 minutes by adding some extraneous scenes such as a formal dance and a rowdy, drunken party at Baldwin's home that tend to slow down the flow of the narrative. Galeen's version also begins and ends with a shot of Baldwin's tombstone with the superimposed title that reads, "Here lies Baldwin, who fought the Devil and lost."

Dr. Caligari himself, the stolid Werner Krauss, imbues the role of Scapinelli with a demonic fervor that suggests the hidden power of his satanic majesty. In one memorable scene he stands on top of a hill next to a twisted tree and directs the actions of his mortal victims with wild, sorcerous gestures as if he is conducting an orchestra. In another scene Kraus's shadow rises out of the darkness until it engulfs the figures of Baldwin and the Countess on a balcony above. Unfortunately, the Scapinelli character disappears in the second half of the film. Fellow *Caligari* alum Conrad Veidt brings a haunted intensity to the part of both Baldwin and his phantom double, his gaunt, corpse-like features being perfectly suited for the role. Unlike the 1913 version, which was shot on location on the streets and monuments of Prague, the remake was largely photographed on subtly distorted sets in the Expressionist style of the period.

In the remake, when Baldwin shoots the doppelganger it vanishes but the mirror is shattered, whereupon Baldwin is able to see his image reflected in a shard of the glass once more before he dies. In contrast to the original movie, the Devil does not appear at the end of the film to claim Baldwin's soul, indicating that the student was able to redeem himself by his actions and avoid eternal damnation. The lack of a mirror reflection is a motif more commonly associated with Count Dracula and other vampires, who are also beings who have lost their souls via black magic.

A third version of Ewers's doppelganger tale was filmed during the early sound period in 1935 by director Arthur Robinson. In this iteration Baldwin is portrayed as a dashing, mustachioed leading man by Anton Walbrook. The student has fallen in love with comely opera singer Julia (Dorothea Wieck) who is being kept on a short leash by her fiancé, Baron Waldis (Eric Fiedler). Once again Baldwin is tempted into trading away his reflection to the sinister Dr. Carpis (Theodore Loos) in order to woo his lady love, with the usual dire results. Robinson's visuals are elegant, but the film was made during the early years of the Nazi era, when the *Schauerfilme* was no longer in fashion. Consequently, the treatment is more that of a historical romance than a horror film, with numerous love scenes, masked balls and operatic arias performed by Julia, (whose singing voice was dubbed by diva Miliza Korjus). Because it downplays the uncanny angle of the plot, it is the least effective of the three screen versions of the story.

One year after the release of *Caligari*, the acclaimed director F.W. Murnau, who would go on to produce some of the greatest films of the German silent period such as *Nosferatu*, *Faust* and *The Last Laugh*, directed an unauthorized version of Stevenson's *The Strange Case of Dr. Jekyll and Mr. Hyde*. Written by Carl Janowitz who had co-scripted *Caligari*, *Der Januskopf* (*The Janus-Head*, 1920) stars Conrad Veidt as the Jekyll-esque Dr. Warren. In the opening sequence the respectable British physician buys a bust of Janus, the two-faced Roman deity of the New Year, as a gift for his girlfriend, Jane Lanyon (Margarete Schlegal). The statuette has a normal face on one side, while the other side has the twisted features of a leering satyr. When he presents the gift to Jane, however, she refuses it, but Warren keeps it and quickly becomes obsessed with the enigmatic work of art.

Some demonic force within the statuette transforms Dr. Warren into an alter ego, the hideous, Hyde-like Mr. O'Connor. Consumed with evil lusts, he kidnaps Jane and brings her to his laboratory and to a brothel in London's seedy Whitechapel district, and later murders a little girl on the street. When O'Conner transforms back into Warren he is horrified by the deeds committed by his doppelganger and tries to sell the Janus head at an auction, but the malevolent force within the statue forces him to buy it back. As the O'Connor personality is on the verge of a complete takeover of the doctor, Warren realizes there is only one way to be free of the influence of the artifact. He locks himself in his lab and takes poison, clutching the hideous two-faced bust to him as he expires.

The Janus-Head is a lost film and any information about it comes from the surviving screenplay, production notes and stills. The similarities to Stevenson's *Jekyll and Hyde* are obvious, but Dr. Warren's transformations into Mr. O'Connor are achieved by supernatural means rather than through scientific experimentation, moving the story from the realm of sci-fi into fantasy, although this was done primarily to avoid copyright infringements. As in Stevenson's source material, O'Conner, the monster from the Id eventually overpowers the civilized superego of Dr. Warren. Stills from the film show O'Conner depicted as a hairy, werewolf-like creature that is not unlike Stevenson's description of the troglodytic Mr. Hyde, and similar to the makeup used in the 1932 Fredric March version of *Jekyll and Hyde*. One of the cameramen on the film was the great Karl Freund, who would shoot a number of the classics of German silent and early sound cinema, and future horror star Bela Lugosi, who appears in the supporting role of Dr. Warren's butler.

Perhaps the most unusual example of the *Schauerfilme* was Arthur Robinson's *Warning Shadows* (*Schatten*, 1923), subtitled *A Nocturnal Hallucination*. The narrative, which unfolds without the use of titles, is set sometime in the 19th century, where a Count (Fritz Kortner) is giving a dinner party attended by four cavaliers. The Count is consumed with jealousy at the thought that his wife (Ruth Weyler) may be having an affair with one of the handsome young cavaliers (Gustav von Wangenheim). As the party progresses, the wife inflames the Count's jealous passions by flirting with the guests and making subtle advances toward the man he thinks is her lover.

Before matters get out of hand an itinerant shadowplayer (Alexander Granach), a mysterious eccentric character, comes to the door and begs permission to entertain the guests with a performance of his art. Projecting silhouette images onto what looks like a movie screen, he beguiles the guests, who seem to fall into a hypnotic trance, whereupon the shadowplayer uses magic to steal their shadows away and draw them into the realm of the unconscious. In this dream state the characters act out their uncontrolled desires.

The wife seduces the cavalier while the count watches their dalliance in another room through an oblique mirror reflection. Provoked to a murderous rage, he orders his sinister servant (Fritz Rasp) to hogtie her like an animal and compels the guests to stab her to death. In the aftermath he is overcome with remorse and starts to fight with the other guests until they hurl him through a window to his death. At this point the characters, who now appear to be projected on a movie screen, fade out and back into reality as the shadowplayer reappears and restores their shadows to them and they awaken. Their negative emotions having been played out by their shadow doubles in the realm of the unconscious, they have exorcized their inner demons and have returned to normalcy. The guests and the young cavalier depart in peace and the enigmatic shadowplayer, his mission accomplished, rides away on a pig (!) as dawn breaks and the husband and wife are reconciled to each other.

One of the more obscure masterpieces of the German silent period, *Warning Shadows* is an artistic tour de force, a phantasmagoric dreamscape of light and shadow brilliantly captured by director Robinson and the great cinematographer Fritz Arno Wagner. Imaginative set design, dramatic lighting setups, optical dissolves and multiple superimpositions all combine to conjure a nightmarish world of fantastic illusion. Fritz Kortner's masterful performance as the cuckolded Count portrays the character's inner torments through a series of wonderfully torturous facial expressions and vivid body language. Ruth Weyher as the count's errant wife oozes sensuality, while Gustav von Wangenheim, who had played the Jonathan Harker character in Murnau's *Nosferatu* a year earlier, is properly oily and handsome as the wife's lover. Alexander Granach brings an air of mystery and a touch of comedy to the role of the shadowplayer, and Fritz Rasp, who would go on to play major-league heavies in Fritz Lang's *Metropolis* and *Woman on the Moon*, exudes menace as the count's malevolent servant. Despite its many cinematic virtues, the film was neither a popular nor critical success as audiences of the time did not warm to its unusual, avant-garde stylistics and bizarre thematics. Robinson would later direct the 1935 version of *The Student of Prague*.

A number of motifs may have been derived from *The Student of Prague*, including the frequent use of mirror images and the mysterious, eccentric figure of the shadowplayer, who has the supernatural ability to steal people's shadow images away in a manner similar to Scapinelli's theft of the protagonist's mirror image in *Student*. This theme also recalls the character Peter Schlemihl, the creation of the 19th-century writer Chamisso, who sells his shadow to the Devil in a Faustian bargain. In this case, however, the count, his wife and the four dinner guests are all transformed into doppelgangers who act out their basest desires in a kind of virtual reality shadowplay. But instead of having their souls stolen, the magician's spell subjects them to a kind of group therapy that ends up exorcising their personal demons and enriching their lives. The film makes exquisite use of mirrors, reflections and unusual shadows to portray the realm of the double, which is associated with the world of dreams as in some occult lore.

Unlike the *Schauerfilmes* of Germany, supernatural and fantastic themes were not popular in American cinema during the 1920s. One of the first major American films in this genre was *Dr. Jekyll and Mr. Hyde* (1920) starring the acclaimed thespian John Barrymore in the dual roles. The screenplay, penned by Clara S. Berenger, follows the plot of Stevenson's novel closely, but also appropriates plot elements derived from an 1887 stage version by Thomas Russell Sullivan. In the play and movie versions, Jekyll is engaged to Sir George Carew's daughter, Millicent, and a love interest for Hyde is also provided in the form of an Italian dancer named Gina.

The film begins with a title proclaiming: "In each of us, two natures are at war—the good and the evil. All our lives the fight goes on between them, and one of them must conquer. But in our own hands lies the power to choose—what we want most to be, we are." We see the noble doctor (Barrymore), dubbed "London's Saint Anthony," selflessly dispensing his healing arts at his clinic for the poor. Jekyll's altruism sticks in the craw of Sir George Carew (Brandon Hurst), the father of Jekyll's fiancé, Millicent (Martha Mansfield), who challenges his prospective son- in-law at dinner one night attended by Dr. Lanyon (Charles Lane), Edward Enfield (Cecil Clovelly) and Mr. Utterson (J. Malcolm Dunn). Decrying Jekyll's saintliness, Carew argues, "In devoting yourself to others, Jekyll, aren't you neglecting the development of your own life?" When Jekyll protests, Carew adds, "A man cannot destroy the savage in him by denying its impulses. The only way to get rid of a temptation is to yield to it" (a line cribbed from Oscar Wilde's *The Picture of Dorian Gray*).

In an attempt to awaken Jekyll's libido, Carew and his friends escort him to a sleazy cabaret in London's low-rent Whitechapel district, where they take in an erotic dance by the attractive Italian performer Gina (Nita Naldi). Having been awakened to the dark side of his nature for the first time inspires Jekyll to begin his experiments. "Wouldn't it be marvelous if the two natures in man could be separated—housed in different bodies?" he muses as he works on a formula that will do just that. The first time he imbibes the potion he suffers a violent reaction almost like an epileptic seizure, as he is transmogrified into his malevolent alter ego, Edward Hyde while a second dose of the drug cocktail transforms him back into Jekyll again. The stooped, unkempt-looking Hyde has scraggly hair, extralong fingers and is unrecognizable as Jekyll. As Hyde, he rents a rundown apartment in a seedy part of town from which he can start living a double life.

Hyde installs Gina, the girl from the dance hall, in his new digs and begins an abusive relationship with her. He begins to savor the heretofore forbidden pleasures of opium dens, sleazy bars and the fleshpots of London. Jekyll's long unexplained absences have caused him to neglect Millicent, who begins to worry about her fiancé, so her father decides to pay a call on him in order to sort things out. When he reaches Jekyll's house he encounters Hyde instead, who he observes in the act of callously knocking down a child playing in the street. An angry crowd gathers and Hyde is forced to produce a check for damages, which Carew notes is signed by Henry Jekyll. Angry and confused, he demands to see the doctor, storming into Jekyll's house to demand an explanation. Hyde has taken the transforming draught and becomes Jekyll once more, and the confrontation with Carew arouses his ire. "What right have you to question me—you who first tempted me?" he asks, as he changes back into Hyde without the formula before Sir George's astonished eyes. The demented Hyde then chases Carew into the courtyard and beats him to death with his heavy walking stick.

Turning back into Jekyll, Hyde evades the police and seemingly gets away with the murder. While Millicent grieves, Jekyll hides in his laboratory, his supply of the transforming drugs having run out, as he fears he will once more change into Hyde without the formula. When Millicent finally comes to see him he starts turning into Hyde again, but takes poison before the transformation is complete so he cannot harm her. At this point Lanyon and Utterson show up in time to witness Hyde's final metamorphosis into Jekyll on his deathbed.

Jekyll and Hyde was a dramatic tour-de-force for Barrymore, as the film is framed around his performance in the dual roles. The actor's initial transformation was accomplished without resorting to either special effects or makeup, relying on nothing but facial expressions instead. Barrymore utilized prosthetic extensions on his fingers to make them longer and more clawlike. As horror film historian Carlos Clarens notes, "Barrymore's Jekyll is the handsome, posturing gentleman of a Whistler canvas, and as such, of little interest to him or the audience. But as Mr. Hyde, Barrymore enjoyed an actor's field day. With his misshapen skull, scraggly hair and clawlike hands, Barrymore does not conform to Stevenson's bestial, apelike conception, but his Hyde is nevertheless a remarkable creation: a leering, demented-looking old man not too distant from the villainous roués of stage melodrama."[4] Jekyll's transformation to Hyde during the murder of Carew is the film's most powerful scene as Hyde's skull-like visage convulses in a homicidal rage. Director Robertson had little to do

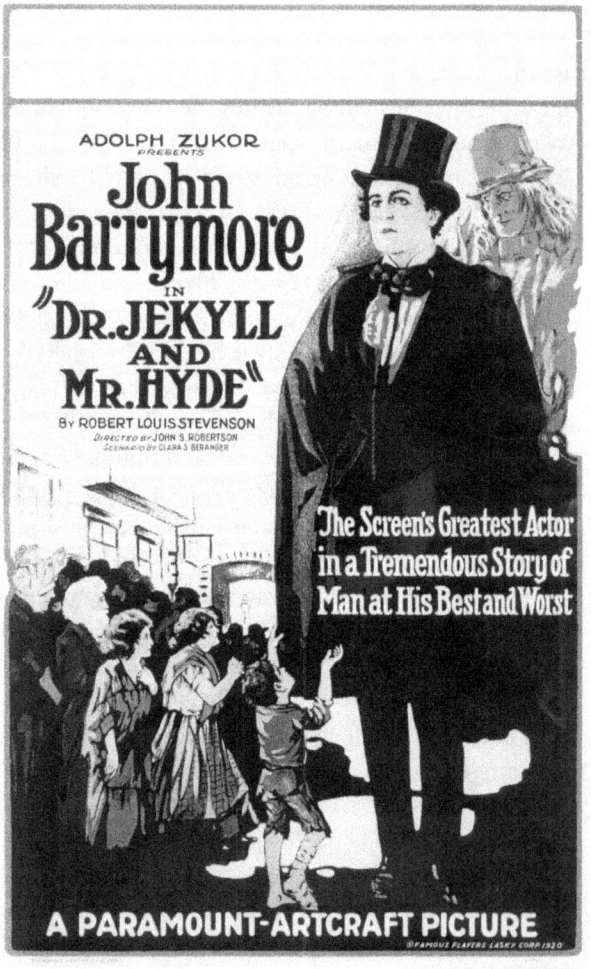

The saintly Dr. Jekyll (John Barrymore) is shadowed by his evil self in the silent version of *Dr. Jekyll and Mr. Hyde* (1920).

except place the camera in front of "the Great Profile" and let it roll, but he nonetheless managed to imbue the proceedings with some finely rendered Victorian atmosphere.

The physical contrast between Jekyll and his doppelganger Hyde is so extreme that they appear to be entirely separate persons, with Hyde being much more flamboyant and appealing than the saintly Jekyll. The introduction of a love interest for both Jekyll and Hyde forms a parallel pair of doubles in an upper class vs. lower class dichotomy, and this good girl/bad girl formula would become much more embellished in subsequent screen versions. The most bizarre imagery in the film occurs during a dream sequence in which Jekyll is lying in bed and attacked by his alter ego in the form of a hairy, man-sized spider or tick (obviously a man in a costume), a ghostly, transparent figure that crawls on top of him as if to suck out his life's blood. This monstrosity is arguably the most outré depiction of a doppelganger in screen history.

A second version of Jekyll and Hyde was also released later that year, produced by Louis B. Mayer and featuring Sheldon Lewis in the title roles. It was set in New York and had a trick ending in which the whole melodrama turned out to be nothing but a dream. This inferior entry was completely overshadowed by the Barrymore version at the box-office. F.W. Murnau's unauthorized adaptation of the Stevenson novel, *Der Januskopf*, was also released in the same year.

During the late 1920s and early 1930s many of the most talented German filmmakers emigrated to Hollywood either for the opportunity to make movies or to escape the clutches of the Nazi regime that had just come to power. The list included Fritz Lang, F.W. Murnau, Karl Freund, Paul Leni, Otto Preminger, Edward G. Ulmer and Robert Siodmak, among others, who brought the terrors of the Germanic "shudder films" with them. Depression-era audiences were primed to accept the relief from grim reality of the everyday that these works of fantasy and imagination offered. In 1931, Universal Studios produced the mega-hits *Dracula* and *Frankenstein* that started the 30s horror film cycle. Paramount's adaptation of *Dr. Jekyll and Mr. Hyde*, released on December 31, 1931, so that its star Fredric March could be considered for an Academy Award for that year, was the third horror sensation in a row. The first sound version of the Stevenson classic is still considered the best screen iteration of the tale due to March's performance and the brilliant direction of Rouben Mamoulian.

The screenplay, concocted by Samuel Hoffenstein and Percy Heath, takes its narrative cue from the 1887 stage adaptation and the 1920 screen version. Jekyll (March), the altruistic protagonist and selfless dispenser of medical care to London's poor, is nonetheless obsessed with the notion that the soul of man is "not truly one, but truly two." Engaged to Muriel Carew (Rose Hobart), the virginal, upper-class daughter of General Carew (Halliwell Hobbes), the staid Jekyll secretly yearns to experience the forbidden pleasures of the lower classes. One foggy London night he is walking through a seedy part of town with his friend and colleague Dr. Lanyan (Holmes Herbert) when they observe a street tough beating up a young girl. Jekyll hastens to offer medical assistance to the victim, the vivacious prostitute "Champagne Ivy" Pearson (Miriam Hopkins). Dazzled by the young nobleman's position and good looks, as well as his kind heart, Ivy offers herself to Jekyll, who is almost seduced by her feminine charms but manages to stay true to his fiancé.

His close encounter with Ivy spurs Jekyll into working on the formula that will separate the good and evil in the human psyche. The first time he drinks the experimental potion his skin begins to darken and his consciousness starts swirling around in a montage of libidinous images and eerie sounds. When his head stops spinning he approaches a mirror to behold his transformation into his alter ego, Mr. Hyde, a brutish-looking individual with beetling brows, a jutting jaw and prominent teeth that bears more than a passing resemblance to a Neanderthal man. "Free, free at last," Hyde exults, regarding his mirror image as he rails against the "deniers of life." He then rushes off into the night in search of Champagne Ivy, who he locates while she is plying her trade in a sleazy dance hall. The aggressive Hyde forces his attentions on the poor girl, dazzling her with Jekyll's wealth as he installs her in a rundown flat in Soho as his mistress.

Jekyll's erratic behavior and frequent absences cause General Carew to break off the engagement to his daughter and take Muriel away from London on an extended vacation. As a result the Hyde persona begins to dominate and his behavior toward Ivy becomes more abusive and sadistic until she begins to fear for her life. Before long, however, Muriel and her father return and Jekyll resolves to abandon his alter ego and double life. His resolution is strengthened when Ivy pays him a visit and reveals wounds on her body that reveal the extent of Hyde's cruelty, whereupon he swears to her that Hyde will never trouble her again.

Jekyll becomes reconciled with Muriel and the engagement is on again, but on the way to his engagement party he observes a cat killing a bird while crossing through a city park, the sight of which causes him to spontaneously transform into his alter ego. Hyde returns to Ivy's flat and taunts her with the knowledge that he is really Jekyll before brutally strangling her to death, then escapes from the scene of the crime by bounding down the building's stairs like an ape. During his struggle he loses his keys and is forced to rely on Dr. Lanyan to retrieve the chemicals from his laboratory that will turn him back to Jekyll once more, but Lanyan holds Hyde at gunpoint, forcing him to reveal his secret. Before Lanyan's astonished eyes, Hyde quaffs the transforming brew and becomes Jekyll once more.

Lanyan offers to keep his friend's dual identity a secret if he refrains from using the potion, and Jekyll agrees. He pays a visit to Muriel with the intent of ending their relationship, although during their tearful encounter he gives no explanation for his actions. Leaving Muriel heartbroken, he spontaneously turns into Hyde once again and returns to attack her, whereupon General Carew comes to her defense and is savagely beaten to death with Hyde's walking stick. The murderer manages to escape and hides himself in Jekyll's lab, drinking the potion once more to affect the perfect disguise. Arriving at the Carew residence, Lanyan recognizes Jekyll's walking stick and realizes that his friend is the culprit. He guides the police to Jekyll's mansion and fingers him as the killer, causing him to transform back into Hyde again, and he is shot while trying to escape from the police.

Considered by critics and horror movie buffs to be the finest of the many screen adaptations of Stevenson's doppelganger tale, Mamoulian's version is enlivened by its avant-garde, almost experimental use of cinematic techniques that are all the more remarkable for occurring in a film made during the early sound period, when static camera setups and pedestrian narrative expositions were the norm. Mamoulian makes brilliant use of the moving camera, subjective camera, optical superimposition, extended dissolves, overlapping dialogue, split screens and other techniques that do not call undue attention to themselves and move the narrative along in a unique way. For instance, in one scene the screen is divided down the middle diagonally, showing Muriel anxiously awaiting Jekyll's appearance at her engagement party on the right side, while on the left Jekyll, having turned into Hyde spontaneously, hurries through the park to murder Ivy. The director famously employed varicolored makeup on March's face that seemed to appear magically during his transitions to Hyde by placing colored filters in front of the lights and then withdrawing them to reveal the previously invisible makeup. Later in the film, time-lapse photography is utilized to depict the transformations between the two characters.

Fredric March earned a well-deserved Best Actor Oscar for his portrayal of the altruistic young scientist and his atavistic alter ego. Unlike Barrymore's Jekyll, who comes off as a bland non-entity, March's Jekyll is a forceful, yet likable characterization. It is his performance as Hyde, however, that dominates the film. Acting in the heavy makeup devised by Wally Westmore, his Hyde is a fantastical creation who sniffs the air like an animal and bounds about like an ape with an almost superhuman vitality. The makeup's one drawback is the elaborate dental prosthesis, complete with canine fangs, that causes Hyde to lisp out his lines of dialogue.

Mr. Hyde looks over the shoulder of Dr. Jekyll (Fredric March) is this poster for the Rouben Mamoulian version of *Dr. Jekyll and Mr. Hyde* (1931).

March's co-star Miriam Hopkins also delivers a powerful performance as the pathetic whore Champagne Ivy, and manages to bring a good deal of audience sympathy to the part. Made before the advent of Hays Office censorship, Hopkins imbues the role with a heady eroticism.

The film's depiction of Mr. Hyde as a de-evolved troglodyte is closer to Stevenson's conception of the character than any other screen version. Stevenson describes Hyde as being smaller and younger than Jekyll, which is also part of March's characterization. As the film progresses Hyde's appearance becomes more hirsute and apelike as his persona begins to dominate Jekyll's. This extreme visual contrast between Jekyll and his doppelganger depicts the two as entirely different persons. Samuel Hoffenstein and Percy Heath's screenplay elevates Hyde's love interest, who had been introduced in the 1920 version, into a major character, thus creating a parallel set of female doppelgangers that underscores the contrast between Jekyll and Hyde.

The Paramount version of *Jekyll and Hyde* was re-released in 1935, but after that MGM purchased the rights to the film and took it out of circulation so it would not be compared to MGM's adaptation, which would be released in 1941. This version starred Fredric March's rival Spencer Tracy in the title roles and was directed by Victor Fleming, who had lensed the 1939 screen classics *Gone with the Wind* and *The Wizard of Oz*. Starring opposite Tracy were leading ladies Ingrid Bergman and Lana Turner. Producing a horror movie was a departure for the family-friendly MGM, a studio that was not known to be friendly to the genre, but the literary classic would benefit from the big budget, quality picture approach that constituted the "MGM touch."

John Lee Mahin's screenplay follows the plot of the Paramount version closely, with the addition of some early scenes involving laborer Sam Higgins (Barton MacLane), who has suffered a serious work injury that has turned him into a boisterous sociopath. After Higgins disrupts a church service attended by Jekyll (Tracy) the good doctor attempts to cure him with an experimental treatment, but the patient dies. These scenes, meant to establish Jekyll's altruistic nature, fall flat and only serve to slow down the narrative. In this version, Ivy Pearson (Bergman) is a waitress, not a prostitute, and her role has been greatly expanded. Her performance as the tormented Ivy upstages Tracy's acting and proved to be a prelude to a similar role as a tortured wife in MGM's psychological thriller *Gaslight* (1944) that would earn her an Academy Award. Sexpot Lana Turner, cast against type as Jekyll's betrothed Beatrice, is photogenic but is relegated to a throwaway part.

Fleming's approach to the material abandons the Expressionist shadows of the horror film (except for a few key scenes) in favor of a flat, realistic approach. Here Stevenson's work is played more as a romantic costume melodrama than a fear fest. The film does benefit from the Oscar-nominated cinematography of Joseph Ruttenberg, who beautifully captured the mysterious fog-bound streets of Victorian London, the period set design of Edwin B. Willis, the lush art direction of Cedric Gibbons and an evocative musical score by Franz Waxman. All of this, however, is not enough to save the picture.

Spencer Tracy's mediocre performance as the title characters is the film's fatal flaw. Unlike March's depiction of a simian version of Hyde, Tracy insisted on playing the character using minimal makeup, instead relying on

Dr. Jekyll (Spencer Tracy) is framed in the image of his nemesis in this publicity still for Victor Fleming's *Dr. Jekyll and Mr. Hyde* (1941).

facial expressions to convey Hyde's evil persona. The result is that there's little difference in their appearance, which works against the notion that they are two separate people. Tracy's Jekyll is bland and colorless, with none of the altruistic passion brought to the role by March. As Hyde, he is merely a brutish, leering lecher, his face frozen in a perpetual Joker-like grin. As Carlos Clarens put it, "Tracy's Hyde, relying on facial expression rather than face make-up, resembled nothing more than a snickering, lusty libertine, a cross between Aleister Crowley and James Cagney."[5] The British novelist Somerset Maugham reportedly visited the MGM soundstage where *Jekyll and Hyde* was being shot, and, watching Tracy's performance, inquired, "Which one is he playing now?"

Unlike the Germans, American film audiences did not have a fascination with the doppelganger, and only a handful of movies on this theme were made during the horror film boom of the 1930s and early 40s. Doppelgangers and even ghosts were pushed aside in favor of more modern creatures spawned in the Universal horror factory: Dracula, Frankenstein, the Invisible Man, the Mummy and the Wolf Man. Playing these movie monsters had made screen icons out of Universal stars Boris Karloff and Bela Lugosi, and other studios began to produce their own genre films to cash in on the horror craze.

Columbia's *The Black Room* (1935) was an historical horror film that starred Karloff (on loan from Universal) in a dual role as a pair of doppelgangers. The film is set in an 18th-century Tyrolean castle, where Baron de Berghmann (Henry Kolker) is awaiting the birth of an heir. When the doctor informs him his wife has given birth to twins, he turns morose. "Don't toast this birth," he exclaims, reminding the assembled guests of a grim prophecy. His baronial line had begun generations ago with a pair of twins and the younger brother had killed the elder. "This house began with murder," the Baron laments, "and it will end the same way." The younger brother committed his fratricide in the dreaded "Black Room" dungeon in the castle, which has long been walled up to prevent further incidents from occurring.

When the children mature, the older brother, Gregor, becomes the new Baron de Berghmann, while the younger brother, Anton, whose right arm is paralyzed from birth, has been away for ten years traveling around Europe. Although they are identical in appearance, they are polar opposites in temperament; Gregor is cruel while Anton is kindly. When Anton returns from abroad, accompanied by his enormous mastiff, Tor, he learns of rumors that his brother is kidnapping women from the town and making them disappear. Alas, the rumors are true, as Gregor is shown murdering a young woman named Maskha (Katherine deMille) and disposing of her body in a pit inside the Black Room, which he gains access to via a secret passage disguised as a fireplace.

Mashka's disappearance causes a furor that ignites a revolt in the town. An angry mob storms the castle seeking vengeance, but Gregor merely offers to abdicate and pass the title to Anton to resolve the situation. Anton becomes the new Baron de Berghmann, but during the transition Gregor lures his brother into the Black Room and hurls him into the pit, where he is impaled on a knife. It has been Gregor's plan all along to dispose of Anton and retain the title by impersonating his twin.

Emulating his brother's sunny disposition and holding his right arm rigid as if it were Anton's paralyzed limb, no one suspects he is Gregor. He sets his sights on the lovely Thea Hassell (Marian Marsh), the daughter of the commander of his armed forces, Colonel Paul Hassell (Thurston Hall), even though Thea is in love with one of her father's officers, Lieutenant Albert Lussan (Robert Allen). The Colonel, however, is amenable having Thea marry "Anton" despite his daughter's wishes, but while he is drawing up the papers to transfer Thea's properties to the Baron, he observes Gregor sneakily signing the documents with his "paralyzed" hand in a mirror and knows that he is dealing with the wrong brother. In order to sustain the ruse, Gregor kills the Colonel and blames the murder on Lt. Lussan, who is tried and convicted of the crime on the basis of circumstantial evidence planted by Gregor and sentenced to death.

With his romantic rival out of the way, Gregor prepares to marry Thea, but on their wedding day he makes the mistake of entering the Black Room once more to gloat over his brother's corpse. Anton's mastiff, Tor, follows him into the dungeon via the secret passageway in the fireplace and, seeing his dead master, begins to hound Gregor, who orders the dog poisoned before departing for the wedding ceremony. The loyal Tor, however, eludes the baron's servants and races after Gregor's carriage. Tor gains access to the church and attacks Gregor as the couple are taking their vows, and Gregor defends himself with his supposedly paralyzed right hand, revealing his true identity to the crowd. Pursued by Tor and the entire town, he flees back to his castle and tries to hide in the Black Room, but the dog leaps on him and pushes him into the pit, where he falls upon the same knife that killed Anton. The prophecy is thus fulfilled, as the younger brother has "killed" the elder and the baronial line of the de Berghmanns is ended.

Director Roy William Neill packs a goodly share of gothic chills, historical ambience and murky atmosphere into *The Black Room*'s brisk 67 minute running time. It compares favorably to the contemporaneous Universal horror product and to classic historical horror movies such as Rowland V. Lee's *Tower of London* (1939) or Robert Wise's *The Body Snatcher* (1944). Neill would go on to helm a number of memorable entries in Universal's Sherlock Holmes series. Horror star Karloff gives two bravura performances in the dual roles of the ill-fated twins. As Gregor, he projects his well-known sinister vibe, but as Anton he shows his versatility as an actor in his portrayal of a kinder, gentler individual, presaging the sympathetic "kindly old scientist" roles he would play in later years. Made during the same year that he played the Monster in *The Bride of Frankenstein*, Karloff's performance in *The Black Room* is one of his finest performances of the decade. His female co-star Marian Marsh, who had starred opposite John Barrymore in *Svengali* (1931) and *The Mad Genius* (1931), adds a touch of beauty and elegance to the proceedings in her role as Thea.

The screenplay by Henry Myers, adapted from the works of Arthur Strawn, plays like a Greek tragedy in which a curse is placed upon a noble house for past misdeeds, along with a dire prophecy and a homicidal conflict between family members. Thus the uncanny twins are linked by destiny to destroy each other in a Jekyll/Hyde polarity. The film makes use of mirrors in many scenes, including the one in which Gregor's true identity is revealed through his mirror image. In addition, the walls of the dreaded Black Room are fashioned from onyx, a dark-colored stone with a mirrored surface in which Gregor regards his evil reflection. As in the German films *The Student of Prague* and *Warning Shadows*, as well as some of Hitchcock's works such as *Vertigo* and *Psycho*, the use of mirrors serves to emphasize the doppelganger theme.

By the early 1940s, Karloff's horror movie rival, Bela Lugosi, had fallen on hard times for a variety of reasons. No longer an A-list actor, he was reduced to starring in cheapie thrillers produced at Hollywood's "Poverty Row" studios like Monogram and PRC. Monogram's *Bowery at Midnight* (1941) featured Lugosi in a schizophrenic double role. During the daytime, he is professor Brenner, who teaches abnormal psychology at a local university and dotes on his wife (Anna Hope); by night he assumes the identity of criminal mastermind Karl Wagner. As Wagner, he runs the Bowery Friendly Soup Kitchen in New York's Skid Row, where he recruits gang members from among the derelicts and reprobates for his criminal enterprises. As a cover for his operation, he employs pretty young nurse Judy Malvern (Wanda McKay), who dispenses her healing arts to the poor while remaining blissfully oblivious to Wagner's nefarious schemes. Meanwhile, in the building's secret sub-basement, demented junkie sawbones Doc Brooks (Lew Kelly) conducts dubious experiments on the corpses of Wagner's victims designed to raise them from the dead.

One night the notorious killer Frankie Mills (Tom Neal), wounded after a botched heist, takes refuge at the Friendly Soup Kitchen and is protected from the police by Wagner. The two psychopaths hit it off, and Wagner decides to make the homicidal Mills into his chief enforcer. Armed with Wagner's brains and Mills's brawn, the gang unleashes a reign of terror on the city in a series of brutal crimes. The police are baffled by these bizarre events until Judy's boyfriend Richard Dennison (John Archer) pays a visit to the soup kitchen disguised as a Bowery bum while doing fieldwork for a paper on the psychology of poverty. Richard recognizes Wagner as professor Brenner and is taken prisoner by the gang, but his disappearance ultimately leads the police to Brenner and exposes his double existence. They storm the soup kitchen and a gun battle follows, during which Frankie Mills goes down in a hail of lead and Wagner attempts to hide in the secret cellar. Unfortunately for him, Doc Brooks leads his hated master down into the chamber where he has been conducting his experiments and Wagner is horribly torn to pieces by the crackpot scientist's reanimated zombies.

Directed by studio hack Wallace Fox from a script by Gerald Schnitzer at the behest of schlockmeister producer Sam Katzman, *Bowery at Midnight* is a typically cheesy low budget horror fare from Monogram. The film combines elements of horror and science fiction with the gangster film, with mixed results. Lugosi, well into his professional decline, gives a lackluster performance in his starring roles and is upstaged by the up and coming actor Tom Neal, who would later go on to cult fame in Edward G. Ulmer's low-rent film noir *Detour* (1945). One of the film's main faults is that there is no discernible difference in Lugosi's portrayal of the saintly professor Brenner and his doppelganger Karl Wagner, nor is any explanation offered for the Jekyll and Hyde relationship between the two characters.

More poverty row doppelgangers appeared the following year in the PRC studio's production *Dead Men Walk* (1943). The film starred British horror actor George Zucco in a dual role as good and evil twins, ably assisted by Dwight Frye, who had made a career out of playing demented assistants in horror flicks, beginning with *Dracula* and *Frankenstein*. Zucco plays the kindly physician Dr. Lloyd Clayton, who is attending the funeral of his twin brother, Elwyn, as the film opens. Elwyn, it seems, was a bad seed who had recently returned from India, where he studied the occult arts and had been accused of practicing "horrible blasphemy" and "unspeakable sorceries" by the townspeople. After the funeral, Dr. Clayton is burning his sibling's books on black magic when he is accused of murdering Elwyn by Elwyn's hunchbacked assistant, Zolarr (Frye), a claim that turns out to be true, as the good doctor threw his brother off a mountaintop to rid the world of his evil.

Nurse Judy Malvern (Wanda McKay) is menaced by criminal mastermind Karl Wagner (Bela Lugosi, left) and gangster Frankie Mills (Tom Neal) as a surly dwarf (unidentified) looks on in *Bowery at Midnight* (1941).

That night Zolarr disinters Elwyn's coffin and transports it to an undisclosed location, where the evil twin rises from the dead and proclaims himself to be a vampire. He visits his brother and threatens to use his black arts to destroy everything Clayton holds dear before vanishing like a wraith. Clayton is the legal guardian of his niece, Gail (Mary Carlisle), who is engaged to the doctor's young medical partner, Dr. David Bently (Nedrick Young). Gail becomes the target of Elwyn's vengeance as he visits her at night to feast on her blood and turn her into his vampire slave.

The film's second act plays like a pale imitation of *Dracula*, with the two male leads striving to free Gail from the vampire's power while his demented slave slinks around doing his unholy bidding. Clayton and David learn that they must immolate the vampire's corpse as the sun rises in order to destroy him. Matters come to a head when Elwyn deliberately shows himself gloating over the corpse of one of the townspeople he has murdered. The townsfolk think that Doc Clayton has turned into "one of them Jekyll and Hyde fellas," and organize a lynch mob to storm the doctor's house. In the meantime, Clayton has followed Zolarr to the vampire's secret crypt and attacks his evil double. During the melee Zolarr gets trapped under a heavy piece of masonry and a candle gets knocked over, causing a fire to spread as the sun rises. David and the mob arrive on the scene to watch as Clayton, Elwyn and Zolarr are consumed in the fiery conflagration.

Despite its wretched production values, *Dead Men Walk* is a neat little thriller enlivened by the performances of veteran horror actors George Zucco and Dwight Frye. Zucco, who was a staple of Universal horror flicks like *The Mummy's Hand* (1940) and *House of Frankenstein* (1944) and portrayed the sinister Professor Moriarty in Fox's *The Adventures of Sherlock Holmes* (1939), shines in his dual role, and most especially as the evil vampire double Elwyn. Dwight Frye, who had played the lunatic Renfield in *Dracula* and the mad scientist's hunchbacked assistant Fritz in *Frankenstein*, brings his special brand of nuttiness to the role of Zolarr, a character who is an amalgam of Renfield and Fritz. Unfortunately, *Dead Men Walk* was the only joint outing for these two titans of terror, whose performances complement each other well. Director Sam Newfield manages to imbue the film with some evocative horror movie atmosphere on a shoestring budget.

The film is built around the idea of a conflict between a pair of good and evil twin brothers, as in *The Black Room* or *Among the Living*. As frequently happens, the murderous deeds of the evil twin are blamed on his innocent double, although Dr. Clayton is not exactly innocent after committing fratricide against Elwyn. Once again, it is fatal for a person to be in the same time and place as one's doppelganger, as Clayton and Elwyn vie against one another and are destroyed by the blazing inferno at the film's climax. Elwyn, although nominally a vampire, appears more like a ghost who materializes and vanishes at will and walks through walls in a manner similar to the doppelganger in *The Student of Prague*. Vampires and black magic would later be linked to good and evil twins in *Black Sunday* (1960) and *Twins of Evil* (1971).

MGM studios, who had not produced a horror film since Victor Fleming's 1941 *Jekyll and Hyde* remake, returned to the genre with an equally prestigious Victorian literary property in their screen adaptation of Oscar Wilde's *The Picture of Dorian Gray* (1945). The screenplay by Albert Lewin, who also directed, follows the plot of Wilde's novel fairly closely, even appropriating large swaths of Wilde's epigrammatic dialogue. Hurd Hatfield plays the eponymous Gray, a handsome youth who is having his portrait painted by the distinguished artist Sir Basil Hallward (Lowell Gilmore). The painting is so lifelike that it seems to capture some of Dorian's soul, causing him to wish, "As I grow old, this picture will remain always young…. If only the picture could change and I could be always as I am now. For that I would give anything." Unbeknownst to Dorian, his wish has been granted by an ancient Egyptian statuette of a cat, "one of the 73 great gods of Egypt," that Sir Basil has included as a detail in the portrait. When the painting has been completed, Sir Basil presents it to Dorian as a gift.

Dorian comes under the baleful influence of Sir Henry Wotton (played to perfection by George Sanders), who leads the lad into perdition by expounding his hedonistic philosophy. Like his Victorian counterpart Dr. Jekyll, Gray begins mucking about with the lower classes in low rent areas of London, where he meets the plucky cockney songstress Sybil Vane (Angela Lansbury) while she is performing at a local bistro. He becomes infatuated with Sybil and even proposes marriage, although she does not even know his name. Before they can consummate their union, however, Sir Henry suggests that Dorian test her morals by proposing that they spend a night together before they are wed. Poor Sybil, out of love for Dorian, fails the test and is humiliated enough to kill herself out of remorse.

The dapper Dorian Gray (Hurd Hatfield) woos cockney songstress Sybil Vane (Angela Lansbury) in this scene from *The Picture of Dorian Gray* (1945).

Because no one knows his identity, Dorian escapes any responsibility for the girl's death. In the aftermath of these events, he notices a subtle change in the portrait, whose features have magically assumed an expression of cruelty. Upset by this strange occurrence, he hides the picture inside a locked room.

This act propels Dorian into a life of wickedness and perversity as he indulges his every sordid whim to the fullest extent. Twenty years later, despite his debauched lifestyle, his features remain unchanged, while the portrait, hidden in its secret nook, shows the horrible ugliness of his many misdeeds. One night he meets Sir Basil by chance and the artist demands to see the portrait once more, and Dorian, acting on some wicked impulse, obliges him. Looking upon the awful countenance of Dorian's sins (shown in grisly Technicolor in this black and white movie), he is horrified by the sight and tries to get Dorian to repent, but he is brutally knifed to death instead. Gray then blackmails another reprobate, chemist Allen Campbell (Douglas Walton) into disposing of Sir Basil's corpse. Campbell complies, but later commits suicide out of remorse, leaving Dorian once more in the clear.

The forever-young nobleman is contemplating a marriage with Sir Basil's niece, Gladys (Donna Reed), much to the chagrin of the young aristocrat David Stone (Peter Lawford), but as he begins to have qualms of conscience about his murderous deeds, Dorian unexpectedly calls off the engagement. In the meantime, the police are investigating the disappearance of Sir Basil and Campbell's suicide, prompting David to sneak into Dorian's hidden room, where he learns the secret of the painting. As David summons Gladys and Sir Henry to confront Dorian, he enters the secret room to dispose of any evidence of his foul deeds. He plunges a knife into the heart of the portrait, but is overcome and falls to the floor. His friends, breaking into the house, find him lying dead, his face having assumed the aged, rotting features of the picture (once again in Technicolor), while his portrait has reverted back to the image of a handsome young man.

Like Metro's earlier *Jekyll and Hyde*, this prestige production lovingly recreates the world of Victorian London via the Oscar-winning cinematography of Harry Stradling and the Oscar-nominated production design of Cedric Gibbons, who had done a similar evocation of the era for the 1941 *Jekyll and Hyde*. Writer/director Albert Lewin delivers a wonderfully faithful adaptation of Wilde's unusual novel, complete with the author's sparkling dialogue lifted verbatim from the text. Lubin had been granted complete artistic control over the project by the studio, along with a generous budget of $2 million (in 1945 dollars). He reportedly insisted that the film be shot scene by scene in sequence, which is a cumbersome and expensive method of filmmaking. The relatively unknown Hurd Hatfield is perfectly cast in the lead role, his handsome features transforming into a drawn, feral mask as Dorian descends into his netherworld of the soul. British actor George Sanders, however, nearly steals the movie as Sir Henry, Gray's acerbic mentor, who acts as a mouthpiece for Wilde's hedonistic philosophy and has many of the best lines. Angela Lansbury garnered her second Academy Award nomination in two years (after 1944's *Gaslight*) for her role as the doomed Sybil Vane.

Like *The Student of Prague* and E.T.A. Hoffmann's works, the doppelganger exists in the form of a mirror image (in this case a vivid painting) that captures the atavistic part of the protagonist's persona in a Faustian bargain. Unlike the novel, in which no explanation of the magical relationship between Dorian and the painting is ever offered, the screen version introduces the plot device of the Egyptian cat statuette that creates Dorian's demonic double through the agency of an ancient sorcery. As in Poe's story "William Wilson," when the protagonist tries to destroy his double, he also destroys himself. The unusual technique of showing the painting in full, vivid color during a few key scenes in a black and white film depicts Dorian's doppelganger to the audience in a hyper-real fashion, a multicolored vision that the characters in the film do not apprehend.

As World War II ended in 1945, so did the popularity of the horror film, as its escapist appeal was no longer necessary and its terrors overshadowed by the grim aftermath of the war. This hiatus lasted until the late 1950s when, after a detour through the realm of sci-fi horror, the genre returned with a vengeance with England's Hammer Studios retreads of the Universal monster formula in *The Curse of Frankenstein* (1957) and *Horror of Dracula* (1958). A flood of Euro-horrors followed from Hammer and other British studios like Amicus and Tigon and the fledgling Gordon Films, who produced one of the best of the lot, *The Haunted Strangler* (1959).

Set during the mid–19th century, the film stars Boris Karloff as James Rankin, a crusading writer who becomes obsessed with the cold case of the so-called "Haymarket Strangler," a serial killer whose real name was Edward Styles. Twenty years earlier, Styles was convicted and executed for the strangulation and stabbing murders of five women, but Rankin believes that Styles was innocent of the crimes and sets out to prove his theory that the real murderer was a physician named Dr. Richard Tenant, who performed the autopsies on the Strangler's victims and seemed to have intimate knowledge of the homicides.

Rankin convinces the police to let him examine records about the case, where he learns that Dr. Tenant suffered a nervous breakdown after Styles's execution and was hospitalized for having hallucinations, bouts of amnesia and the partial paralysis of one arm. Furthermore, the doctor, along with one of the nurses, mysteriously disappeared from the hospital three days later and the two were never seen again. His investigation also leads him to a bawdy music hall called the Judas Hole, where he interviews the proprietress Cora Seth (Jean Kent), who had identified Styles as the killer, but finds her eyewitness description inconclusive.

Finally, Rankin locates Tenant's medical kit in a hospital storeroom, and notices that it is missing one scalpel. Reasoning that the missing item may have been buried with Styles, he makes plans to exhume the coffin to find the missing evidence that will prove that the doctor was the real killer. Rankin's wife Barbara (Elizabeth Allen) is disturbed by her husband's obsession, but Rankin will not be dissuaded. He bribes an official at Newgate Prison to allow him to dig up Styles's coffin in the prison cemetery, where he finds the missing scalpel and undergoes a strange transformation. His face contorts into a hideous expression and one of his arms seems to shrivel as if paralyzed. The transmogrified Rankin returns to the Judas Hole, where he murders one of the dancers and is recognized by Cora as the Haymarket Strangler, who seems to have returned from the dead.

When he returns to being himself, Rankin has partial amnesia about the transformation and the killing. He confesses his misgivings to Barbara, who reveals the awful truth that he is in reality Tenant. The two had met in the hospital two decades earlier, when she was a nurse and Tenant had suffered amnesia about the murders. She had fallen in love with him and spirited him away to start a new life as Rankin. Memory fragments about his old identity began to surface, however, leading Rankin to become obsessed with his former identity, which has emerged once more at the sight of Tenant's murder weapon. Unfortunately, these revelations cause the effect of transforming Rankin into his alter ego once more, and as the Strangler he brutally murders Barbara and escapes from the house.

Reverting back to the Rankin identity once more, he turns himself in to the police and confesses to the homicides, but ironically the authorities refuse to believe him. The family servant cannot identify him as the killer due to his altered appearance, and the prison official he bribed to let him dig up the graveyard will not admit to it. Rankin is locked in a padded cell in a sanitarium, where he turns into the Strangler and manages to escape, but the police track him down and shoot him to death on top of Styles's grave, where he has, ironically, proven his theory at last.

The Haunted Strangler offers a highly original twist on the Jekyll and Hyde theme by screenwriters John C. Cooper and Jan Read. Director Robert Day crafts an intelligent, finely wrought costume horror thriller that offers fine period detail, tight pacing and fear-inducing Gothic shadows rendered by cinematographer Lionel Banes. Boris Karloff gives one of his best 1950s era performances in the dual role, his portrayal of the Strangler taking a page from Barrymore's transformation in the 1920 *Jekyll and Hyde* by relying mostly on contorted facial expressions to convey the switch in identities. The Strangler's withered arm recalls his character's similar paralyzed limb in Karloff's portrayal of Gregor in *The Black Room*, filmed decades earlier. All the film's cinematic elements work together perfectly to produce a minor classic of the horror genre.

On the other hand, the film never explains how a doctor, who had presumably taken the Hippocratic Oath, could become a mute homicidal maniac with a withered arm and grotesquely twisted features, and later transform yet again into a kindly, socially-conscious writer. A possible explanation lies in a "three faces of Eve" type of multiple personality disorder, but this is never suggested, although some form of amnesia is involved. Note that the "original" personality, that of Dr. Tenant, is never shown to the audience, although he must have been wicked enough to cover up his crimes and implicate an innocent man who was tried and executed for them in his stead. The doppelganger relationship as depicted is therefore between the kindly Rankin, who seems to be an artificially created persona and that of his serial killer opposite number.

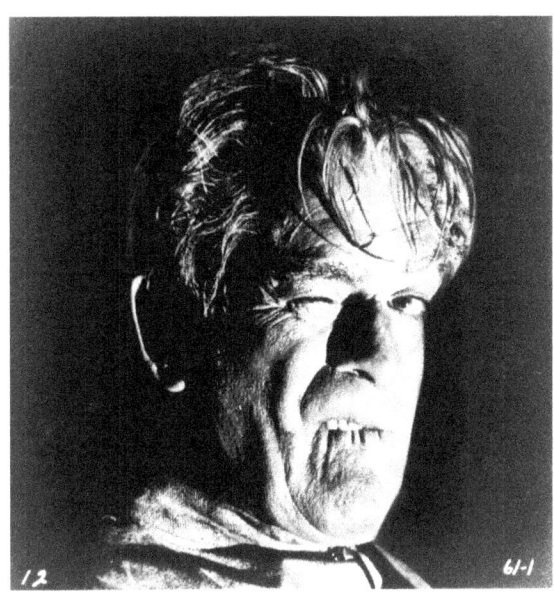

Boris Karloff as the title character in *The Haunted Strangler* (1957).

Another 1950s doppelganger-themed film from abroad was the Japanese-American co-production of *The Manster* (*Soto no Satsujinki*, 1959). The film begins with the lurid killing of several young Japanese girls at a bathhouse by a yeti-like hairy monster. The creature turns out to be the brother of scientist Dr. Robert Suzuki (Tetsu Nakamura), who has been conducting experiments with chemically induced mutations in a laboratory atop an active volcano. Suzuki's lab is filled with giant mutant plants and futuristic machines, along with his wife, Emiko (Toyoko Takechi), who has been transformed into a hideous monster by another experiment gone awry and is kept in a cage like an animal. When the ape-man returns to the lab, Suzuki shoots it dead and throws its furry corpse into the flaming maw of the volcano.

Larry Stanford (Peter Dyneley) an American foreign correspondent working in Japan, is assigned to do a story on the scientist's work by his newspaper and duly trudges up the mountain to the doctor's lab. Suzuki quickly sizes up Larry as his next experiment, slips him a sedative and gives him an injection of an experimental serum into his shoulder. The unsuspecting journalist, who has confided to the scientist that he plans to return home in the near future, is cajoled into staying in Japan by the wily Suzuki and his sultry Eurasian assistant Tara (Terri Zimmern), as the two beguile him with the charms of Tokyo's geisha joints, co-ed bathhouses and lavish nightclubs that serve to forestall his trip home.

As the serum begins to work, Larry's body begins to experience a startling metamorphosis. His right hand starts having convulsions and grows hair like the paw of an ape, and he develops an itch on his shoulder on the spot where Suzuki injected him. Larry's persona is also undergoing a change, becoming more moody and withdrawn. His wife Linda (Jane Hylton) arrives from New York to reconcile with her husband, but he rejects her and goes off with Tara. Later that evening, after a night of carousing, Larry returns to his hotel room and feels a sharp pain in his shoulder. In the film's most surrealistic and memorable scene, he loosens his shirt to reveal an eyeball growing out of his shoulder reflected in a mirror.

Becoming ever more morose and solitary, Larry begins wandering the streets of the city at night and indulging his homicidal impulses. He kills two women he happens to meet on the street for starters, then murders a monk (Shinpei Takagi) in an eerie scene in a Buddhist temple, and finally dispatches a psychiatrist (Alan Tarlton), who tried to treat him. Police Superintendent Aida (Jerry Ito) is on the case, but is baffled by the senseless crimes until a set of prayer beads from the Buddhist temple is found in Larry's possession. In the meantime, Larry has grown a second, ape-like head, and the two-headed freak is running around Tokyo wrecking havoc. He makes his way back up the mountain to Dr. Suzuki's lab, where he kills the doctor and sets fire to the place as Tara flees. Chasing her out on the mountainside, he splits down the middle, dividing in two like an amoeba into a normal Larry and a furry ape monster. The creature grabs Tara and hurls her into the volcano, then Larry and his hairy counterpart grapple until the beast falls to his death in the molten hot magma and Linda and the cops arrive to take Larry into custody.

This Japanese-American oddity is frequently lumped together with other two-headed horror films such as *The Incredible Two-Headed Transplant* (1971) and *The Thing with Two Heads* (1971), but the difference here is that the monster's second noggin is not the result of transplant surgery but is due to the injection of an experimental chemical, as in *Jekyll and Hyde*. Like Stevenson's character, *The Manster*'s protagonist is transformed into a homicidal psychopath under the effects of a drug. Writer/producer/director triple-threat George Breakston turns out a surprisingly effective low-budget horror thriller with several memorable scenes, including Larry's discovery of an eyeball on his shoulder and the murder of the Buddhist priest in a creepy temple amid a multitude of strange statues and eerie, atonal chanting. The exotic Japanese locale lends a jarring East meets West ambience to the proceedings. Peter Dyneley's standup performance as the dour Larry Stanford carries the film, with an able assist from the lovely Terri Zimmern as the oriental temptress, Tara.

The Manster goes *Jekyll and Hyde* one better by having the two warring halves of the protagonist's personality physically separate into two separate beings. Like Mr. Hyde, the main character's evil counterpart is depicted as a de-evolved troglodyte-like creature. As in many tales of the doppelganger, the narrative climaxes with a one-on-one physical confrontation between the two beings resulting in the annihilation of one of them. The film exploits the anxieties of "body horror" in a manner similar to the later films of director David Cronenberg such as *Videodrome* (1983) and *The Fly* (1986).

Britain's Hammer Studios, who had revitalized the horror film with their color retreads of Universal's Frankenstein and Dracula series, took a stab at another classic in *The Two Faces of Dr. Jekyll* (1960). As they had done in their remake *Horror of Dracula* (1958), the studio radically altered the source material. The film is set, for no discernible reason, in 1874, 14 years before the events of Stevenson's 1888 novel. Dr. Henry Jekyll (Paul Massie) is a gruff, bearded recluse who spends all his time working in his secluded lab on an experimental serum that will separate the good and evil natures in mankind, much to the chagrin of his neglected wife, Kitty (Dawn Addams). Her husband's inattentions have driven Kitty into the arms of the doctor's suave friend, Paul Allen (Christopher Lee). A notorious libertine, Paul is continuously hitting Jekyll up for money to cover his extensive gambling debts.

Jekyll finally perfects the formula, which he administers to himself (via hypodermic injection rather than orally). The drug transforms him into his alter ego, Mr. Hyde, a younger, handsomer, more vital and clean-shaven version of himself. Hyde wastes no time in partaking in the tawdry pleasures of London's demimonde at the Sphinx, a wretched hive of scum and villainy frequented by drunks, cutpurses and whores. As fate would have it, Hyde encounters Allen and Kitty at a table and approaches them, introducing himself to the couple as a friend of Jekyll's. Hyde tries to put the make on Kitty, but his attempt at seduction is thwarted by a confrontation with the club's bouncer (future star Oliver Reed in his first Hammer role), who he almost beats to death during a violent altercation. As a result, kindred spirits Allen and Hyde become fast friends, drinking buddies and partners in depravity.

On his next visit to the Sphinx with Allen, they watch an erotic performance by the masked snake dancer Maria (Norma Marla), and after the show Hyde manages to seduce her and make her his mistress. Hyde has other ambitions, however, which include bedding Jekyll's wife Kitty, but she finds Hyde repugnant and rejects him. In an attempt to get Allen under his thumb, Hyde offers to bankroll his gambling debts in exchange for Allen initiating him into the delights of London's sleazy underbelly, and the two begin a tour of the city's whorehouses, fight clubs and opium dens.

When he returns to his other self, Jekyll finds that the transformative drug is having an adverse effect on his metabolism and is making him age more rapidly. Consequently, he plans to abandon his primary identity and become Hyde forever. As Allen's debts mount, Hyde proposes that he give Kitty over to him in exchange for money, but Allen has fallen deeply in love with her and he refuses the request. Likewise, Kitty is repulsed by his advances, causing Hyde's sociopathic personality to go on a homicidal rampage. He gets hold of Maria's snake and locks Allen in an upstairs room with the deadly serpent, then abducts Kitty into an adjacent room and rapes her. Kitty awakens to find Allen's corpse with the snake crawling over him, and the sight drives her to jump from a balcony to her death. For good measure, Hyde also strangles Maria to cover any loose ends related to Allen's murder.

As a police inspector (Francis de Wolff) assigned to investigate the serial killings closes in on Hyde, he concocts a plan to frame Jekyll for the crimes. He kills an unsuspecting worker and torches Jekyll's lab to make it seem like Jekyll died in the blaze while Hyde escaped from the maniac with his life as the cops and firemen arrive. An inquest is held in which Jekyll's death is ruled a suicide, causing an exultant Hyde to think that he has gotten away with mass murder. But before he can leave the courtroom the Jekyll personality reasserts itself, and Hyde transforms back to the bearded scientist before the astonished eyes of the court officials, and Jekyll confesses to the crimes before dying from the deleterious effects of the drug.

Poster art for the film promised an "Enthralling New Screen Presentation of R.L. Stevenson's Spine-Tingling Story!" and the screenplay by playwright Wolf Mankowitz offers some new twists on the Stevenson classic by introducing a brand new set of characters, dramatic entanglements and ironies that serve to make the story more complex. By making Jekyll into an unpleasant boor and Hyde into a charming psychopath, however, this clever role reversal only serves to confuse the moral aspects of the tale. Hammer wanted to make the film a prestige production, and therefore toned down the explicit gore and violence that had made their previous efforts more profitable. The result is a film that is curiously lacking in effect that has been relegated to a minor status in the Hammer canon, and was a commercial failure upon release despite the best efforts of ace Hammer director Terence Fisher. Hammer repertory players Christopher Lee and Dawn Addams turn in adequate but unmemorable portrayals of characters who do not appear in Stevenson's novel. Particularly execrable is the scene in which Lee is discovered dead with the supposedly poisonous python crawling atop his body, the image being nothing short of laughable.

The best thing about *The Two Faces of Dr. Jekyll* is Paul Massie's masterful performance as the altruistic scientist and his deadly alter ego. Massie truly makes Jekyll and Hyde appear to be two different people, and his version of Hyde as a handsome, leering psychopath is refreshing and original. The depilatory effect of the drug that transforms the bearded Jekyll into the smooth-faced Hyde is never explained, however, and tends to strain credulity. In one odd scene, Jekyll sees his image as Hyde reflected in a mirror and has a conversation with his doppelganger as if Hyde is an entirely separate entity. The re-emergence of Jekyll at the moment when Hyde is poised to escape punishment for his multiple homicides is an ironic twist that is dramatically satisfying.

The international gothic horror revival of the 1960s continued with one of the all-time classics of the genre in the Italian director Mario Bava's *Black Sunday* (*La maschera del demonio*, 1960). The film begins in the Eastern European country of Moldavia in the year 1630, where a witch named Asa Vadja (Barbara Steele) is about to be burned at the stake along with her lover, Igor Javuto (Arturo Dominici). The malevolent sorceress curses her descendants for all time before a hideous metal mask is nailed to her face and the fire is lit, but a freak rainstorm, caused by the witch's magic puts out the flames before they can consume her body, which is interred in an unhallowed crypt.

Two hundred years later, in 1830, Dr. Thomas Kruvajan (Andrea Checchi) and his young assistant Dr. Andre Gorobec (John Richardson) are traveling through the same area on their way to a medical conference when their coach breaks down and the two physicians decide to take a walk while it is being fixed. By fate or some dark design they wander into Asa's crypt, where they remove the hideous mask of Satan and observe that the witch's body is remarkably well preserved even though it is crawling with vermin. When Dr. Kruvajan accidentally cuts his hand on a piece of glass, a drop of blood falls upon Asa's face.

Exiting the tomb, the doctors encounter Princess Katia Vajda (Steele), a descendent of the witch who is Asa's exact lookalike. She informs them that she lives in a nearby castle with her father, Prince Vajda (Ivo Garrani) and her brother Constantine (Enrico Olivieri) and that today is the feast of St. George, an accursed day when witches and evil spirits roam the land. Kruvajan and Gorobec, their carriage repaired, continue on to a local inn. In the meantime, the drop of Kruvajan's blood has partially revived the witch, who uses her powers to reanimate the corpse of her servant, Javuto, who she dispatches to the castle to murder Prince Vadja. The old man manages to ward off the undead Javuto with a crucifix, but is so traumatized that Katia and Constantine send a servant to the inn to summon Dr. Kruvajan to the castle. Unfortunately, Javuto kills the servant and arrives at the inn to escort Kruvajan to the castle, but when the doctor arrives he is delivered to Asa, who drinks his blood and makes him her slave and then commands him to murder Prince Vadja.

Searching for his colleague, Gorobec consults with the village priest (Antonio Pierfederici) to try to unravel the mysteries. The wise cleric has an inkling as to what's behind the strange goings-on and leads the doctor to Javuto's grave, where they find the undead Kruvajan in the coffin instead. The vampire is put to rest by being staked through the eye socket with a piece of wood in a gory scene. Back at the castle, Javuto abducts Katia and takes her to Asa's tomb, where the witch is planning to drink her blood, take her life and possess her body. "Your life was consecrated to me by Satan," she exults as Katia is stricken unconscious, but the witch is unable to consummate the unholy union because Katia is wearing a crucifix around her neck.

Gorobec, seeking Katia, enters the crypt and finds Asa who pretends to be her double. The witch urges him to stake the unconscious princess, and he is on the point of doing so when he notices the cross around Katia's neck and becomes suspicious. He rips open Asa's robe to reveal the fleshless bones of the undead concealed underneath. Just then the priest arrives with a contingent of villagers armed with torches and pitchforks who seize Asa and burn the sorceress for good this time, and the Vadja family curse is broken as Gorobec rescues Katia from the witch's tomb.

In his first credited directorial effort, director Bava crafts one of the last great black and white horror films and a true classic of horror cinema. One of a very few directors who also do their own cinematography (Nicholas Roeg and Ridley Scott are other examples), Bava uses his camera to create exquisite chiaroscuro visuals that conjure a dark universe of Gothic terror that harks back to the glory days of the great Universal programmers. Some images, such as scorpions and insects crawling over the death mask of Asa, are unforgettable. Unlike its Universal predecessors, however, *Black Sunday* contained visuals considered too gruesome and gory for U.S. consumption that were censored in the American version.

The source material was reputedly an 1865 short story by the Russian writer Nikolai Gogol entitled "The Vij," but screenwriters Bava (uncredited), Ennio de Concini and Mario Serandrei jettisoned most of Gogol's story except for its Eastern European locale and the notion of a witch being reincarnated. Much of the film's success must be credited to the remarkable performance of British actress Barbara Steele, whose wonderfully expressive features convey virginal innocence as Katia and primal evil as Asa. Only 19 years old at the time, she was catapulted to cult fame as an international scream queen.

Here the doppelganger is associated with both witchcraft and vampirism. It is Asa's black magic that causes her double to be reincarnated every hundred years so that she may possess her descendant's body and return to life. The film reaches its climax when Katia finally comes face to face with her double in time-honored fashion. There are similarities with the plot of Hammer's *Twins of Evil* (1971), which also featured a pair of beauties, one of whom becomes a vampire, and a witch resurrected through a black magic blood ritual.

Antonio Margheriti's *The Long Hair of Death* (*I lunghi capelli della Morte*, 1964) continued in the rich vein of Italian Gothic that had been opened up by *Black Sunday,* and also starred the reigning queen of 60s gothic horror, Barbara Steele. The film is set in an unnamed Roman Catholic country at the end of the 15th century, where a woman reputed to be a witch, Adele Karnstein (Halina Zalewska) is being burned for murdering the nobleman Count Franz. Proclaiming her innocence, Adele curses his successor, Count Humboldt (Guiliano Raffaeli) and promises vengeance as the flames consume her. In reality, Humboldt's amoral son Kurt (George Ardisson) is the real murderer, and to further cover up their crimes, Humboldt kills Adele's younger sister Helen Rochefort (Barbara Steele), who may have knowledge of the Count's murder.

After a few years Adele's youngest daughter, Lisabeth (also played by Zalewska) grows up to be the spitting image of her mother. "Her face constantly reminds me of that witch," Humboldt grouses, but Kurt has become irresistibly attracted to her and forces her to marry him against her wishes. Soon afterward a plague strikes the village that is finally broken by a torrential rainstorm, and during the tempest a lightning bolt strikes Helen's grave and magically resurrects her. As Humboldt, Kurt and the village elders are giving thanks for being delivered from the pestilence in their church, the wraithlike Helen wanders in from the storm, whereupon Humboldt, seeing the doppelganger, promptly dies of a heart attack.

Helen claims to be a person named Mary who was traveling to a nearby town looking for her father when her carriage suffered an accident and she wandered into the church. Kurt, who has become the new count, offers his hospitality but secretly contrives to keep her at the castle to satisfy his extramarital lust for the doe-eyed beauty. Kurt seduces Mary and the two enter into an illicit affair and begin planning to do away with Lisabeth. Kurt slips poison into her goblet and after she is dead Kurt and Mary conceal the body in the family crypt deep in the bowels of the castle.

Funny thing is, Lisabeth refuses to stay dead. Her body is missing from the crypt, and servants report seeing her around the castle, but somehow Kurt never seems to encounter her face to face. During a nightmare Kurt watches Lisabeth approach his bedside, then wakes up clutching a fistful of her hair. The strange cat and mouse game starts to drive him insane until finally Lisabeth and Mary confront him with the truth. Lisabeth is alive and Mary is Helen's ghost come back from the grave to avenge her sister. The living wife and the dead lover manage to trap Kurt inside a skull-faced effigy in which he is burned alive during a ceremony to celebrate the end of the plague, and the sisters finally have their revenge.

The Long Hair of Death is a well-made but not particularly inspired Italian Gothic thriller. For one thing, the screenplay by director Margheriti and Tonino Valeri derives too much from Bava's much superior *Black Sunday*. Borrowed plot elements include a witch burning, a family curse, a vengeful ghost, and Barbara Steele in dual roles. The narrative is poorly focused and overly complex and goes back and forth between the poles of costume mystery and supernatural horror. On the plus side, Margheriti delivers a good deal of spooky Gothic atmosphere as his camera glides through the musty crypts and ornate rooms of the count's palace. Many exteriors and interiors were filmed at the 12th-century Castle Collato Sabino in Lazio, located about 30 or 40 miles outside of Rome, which the director had used in his earlier Gothic thriller *Castle of Blood* (1963) to provide historical verisimilitude. The lovely and mysterious Barbara Steele graces the film with her magnetic screen presence, although her performance is not as dynamic as it was in *Black Sunday* or some of her other genre efforts. Italian thesps George Ardisson and Halina Zalewska acquit themselves well as the other two parts of the love triangle.

Once again Steele is cast in a dual role as a mortal woman and an undead being seeking vengeance from beyond the grave. She is a flesh and blood incarnation during most of the film but morphs into an insubstantial phantom during the climax. Helen's surname of "Karnstein" is a reference to the female vampire character in Sheridan Le Fanu's classic novella *Carmilla*. In the 1970s Hammer would produce a series of lesbo-vampire flicks loosely based on Le Fanu's story dubbed the "Karnstein Trilogy," consisting of *The Vampire Lovers* (1970), *Twins of Evil* (1971) and *Lust for a Vampire* (1971). Note that there are two pairs of doppelgangers: the witches Adele and Lisabeth, and Helen and the spectral Mary. Once again the double is associated with witchcraft, ghosts and a family curse.

Italian horror movie directors couldn't get enough of Steele, who director Mario Caiano cast in yet another dual role in *Nightmare Castle* (*Amanti d'oltretomba*, 1965). Sometime during the 19th century, in Hampton Castle (presumably somewhere in England), mad savant Dr. Stephen Arrowsmith (Paul Muller) conducts experiments into "electrolytic treatment of the blood," while his wife Muriel (Steele) carries on an affair with the castle gardener, David (Rik Battaglia). In retribution for his wife's infidelity, Arrowsmith subdues the pair, ties them up and tortures them, disfiguring half of Muriel's face with acid. During her agony, however, Muriel taunts him by revealing that she has changed her will and left the entire estate to her twin sister, Jenny. Arrowsmith electrocutes the lovers and uses Muriel's blood to restore youth to his elderly servant, Solange (Helga Line).

A short time later Arrowsmith marries Jenny (Steele in a blond wig) and brings her to Hampton Castle, much to the chagrin of Solange, who has become the doctor's lover and co-conspirator. They intend to gaslight Jenny, who has a history of mental problems, and drive her insane so that he will inherit the castle and Muriel's assets. He gives her psychedelic drugs that produce terrifying hallucinations and nightmares, then brings in psy-

Mad scientist Stephen Arrowsmith (Paul Muller, left) prepares to electrocute his wife Muriel (Barbara Steele) and her lover, David (Rik Battaglia), in *Nightmare Castle* (1965).

chiatrist Doctor Jerry Joyce (Marino Mase) to certify that she is *non compos mentis*. But instead of going along with her husband's plan, the handsome young headshrinker tries to restore Jenny's sanity, and even comes to believe that some of her visions are due to a supernatural agency.

Realizing that some sort of plot is afoot and fearing for his and Jenny's safety, Dr. Joyce arranges to leave Hampton Castle on a pretext, but secretly plans to return later that evening. With the psychiatrist gone, Arrowsmith and Solange plan to make their move to dispose of Jenny by transfusing her blood into Solange, who has started to age once more. The two women are strapped into adjacent operating tables in the mad doctor's lab, but as the transfusion is taking place the ghosts of Muriel and David appear to take their revenge. David cuts off the flow of Jenny's blood, which turns Solange into a skeleton, while Muriel reveals her scarred features to Arrowsmith before burning him to death. In the meantime, Dr. Joyce has returned to the castle and found his way to Arrowsmith's laboratory, where he rescues Jenny as the ghosts vanish.

Working with a modest budget, director Caiano still manages to deliver an atmospheric Gothic thriller through the use of high-contrast chiaroscuro cinematography and extreme close-ups that showcase Barbara Steele's extraordinarily expressive physiognomy, particularly her expressive eyes that alternately convey fear and malignancy. Steele's magnetic performance in the dual roles of Muriel and Jenny dominates the film as she portrays both the vulnerable victim of a heinous plot to rob her of her sanity, and a promiscuous wife seeking revenge on her husband from beyond the grave. She appears in several scenes wandering through the haunted spaces of Hampton Castle clad in a diaphanous nightgown while holding a candelabra, the very image of a Gothic heroine in peril from supernatural forces. Co-star Paul Muller's portrayal of the twisted mad scientist Dr. Arrowsmith conveys cold menace in the principal characterization that drives the plot. In the minus column, the screenplay by Caiano and Fabio De Agostini tends to bog down in repetitive scenes in the latter half of the film.

The Gothic doppelganger is once more in evidence in the depiction of identical twins representing darkness and light. As in *Black Sunday* and *The Long Hair of Death*, there is an association with vengeful female ghosts, which was perhaps becoming something of a cliché. *Nightmare Castle*'s 19th-century British setting, however, introduces an element of Victorian science fiction into the mix. Unlike the earlier Italian Gothics, the supernatural double co-exists with the technologies of hallucinatory drugs, electricity, and unorthodox medical experimentation a la *Frankenstein* or *Jekyll and Hyde*.

During the 1960s producer/director Roger Corman made a series of adaptations of the works of Edgar Allan Poe featuring horror star Vincent Price for American International Pictures. *The Masque of the Red Death* (1964) is widely considered the best of the lot for its lavish production design by Daniel Haller, the lush Technicolor cinematography of Nicholas Roeg, and an intriguing script by Charles Beaumont and R. Wright Campbell. The screenplay greatly expands the plot of Poe's short story by adding sub-plots concerning the brutal revenge of a slighted dwarf (taken from the Poe story "Hop Frog"), the satanic worship of a noblewoman (Hazel Court) and a doppelganger, while keeping the basic narrative of the story intact.

Price plays Prince Prospero, a decadent 12th-century Italian noble who has taken refuge from the deadly plague of the red death by barricading himself in his castle with a group of equally degenerate sycophants. From a local village, Prospero plucks a comely lass named Francesca (Jane Asher), whom he imprisons in the castle and hopes to corrupt to the worship of Satan. Francesca's heart remains true, however, despite Propsero's many trials of her virtue, while the sadistic prince devises a series of cruel and murderous ordeals for his guests to endure. His consort Juliana (Hazel Court) consecrates her soul to Satan during a hallucinatory ceremony, but Prospero unleashes his hunting falcon upon Juliana, causing her to be slashed to death by the bird's talons, and his court jester, the dwarf Hop Toad (Skip Martin), arranges for a man to be burned to death for the prince's amusement.

Prospero throws an elaborate masked ball during which his guests all wear costumes, but he has forbidden any of the revelers to wear red. Spying a masked figure clothed in red robes and a red cowl like a monk, the prince is furious and pursues him through the rooms of the castle. When he finally confronts the robed one, Prospero at first believes the forbidding person to be Satan himself, but soon has his doubts. "Who are you beneath that mask?" he ponders, and when the mask is ripped away he beholds that the figure has his

Stephen Arrowsmith (Paul Muller) attempts to gaslight his wife's identical twin sister Jemmy (Barbara Steele) in *Nightmare Castle* (1965).

own face. "There is no face of death until the moment of your own death," the being replies. The doppelganger, who is the red death personified, pursues the prince through the castle until he and the other guests expire in a macabre dance of death. The innocent Francesca, however, is spared their grim fate.

Corman is at the top of his directorial form in this lavish Poe adaptation that is truer to the source material than many of the other films in the series despite its embellishments. Filmed in England, Corman, who also produced, made good use of the superior technical facilities there, along with a decent budget, to craft a film that unreels like a Technicolor nightmare. Price is superb as the demonic Prince Prospero, while British actresses Hazel Court and Jane Asher (Paul McCartney's girlfriend at the time) shine in supporting roles. In collaboration with production designer Daniel Haller and cinematographer Nicholas Roeg, *The Masque of the Red Death* represents the apex of Corman's directorial career.

One of the major departures from Poe's tale is the inclusion of the doppelganger motif as a plot element at the climax of the film. The robed and hooded figure of the Red Death is an obvious homage to the grim reaper character in Ingmar Bergman's medieval allegory *The Seventh Seal* (1957). As in doppelganger folklore, Prospero's double acts as a kind of psychopomp, a *fetch* that arrives at the threshold of mortality to escort him to the netherworld, or as the Red Death himself explains, "there is no face of death until the moment of your own death."

Possibly inspired by the popularity of American International's Poe series, European producers Alberto Grimaldi and Raymond Eger conceived of the idea of making an anthology horror film based on Poe's tales that would be directed by some of Europe's hottest talents. Trend-setters such as Claude Chabrol, Joseph Losey and Luciano Visconti, along with Hollywood legend Orson Welles were considered, but ultimately bowed out in favor of French directors Roger Vadim and Louis Malle, and Italian superstar Federico Fellini. The result was the French/Italian co-production *Spirits of the Dead* (French: *Histoires extraordinaires*; Italian: *Tre passi nel delirio*, 1968). Fellini's segment, based on Poe's "Toby Dammit," concerned a famous but world weary actor who is haunted by the Devil, who appears in the form of a weird little girl, but the Vadim's and Malle's contributions deal with Poe's concepts of the doppelganger.

Vadim's adaptation of "Metzengerstein" is set in an unnamed European country several hundred years ago (Poe's story takes place in Hungary during the 15th century). Jane Fonda plays the Countess Frederique de Metzengerstein, a decadent young noblewoman described as a "petty Caligula" who indulges in "unheard of cruelties" and various promiscuous pleasures. Her cousin, the Baron Wilhelm Berlifitzing (Jane's brother Peter Fonda), lives as a recluse on an adjacent estate, but the two have no contact due to a long-standing family feud. One day, while riding through the forest, Frederique unexpectedly encounters Wilhelm and feels drawn to him, but when she attempts to seduce him he refuses her, knowing her reputation, and the countess returns to her castle in high dudgeon.

Stung by the rejection, Frederique orders her servants to set fire to Wilhelm's stable, and while he is attempting to rescue his horses he perishes in the flames. Afterward, she is attracted to the vivid image of a charger rampant woven into one of her palace tapestries, but the picture of the horse mysteriously gets burned. As she orders her master weaver (Georges Douking) to repair the tapestry, a beautiful black stallion arrives at Castle Metzengerstein. The animal is wild and unpredictable but exerts a strange fascination over the Countess.

Forsaking all other human contact, Frederique becomes totally obsessed with the black stallion, riding it through the countryside at full gallop and spending every waking hour under the spell of the uncanny creature. Finally, the weaver fully restores the image of the horse to the tapestry, and on that day a lightning strike causes a brush fire near the castle. Realizing her destiny and longing for death, the countess takes one final ride as the stallion plunges into the flames as she shares Wilhelm's grim fate, as he had, through some magic, transmigrated his soul into the body of the horse in order to exact his revenge.

In the Poe story Metzengerstein is a youth and Berlifitzing is an old man, but scripters Vadim and Pascal Cousin change the characters around to create an erotic attraction and rejection scenario that actually improves the dramatic tension of the narrative. Vadim was married to Jane Fonda at the time and had just directed her in the sci-fi spoof *Barbarella* (1968); thus, the camera lingers on her lissome form attired in a variety of revealing outfits as she strikes lascivious poses with exotic animals. Brother Peter, on his way to stardom in the hippie anthem *Easy Rider* (1969), projects an otherworldly aloofness that perfectly captures the essence of the mysterious Wilhelm. Vadim uses lush, highly saturated colors and brightly lit exteriors rather than Expressionist shadows to convey a Poe-esque, dreamlike *mise en scene*. Evocative use is made of ruins and seashore locations, and the characters are often framed in extreme long shots against the picturesque European landscapes.

Wilhelm's doppelganger is the forbidding black stallion, a creature at once beautiful and terrifying that is fated to be the instrument of Frederique's death and Wilhelm's revenge. As such, it represents one of the most unusual variations of the theme in all of film. It is also a kind of ghost, as Wilhelm's spirit has been transferred into the beast, as Poe indicates in his story, via the ancient Greek doctrine of metempsychosis, or the transmigration of souls. There is also the matter of the image of the horse in the tapestry that has some mysterious link with the deadly stallion in a manner that recalls the uncanny painting in *The Picture of Dorian Gray*.

Louis Malle's segment, an adaptation of "William Wilson," stars Gallic leading man Alain Delon in the title role of a man haunted by his double. Malle's version is set in Austrian-dominated northern Italy during the 19th century, where Austrian army officer Wilson runs into a church and demands that a priest (Penzo Palmer) hear his confession. In the confessional, Wilson reveals that he has just killed a man and is seeking absolution for the crime. The rest of the story unreels in flashback, as Wilson relates the circumstances of the murder. It seems that for most of his life, Wilson has been plagued by a double that interferes with his life at key junctures.

Even as a little boy Wilson had a streak of cruelty and a propensity for corrupting others. He first encounters the second Wilson as a schoolboy while he is performing the sadistic prank of lowering a fellow student into a well filled with rats. The doppelganger arrives in a timely fashion to interfere with his fun, and that night Wilson tries to strangle his counterpart, an act that leads to both of them being expelled. Years later, when Wilson is an adult studying in medical school, he cajoles his fellow students into waylaying a young woman (Katia Christine) they encounter in the street one night and strapping her naked body to a table in the school's operating theater where Wilson threatens her with a scalpel. Once again the second Wilson arrives to interfere with his fun by freeing the intended victim. As a result of these atrocious actions, Wilson is forced to leave the school and enlists in the Austrian army where he becomes an officer.

Several years later, Wilson goes to a party where he sits down for a high-stakes card game with the wealthy courtesan Guiseppina (Brigitte Bardot) that lasts all night into the next day until her losses are so heavy that she can no longer cover her bet. Wilson then proposes they play for double or nothing for her body, and she agrees. When she loses the final hand, Wilson exacts his pound of flesh by viciously flogging her naked back before offering her to his friends as a sexual plaything, but at that moment his double arrives, wearing a mask, and exposes him as a card cheat. For this transgression, Wilson is disgraced, forced to resign his commission and leave town.

Enraged by his double's interference in his affairs, Wilson rushes outside to confront his tormentor and challenges him to a duel. The two fence with swords and the double wins, but Wilson treacherously stabs him in the back with a dagger, killing him. When he unmasks the doppelganger, he finds that it has his own face. Expiring, he quote's Poe's lines, "From now on you are dead—dead to the world, to heaven, and to hope." Flash forward back to the confessional, where the priest, hearing this strange tale, insists that Wilson has been drinking or hallucinating, whereupon Wilson loses his composure, runs to the top of the bell tower of the church, and throws himself off. When his body is examined, however, the dagger used to stab the other Wilson to death is found sticking in his back.

Malle, who co-wrote the segment with Clement Biddle Wood, had reportedly conceived a scenario that was closer to Poe's tale, but the story was altered at the behest of co-producer Raymond Eger to include scenes of gratuitous violence and nudity that do not appear in the original, such as the nude woman being threatened in the dissecting room and the whipping of Guiseppina. The Guiseppina character seems to have been inserted into the plot solely to exploit the box-office appeal of Brigitte Bardot, and as a counterweight to fellow "sex kitten" Fonda in Vadim's segment. Nonetheless, Malle's direction is sure and true to Poe's basic concept of the story. French sex idol Alain Delon cuts a dashing figure as the unctuous and sadistic Wilson, while Bardot is glamorous and forceful in the supporting role of Guiseppina.

As in the Poe story, no clear explanation for the existence of the second Wilson is offered, but the film does imply that the double represents Wilson's conscience, as it only appears at climactic moments in order to rescue Wilson from indulging in his most egregious iniquities. The two Wilsons exist within the usual good versus evil polarity, but the narrative is unusual in being shown through the perspective of the evil twin. The detail of the dagger being found in the dead Wilson's back does not appear in Poe's tale, nor does the suicidal plunge from the church's bell tower, which may have been lifted from Hitchcock's *Vertigo*.

By the 1970s Hammer Studios was beginning to go into decline as audiences began to tire of their formulaic product. The final film in their "Karnstein trilogy" of lesbian-themed vampire flicks derived from Sheridan Le Fanu's *Carmilla* was *Twins of Evil* (1971). Former Playboy Playmates Mary and Madeleine Collinson star as Maria and Frieda Gellhorn, orphaned twin sisters who have left their native Vienna to live in the bucolic province of Karnstein with their uncle Gustav Weil (played by Hammer stalwart Peter Cushing) and aunt Katy (Kathleen Byron). The puritanical Gustav is the province's witchfinder general, who believes he has been called by God to eradicate all evil in their midst, aided by a fanatical crew of locals called "The Brotherhood." Gustav and his lynch mob keep busy by burning innocent girls they suspect of being witches at the stake in an exercise of puritan sexual repression.

Gustav's attentions are misdirected, however, as there is a diabolical menace in their midst in the form of Count Karnstein (Damien Thomas), who dabbles in black magic, but the degenerate nobleman is in the Austrian Emperor's favor and therefore untouchable. In Castle Karnstein high above the village the Count sacrifices a young girl (Kirsten Lindholm) to the powers of darkness and her sacrificial blood reincarnates the vampire Countess Mircalla Karnstein (Katya Wyeth), who wastes no time turning the Count into one of the undead.

Frieda, who has a rebellious streak, is attracted to the dashing Count and decides to accept his invitation to visit him secretly despite the admonitions of her sister, the morally upright Maria. The Count, under Mircalla's direction, transforms Frieda into a vampire, and when she returns to her uncle's home she forces her sister into keeping silent about her nocturnal visits to the castle by threatening to put the bite on her. While Frieda continues her midnight rambles, Maria falls for Anton Hoffer (David Warbek), a young schoolteacher, but he is more attracted to Frieda and can usually tell the difference between the twins.

Identical twins Mary and Madeleine Collinson face off as Count Karnstein (Damien Thomas) offers up a human sacrifice (Kirsten Lindholm) in this poster for Hammer's *Twins of Evil* (1971).

One night Frieda is caught sinking her fangs into a member of the Brotherhood and she is captured by her uncle and imprisoned. "The Devil has sent me twins of evil!" Gustav rants as he and the Brotherhood prepare to burn her at the stake, but while they are otherwise occupied Count Karnstein kidnaps Maria and substitutes her in Frieda's place, while Frieda pretends to be the innocent Maria. When the vampire sister tries to seduce Anton however, he notices her lack of reflection in a mirror and fends her off with a crucifix. She flees back to Castle Karnstein while Anton rushes to save Maria, who proves her innocence by kissing a cross before she can be consigned to the flames. Anton and Gustav lead the Brotherhood to the castle where they do battle with the Count and his minions. Frieda is beheaded by Gustav, but is killed by Karnstein, who in turn is staked by Anton.

One of the livelier of the 70s Hammer productions, *Twins of Evil* benefits from the competent direction of John Hough and an intriguing screenplay penned by Tudor Gates. The scene in which the Countess Mircalla is resurrected is the strongest part of the film and is replete with Gothic chills and atmosphere. Hammer trouper Peter Cushing comes through with another solid performance, while Damien Thomas's Count Karnstein exudes decadent vampiric menace. The Collinson twins offer up innocence and evil in equal measures. Although the former Playmates bare some flesh during the proceedings, the Sapphic themes of the earlier Karnstein flicks are absent, and would have involved an onscreen incestuous relationship between the sisters had it been included.

The plot involves the usual "good twin" versus "bad twin" dichotomy, or as poster art for film queried, "Which is the Virgin? Which is the Vampire?" Once again the doppelganger is associated with vampirism and black magic. As previously noted, there are similarities with the plot of Bava's *Black Sunday*, in which a sorceress is reincarnated via a blood ritual and turns the men around her into vampire slaves, and a scene where the evil vampire woman masquerades as her human double whose ruse is uncovered by the innocent woman's veneration for the cross.

Hammer took another stab at retooling the Jekyll and Hyde story with *Dr. Jekyll and Sister Hyde* (1971), a film that promised to depict, "the sexual transformation of a man into a woman ... before your very eyes." In Victorian London, in the year 1888, the reclusive Dr. Henry Jekyll (Ralph Bates), labors to find cures for all of humankind's maladies, but is frustrated by the notion that he might not live long enough to accomplish this noble goal. Accordingly, he decides to concentrate on a formula that will extend his life span, and accidentally discovers that female hormones are the key to longevity. The only problem is that he must obtain these hormones from fresh female cadavers supplied by the notorious grave robbers and murderers William Burke (Ivor Dean) and William Hare (Tony Calvin).

A pair of siblings, Howard Spencer (Lewis Fiander) and his sister Susan (Susan Brodrick), live upstairs from Jekyll, and Susan has developed a romantic attraction for the mad doctor that remains unrequited. In the meantime, Jekyll has developed a new serum that he intends to test upon himself, and when he drinks the potion is transformed into a vivacious young woman, Mrs. Hyde (Martine Beswick). Amazed and delighted by the transformation, Hyde explores her newfound physiognomy as she fondles her breasts lasciviously before a mirror. Jekyll passes off Mrs. Hyde as his widowed sister to the Spencers, but Susan is upset by what she perceives as a female rival, yet Howard is drawn to the physical charms and libidinous persona of the seductive Mrs. Hyde.

Unfortunately, Jekyll's supply of estrogen is abruptly cut off when Burke and Hare are lynched by a street mob as they are caught performing their nefarious activities. In order to obtain more raw material for the transformative serum, Jekyll must get it by murdering women, and while he balks at this, his alter ego is only too willing to oblige. Mrs. Hyde begins wielding the scalpel on prostitutes in London's seedy Whitechapel district in a series of grisly homicides that come to be known as the "Ripper murders." During the murder spree, the Hyde personality begins to dominate Jekyll's, and he begins to transform into her without benefit of the serum.

When Jekyll invites Susan to a night at the opera, Mrs. Hyde emerges instead to stalk her through the fogbound streets of London seeking to acquire her vital fluids for another dose of the youth serum. As she is about to murder Susan, however, Jekyll's personality re-asserts itself and he changes back to his male self once more and seeks out another victim, but he is caught in the act by the police, who give chase. Jekyll tries to escape by climbing up the façade of a building, but spontaneously becomes Hyde once more and, deprived of his male strength, plunges to the ground. In death, the male and female elements of the double-gendered being combine to become a grotesquely hermaphroditic corpse.

The most radical iteration of the Jekyll and Hyde story that had so far been attempted, the film is a far cry from Hammer's mediocre prestige production *The Two Faces of Dr. Jekyll* lensed a decade earlier. This lurid, gender-bending version of Stevenson's tale introduces an element of sexual ambiguity into the mix that viewers uncomfortable about their own sexuality might find disturbing. The mass murder of helpless females by a psychopathic killer was an element that ran counter to the burgeoning women's liberation movement. Additionally, Brian Clemens's screenplay weaves the exploits of the real-life murders of Burke and Hare and Jack the Ripper into the plot. Burke and Hare plied their gruesome trade in murder and grave-robbing in Edinburgh decades earlier, and were the inspiration for R.L. Stevenson's short story "The Body Snatcher." Oddly, there is also a connection between Stevenson's *The Strange Case of Dr. Jekyll and Mr. Hyde* and Jack the Ripper in that the Ripper murders occurred shortly after the publication of the novella and its stage adaptation, and were thought to be the work of a physician and a respectable member of London society.

Veteran Hammer director Roy Ward Baker vividly evokes the gaslit, perpetually foggy environment of Victorian London, especially in the murder scenes that take place on the seedy cobblestone streets of Whitechapel. The gaunt features of Ralph Bates as Jekyll meld seamlessly into those of Martine Beswick during the initial transformation scene, which only obliquely depicts the promised "sexual transformation of a man into a woman." Ms. Beswick steals the show as "sister" Hyde with her deliciously devilish performance as the psychopathic ripper murderer.

In this bizarre but original treatment of the doppelganger theme, the

Dr. Jekyll (Ralph Bates) is transmogrified into Mrs. Hyde (Martine Beswick) in Hammer's gender-bending twist on the classic R.L. Stevenson tale *Dr. Jekyll and Sister Hyde* (1971).

double is associated with an instantaneous gender switching transmogrification that borders on the scientifically impossible. Modern day sexual reassignment therapy is a long, involved process that involves extensive surgery, hormone injections and a series of lengthy medical procedures to achieve its goal. Once again the double represents an Id-force that manifests itself in Mrs. Hyde's persona as a homicidal, sexually promiscuous femme fatale. The similarly-themed *Dr. Jekyll and Ms. Hyde* (1995) involved the same gender-bending take on the Stevenson classic for comedy rather than horror.

Actor-turned-writer Tom Tryon's American gothic novel *The Other* (1970) was a horror hit that was part psychological thriller and part ghost story. Tryon wrote the screenplay for the 1972 screen adaptation of his novel directed by Robert Mulligan. The story is set in the small rural community of Pequot Landing, Connecticut during the summer of 1935, where the Perry twins Niles (Chris Udvarnoky) and Holland (Martin Udvarnoky) live an idyllic life on a farm. All is not peaches and cream in this bucolic paradise, however. The twin's mother, Alexandra (Diana Muldaur), is an agoraphobic recluse with mental problems caused by the death of her husband who confines herself to her room, and their Aunt Ada (Uta Hagen) is a kindly witchy-woman from the old country. In the farm's apple cellar, Niles whispers in the dark to his brother Holland and displays his secret trophy, a severed human finger wearing a ring that he keeps hidden in a tobacco tin. It is also the summer when the kidnapping/murder of aviation hero Charles Lindbergh's son by German immigrant Bruno Hauptmann electrified the nation.

The sweet natured Niles is constantly being tempted into committing antisocial deeds by his older, dominant brother, Holland. When their obnoxious cousin Russell (Clarence Crow) finds out about the contents of the tobacco tin and threatens to tell, Holland instructs Niles to conceal a pitchfork under a pile of hay in the barn that Russell likes to jump in, and the child is impaled upon the instrument and killed. When a carnival comes to town, Holland cajoles Niles into sneaking inside the tent, where they view the corpse of a "hydrocephalic baby" preserved inside a jar and watch a magic show. Afterward, Holland has Niles dress up like a magician and offer to perform tricks for the elderly widow Mrs. Rowe (Portia Nelson), with whom the twins have a long-standing gripe. At the climax of the act, Niles reaches into his top hat and instead of pulling out a rabbit pulls out a dead rat, the sight of which causes Mrs. Rowe to drop dead from a heart attack.

Later that night Alexandra accidentally finds the ring inside Niles's tobacco tin and realizes that it is a family heirloom supposedly buried with a loved one. When she confronts her son about the ring he tells her that Holland gave it to him, and as they struggle over his prize possession she falls down a flight of stairs and is left mute and partially paralyzed in the aftermath. Several days later, Grandmother Ada discovers the corpse of Mrs. Rowe along with Holland's harmonica at the scene. Ada, who has been teaching Niles ancient Russian clairvoyant techniques she calls "the game," quizzes the child about Mrs. Rowe's death. When he insists that it was Holland who was responsible, she forces him to confront the truth: Holland died months ago in an accident and continues to haunt his brother through their psychic link. Niles relates how Holland spoke to him during the funeral and told him to cut off his finger and take the ring, and Ada comes to suspect that Niles may even have been responsible for murdering his own father.

Ada realizes something is terribly wrong, that Niles has used the "mystic transference" techniques she has taught him, along with the telepathic link that exists between twins, to create a psychological simulacrum of the dead Holland, or to resurrect his ghost. Matters come to a head when the newborn baby of Niles's older sister Torrie (Jenny Sullivan) and her husband Rider (John Ritter) goes missing in a situation similar to the Lindbergh kidnapping. After a search the baby is discovered drowned inside a wine cask, and the farm's immigrant handyman, Mr. Angelini (Victor Franch) becomes the prime suspect. Ada, however, overhears Niles and Holland discussing the murder and decides to take action. She starts a fire in the farm's fruit cellar, hoping to trap Niles inside and exorcise the evil, but the child survives and his grandmother dies, and with his mother in a vegetative state Niles has gotten away with mass murder.

Literary critics have pointed out that Tryon's *The Other*, along with Ira Levin's *Rosemary's Baby* (1967) and William Peter Blatty's *The Exorcist* (1971) led to a revival of the popular horror novel in the early 1970s. All of these books exploited the theme of demonic children, and all of them were made into movies. Director Mulligan's screen version of *The Other* perfectly captures Depression-era life on a country farm, shooting in rich, naturalistic colors and eschewing dark, Expressionistic shadows to convey the primal evil lurking just below the surface of the sleepy, bucolic environment. Results are mixed, however, and Tryon, who scripted, was reportedly unhappy with the finished film, which had been heavily edited. In any event, the film fails to evoke the richness of description and eerie mood of the novel, which is narrated in the first person by Niles. The Udvarnoky twins are merely adequate as the dynamic duo of Niles/Holland, and Diana Muldaur gives a haunting portrayal of the withdrawn and vulnerable Alexandra, but veteran actress Uta Hagen gives the most memorable performance as the witchy Russian grandmother Ada.

The narrative of *The Other* presents the familiar good twin versus evil twin dynamic, only in this case one of the twins is dead and one is alive. The doppelganger situation arises partly through the mind-meld relationship thought to exist between twins, and partly by the use of the "mystic transference" psychic techniques Ada taught to Niles while showing him how to play "the game." There are similarities between *The Other* and Hitchcock's *Psycho* in that in both works a living person creates the doppelganger of a deceased close relative whose dominant personality compels them to commit a series of homicidal acts. As David Fincher had done in *Fight Club*, director Mulligan never shows the two doppelgangers in the same frame at the same time, a technique that emphasizes the idea that one of the characters is real and the other imaginary.

Brian de Palma's *Sisters* (1973), released in the following year, had a strikingly similar take on the doppelganger theme. The film begins on the set of the reality TV show *Peeping Tom*, where contestant Philip Woode endures a hidden camera prank played on him by aspiring French-Canadian actress Danielle Breton (Margot Kidder) and wins a dinner for two at a swanky New York restaurant as a prize. Philip invites Danielle to share the prize with him, and after dinner the couple wind up in her apartment in New York's Staten Island. After a night of torrid lovemaking, Philip wakes up the next day to hear Danielle arguing with a woman in another room in French. Danielle emerges to explain that her twin sister Dominique has arrived to celebrate their mutual birthday, so Philip slips out to a local bakery to buy a cake as a peace offering for the antagonistic siblings. When he returns to the apartment, however, he is brutally knifed to death by the crazy twin Dominique. In the aftermath of the killing, a man who claims to be Dominique's husband Emil (William Finley) arrives on the scene to conceal all traces of the crime, hiding Philip's body inside a fold-out sofa bed.

The murder has been witnessed by local news reporter Grace Collier (Jennifer Salt) from a window in an adjacent apartment. She calls the police, but upon examining the apartment, they can find no trace of the murder, and Danielle insists she has been alone all day. Grace does find the cake inscribed to Danielle and Dominique, but accidentally destroys the evidence before she can show it to the cops. With nothing to go on the detectives depart, but Grace's reporter's instinct has been tweaked, and smelling a good story she teams up with avuncular private investigator Joseph Larch (Charles Durning) to uncover the truth.

Disguised as a window cleaner, Larch gains access to Danielle's apartment, where he finds a medical file revealing that Danielle and Dominique were conjoined Siamese twins who were only recently separated and that Dominique is currently residing in a nearby mental hospital. Grace begins snooping around the sanitarium, but is apprehended by Emil, who is a doctor at the hospital and forcibly admitted under the guise of being an escaped mental patient. She is confined and kept heavily sedated with hypnotic drugs while Emil brainwashes her into thinking that the killing was all in her mind by endlessly repeating the phrase "There was no body because there was no murder."

In a hallucinatory dream sequence brought about by the effect of the drugs, Grace witnesses a confrontation between Emil and Danielle and learns the bizarre truth that the evil twin Dominique died during the separation operation and that Danielle is psychologically recreating her sister's personality out of guilt over her death. Whenever a man tries to make love to her, Danielle becomes the homicidal Dominique. Grace wakes up and watches helplessly as Emil attempts intimacy with Danielle and Dominique emerges to slice and dice him to death with a scalpel. The police arrive to arrest Danielle, who denies she is a murderer or that she has a sister, and when they question Grace about the events she can only mindlessly repeat, "There was no body because there was no murder."

This was De Palma's first stab at imitating Hitchcock, and plot elements from Hitch's thrillers *Rear Window* and *Psycho* were incorporated into his screenplay. In addition, the hilly, bayside landscape of Staten Island was used as a low-rent stand-in for *Vertigo*'s San Francisco. De Palma tries to outdo Hitch by utilizing 70s-era nudity, gore effects and split screens, but despite the film's derivative elements the director crafts an effective thriller in its own right. The extended dream sequence, however, is overlong and confusing, and presents story exposition in a psychedelic mode. A cast of relative unknowns turn in solid performances, headed up by Margot Kidder, who projects vulnerability as the sweet-natured Danielle, and Jennifer Salt as the intrepid newshound who winds up in a state of hypnotically-induced delusion, while Charles Durning provides some comic relief as P.I. Joseph Larch. De Palma coaxed longtime Hitchcock musical collaborator Bernard Hermann out of semi-retirement to contribute a chilling score that is one of the best of his later efforts. The director would later work with the composer on De Palma's homage to *Vertigo*, *Obsession* (1976).

As in *The Other*, the doppelgangers are a pair of twins, one of whom is living and the other dead. Like Norman and his mother in *Psycho*, the deceased personality of Dominique is being kept "alive" because of the survivor's guilt. The homicidal Dominique, however, gets very little screen time and seems more like a clever plot device than a real character, and no backstory is provided to explain her murderous behavior towards men, or any other facet of her persona. The psychological relationship between Danielle and her dead twin is explainable as a case of multiple personality.

Polish-American expatriate director Roman Polanski is best known for a trio of horror thrillers that have been referred to by critics as his "apartment trilogy." In *Repulsion* (1965), Catherine Deneuve plays a young woman with mental problems who descends into murder and madness when left alone in her sister's London apartment for a weekend. *Rosemary's Baby* (1968) was a supernatural chiller about a cult of Satanists menacing Mia Farrow in New York's infamous Dakota apartment complex. The third film in the trilogy, *The Tenant* (*Le Locaitaire*, 1976), featured Polanski himself in the lead role as a Parisian apartment dweller who enters into a doppelganger relationship with the flat's previous occupant.

Polanski plays Trelkovsky, an Eastern European immigrant who rents a ratty Paris walk-up from curmudgeonly landlord Monsieur Zy (Melvyn Douglas). Trelkovsky soon learns that the previous tenant was an Egyptologist named Simone Choule, who threw herself out of the apartment window and is clinging to life but not expected to survive. Visiting her in the hospital, he

Margot Kidder appears as a pair of Siamese twins in this poster for Brian De Palma's Hitchcockian thriller *Sisters* (1973).

finds Simone almost completely swathed in bandages and barely conscious. He is joined at her bedside by Simone's friend Stella (Isabelle Adjani), who tries to get Simone to recognize her, but Simone seems to recognize Trelkowsky instead and lets out a horrible cry of anguish. In the aftermath of the visit the pair enter into a somewhat confused love affair.

Trelkowsky is a shy individual who suffers from a severe lack of assertiveness. He allows himself to be bullied by his co-workers, by Zy and the apartment's unpleasant concierge (Shelley Winters) and by the other tenants in the complex. The drab, confining apartment, which still contains many of Simone's things, takes on a malevolent aspect that makes Trelkowsky increasingly disturbed. He becomes more and more withdrawn and isolated and begins to think that his neighbors are trying to control him. He discovers a human tooth inside a hole in the wall, and observes the tenants watching him from a window in the toilet.

Fear and paranoia begin to draw Trelkovsky into a delusional, subjective reality. One night when he is using the toilet he finds columns of hieroglyphics inscribed on the wall and sees his own double regarding him through the window of his apartment. He comes to believe that the other tenants are trying to transform him into Simone, and their will seems to be affecting him as he buys a wig, lipstick and nail polish and starts wearing the dead woman's clothes. He suffers from bizarre hallucinations, seeing a vision of the other tenants performing a sadistic ritual in the courtyard below, and a frightening apparition of Simone's ghost unwinding her bandages while standing in front of the toilet window.

As his sanity crumbles, Trelkowsky can no longer distinguish fantasy from reality and can no longer fight the strange impulses that are overwhelming him. Dressing up in drag once more, he looks out of his window to observe the other tenants gathered in the courtyard below urging him to defenestrate himself for their amusement. He takes the fatal plunge but survives, waking Zy and the other tenants who have in reality been asleep the whole time. They crowd around to try to aid him, but he sees only twisted, demonic faces that drive him back up to his room to attempt suicide a second time. He awakens in a hospital bed completely wrapped in bandages like Simone, and when he is visited by Stella and his own doppelganger he lets out the same horrible, piercing cry that she had uttered as the exchange of personalities is now complete.

Polanski and co-scripter Gerard Brach adapted *The Tenant* from the novel *Le locataire chimerique* by Roland Topor. Compared to the other works in his "apartment trilogy" it's not as focused and is overlong, more slow-moving, and not as effective as horror. It has its moments, however, such as Trelkowsky's eerie vision of Simone's ghost, which is the only time her face is seen in the movie. Polanski brilliantly sets up the claustrophobic space of Trelkowsky's haunted apartment, which is infinitely more suffocating than a haunted mansion, by using drab, washed-out colors and evocative sounds such as dripping water or the nervous ticking of a clock. As an actor, Polanski manages to carry the film in what is practically a one-man show, evoking sympathy for the doomed plight of the film's hapless protagonist. Screen veterans Melvyn Douglas and Shelley Winters provide able assistance in supporting roles. The film seems to have influenced Richard Ayoade's 2013 adaptation of Dostoyevsky's *The Double*, which also features a tormented main character who is compelled to take a suicidal plunge from his apartment window at the film's climax.

The unusual and tragic events depicted are never explained to the viewer and remain an enigma throughout. Is the apartment haunted by Simone's ghost who is looking to possess Trelkowsky from beyond the grave, or is everything a paranoid delusion caused by his imagination? The film works as both a supernatural thriller and a psychological horror film. As in *Psycho*, the protagonist's introverted personality is overwhelmed by that of a dominant woman who is dead yet compels him to cross-dress and assume her persona. "At what precise moment," Trelkowsky wonders at one point, "does an individual stop being who he thinks he is," and this dilemma is at the soul of the plot. Like Norman Bates in Hitchcock's film, Trelkowsky is transformed into the dead character at the very end. Note that Trelkowsky sees his own double observing him twice during the film. Here again, the doppelganger is associated with madness, death, possession and ghosts.

In Celtic folklore a *changeling* is a fairy child exchanged for a human baby by the little folk. Peter Medak, who would later direct the evil twin melodrama *The Krays* in 1990, first explored the doppelganger theme in his modern ghost story *The Changeling* (1980). George C. Scott stars as John Russell, a New York composer whose wife and daughter are killed in a freak traffic accident. After the tragedy Russell relocates to Seattle in an effort to psychologically recover from the deaths. Learning of a vacant mansion in the Chessman Park area from real estate agent Clair Norman (Trish Van Devere), he moves into the imposing home while he tries to continue his work while putting his life back together.

It soon becomes apparent that there is an unseen presence inhabiting the house. Doors open and shut by themselves, strange sounds are heard, water taps turn on and off and windows shatter as if directed by an invisible hand. Russell discovers a hidden room in the attic where he finds a child's antique wheelchair and a music box that plays a melody identical to one he has been composing. After catching a glimpse of the face of a drowned boy in the attic, he realizes that there is paranormal activity going on and invites a medium, Leah Harmon (Helen Burns) to conduct a séance in the house. Russell later finds that responses to the psychic's questions are recorded on audio tape left running during the séance, which reveals that the house is haunted by a boy named Joseph who died there around the turn of the century.

Russell becomes obsessed with learning the identity of the dead boy and unlocking the secret behind the haunting. Searching through old records he manages to locate Joseph's remains, along with a religious medallion on another property where Joseph's ghost has recently been seen. His investigation eventually leads him to the grim truth, that the deceased, Joseph Carmichael was murdered in 1906 by his father, Richard. A sickly child confined to a wheelchair and isolated in the house's attic room, Richard had doubts about Joseph being able to reach his 21st birthday, in which case he would lose the family inheritance, so he secretly drowned his son and concealed his body in a well on another property owned by the family. Adopting a boy from a local orphanage, he spirited the lad off to Europe for a few years, then brought the child home, supposedly restored to health, and passed him off as his own son.

The bogus Joseph Carmichael is now a rich and powerful U.S. Senator (Melvyn Douglas from *The Tenant*) who gets terribly upset when confronted with these facts by Russell. He knows, however, that it is all true when Russell produces the birth medallion, which is identical to one in his possession. At first he thinks that Russell is trying to blackmail him, but the composer disabuses him by leaving the ghostly tape recording, his research files and the medallion with him. In the meantime, Claire returns to the mansion looking for Russell and is chased down the main stairway by Joseph's empty wheelchair. Russell arrives to rescue her, but when he goes back inside the entire house begins to shake and a mighty wind blows him onto the floor. Back in Carmichael's office, the senator undergoes severe paroxysms of guilt over being revealed as the beneficiary of a murder for profit. As he goes into cardiac arrest, Russell sees his doppelganger going up the stairs toward the attic room as flames suddenly engulf the house. The senator dies of a heart attack while Russell manages to escape and the building is destroyed in a fiery conflagration.

Considered by critics to be one of the most memorable ghost stories ever filmed, *The Changeling* is a class act enlivened by expert direction and fine performances. Director Medak's moving camera swoops through the haunted mansion like a disembodied spirit. In contrast to *The Tenant*'s confined spaces, the characters are frequently filmed in long shots, or even extreme long shots, and wide-angle lenses are used to distort perspective to make it seem as if the human figures are lost within the vastness of the spooky house. Taking a cue from Robert Wise's classic ghost story *The Haunting* (1963), sounds such as a loud rhythmic thumping or the ghostly whispers of the dead child are used to heighten the tension. The original screenplay by Russell Hunter, William Gray and Diana Maddox presents an intriguing blend of haunted house chills and supernatural mystery. Oscar winning actor George C. Scott delivers a perfectly understated portrayal of a man tormented by personal tragedy who is thrown into a mysterious and unnerving situation, while Trish Van Devere and Melvyn Douglas serve up solid performances in supporting roles.

The Changeling presents another example of the connection between the doppelganger tale and the ghost story. The aged Senator Joseph Carmichael, who has enjoyed the fruits of his wealth and position all his life, is the titular "changeling" of the real Joseph Carmichael. When Russell moves into the Chessman Park house, his anguish over the loss of his family acts as a catalyst that conjures up Joseph's ghost and sends it out to visit vengeance on the beneficiary of his murder. The pair of birth medallions constitute a visual metaphor for the twinned Joseph Carmichael identities. At the film's climax Senator Carmichael's double is summoned to the mansion to face the ghost's revenge while his flesh and blood self is annihilated in the encounter.

On July 17, 1975, the tenants of the deluxe apartment building at 450 East 63rd Street in New York City's tony Sutton Place neighborhood complained of a horrible smell emanating from the tenth floor apartment of Cyril Marcus, who shared the flat with his twin brother, Stewart. The twins were gynecologists who had once been prominent in their field but had lately become reclusive. Opening the door with a pass key, the building's super was hit by the overpowering stench of death as he waded into a foot-thick pile of dirty clothes,

Claire Niveau (Genevieve Bujold) is flanked by twin gynecologists Beverly (left) and Eliot Mantle (both Jeremy Irons) in David Cronenberg's *Dead Ringers* (1988).

soda cans, empty liquor bottles, rotting food and other refuse that littered the floor and made his way to the bedroom. There, on adjacent mattresses, he found the decomposing corpses of Cyril and Stuart Marcus, who, it was later determined, had both died in the throes of barbiturate drug withdrawal. The horrific story of the Marcus twins became the basis for the novel *Twins* by Bari Wood and Jack Geasland, which in turn was adapted for Canadian horrormeister David Cronenberg's screen version entitled *Dead Ringers* (1988).

Jeremy Irons stars as Elliot and Beverly Mantle, identical twin OB-GYN doctors who operate a prestigious Toronto clinic devoted to the treatment of women's fertility problems. They are abnormally close, even for twin brothers; they live together, work together and even share the same women. The Mantle twins are brilliant scientists who conduct cutting edge research in their field, and work together flawlessly as a team. Elliot, the elder and more dominant of the twins, handles the P.R. and administrative chores, while Beverly, who is shy and retiring, does most of the research.

The twin's relationship begins to change when Claire Niveau (Genevieve Bujold), a highly-strung, drug-addicted actress who nonetheless wants to have a baby, comes to the Mantle Clinic for an examination. She is found to have a very rare condition known as a "trifurcate uterus," in which her womb is divided into three sections, a condition that renders her unable to conceive children. Eliot seduces Claire, then passes her on to Beverly according to their practice of sharing women, even among their patients. When Claire accidentally discovers that Beverly has a twin, she demands to meet Elliot and humiliates the twins while the three of them are having dinner at a posh restaurant. After a while, however, she resumes her relationship with Beverly, but tells him, "You two have never come to terms with the way it really does work between you."

Beverly's emotions for Claire become obsessive, and threaten to upset the psychic equilibrium between the twins. Under her influence, he starts doing drugs with her and compromises his professional ethics by writing her prescriptions for amphetamines and barbiturates. When she has to go out of town for a few weeks he becomes unhinged and begins suffering from drug-induced delusions that she has been unfaithful to him, and he becomes unable to perform his medical duties at the clinic as he sinks into a major depression. Worst of all, he commissions local sculptor Anders Wolleck (Stephen Lack) to fashion a set of grotesque gynecological tools designed for "working on mutant women." When he attempts to use these implements, which resemble medieval instruments of torture, on a patient during an operation, his professional license is suspended and he is placed on administrative leave pending further action by the medical board.

His brother's drugged-out condition begins to affect Elliot via some telepathic process between the twins. He starts taking the same drugs himself in order to "synchronize" their mental states and soon follows his brother into addiction. When Claire returns to Toronto she is appalled to find Elliot and Beverly living together in Beverly's apartment, which has sunk into filth and decrepitude. Amid the garbage and refuse strewn about the place, she discovers Beverly's obscene gynecological tools and is even more repulsed. Once Claire is out of the picture the Mantle twins descend into their own private hell together until they decide to perform an operation that will "separate the Siamese twins" forever. In a bizarre murder/suicide ritual, Beverly operates on Elliot using the set of twisted OB/GYN instruments he created to cut his brother's guts out before joining him in death.

Considered one of shockhound Cronenberg's more restrained efforts, *Dead Ringers* exploits the director's signature use of visceral "body horror" while also offering up a psychological study of the insular private world and strange medical obsessions shared by a pair of brilliant twins. Jeremy Irons delivers two knockout performances as the Mantle siblings, his dual portrayal conveying subtle difference between their characters that are almost subliminal. Elliot, the elder twin, is domineering and acerbic, while Beverly comes off as being warmer and more vulnerable. Irons reportedly used two separate dressing rooms and two sets of wardrobes, one for each twin, which enabled him to slip into the contrasting roles of the two Mantle brothers. Later on during the production he used the dramaturgic Alexander technique to portray the twins by finding the "different energy points" between their characters. Canadian actress Genevieve Bujold also comes through with a strong performance as the hard-edged, cynical Claire.

Cronenberg's screenplay, which he co-authored with Norman Snider, avoids the usual cliché of the "bad twin" versus the "good twin" narrative, opting instead to explore the unusual psychological mechanics of their inner world. The tag line for the film read "Two Bodies, One Mind, One Soul," and this perfectly expresses its underlying theme. The Mantle brothers are caught up in the syndrome psychologists call *folie a deux*, a fantasy world that is shared by two individuals who are extremely close, usually a parent and child or husband and wife. In this case the extreme mental and emotional intimacy exhibited between identical twins amplifies the delusion. In *folie a deux*, one of the two personalities dominates the other, as the elder Elliott dominates his younger brother Beverly. Ironically, it is Claire who disrupts the equilibrium between the twins and puts them out of "synchronization" with each other and ultimately leads to their dissolution and destruction.

After *Sisters* and *Obsession*, director Brian De Palma's third cinematic foray into the realm of the doppelganger was the psychological thriller *Raising Cain* (1992), whose plot explored another fascinating psychological condition, multiple personality disorder or MPD. John Lithgow stars as child psychologist Dr. Carter Nix, who is married to Jennie (Lolita Davidovich), a nurse at a local hospital. Carter spends an inordinate amount of time conducting scientific studies of their daughter, Amy (Amanda Pombo), and Jenny is concerned that her husband's obsession with Amy's development is unhealthy.

Jenny is blissfully unaware that Carter suffers from MPD and has an alternate personality named Cain (also played by Lithgow) who describes himself as a "cheap hoodlum" and whose violent, aggressive personality dominates Carter's. Cain is not an internal phenomenon, but appears as an entirely separate being, a grinning, demonic avatar of Carter. In the film's opening scenes Cain helps Carter abduct a young mother and her little boy from a playground. Cain kills the mother and disposes of the body, then brings the child to a local motel, where it is delivered to Dr. Nix, Sr. (also Lithgow), a savant who is conducting research into child development at a secret laboratory in Norway and needs a supply of children for his experiments.

Soon afterward, Jenny has a chance meeting with old flame Jack Dante (Steven Bauer) that leads to a tryst in the neighborhood playground. Unfortunately, Carter secretly observes their brazen lovemaking in the woods behind the playground, and his rage allows Cain's personality to take over. He suffocates Jenny with a pillow, then stuffs her body in the back seat of her car and sinks it in a local bog, only to watch Jenny awaken as the car slips beneath the water. Her body is discovered and laid out in the county morgue, while Carter cleverly directs suspicions about the murder onto Jack, who has been observed hanging around the playground waiting for Jenny. While the police arrest Jack, Jenny, having somehow come back to life, returns home to find that Amy is missing and threatens Carter, who is now back in control, but he can only say that Amy was taken to his father, but since Cain was controlling the consciousness at that time, Carter has no memory of where she was taken.

In order to try to unlock the multiple's memory, the police call in psychologist Dr. Lynn Waldheim (Frances Sternhagen), a garrulous MPD specialist who is undergoing chemotherapy and wears a hideous wig that makes her "look like a transvestite." Dr. Waldheim explains that she was involved in a child development study with Carter's father and suspects that Nix Sr. performed personality experiments on his own son. She hypnotizes Carter, hoping to access Cain's memory, but instead draws out two of his other personalities, Josh, a shy ten-year-old boy and the creepy middle-aged Margo who knocks her unconscious and steals her clothes and wig. Disguised as Waldheim, the multiple escapes from the police station and goes to the motel to join the elder Nix.

Believing she is following Waldheim, Jenny trails the multiple to the motel, riding up in the elevator with the strange figure, whose face is obscured behind a bag of groceries. When the elevator door opens, she encounters Nix Sr., who is holding Amy. While the mother is struggling to free her child, the Carter/Cain/Margo entity comes from behind and stabs Nix in the back with a knife. Amy is rescued and Jack is cleared, but in the confusion the multiple quietly slips away. Sometime after the events, Jenny is playing in the park with Amy when the child is lured away by the Margo personality who is now in complete drag.

De Palma, who also scripted, turns in a tight, effective thriller that steals some key elements from Hitchcock's *Psycho*, including the grisly "car in the lake" scene and the killer being a mentally ill transvestite. Another major influence was Michael Powell's infamous psychological horror film *Peeping Tom* (1960), in which a father conducts morbid experiments on his own son that turn him into a serial murderer. While the film's suspense narrative hangs together well, there are several gaping holes in the plot. How come Jenny never noticed that her husband had multiple personalities? How does Jenny come back to life after being killed not once but twice, asphyxiated, drowned in the back of a car and laid out in the morgue? Why does Nix Sr. suddenly reappear after being in hiding for two decades? John Lithgow's performance in multiple roles drives the film, especially as the spooky Margo character, who seems to glide through the film like a ghost.

Raising Cain exploits the psychological enigma of multiple personality disorder (now referred to as "dissociative identity disorder" by shrinks) by making the multiple into a psycho-killer. In real life, MPD is not considered a psychosis and is not associated with mass-murder or even homicide. De Palma depicts Carter and Cain as doppelgangers and entirely separate entities on the screen instead of having the personalities converse via interior mental dialogue. This technique was previously used in the popular MPD drama *Sybil* (1976), and while it serves to create a visual means of showing the personalities to the audience, it does not accurately reflect the subjective experience of people who suffer from the disorder. Lithgow does a good job of portraying the process of "switching," in which one personality suddenly replaces another. His features go slack for a moment before another persona emerges with its own set of facial expressions. The use of MPD as a plot device to create a series of doppelgangers is a novel and effective concept.

The idea of a man haunted by his own unborn twin was the premise of *The Dark Half*

(1993), based on a novel by horrormeister Stephen King and directed by George Romero, who had given the world *Night of the Living Dead* (1968) and its many sequels and spinoffs. The film begins in 1968, when junior high school student Thad Beaumont is undergoing brain surgery for an epileptic condition. When the doctors open up his skull they find a living human eye staring at them, a remnant of an unborn twin brother that was not completely absorbed into Thad's body. As they surgically remove the excess tissues from the boy's brain, a freak flock of sparrows attacks the hospital.

Twenty-three years later, Thad Beaumont (Timothy Hutton) is a creative writing teacher at a small New England college and also writes highbrow but poorly-selling literary fiction under his own name. Under the pseudonym of George Stark, however, he cranks out a series of best-selling but lowbrow, ultra-violent mystery thrillers. He is careful to conceal his identity as Stark from the public until one day a fan named Fred Clawson (Robert Joy) learns the truth and attempts to blackmail him by revealing his dual authorship to the public. Beaumont reacts to the threat by owning up to his dual literary identity, even staging a mock burial and gravestone for Stark in the local cemetery as a PR stunt.

That night the photographer for the event, Homer Gamache (Glenn Colerider), is brutally killed and Thad's fingerprints are found on Homer's truck. Local sheriff Alan Pangborn (Michael Rooker) investigates the killing, but finds Thad has an airtight alibi. Visiting Stark's mock grave, Thad is stunned to find a hole in the earth that looks as if someone has dug their way out. Next, Clawson is found murdered and a message scrawled in his blood reads, "The sparrows are flying again." Once more Thad is implicated in the crime, but no proof of his guilt can be found. Thad slowly comes to the realization that somehow, his literary alter ego has taken on a life of its own and George Stark has refused to die and is committing the murders. To make matters worse, clouds of sparrows mysteriously begin to flock around the Beaumont home.

Several more murders follow until Stark (also played by Hutton) invades Thad's home and kidnaps his wife, Liz (Amy Madigan), and his

Child psychologist Dr. Carter Nix and his alternate personality Cain (John Lithgow) are pictured in this poster for Brian De Palma's thriller *Raising Cain* (1992).

twin boys. He will free them only if Thad will complete the latest book he has been writing as Stark, because Stark is afraid he will die if the book isn't finished. Thad agrees to the proposal, but during the writing of the book he gets into a physical struggle with his evil doppelganger. As they fight, a huge swarm of sparrows, who are supernatural agents of destruction and retribution, arrives to attack Stark and shred his body into non-existence before winging away into the night.

This collaboration between two of the titans of modern horror should have been better than it was. While Romero's direction is steady, suspenseful and tightly paced, the main problem is King's novel and its screen adaptation by Romero, Paul Hunt and Nick McCarthy. The narrative tries to walk the line between serial killer thriller and supernatural horror, with mixed results. The basic premise of an unborn twin becoming a literary alter ego and then a flesh and blood revenant and serial murderer doesn't quite jell, and the deadly flock of sparrows who peck Stark back to the netherworld is not exactly a menace that inspires terror. The Thad Beaumont character is obviously based on that of King himself, who also taught English literature in a New England school while churning out popular horror chillers, and reflects the author's angst about being accepted as a serious novelist by the literary establishment. Timothy Hutton does a workmanlike job portraying both Thad and Stark, but overall the acting in the film is not especially memorable.

The unborn twin doppelganger in *The Dark Half* combines the concept of the ghostly double with the notion of a literary Jekyll and Hyde relationship. It's not clear if George Stark is supposed to be the author of his books or the psychopathic killer who is their subject, as he seems to fill both roles simultaneously. The double emerges as an aspect of Thad's literary persona. "Each of us," he explains to his creative writing class, "is two separate beings," an outer and inner self, and it is the responsibility of the writer to let loose the inner being so it can have a voice in his work. The unborn twin angle also features into the explanation of Thad's doppelganger. Thad's doctor explains that one in ten of us has a twin and that the stronger fetus usually absorbs the weaker. Naturally, the film climaxes with a confrontation between the protagonist and his double that concludes with the annihilation of one of them. Note that Thad is the father of twin boys, and Romero utilizes the music of Elvis Presley on the soundtrack, who also had an unborn twin.

Eight decades after *The Student of Prague* introduced movie audiences to the legend of the supernatural doppelganger, Hollywood finally discovered the concept in *Doppelganger: The Evil Within* (1993). The up-and-coming actress Drew Barrymore starred as Holly Gooding, a troubled young woman who seems to be haunted by a murderous double. The film opens in New York City, where black clad femme fatale Holly (or is it her doppelganger?) pays a visit to her mother (Jaid Barrymore), who is plotting to kill the girl and inherit the estate left to her by her dead father. Before she can carry out this nefarious plan, however, Holly steps in and slashes her to death with a knife.

The scene shifts to Los Angeles, where Holly, now a sweet-natured young thing, arranges to sublet an apartment with aspiring screenwriter Patrick Highsmith (George Newbern) while she's in town to settle her family's estate. His platonic friend and collaborator Elizabeth (Leslie Hope) has doubts about the setup, which prove to be well founded when a series of uncanny events ensue. On several occasions Patrick spies a Holly-like figure dressed in black who seems to vanish before he can confront her. One night Holly seduces him, but the next morning insists that it was her double who initiated the lovemaking. "She may look like me," Holly informs him icily, "but she's not me. Don't confuse me with her." Soon afterward, FBI agent Stanley White (Dan Shor), who is staking out Patrick's apartment, tells him that Holly is still a suspect in her mother's death.

One night while Patrick is otherwise occupied, Holly's black-clad double pays a visit to Holly's brother, who is confined to a nursing home, and attacks him with a knife. Hearing of the incident, Patrick hastens to Holly's side, where he encounters her psychiatrist, Dr. Heller (Dennis Christopher), who informs him that his patient is being treated for multiple personality disorder. Confused and desperate, Patrick decides to consult a friend who may have some knowledge of the supernatural, an ex-nun named Sister Jan (Sally Kellerman), who has become a phone sex worker for an outfit called Intimate Strangers. In between phone calls, Sister Jan enlightens him with her pearls of occult wisdom. "Every element is dual," she tells him, explaining that doppelgangers exist in a state between life and death, where they have been forced out by extreme trauma and do not want to reunite with the original person. Only love can pacify the doppelganger because "love allows both halves to co-exist peacefully."

Soon afterward Holly receives a phone call from the double who tells her to meet her at the Gooding estate, a gloomy old mansion that has been shuttered for years. Patrick decides to follow her, and once inside the double grabs Holly, injects her with a soporific drug, and goes after Patrick with a knife. As they struggle the double's mask slips, revealing that it is in reality Dr. Heller, who has been impersonating her while giving her subliminal commands to murder her mother and brother in a scheme to get his hands on the Gooding estate. In the mind-numbing climax, as Heller menaces Patrick, Holly suddenly awakens and physically splits into two slimy, skeletal creatures that kill Heller before re-uniting with each other, driven by the force of her love for Patrick. In the aftermath, Holly, now whole again, is shown recuperating in a hospital with Patrick by her bedside.

This hallucinogenic mish-mosh of mystery thriller and supernatural horror ultimately collapses under the weight of its own absurdity. The work of writer/director Avi Nesher, *Doppelganger* sets up a series of confusing and self-contradictory situations that are never satisfactorily explained. The film is larded with a number of dream/hallucination sequences such as a shower scene in which blood pours out of the showerhead that drenches Barrymore's naked body, and an episode in which Barrymore is suspended in a Christ-like pose during a mock crucifixion. It's basically an exploitative Barrymore vehicle in which the up and coming young starlet displays her acting range by playing Holly as a sweet *naïf* and her double as a homicidal *femme*. Sally Kellerman, late of the TV sitcom *M.A.S.H.*, offers a new take on her "Hot Lips" character as the nun turned phone sex operator Sister Jam, and the suave George Maharis has about 20 seconds of screen time as the Gooding family lawyer, Wallace.

Whatever its shortcomings, however, it is the first American horror film to exploit the Germanic concept of the supernatural doppelganger. The audience is kept guessing as to whether Holly really has a ghostly double, if the whole thing was a ploy wherein Dr. Heller impersonated her (a scenario that seems highly unlikely) to gain control of her estate, or if she is suffering from multiple personality disorder and has committed the murders herself. None of these theories are ever explained in the film, yet the bizarre ending where Holly splits in two like an amoeba (which seems to have been cribbed from *The Manster*) suggests that some kind of supernatural agency is involved.

In Jewish folklore, a *dybbuk* is the spirit of a dead person that possesses the body of a living person. This ghostly being is the subject of a number of works of Jewish literature, including S. Ansky's 1916 play *The Dybbuk* and in the macabre short fiction of Isaac Bashevis Singer such as "The Last Demon" and "The Dead Fiddler." In *The Unborn* (2009), writer/director David S. Goyer taps into a rich vein of Kabalistic mysticism to fashion a horror tale involving ghosts, possession and the doppelganger. The film's protagonist is Chicago-area college freshman Casey Beldon (Odette Yustman), who begins to be plagued by terrifying nightmares and strange hallucinations that center around the figure of a ghostly little boy. One night when she is babysitting her neighbor's son Matty Newton (Atticus Shaffer), she observes the child flashing a hand mirror at his infant brother, and when she approaches him, Matty smashes the mirror over her head and utters the mystifying phrase "Jumby wants to be born now."

Her best friend Romy (Meagan Good) tells her about a superstition that infants should not see their mirror reflection until they are one year old or they will die, and soon afterwards the Newton baby dies. Next, Casey's eyes begin to change color, a condition that her doctor tells her is usually associated with twins called genetic mosaicism. Confronting her father (James Remar) about the anomaly he tells her that she indeed had a fraternal twin, a brother who died in childbirth because Casey's umbilical cord had wrapped around his neck and strangled him. He further informs her that he and Casey's mother had nicknamed the unborn child "Jumby." In light of this conversation, Casey begins to suspect that her mother's suicide years earlier might have something to do with her dead fraternal twin.

Casey is frequently left alone while her dad is out of town on business, and her dreams and hallucinations begin to intensify with his absence. She has horrific visions of Jumby leaping out at her through the bathroom mirror and is assaulted by hordes of slimy insects. Going through her mother's things, Casey finds out that her mother had consulted an elderly woman named Sofia Kozma (Jane Alexander), a Holocaust survivor who is currently residing in a nearby nursing home. Upon visiting Kozma she learns that the old lady is in fact her grandmother, who was subjected to occult experiments while interned in a concentration camp along with her twin brother Barto (Ethan Cutowsky). The Nazi doctors were obsessed with twins, who they thought held some mystical power, and eventually killed Barto during one of their infernal rituals and caused him to be possessed by a *dybbuk*.

Kozma further explains that she was forced to kill her brother a second time to prevent the spread of the undead evil, but the *dybbuk* still haunted their family while seeking a pathway back into the world of the living. It tried to re-enter the world through the body of her twin brother, but since "Jumby" died during childbirth he is now trying to possess Casey's body. She warns that the malignant spirit will try to weaken her by killing those around her and is given an amulet called the "hand of Miriam" to protect her. She also suggests that Casey obtain a Hebrew text called the *Sefer Ha-Marot*, or *Book of Mirrors*, and directs her to a local rabbi who may be able to help with her predicament.

Obtaining a copy of the book, Casey approaches learned Rabbi Joseph Sendak (Gary Oldman) and requests that an exorcism be performed, but he is skeptical until he observes paranormal activity while he is translating the book. In the meantime the *dybbuk* kills Kozma and, possessing Matty, stabs Romy to death. Casey's exorcism is conducted in a ruined church, with a team present that includes Episcopal priest Arthur Wyndham (Idris Elba) and Casey's boyfriend Mark Hardigan (Cam Gigandet). The ritual soon spins out of control as supernatural forces are unleashed and the *dybbuk* possesses Wyndham, who attacks Casey but is killed by Mark. The spirit then enters Mark, but Casey winds up killing him by stabbing him in the neck with the protective amulet. Rabbi Sendak and Casey manage to complete the rite and drive out the evil Barto/Jumby entity, but in the aftermath Casey learns that she has been impregnated by Mark with a set of twins.

Clocking in at a brisk 80 minutes of running time (sans credits), *The Unborn* is a fright fest consisting of nightmare dream sequences, horrifying visions and paranormal goings-on that assault the viewer almost nonstop. Goyer's script borrows heavily from *The Exorcist*, with Jewish religious symbolism substituting for the Catholic motifs in the earlier film. As director, Goyer piles on a series of shock and suspense sequences that are frightening and effective, but lack narrative cohesion because the audience sometimes cannot distinguish the real from the unreal. Newbie star Odette Yustman's portrayal of the supernaturally besieged Casey is merely adequate and is overshadowed by the more polished performances of screen veterans Jane Alexander as Kozma and Gary Oldman as Rabbi Sendak.

The film preceded several recent movies on the *dybbuk* theme such as *The Possession* (2012) and *Demon* (2015). In *The Unborn*, however, the *dybbuk* is associated with the doppelganger via its connection with twins, where the malignant spirit attempts to use the intimacy of twinship as a bridge from the netherworld to our world. Harking back to *The Student of Prague*, mirrors are also used as a gateway for the demonic double to pass into our reality. Once again the doppelganger is connected with the Devil, black magic, death, mirror images and possession.

The Aokigahara Forest, located at the northwest base of the famous Mt. Fuji, is known as one of the most haunted places in Japan. In his book *Yurei: The Japanese Ghost*, author Zack Davisson describes it thus: "Also known as the jukai, or sea of trees, Aokigahara was described as 'the perfect place to die' in Wataru Tsurumui's bestselling book *The Complete Manual of Suicide.* Close to a hundred people a year kill themselves in the jukai, travelling from far away to die in this destination suicide spot…. As the fame of Aokigahara spreads, the number of suicides only increases. Signs emblazoned with messages such as *'Please Reconsider'* and *'Please consult the police before you decide to die!'* are nailed to trees throughout the forest."[6] The suicide haunted Aokigahara was the grim setting for the horror thriller *The Forest* (2016).

Jess and Sara Price (both played by *Game of Thrones*'s Natalie Dormer) are identical twin sisters whose parents were killed in a bizarre murder-suicide several years earlier. Jess witnessed the accident and suffered psychological trauma, while Sara did not. Possibly wishing to cut her ties with the past, Jess takes a job teaching English in a provincial school in Japan, while Sara remains in the States. One day Sara gets a call from the Japanese police informing her that they believe Jess is dead, having last been seen entering the suicide forest.

Sensing that her sister is still alive through an intuitive psychic bond between the twins, Sara sets off for Aokigahara to find Jess. Staying at the hotel where her sister had been lodging, she takes up with Aiden (Taylor Kinney), an American travel writer who wants to do a story on her quest. Together with a local guide, Michi (Yukiyoshi Ozawa), they plunge into the depths of the haunted forest, and discover Jess's tent deep in the woods. With night coming on Michi must leave, but Sara insists on staying at the tent in case her sister returns, and Aiden volunteers to stay with her. That night, Sara hears a noise outside the tent and rushes off into the woods to investigate, but instead of Jess she encounters a mysterious schoolgirl named Hochiko (Rina Takasaki), who warns her not to trust Aiden before running away into the darkness.

When morning comes, Sara and Aiden set off, but without Michi to guide them they soon get lost in the woods. Sara tries to make a call on Aiden's cell phone, but is horrified to find a picture of Jess on it. She runs away from him while starting to hear voices in her head and falls into a cave, where she is confronted once more by Hochiko, who reveals herself to be a ghost. Aiden arrives to rescue her, and he convinces her to accompany him to an old ranger station he has discovered. Once they are inside, however, Sara finds a note from Jess telling her that Aiden is keeping her captive in the station's basement. Thinking that he is out to kill them both, she attacks him and stabs him to death with a knife, but at that point realizes that she has been experiencing hallucinations.

Looking to see if Jess is really in the basement, Sara instead encounters the ghost of her father, who clutches at her wrist. She cuts at his fingers with the knife and once freed from his grip flees out into the night, where she sees Jess running toward the lights of a rescue party led by Michi. She tries to call out to her sister, but Jess cannot hear her. Then Sara realizes that while she was cutting at her father's ghostly fingers, she had in reality slashed her own wrists and is dying from loss of blood. As Jess is rescued, she tells the members of the party that she knows her twin is dead, and Michi has a final vision of Sara's forlorn spirit, which has now become one more ghost in the haunted forest.

The genesis of the film came from producer David S. Goyer, who read an article about the Aokigahara forest and became obsessed with making a movie about it. The screenplay was authored by a team consisting of Ben Ketai, Sarah Cornwell and Nick Antosa, and first-time director Jason Zada was assigned to direct. Unfortunately for the project, the Japanese government would not allow filming in the Aokigahara, so woods near Tara Mountain in Serbia had to stand in for the suicide forest. In his directorial debut, Zada constructs an intelligent thriller in the first half that descends into standard horror movie tropes in the second. The scenes of the characters wandering about lost in the haunted woodland recall similar treks in *The Blair Witch Project* (1999). Lead actress Natalie Dormer has little opportunity to display her acting range as twins, as the more psychologically troubled Jess is afforded little screen time in favor of her more well-adjusted sister, Sara. All in all, *The Forest* is a competently made but ultimately mediocre horror film, although its fact-based subject matter is original and intriguing.

The doppelganger angle consists of the use of the telepathic bond between identical twins that drives the plot. As usual, the twins are contrasting personalities, with Sara being the level-headed sister while Jess is psychologically scarred by viewing the murder-suicide of their parents. However, little in the way of explanation is offered for Jess's suicidal actions, and her motivations for adopting a strictly Japanese mode of suicide likewise remains unexplained. A sort of personality shuffle between the siblings occurs as the narrative progresses, with Sara experiencing her twin's horrific memories and assuming the guilt over them that leads to madness and self-destruction. The psychic bond between identical twins is a typical doppelganger motif.

The 1913 production of *The Student of Prague*, which was the first feature-length horror film, introduced movie audiences to the legendary doppelganger. Over a century later, this uncanny theme is still vital and viable. In the realm of horror, the double is a shape-shifter that takes many forms. The numerous variations on the theme include vampires (*Dead

Men Walk, Black Sunday, Twins of Evil), malignant twins (*The Other, Sisters, Dead Ringers*), ghosts (*The Long Hair of Death, Nightmare Castle, The Tenant*), unborn twins (*The Dark Half, The Unborn*), multiple personality (*Bowery at Midnight, The Haunted Strangler, Raising Cain*), and even more bizarre variants (*Warning Shadows, The Picture of Dorian Gray, The Manster*).

As fantastic as these myriad forms are, the doppelganger is also found in yet another realm, within the strange alternate realities of the science fiction film.

CHAPTER FIVE

Human Duplicators
Science Fiction Films

While the doppelganger had started out as a supernatural concept, it easily adapted itself to the techno-reality of the science fiction universe without losing its connection to the uncanny. The new alchemies of science allowed the fantastic double to evolve into novel and unexpected forms by fitting itself inside a number of established sci-fi concepts.

The earliest of these was the extraterrestrial doppelganger, which had first appeared in John W. Campbell's classic 1938 novella *Who Goes There?* Campbell's story featured a shape-shifting alien that had the power to disguise itself as human beings. Decades later, Jack Finney's 1955 novel *The Body Snatchers* also featured E.T.s who mimicked the human form. Both of these works would be translated into memorable sci-fi films featuring science fiction iterations of the doppelganger. In the popular imagination, aliens are fantastic creatures with unknown abilities, including the power to mimic humans.

Another science fiction invention that was capable of duplicating humans was the robot, at first a metallic simulacrum of the human form that was later refined into the concept of the "android," an intelligent machine that could be made to appear indistinguishable from a human being. Sci-fi author Philip K. Dick was reportedly obsessed with this concept, incorporating it into his novel *Do Androids Dream of Electric Sheep?* which was later filmed as *Blade Runner*, a tale of a future society that can create androids that are "more human than human." Robotic doppelgangers are able to perpetrate all kinds of mischief while impersonating their human counterparts, and usually do. The robotic double had its origin in the very first science fiction epic in movie history.

H.G. Wells's 1895 novel *The Time Machine* introduced the notion of time travel to science fiction literature. Later on, other sci-fi writers speculated on theories of the "temporal paradox," in which journeying back in time could change the present or the future. The question then arose as to what would happen if a time traveler met themselves back in the past and interacted with their earlier self. This conundrum created the notion of the time travel doppelganger.

Cloning, the production of genetically identical offspring in the laboratory, was a sci-fi concept that had been kicking around in SF literature for decades before scientists at the University of Edinburgh created the first cloned higher animal, Dolly the sheep, in 1996. This led to speculation as to whether human beings could also be cloned, but to date this has not happened, and laws forbidding human cloning have been enacted by governments around the world. Sci-fi filmmakers, however, have hit on the idea of cloning as another avenue for the creation of human doppelgangers.

A more recent sci-fi theme is a technology that allows a person's consciousness to be projected outside their body into a double that possesses superhuman powers. This technology involves a machine that provides a hookup between the two while the subject is in a sleeping or comatose state. Their doppelganger can be an android, a genetically engineered alien life form or even a digital construct. This idea harks back to the folkloric notion of the double as the dreaming self.

In addition to these basic ideas, sci-fi doppelgangers can also be produced by other, more exotic means, many of which were exploited by the writers of the classic 1960s-era TV series *Star Trek*. An episode entitled "The Enemy Within," written by sci-fi luminary Richard Matheson, featured Captain Kirk getting split into two separate beings by a transporter malfunction. One of the Kirks is aggressive and belligerent, while the other is passive and indecisive. In "What Are Little Girls Made Of?" by sci-fi/horror writer Robert Bloch, a renegade archaeologist uses rediscovered alien technology to create an android double of Kirk, while in "Mirror, Mirror" another technological glitch sends Kirk, McCoy, Scotty and Uhura into a "mirror universe" in which the United Federation of Planets is a fascist empire, while doppelgangers of the same four crewman are teleported aboard the starship *Enterprise*. In this alternate universe, Mr. Spock sports a charming Vandyke beard. "Whom Gods Destroy" featured an escaped inmate from an insane asylum making himself into a double of Kirk by using an illusion-creating device, while in "Turnabout Intruder" a renegade female scientist trades bodies with the Captain in a bid to take over the starship *Enterprise*.

Doppelgangers also infested the follow-up series, *Star Trek: The Next Generation*, which featured doubles of the various characters in several episodes. This trend culminated in the feature film *Star Trek Nemesis* (2002), in which TNG's Captain Jean-Luc Picard (Patrick Stewart) battles Shinzon, a clone of himself created by the Romulans (played by *Legend*'s Tom Hardy) and android crewman Data (Brent Spiner) squares off against an identical prototype model designated B-4.

Many science fiction movies featuring superheroes involve the doppelganger motif. The classic heroes such as Superman and Batman have dual identities that allow them to function in the everyday world while disguised as normal people. Superman's alter ego is Clark Kent, mild-mannered reporter for a great metropolitan newspaper, a ruse that allows him to gather info on the crises that threaten the city of Metropolis, while Batman disguises himself as millionaire Bruce Wayne, an effete playboy whom no one would suspect of being a caped crime fighter. These "secret identities" constitute alternate selves, which are quickly cast off when they wield their heroic powers. More recently, however, with the ascension of the Marvel Comics superheroes to mega-popularity, the trend has been away from characters having secret identities. None of the heroes in the Marvel super teams The Avengers, The X-Men or the Fantastic Four have them. Only Spider-Man, who masks his identity as boy genius Peter Parker, persists in having one. While the exploits of these super folks are extensively chronicled elsewhere, there is one movie based on a Marvel character that features the doppelganger in a more recognizable form.

The history of the science fiction feature film begins in Germany during the First World War, in the same milieu that produced the genesis of the horror film. The imaginations of these early filmmakers and their attraction toward the fantastic led to the first wave of science fiction films in cinema history. Audiences of the time were thrilled by such sci-fi classics as *Homunculus* (1916), *Algol* (1920), *The Hands of Orlac* (1924), *Alraune* (1928), *Woman in the Moon* (1928) and *Floating Platform One Does Not Reply* (1933). The most memorable of these was the first epic science fiction blockbuster, Fritz Lang's *Metropolis* (1927), a classic that continues to resonate into the 21st century.

Metropolis is set in a futuristic mega-city in the year 2026, where enormous buildings tower into the sky, traffic flows along elevated highways and airplanes fly overhead. But deep beneath this mechanized utopia, armies of faceless workers slave away at the machines that power the megalopolis and live in vast underground cities hidden in gigantic, man-made caverns. In the city far above, the privileged "Club of the Sons" of the wealthy frolic in the Eternal Gardens among half-naked courtesans, tropical plants and exotic birds. One day, as rich scion Freder Fredersen (Gustav Frohlich) is enjoying himself in the Gardens, a door opens up and Maria (Brigitte Helm) appears, leading a group of ragged children of the workers. "Look, these are your brothers," she explains to her charges before being hustled away by the Garden's security, but Freder is mesmerized by Maria's saintly demeanor and the sight of the children's poverty and decides to see their world for himself.

Gaining access to the worker's city, he witnesses the explosion of one of its giant machines and realizes how brutally the slaves are being exploited. He takes his concerns to his father, Joh Frederson (Alfred Abel), the mega-industrialist who built the city, in his headquarters in the "New Tower of Babel" where he directs its affairs. Freder is rebuffed by his father and secretly placed under surveillance, as he has discovered that the workers are conducting clandestine meetings and may be planning a revolt.

Inspired by a sense of mission, Freder sneaks back to the subterranean city and changes places with one of the workers, and after a grueling shift tending the machines, finds his way to a secret meeting where Maria is preaching a message of patience and reconciliation. She foretells the coming of a "Mediator" who will emerge to bring peace and harmony between the classes, and Freder becomes convinced that he is that mediator. In the meantime, Joh Frederson consults with the genius inventor Rotwang (Rudolf Klein-Rogge), who proudly displays his latest creation, an exquisitely crafted robot woman. "I have created a machine in the image of man that never tires or makes a mistake," he boasts, adding that in 24 hours, "no one will be able to tell a machine man from a mortal." Eventually these robots will make human workers obsolete, but for the short term Rotwang plans to make the metal woman into a simulacrum of Maria in order to counter the worker's revolt. Rotwang kidnaps Maria and takes her to his hi-tech laboratory and, in the most memorable and seminal sequence in the film, transfers her likeness onto the robot as his machines spit out bolts of artificial lightning.

Maria's robot doppelganger is an amoral femme fatale who delights in chaos and destruction. She performs an erotic dance at the posh Yoshiwara nightclub that drives the audience into a frenzy of lust and murder. Seeing that the robot is indistinguishable from the real Maria, Joh Fredersen unleashes her on the workers, where she beguiles them with her charisma and inspires them to revolt. As they riot and destroy the machines, Freder rescues the real Maria from Rotwang's lab, and the couple descends into the worker's city, which is being flooded because the machines have been turned off.

While the workers revel in an orgy of destruction led by the double, Freder and Maria manage to save the worker's children from drowning and lead them to safety. When the revelers finally come to their senses they realize that their children have been placed in mortal jeopardy and turn on the false Maria. She is burned at the stake like a witch and the flames consume her disguise, revealing the metal concealed beneath the artificial skin. While the crowd is thus distracted, Rotwang appears and chases the real Maria into the city's cathedral, where Freder pursues them to rescue her and throws the mad scientist to his death. The film ends with the reconciliation between the workers and Joh Fredersen, as Freder becomes the promised mediator who unites "the brain, the heart and the hand" to bring the future society into harmony.

Metropolis was the first science fiction blockbuster in screen history, costing UFA studios more than a million marks (in 1927 Weimar money). The film utilized monumental sets, forced perspective, crowds of extras and the "Shuftan process," a technique that used mirrors to magnify small models and make them appear large onscreen, to create its futuristic imagery. Lang's visuals are marred, however, by the loopy screenplay authored by his wife, Thea von Harbou, that presented a muddled political parable of class struggle and social reconciliation. Brigitte Helm, who was in her teens during the filming, steals the show in her dual role, especially as the inhuman robotic temptress. Perennial heavy Rudolf Klien-Rogge provided the template for countless mad scientists who would follow in his footsteps as the manic inventor Rotwang.

Despite its flaws and retro-kitsch technology, the influence of *Metropolis* on science fiction cinema was enormous. The laboratory scene in which Maria's double is created was

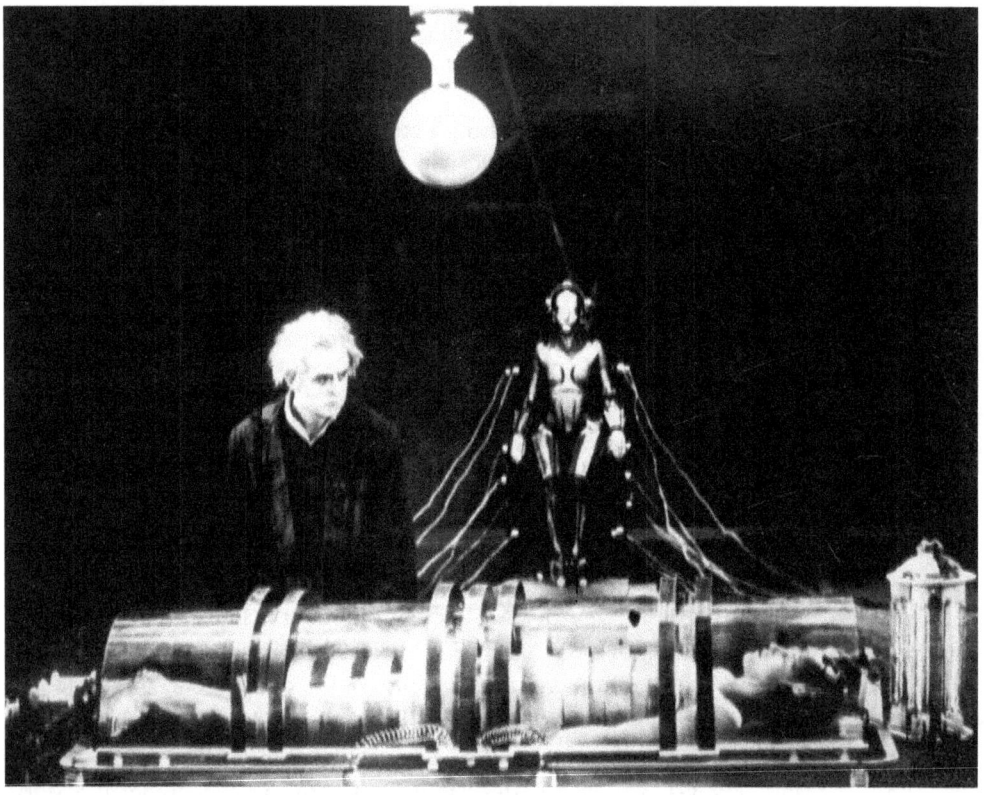

Mad savant Rotwang (Rudolph Klein-Rogge) creates a robot double of social activist Maria (Brigitte Helm) in Fritz Lang's silent-era science fiction epic *Metropolis* (1927).

copied in James Whale's *Frankenstein* (1931) and its legions of sequels, remakes and imitators. The robot bears a striking resemblance to protocol droid C3P0 in George Lucas's sci-fi megahit *Star Wars* (1977), while the futuristic city provided the blueprint for Ridley Scott's urban dystopia in *Blade Runner* (1982).

The robot Maria is the first example of a science fiction doppelganger in screen history, the Teutonic double making a seamless transition from the realm of the supernatural to that of the technological. Instead of being conjured by the Devil, or being a ghost or vampire, the doppelganger is produced in a laboratory. But while *Metropolis* is ostensibly a science fiction film, Lang and von Harbou also wove a number of supernatural elements into the plot. In an interview with director Peter Bogdanovich, Lang stated, "I dabbled in so many things in my life, and I also dabbled in magic. Mrs. Von Harbou and I put into the script of *Metropolis* a battle between modern science and occultism, the science of the Middle Ages."[1] Rotwang's lab is located in a medieval house nestled in the midst of the towering futuristic skyscrapers and the pentagram, the ancient symbol of magic, is inscribed on his door. In the film's climactic scene, the doppelganger is burned at the stake like a witch. The two Marias are diametric opposites; the real Maria is virginal and altruistic, while her double is an amoral, hypersexual femme fatale.

The German sci-fi wave fizzled out in the early 1930s, and the genre remained in decline until its resurgence during the American science fiction boom of the 1950s. In between, SF film inhabited the limbo of the Saturday afternoon serial, where children of all ages thrilled to the exploits of space opera heroes like Flash Gordon, Buck Rodgers and their heroic ilk. The serials were shot on shoestring budgets and featured low rent robots, aliens, spaceships, death rays and other technological marvels of the modern age. Their two-fisted heroes packed a mean wallop and their damsels in distress needed rescuing at the end of each chapter.

One of the oddest of these was Republic's 15-chapter serial entitled *The Purple Monster Strikes* (1945), the first American film to feature an alien invasion. The narrative begins with the distinguished astronomer Dr. Cyrus Layton (James Craven) observing a purple-colored meteor approaching the Earth through his telescope. In reality it is a spaceship on a one-way trip from the planet Mars that crash-lands near the observatory and disgorges a husky Martian in a form-fitting suit and hood known only as the Purple Monster (played by stunt man Roy Barcroft). Making his way to the astronomer's observatory, he murders Dr. Layton and assumes his identity by holding a smoking phial of Martian gas under his nose, which renders him transparent and takes possession of Layton's body.

As Layton, the alien pilfers the plans for an interplanetary rocket plane that will enable him to return to Mars and build a fleet of spaceships to launch a full-scale invasion. Opposing him is intrepid hero Craig Foster (Dennis Moore) and Layton's niece Sheila (Linda Sterling), who work for a scientific outfit called "The Foundation." Stealthily switching back and forth between Layton and his true identity, the Purple Monster enlists the help of mob boss Hodge Garrett (Bud Geary) and his gang of hoodlums in constructing the spaceship. Foster and Sheila labor mightily to keep the Foundation's hi-tech gizmos, such as the "electro-annihilator," the "atmospheric stabilizer," and the "electronic torch" out of the Monster's slimy grasp. In Chapter Eleven a female Martian, appropriately named Marcia (Mary Moore), arrives to assist her purple colleague and takes over the body of one of the Foundation scientist's secretaries, Helen (Rosemonde James). After a seemingly endless series of fistfights, car chases, shootouts and last minute escapes, the earthlings manage to thwart the Martian invasion plot and save the world.

A typical kiddie matinee serial of the period, *The Purple Monster Strikes* is built around a series of action setpieces and last minute escapes. As the titular Purple Monster, stuntman Roy Barcroft is a two-fisted Martian brawler in a silly costume, while his nemesis, the vertically challenged Dennis Moore, makes an unlikely opponent. Leggy Linda Sterling makes a fine damsel in distress as Sheila, while screen veteran James Craven provides some acting grit. Perhaps the most intriguing character is Mary Moore's sexy Marcia the Martian, the first femalien invader in cinema history, but unfortunately she is removed from the plot after a couple of episodes. Co-directors Spencer Gordon Bennett and Fred C. Brannon keep the action running smoothly through 15 chapters, and the film was later re-edited into a feature version entitled *D-Day on Mars* shown on television during the 1960s.

The Purple Monster Strikes was unusual in one sense, however. It was the vanguard of a veritable army of alien invaders who began arriving on Earth half a decade later in the wake of the first wave of flying saucer sightings during the 1950s. Many of these invaders had a propensity for turning themselves into doppelgangers of earthlings in order to infiltrate our society. While the Purple Monster's *modus operandi*, involving the smoking phial of Martian air held under the nose that turns him into a phantom, is hokey, he was the first in a long line of alien body snatchers that have persisted into the 21st century.

Roy Barcroft and Mary Moore pose as the body-snatching Martians in the Republic serial *The Purple Monster Strikes* **(1945).**

Across the pond in England a British science fiction film wave was in the making. A very early example was *The Perfect Woman* (1949), a comedy with sci-fi overtones. In the film, eccentric inventor Professor Belman (Miles Malleson) has created an artificial female that is "a robot indistinguishable from a normal woman." He has fashioned the robot, dubbed Olga (Pamela Devis), in the likeness of his niece, Penelope (Patricia Roc). In order to prove that Olga cannot be distinguished from a real woman, he hires screwball socialite Roger Cavendish (Nigel Patrick) and his goofy butler Ramshead (Stanley Holloway) to escort Olga to a hotel and see if anyone can tell the difference before he exhibits her to his fellow scientists.

A series of comic misadventures ensues when Penelope, to spite her uncle, pretends that she is the automaton and goes to the hotel suite with Cavendish and Ramshead. She playfully mimics the automaton until Cavendish's aunt Mary (Anita Sharp-Bolster) pricks her with a pin and she reacts. In the meantime, the professor's servant Mrs. Butters (Irene Handl) brings the real Olga to the hotel to add to the confusion. The most memorable scene in the film occurs when Ramshead attempts to dress Olga and the robot, who can only obey simple commands, gets him into a series of compromising positions in the bedroom. The butler manages to get her into bed so that Cavendish can prove to his aunt that a robot was really involved, but when she applies the pin test a second time it causes Olga to malfunction. Walking stiff-legged like Frankenstein's monster and trailing a shower of sparks, the professor's creation stalks through the hotel lobby and explodes offscreen.

Unlike the crime melodrama or horror genres, the science fiction film can offer a comic take on the doppelganger theme. *The Perfect Woman* is an example of the bedroom farce, with its plot being driven by mistaken identities and sexual situations. Based on a 1948 stage play by Wallace Geoffrey and Jeannie Frances Mitchell, the film's theatrical origins are obvious in its limited use of locations and its reliance on dialogue. British film star Patricia Roc is impish and sexy as Penelope, especially in the scenes where she impersonates the robot, while Pamela Devis, who was a dancer and choreographer, plays the role of Olga using physical comedy that borders on slapstick. The one standout performance, however, is by British musical comedy star Stanley Holloway, best known to American audiences as Liza Doolittle's cockney father in *My Fair Lady* (1963), in his role as the hapless butler, Ramshead.

Like *Metropolis*, *The Perfect Woman*'s plot revolves around the idea of a robotic woman who is indistinguishable from the real thing. A more recent variation on this theme is found in the sci-fi thriller *Ex Machina* (2015), in which a man must apply the "Turing test" of artificial intelligence to determine whether a being is either a woman or a machine. In *The Perfect Woman* the close resemblance between Penelope and Olga causes a series of double takes and creates a number of risqué situations. Unlike *Metropolis*, it is the real woman who has a libidinous side, while her robot counterpart is cold and asexual and wears an outfit that looks like a cross between a medieval corset and a chastity belt. There are a number of amusing scenes involving Olga, including one in which she inhales cigarette smoke and blows it out of her ears, and another when she is given the command to sit and blithely sits on a man's lap during a trip on the London subway. Modern feminists would surely balk at the notion of a "perfect woman" whose attributes are that she looks pretty, keeps her mouth shut and does whatever she is told.

During the 1940s and early 50s Britain's Hammer Studios was busy cranking out crime melodrama B-features, but beginning in 1953 they began to diversify their product by producing a number of modestly budgeted science fiction pictures such as *Spaceways* (1953), *The Quatermass Xperiment* (1955), *X-The Unknown* (1956) and *Quatermass II* (1957). Another of their early efforts was *Four Sided Triangle* (1953) based on a classic SF novel by William F. Temple. The story centers around a pair of British scientists, Bill Legatt (Stephen Murray) and Robin Grant (John Van Eyssen), who are rivals for the affection of their childhood sweetheart, Lena Maitland (Barbara Payton), who is working as their lab assistant. Bill and Robin invent a machine they call the "Reproducer," that can convert energy into matter and thus duplicate any material object.

Being conservative about the revolutionary nature of their device, the two scientists agree to keep their invention under wraps until it can be properly introduced to the world at large, but things get dicey when Robin announces his engagement to Lena and Bill is left out in the cold. In an effort to resolve the love triangle, Bill comes up with the idea of using the Reproducer to create a duplicate of Lena so that he can also marry her. He experiments with replicating animals and finds that after duplication he must perform an additional procedure to bring the organism fully to life. Once this is perfected he convinces Lena to undergo duplication and a double of Leah is created in a dramatic laboratory scene that recalls the creation of the robot Maria in *Metropolis*. Lena's doppelganger is brought to full consciousness by Bill's machine and he names the duplicate Helen.

Bill marries Helen and takes her on a honeymoon, but the couple soon encounter problems because Helen, being an exact copy of Lena, has inherited all of Lena's emotions and memories and is still in love with Robin. After Helen goes into a deep depression and attempts suicide, Bill believes that his last hope to save the marriage lies in erasing Helen's memory using electroshock treatments. Explaining his plight to Lena, she agrees to assist in the procedure in order to resolve the situation, but something goes wrong during the experiment and the laboratory is engulfed in flames. Bill and one of the women die in the fire, but the survivor is suffering from amnesia, making it impossible for Robin to know if it is Helen or Lena until the absence of two small marks on the back of her neck, markings made by Bill's resuscitation machine is noted proving that it is Lena who survived.

This early Hammer SF entry was directed by Terrence Fisher, who would go on to glory as the director of *Curse of Frankenstein* (1957) and *Horror of Dracula* (1958), the megahit shockers that revolutionized the horror movie and established Hammer as the leading purveyor of the fright film genre. Although *Four Sided Triangle* is cerebral science fiction, it was marketed as a lurid horror film, with poster ads that read "He Outdid Frankenstein" and "She Lived Two Amazing Lives Under His Evil Spell." In actually it was a faithful adaptation of William F. Temple's novel that combined hard SF with the everyday drama of a human predicament. Principals Stephen Murray, John Van Eyssen and Barbara Payton all turn in solid dramatic performances, and the laboratory scenes, which invoke those in *Metropolis*, are fun.

The central premise of the film anticipates cloning, but instead of employing a biological process of replication, the Reproducer duplicates the original material through an energy to matter conversion. When Lena's body is duplicated, the machine also copies her wedding ring, showing that Lena's doppelganger is not her diametric opposite but simply an imitation. Helen is merely a love object created to fulfill the longings of an insecure man and has an aura of inferiority about her, and she is portrayed as an unfulfilled individual doomed to a life of unhappiness and desperation. The audience is supposed to be relieved to find that it is Lena, not Helen, who has survived the fatal accident at the end of the film. Lena and her double have minimal interaction and hardly appear onscreen together.

American science fiction cinema enjoyed a popular renaissance during the 1950s, inspired by anxieties of the era related to postwar technological advances such as the rocketship and the atomic bomb. Another source of anxiety sprang from the enigmatic phenomenon of "flying saucers," or UFOs, that were observed zipping through our skies beginning in the late 1940s. Hollywood filmmakers were quick to exploit the mind-bending implications of alien beings visiting the Earth in a series of saucer-themed thrillers beginning with *The Thing from Another World* and *The Day the Earth Stood Still* in 1951. By 1953 the first extraterrestrial invaders arrived on movie screens in color in *The War of the Worlds* and *Invaders from Mars*, and in 3-D in *It Came from Outer Space*.

Scientists Bill Legat (Stephen Murray) and Robin Grant (John Van Eyssen) prepare to duplicate Lena Maitland (Barbara Payton) in Hammer's *Four Sided Triangle* (1953).

It takes place in the little town of Sand Rock, Arizona, where writer and amateur astronomer John Putnam (Richard Carlson) is stargazing with his girlfriend, schoolteacher Ellen Fields (Barbara Rush), when they observe a gigantic meteorite flash through the sky and impact near an abandoned mine outside of town. Rushing to the impact site, Putnam finds a gigantic crater still smoking from the crash, and when he descends into the crater to investigate he discovers an alien spaceship that quickly becomes buried under a landslide. When Putnam reports what he has seen to the authorities, he is ridiculed by the local press and by Sand Rock's skeptical lawman, Sheriff Matt Warren (Charles Drake) due to lack of evidence for his wild claims. But unknown to the townsfolk, one-eyed alien creatures from the spaceship are roaming through the desert leaving slime trails in their wake.

Two telephone linemen, Frank (Joe Sawyer) and George (Russell Johnson) who are working in the desert fall victim to the monstrous creatures that engulf them in a fog and duplicate their bodies. Putnam encounters George and his doppelganger in a remote area, where the alien body snatcher explains to him that "it is within our power to transform ourselves to look like you or anybody" and that "for a time it will be necessary" so that they are able to move about freely. The alien insists that they are not hostile invaders but are only taking humans hostage so they can repair their ship, which was damaged during a journey to another star system and had to make an emergency pit stop on Earth.

Putnam believes that the aliens are being truthful, but when other townsfolk are abducted Sheriff Warren remains skeptical. One of these abductees is Ellen, who lures Putnam out to the old Excelsior Mine, where he is confronted by her alien double in one of the mine shafts. Putnam quickly sees through the ruse, telling her, "You're wearing her clothes, but you're not Ellen." The extraterrestrial doppelganger becomes convinced that he is an enemy, and the creature fires an energy beam weapon at him but the shot goes wide and the faux Ellen is dispatched by a bullet from Putnam's revolver.

In the meantime the sheriff has put together a posse who are determined to drive out to the mine with the intention of blowing the spaceship to smithereens, while Putnam, penetrating deeper into the shaft, encounters the alien doppelgangers, including his own, who are nearly finished with their repairs. He persuades the aliens to release the humans they are holding hostage as a gesture of good faith, and they agree, whereupon he leads the people to safety before sealing the mine shaft with dynamite to prevent the posse from carrying out their threat. The grateful extraterrestrials then take off in their ship and leave the Earth peacefully.

Alien "xenomorphs" that can transform themselves into copies of human beings threaten earthlings in this poster for Jack Arnold's 50s sci-fi classic *It Came from Outer Space* (1953).

One of the finest SF films of the 50s cycle, *It Came from Outer Space* was the work of director Jack Arnold, who would go on to lens genre classics such as *The Creature from the Black Lagoon* (1954) and *The Incredible Shrinking Man* (1957). Outdoor desert locations and aerial photography are used to great effect to create a surreal backdrop for the dreamlike events of the plot, and the haunted desert landscape would become a fixture of many subsequent sci-fi films of the period. Despite its modest special effects budget, Arnold conjures visions of memorable extraterrestrial beings and advanced alien technology. A number of scenes were shot from the one-eyed E.T's point of view, through a shimmering circle positioned at a high angle, as the aliens slither through the desert stalking their human prey. Arnold frequently has a hand or other object suddenly enter the frame to create a visual shock, especially when viewed in the film's original 3-D format.

Originally scripted by sci-fi luminary Ray Bradbury, most of Bradbury's screenplay was discarded and the bare bones of the narrative revamped by Harry Essex. Some of the Bradbury dialogue that survived the rewrite, however, lends an air of poetry to the proceedings. The plot offers a thoughtful exploration of the theme of first contact between humanity and an alien culture instead of the usual E.T. invasion fare, although it does play as a standard horror film at times. Richard Carlson carries the film with his portrayal of the alien-friendly amateur scientist Putnam, the first of many roles he would later play in a number of genre films of the period. Barbara Rush lends an ethereal beauty to the part of Ellen, particularly in the scene where she portrays Ellen's otherworldly doppelganger. Russell Johnson, who would later play the Professor on the TV sitcom *Gilligan's Island*, is surprisingly effective as the eerie double of the telephone lineman George.

It Came from Outer Space is significant as the first SF feature to depict alien "xenomorphs," E.T.s who are able to alter their appearance to precisely mimic specific humans. Their stated reason for doing this are so that they can move around the town to gather materials needed to repair their ship. To the humans, however, they are, "hiding behind other men's faces," as Putnam puts it, and are as freakish and uncanny as the doppelgangers of the fantasy realm. Science fiction film historian John Baxter notes, "All those people who have been 'taken over' behave in a way slightly but eerily out of key ... one of the men, his attention drawn to the blazing sun, looks up and stares unblinking into it. When Putnam faces his girl on a windy hillside at dawn, she stands untroubled by the chill desert wind, while he must pull up his collar and flinch

An alien being has assumed the form of schoolteacher Ellen Fields (Barbara Rush) in *It Came from Outer Space* (1953).

against its bite. Economically we are told that there is something outside our experience, a 'different-drummered' world beyond our own."[2]

The film almost certainly provided inspiration for Jack Finney's novel *The Body Snatchers*, which was published in magazine form just one year later in 1954. Two years later, the film version of the novel, re-titled *Invasion of the Body Snatchers* (1956), was released, a film that would eventually be recognized as another classic of 50s sci-fi cinema. While the locale has been switched from the real life northern California town of Mill Valley to the fictional southern California town of Santa Mira, the film follows the narrative of the novel closely. Our protagonist is country doctor Miles Bennell (Kevin McCarthy), who has just returned to town from a medical conference at the insistence of his nurse, Sally (Jean Willes), because his office has been besieged by patients who all share the same odd delusion that their loved ones have been replaced by lookalike strangers.

One of his patients is Jimmy Grimaldi (Bobby Clark), a child who thinks that his mother is no longer his mother and has gone hysterical. Miles's hometown former flame Becky Driscoll (Dana Wynter) refers him to another case, that of her cousin Wilma (Virginia Christine), who insists that her uncle is an imposter. Baffled by what appears to be an outbreak of mass hysteria, Miles confers with local psychiatrist Dr. Dan Kaufman (Larry Gates) about the problem, but there are no easy answers. Oddly, Miles's other patients stop showing up for the appointments,

Miles takes Becky out to dinner at a local restaurant when they get a call from his close friend Jack Belicec (King Donovan) requesting that he come over immediately, so he and Becky ride over to the Belicec's, where they find Jack and his wife Teddy (Carolyn Jones) in a state of agitation. The reason for their nervousness is laid out on Jack's pool table, something that resembles a naked corpse but appears to be an unfinished simulacrum of Jack. Miles is stunned, but he and Jack agree not to inform the authorities just yet, and to keep the body under observation. He drives Becky home then tries to get some rest, but he is interrupted by Jack and Teddy, who got spooked when Jack's doppelganger opened its eyes and showed signs of life, causing them to flee in a panic. Acting on a sudden impulse, Miles drives back to Becky's house and discovers another partly-formed "blank" of her in the basement. He finds the real Becky in a comatose state and carries her away to safety.

Later on, the town's police chief (Ralph Dumke) explains away Jack's blank as the body of a murder victim subsequently found burned in a haystack, while Dr. Kaufman debunks Miles's sight of Becky's blank as an hallucination caused by nerves. These explanations are convincing enough to reassure everyone involved, but on the following evening Jack, Teddy and Becky are at Miles's house for a barbecue when they discover four enormous seed pods growing in the greenhouse. As they watch in horror, the pods pop open and disgorge more of the blanks, one for each of them. They realize that the alien pods are birthing the monstrous doubles that have replaced many of the townsfolk, and that the original person is somehow destroyed as part of the duplication process. Miles stabs each of the doubles with a pitchfork, destroying them.

Their plan is to have Jack and Teddy escape from the town and get help, while Miles and Becky elect to stay in Santa Mira, but they are soon discovered by the pod people and are chased through the nighttime streets before hiding themselves in Miles's medical office. The next day they observe trucks arriving in the town square filled with the giant seed pods and the townsfolk gathering to disseminate them into nearby communities. Just then

Jack and Dr. Kaufman burst into the office and it soon becomes clear that they have become pod people. Before Miles and Becky can be taken over by the pods, they manage to escape and are chased into the hills on the outskirts of town where they hide from their pursuers in an old mine shaft. Their sanctuary is short-lived however, as Becky slips into an exhausted sleep and is taken over by the pods, and Miles races onto a busy highway where he tries to warn the passing motorists who ignore him or laugh at his dire pronouncements.

This was the way the film was originally scripted by Daniel Mainwaring and shot by director Don Siegel, but producer Walter Wanger thought the ending was too downbeat and insisted on adding a framing story in which Miles is telling his fantastic tale in flashback to a police psychiatrist. The authorities are finally convinced when a truck filled with the pods is accidentally discovered during a traffic accident and the government is alerted in time to stop the invasion of the body snatchers.

Cult director Don Siegel, best known for his hard-edged films noir such as *The Verdict* (1946), *Crime in the Streets* (1956) and *The Lineup* (1958) brought this visual sensibility to *Body Snatchers*. Low camera angles, wide-angle shots and high contrast lighting are used to heighten the tension and induce a mood of manic fear. Most of the exterior shots were filmed on location in the small southern California town of Sierra Madre, which lends a chilling verisimilitude to the proceedings. Unlike many of the other SF movies of the period, there is virtually no reliance on special effects. Siegel reportedly considered it his favorite film, although he never directed another science fiction picture. Tight pacing, vibrant performances and stylish visuals all combine to form a sci-fi masterwork. Daniel Mainwaring's screenplay is faithful to Finney's novel and improves upon the book's unsatisfying ending, in which the pods admit defeat and leave the Earth en masse to seek out another planet to dominate. Dana Wynter, King Donovan and Carolyn Jones turn in strong supporting performances around Kevin McCarthy's intense portrayal of a man hunted by an entire community.

As noted in Chapter One, both the novel and the movie were likely inspired by the medical condition known as Capgras Syndrome or Capgras Delusion, in which the sufferer believes that their loved ones have been replaced with lookalike imposters. Over the years critics have offered a number of interpretations of the film's underlying themes, including loss of identity, conformity vs. individualism and anti-communist paranoia, but taken at face value it most clearly exploits the horror of the doppelganger. Many of the most disturbing scenes in *Body Snatchers* are when the alien "blanks" are revealed to the audience as corpselike simulacra poised to suck the very life force out of the characters. The film also exploits the folkloric notion of the double emerging during a sleeping state, and of occupying the same time and place as one's doppelganger leading to the annihilation of the self. Note that in this case the doppelgangers do not represent the Id force of unrestrained passion, but instead are emotionless, passive vegetable creatures.

The year 1956 also saw the release of another science fiction classic that took a diametrically opposite approach, MGM's high-concept, high-technology space opera *Forbidden Planet*. Set far in the future, the film takes place entirely in outer space, as the star-faring crew of United Planets Cruiser C57-D come out of hyperdrive near the planet Altair-4. Their mission is to check up on the *Bellerophon* expedition, a group of colonists who had landed on the planet nearly two decades earlier and haven't been heard from in years. Leading the intrepid spacehounds is Commander J.J. Adams (Leslie Nielsen), who is warned away from the forbidden planet while the ship is still in orbit by one Dr. Edward Morbius (Walter Pidgeon), the only survivor of the *Bellerophon* expedition. Adams chooses to disregard the warning and insists on landing his ship, which resembles a gigantic flying saucer, at co-ordinates provided by Morbius.

Upon landing on Altair-4, Adams and his crew are met by a robotic entity whose name is "Robby," who chauffeurs Adams, along with his second in command, lieutenant Jerry Farman (Jack Kelly), and the ship's medical officer, Doc Ostrow (Warren Stevens) to meet with the expedition's sole survivor. Morbius, who proves to be an elegant, charming and very intelligent scientist, explains that the *Bellerophon* colonists were all killed, literally torn to pieces, by some "dark, terrible, incomprehensible force," during the first year of the expedition, and was the reason why he issued the warning to stay away. He offers no explanation as to why he was spared by this murderous force, which leads the officers to have suspicions about Morbius's story. More suspicions are aroused when they learn that Morbius has a beautiful young daughter, Altaira (Anne Francis), who was born on the alien world and has never seen other people. Adams tells Morbius that he will have to remain on the Altair-4 while they contact Earth for further orders.

Commander J.J. Adams (Leslie Nielsen, left) confers with scientist Dr. Morbius (Walter Pidgeon) and his daughter Altaira (Anne Francis) as Robby the Robot stands by for driving instructions in *Forbidden Planet* (1956).

Communicating over interstellar distances proves to be a tricky process that involves removing the ship's energy core, so Morbius assigns Robby to lend a hand in fabricating the materials necessary for the operation. When Robby escorts Altaira to the ship while he is making a delivery, romantic sparks begin to fly between her and Lt. Farman. That night, the ship is attacked by an invisible entity that damages the communication equipment. Adams suspects that somehow Morbius is responsible and orders a force field barrier to be erected around the ship to prevent further intrusions. When the Commander and Doc Ostrow confront Morbius with their concerns, he decides to reveal the nature of his research. Eons ago, Altair-4 was the home of a super-advanced alien race called the Krell, and Morbius has devoted himself to recovering the technology of their civilization, which seems to have vanished in a single night due to some unimaginable cataclysm.

Morbius takes the two officers on a tour of the Krell techno-marvels, starting with an education device that doubled the scientist's I.Q. but nearly killed him in the process. They are shown a gigantic machine capable of harnessing the "power of an exploding planetary system" that is still operating and self-sustaining, but whose function is unknown. While they are touring the machine, night has fallen on the planet's surface and the invisible creature returns to the ship, easily slips through the force field perimeter, and tears one of the crewman to pieces.

Fearing that the mysterious force that destroyed the *Bellerophon* expedition has returned to wreck havoc, Adams orders the crew to stand sentry duty fully armed with blaster weapons. That night the invisible entity returns and gets caught between the force field and the crossfire from the ship's neutron beam weapons. Becoming semi-visible inside the energy streams, the being somewhat resembles a bipedal lion. After killing and maiming several crewmen, the creature suddenly vanishes just as Morbius awakens from a dream back at his home.

The next day Adams and Ostrow attempt to confront Morbius once more, but while the Commander tries to convince Altaira that she is in danger, Ostrow slips away and subjects himself to the Krell brain boost machine. When Adams finds him he is dying from the effects of the machine, but his artificially enhanced intelligence has given him some clues to the puzzle. The great Krell machine's purpose was intended to create "civilization without instrumentalities," that could convert their thoughts into anything they desired, but they were destroyed by "monsters from the Id." As Ostrow expires, Adams turns to Morbius for clarification of the term, and is told it is an obsolete term that refers to "the elementary basis of the subconscious mind." Adams theorizes that the Krell were destroyed on the first night the big machine became operational, as "the mindless primitive" buried inside their psyches was released and the machine amplified their subconscious desires in an orgy of destruction.

The discussion ends when Morbius's compound comes under attack by the invisible creature and Adams, Morbius and Altaira take refuge inside Morbius's lab, behind seemingly impenetrable blast doors made of Krell metal, but they watch in horror as the giant doors begin to glow white hot as the monster from the Id punches its way through to them. "Morbius, that thing out there—it's you!" Adams proclaims, explaining that the scientist's subconscious mind had activated the powers of the Krell machine and created the invisible, invincible being that destroyed the crew of the *Bellerophon* when they opted to return to Earth and interrupt his research. Then, when Adams and his crew showed up and threatened to take his daughter away from him, the Id monster reappeared to murder the crewmen.

Morbius is overcome with guilt after these revelations. "My evil self is at that door and I have no power to stop it," he laments as the invisible creature forces its way into the lab. "I deny you, I give you up!" he screams at the Id monster as he hurls himself at it and both of them are destroyed. With his dying breaths, Morbius directs Adams to a self-destruct mechanism that will vaporize the planet in 24 hours, when Altaira and Adams witness the destruction of Altair-4 and the Krell machine on the starship's viewing screen from millions of miles out in space.

The first science fiction film shot in color and widescreen Cinemascope, *Forbidden Planet* had a high gloss 1950s pulp sci-fi ambience that benefited mightily from the resources of the MGM production team headed by Oscar winning production designer Cedric Gibbons, special effects whiz Buddy Gillespie and cinematographer George Folsey. The film was shot entirely on studio sound stages instead of using outdoor locations to simulate an alien planet. The result was an entirely artificial environment which was quite

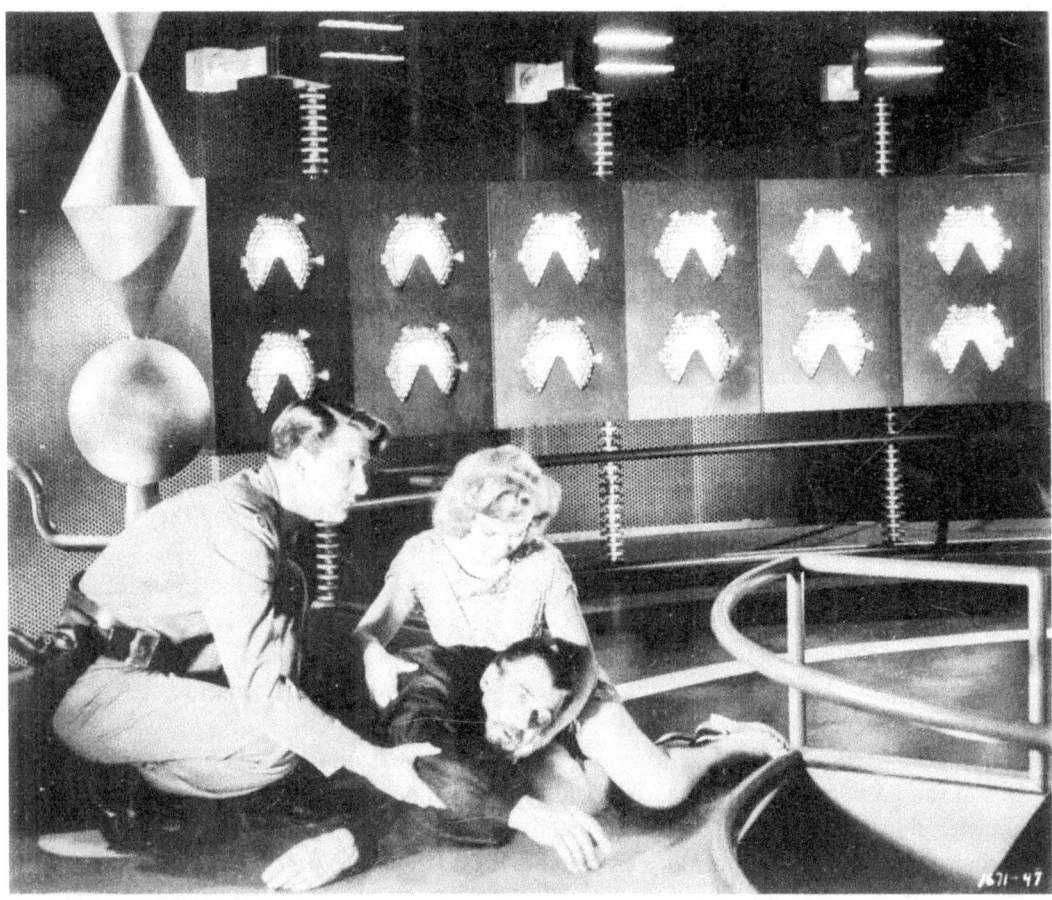

Dr. Morbius (Walter Pidgeon, center) is mortally wounded after confronting his invisible "evil self" and has collapsed into the arms of his daughter, Altaira (Anne Francis), as Commander Adams (Lelsie Nielsen) offers moral support in *Forbidden Planet* (1956).

unique and different from the sci-fi fare of the period. Disney animator Joshua Meador was brought in to bring the "monster from the Id" to life and create other animation special effects sequences. Avant-garde musicians Louis and Bebe Barron contributed an electronic "tonalities" score, a haunting aural soundscape that provided both music and futuristic sound effects. Gillespie's ingenious creation Robby the Robot was the first in a long line of amiable automata that would grace movie screens for decades to come.

But it is Cyril Hume's original screenplay, based on a story by Irving Block and Allen Alder, that is at the science fiction heart of the film. Machines seem to overshadow the humans in its futuristic landscape, with the palatial flying saucer star cruiser, Robby the robot and the Krell mega-machine taking center stage. Critics have long noted the resemblance between the film's narrative and the plot of Shakespeare's *The Tempest*, with Morbius as the wizard Prospero, Altaira as his daughter Miranda, and Robby standing in for the sprite Ariel. Director Fred Wilcox, whose career was otherwise undistinguished, holds the various cinematic elements together expertly and keeps the pacing tight. Hollywood leading men Walter Pidgeon and Leslie Nielsen vie against each other nicely, while the comely Anne Francis, the only female in the cast, shines as the virginal and otherworldly Altaira. Robby the robot is one of the most endearing and interesting characters who manages to steal most every scene he's in.

The film's Id monster is one of the most fantastic conceptions of the doppelganger in all of cinema, and comports with the traditional idea of the double being a manifestation of a person's subconscious and sociopathic impulses. Morbius's "evil self" is an invisible being composed of pure energy that focuses the savant's homicidal impulses into an all-powerful killing machine fueled by his incestuous sexual passion for his daughter and his desire to be left alone with his research, an occupational hazard for 50s-era mad scientists. As originally conceived in the screenplay, the Id monster was a massive, sluglike creature, which was later changed into a bloated insectoid before the MGM art department settled on the form in which it appears in the film. Critics have pointed out that the monster's features bear a resemblance to those of Morbius himself. As with folkloric conceptions of the doppelganger, the double emerges from a dream state, and it is fatal for a person to directly confront one's alternate self.

Perhaps the most atrociously titled SF film of the period was surely *I Married a Monster from Outer Space* (1958), but despite its lurid title it proved to be an intriguing and effective sci-fi thriller. Set in the small town of Norrisville, California, the film stars Gloria Talbott as the titular "I" Marge Bradley, who is engaged to be married to insurance salesman Bill Farrell (Tom Tryon). One night shortly before the wedding Bill is driving home from a local bar when his body is snatched by an alien being who assumes his form. In the aftermath Bill's double appears to be absent-minded, distracted, and unfamiliar with facets of everyday life. After their wedding Marge realizes that Bill is not the man she fell in love with, and seems like "Bill's twin brother from another place." Adding to her frustration is her inability to conceive a child despite their best efforts.

The mystery deepens as other townsfolk are abducted and replaced with alien clones that begin to take over the little community, starting with the town's police force. Puzzled and hurt by her husband's odd behavior, she follows him one night when Bill goes out for a ramble. Trailing him into a wooded area, she watches in horror as he stands still like a zombie and a strange vapor emerges from inside his body that coalesces into the form of a weird alien humanoid. As the monster walks into a landed flying saucer, she approaches Bill and touches him, whereupon he falls to the ground stiff as a board with his eyes wide open and an insect crawls across his face. Terrified, she runs to police chief Collins (John Eldredge), an old, trusted family friend and blurts out her story, but the chief has become an alien doppelganger and expresses skepticism about her story.

Marge attempts to phone the FBI in Washington, but her calls are blocked, then tries to send a telegram, but the telegrapher tears up her message, and when she attempts to drive out of town she is turned back by a police roadblock. Realizing that she is trapped, she finally confronts her husband. "I know you're not Bill," she tells him and he admits the truth. The aliens belong to a race from the Andromeda Galaxy whose women have all been annihilated in a catastrophe, and their mission on Earth is to impregnate Earth women to prevent their race from becoming extinct. So far, however, the Andromedans have proven to be sterile,

In desperation, Marge turns to her family physician, Dr. Wayne (Ken Lynch) who believes her story. Reasoning that they can only be sure that fertile men have not been taken over by the aliens, he rounds up a posse of expectant fathers from among his patients and leads them to the saucer. The townsmen do battle with the creatures, who prove impervious to bullets but are dispatched when attacked by a pair of fierce German shepherds. The posse enters the saucer to find the abductees in suspended animation, attached to machines that broadcast their physical forms and memories as electrical impulses that create the Andromedan's human disguises. When the plugs are pulled on the machines the alien doppelgangers disintegrate into piles of a revolting gelatinous substance. Marge is reunited with the real Bill, and the extraterrestrial saucer fleet in space departs from Earth to seek a less complicated invasion venue.

The film's silly title, perhaps borrowed from 1950's *I Married a Communist*, precluded any serious critical consideration of its virtues for years, but as John Baxter notes, "yet behind this grisly label lies a work of more than usual brilliance, directed by ex-editor Gene Fowler, Jr. with the crisp efficiency that characterized the work of Arnold and Siegel."[3] While the screenplay by Louis Vittes borrows elements from *It Came from Outer Space* and *Invasion of the Body Snatchers*, Fowler's treatment of these derivative plot elements creates a vibrant atmosphere of apprehension and mystery through the use of low-key lighting and razor-tight pacing. Much of the film takes place at night within the claustrophobic spaces of the couple's domicile and the darkened streets of the small town. As in *Body Snatchers*, the plot centers around a single individual oppressed by a secret coven of alien monsters. Gloria Talbott projects both strength and vulnerability as the tormented wife, while Tom Tryon is sinister and even a little sympathetic as the Andromedan invader and faux husband. After playing an alien doppelganger on the screen, Tryon would go on to become the author of the novels *The Other* and *Fedora*, which were made into two memorable films on the theme.

As in *It Came from Outer Space*, aliens abduct humans and are able to form themselves into physical doubles of them while the originals are held captive. The difference here is that a machine is used to transmit the abductee's appearance, memory and personality into their doppelgangers, but once the connection with the device is broken the doubles are annihilated. The aliens are able to leave their human host bodies in the form of a vapor, and when this happens the humans remain in a comatose state. Director Fowler reveals the presence of the Andromedans inside their human hosts by superimposing a quick, almost subliminal shot of the horrific alien's face over the features of those who have been taken over in a lightning flash during a storm.

By the end of the decade, the 1950s sci-fi film boom had gone bust. Movie audiences had been saturated with flying saucers, giant bugs, atomic mutants, prehistoric monsters and the like for the time being, and the genre would morph into new forms during the 1960s, but the transition was slow. *The Day Mars Invaded Earth* (1963) was an anachronism that could easily have been made during the 50s science fiction cycle. Shot in black and white Cinemascope, the film starred the venerable Kent Taylor as Dr. Dave Fielding, a NASA scientist heading up a team that has just landed an unmanned probe on Mars. Shortly after the successful landing, however, the automated probe is completely destroyed by an anomalous burst of high energy and Fielding experiences a momentary feeling of dissociation.

His work on the project completed for the time being, Dr. Fielding leaves Cape Canaveral to join his family in California for Christmas vacation. His wife Claire (Marie Windsor), teenage daughter Judi (Betty Beal) and ten-year-old son Rocky (Gregg Shank) are staying in the guest house of the empty Wainwright Mansion in Beverley Hills, which

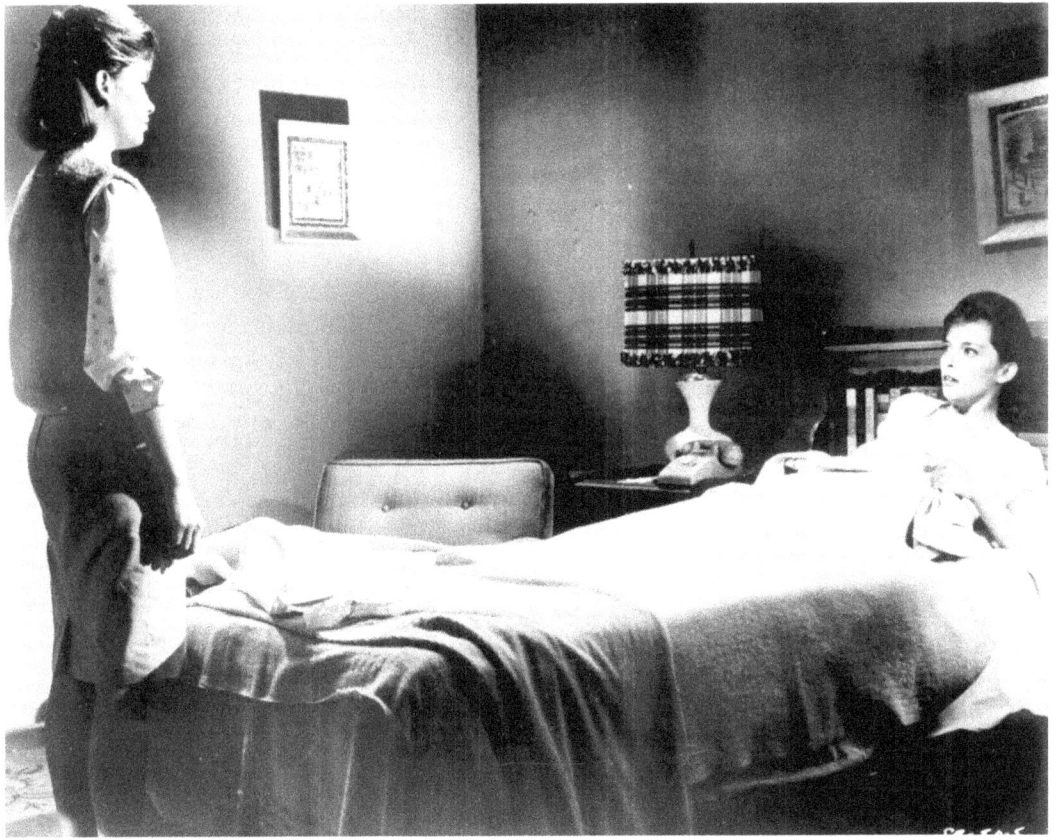

Judi Fielding (Betty Beal) confronts her Martian doppelganger in *The Day Mars Invaded Earth* (1963).

is owned by his wife's family, pending the purchase of a new home. Soon after he arrives, the family members begin seeing what appear to be their doubles haunting the empty estate. Things come to a head when Judi's boyfriend Frank (Lowell Brown) swerves off the road to avoid hitting a figure that he thinks is Judi and is killed. Later that night, Judi awakens to find that the doppelganger has invaded her bedroom, but the double disappears before the others can witness it.

When the automated front gate to the estate cannot be unlocked and the phones go dead the family finds itself trapped inside the deserted estate by some mysterious force. As Fielding searches through the rooms of the empty mansion he encounters his double, who explains that it is a "manifestation of intelligence," a being of pure energy who came to Earth via the radio transmissions from the Mars probe. "You invaded us," the doppelganger explains, further relating that the Martian mission on Earth is to sabotage the space program to insure there are no further incursions on their planetary territory. Toward this end, Fielding and his family are to be eliminated and replaced with exact lookalikes. Imprisoned inside the mansion and its grounds, the family seems to have an avenue of escape when Fielding's fellow scientist Dr. Web Spencer (William Mims) shows up and jimmies the main gate open. The film's final shot, however, shows five human-shaped piles of ash lying on the concrete bottom of the mansion's empty swimming pool as Web's car drives away with the Martian doubles who have successfully replaced the humans.

This low-rent rip-off of *Invasion of the Body Snatchers* is pretty dull stuff, marred by the glacial pacing of producer/director Maury Dexter and a lackluster, overly derivative screenplay by Harry Spalding. The actors appear to be sleepwalking through what is supposed to be a nightmarish situation with little tension or emotion. Exteriors were shot at the historic Greystone Mansion in Los Angeles, which provides a claustrophobic backdrop for the strange goings-on as a typical nuclear family of the period struggles against a covert alien invasion. Poor production values don't help matters, nor does the downbeat ending that recalls the original denouement of *Body Snatchers* in which the invasion succeeds. Veteran thesp Kent Taylor is wasted in the stolid part of Dr. Fielding, and B-movie queen Marie Windsor, best known for her quirky roles in films noir like *The Narrow Margin* (1952) and *The Killing* (1956), is likewise wasted. While the family's close encounters with their doppelgangers is eerie, the film never explains just how the Martians are able to duplicate their human victims.

More alien invaders were on the way to Earth in *The Human Duplicators* (1965). The film begins with a cheesy-looking UFO approaching our planet from interstellar space piloted by a seven foot-tall alien named Kolos (Richard Kiel), who has been instructed by his superiors to establish a colony on Earth as a prelude to world domination by the galactic hegemony. Kolos beams down to the surface from his spaceship and pays a visit to the reclusive cybernetics expert Professor Vaughn Dornheimer (George Macready), who lives with his blind daughter Lisa (Dolores Faith). The giant alien wastes no time dominating the professor and taking over his robot research operation.

A short time later the theft of electronic equipment from a high security laboratory arouses the suspicion of National Intelligence Agency operative Glenn Martin (George Nader), his boss Austin Welles (Hugh Beaumont), and his assistant Gale Wilson (Barbara Nichols). Welles has been following a series of similarly unusual events that may have high security implications and orders Glenn and Gale to investigate. The trail soon leads Glenn to Dornheimer's secluded mansion, where the professor gives him the brush-off but Lisa seems to intimate that something unusual is going on in her father's basement lab.

Glenn returns to the mansion a second time and manages to speak to Lisa, who tells him that Dornheimer is building robotic doppelgangers in the basement, and that her father has been replaced by a cybernetic double. Before he can communicate this info back to NIA HQ, however, he is taken captive by Kolos and imprisoned in the mansion's basement awaiting his turn in the duplication chamber, after which his double will be sent to Washington as one of Kolos's agents to infiltrate the U.S. government. Before this can happen, however, Lisa visits him and helps to free him with the aid of one of Glenn's spycraft gizmos, a hacksaw blade concealed inside a coin.

In the meantime, Kolos's superiors, the "Masters of the Galaxy," order Kolos to duplicate Lisa, but the alien balks at the prospect because he has developed an affection for her. This causes the Masters to command the robots to overcome the errant alien, shackle him in chains, and carry out their orders without his interference. While the robots are prepping Lisa to be duped, Glenn encounters the real Professor Dornheimer, who tells him about a pulse beam device in his lab that can scramble the delicate electronic brains of the androids. Armed with this weapon, Glenn starts frying the brains of the robots and Kolos breaks free of his chains. Together they destroy the duplicates and rescue Lisa, after which Kolos beams himself back up to his starship and departs into deep space.

This cheapo Woolner Brothers production was so sordidly awful that it was satirized on TV's *Mystery Science Theater* program. Production values are bargain basement, the acting is laughable and the plot and dialogue by scenarist Arthur C. Pierce are unintentionally hilarious. Barbara Nichols's performance as Gale is particularly laugh inducing as she speaks her lines with a thick Brooklyn accent, while B-actors George Nader, Hugh Beaumont and George Macready go about their business with comic earnestness. Only the oversized Richard Kiel, best known as James Bond's toothy nemesis "Jaws," generates any interest as the giant extraterrestrial Kolos. Director Hugo Grimaldi tries but fails to rise above the juvenile material.

In *The Human Duplicators* alien technology combines with cybernetics to produce the film's doppelgangers. The film makes use of the concept of the android, a mechanical being indistinguishable from a human being, an idea that harks back to *Metropolis*, as Glenn ponders the question "Would you know an android if you saw one?" As it turns out, even Kolos learns in the end that he is also an android. After they have been duplicated, the original people are placed in suspended animation in a freezer in case they must be recopied. The film has affinities with the sci-fi thriller *Futureworld* (1976), in which a secret cabal plots world domination by creating cloned duplicates of world leaders.

Beginning in the early 1960s the brilliant filmmaker John Frankenheimer directed a series of science fiction thrillers that combined a distrust of high technology with a distinctly American brand of paranoia. In *The Manchurian Candidate* (1962), scientists from Communist nations conspire to take over the government of the United States by arranging an assassination committed by a brainwashed dupe, while in *Seven Days in May* (1964) a group of military leaders attempt a *coup d'etat* by taking control of hi-tech communication systems. *Seconds* (1966) posits a secret society that provides wealthy clients with a second chance at life.

Seconds begins with middle-aged banker Arthur Hamilton (John Randolph) traversing New York's Grand Central Station on his way home from work. As he is about to board a commuter train he is accosted by a man who calls his name and hands him a slip of paper before fading back into the crowd. When he gets home his wife Emily (Frances Reid) perceives that something is troubling him, but Hamilton remains sullen and uncommunicative. That night he receives a phone call from a supposedly deceased friend, Charlie (Murray Hamilton), who instructs him to go to the address written on the piece of paper he was handed at a specific time and to use the code name "Wilson."

The next day Hamilton takes a cab to the address provided and, after several misdirections, finds himself inside a building that resembles a deserted hospital. He is ushered into an office where he confers with Mr. Ruby (Jeff Corey), an executive of a shadowy corporation known only as "The Company," who explains the unique service they provide. For $30,000 they will arrange for him to be "reborn" into a new life and a new identity. A carefully staged "death" will be arranged for him and a surgically-altered cadaver substituted in his place, and he will undergo advanced medical procedures that will alter his appearance and restore his youth. He is obliged to sign a contract that transfers his assets to The Company as trustee to provide for his family and bankroll his new life.

Hamilton undergoes the procedures and is transformed into Tony Wilson (Rock Hudson), and begins his new existence as an artist in a Malibu beach house, his name and profession having been decided by the Company. Guided by his butler and minder John (Wesley Addy), he tries to adjust to life as Wilson, but his paintings are all provided for him and he soon realizes he has no talent as an artist. One day while walking on the beach he encounters a free-spirited young woman named Nora Marcus (Salome Jens),

This poster captures the super wide-angle horror at the conclusion of *Seconds* (1966), as the helpless Wilson (Rock Hudson) is wheeled to his doom.

and the two begin to drift into a love affair. Nora invites him to a wine festival in Santa Barbara that turns into a wild, bacchanalian affair in which the staid Wilson's reserve is broken and he winds up participating in a naked orgy and having sex with Nora in a wine-stomping vat, but there is an unpleasant edge to the revelry like a bad LSD trip.

In another attempt to loosen Wilson up, John arranges a cocktail party for his Malibu neighbors, but Wilson gets too drunk and starts babbling about his former life as Hamilton, whereupon a number of guests pick him up bodily and haul him into the bedroom. Looking at their hostile faces he realizes with a shock that they are all reborns like himself who are there to keep him in line, and that Nora is also an agent of the Company. In the aftermath he realizes that his reborn life is even emptier than the one he left behind, and he tries to reconnect with his former identity by flying back to New York and visiting his wife. He finds, however, that she has moved on with her life and has discarded his things.

These transgressions provoke a response from the Company, and after the meeting a car is waiting outside to take him back to their office, where he awaits another turn at rebirth. Mr. Ruby urges him to recruit another reborn client for them, but he refuses while demanding to have more control over the conditions of his next rebirth. One night Wilson is awakened by the chief (Will Geer), the elderly founder and CEO of the company, who discusses his visions and acknowledges the failures of the reborn project. When he finishes

Wilson (Rock Hudson, left) is under the scrutiny of agents of "the Company" in John Frankenheimer's *Seconds* (1966).

with his spiel, two orderlies wheel a hospital gurney into his room and Wilson, thinking he is going to be reborn again, happily gets on board, but when he is strapped in he begins to suspect that something is wrong. As he is being wheeled into surgery a clergyman appears and begins to intone a series of requiem prayers he apprehends the truth—that he is going to be disposed of and his body used as a cadaver for the bogus death of another reborn. Struggling piteously, he is wheeled into the operating room as a surgeon uses a cranial drill on his skull to simulate a cerebral hemorrhage.

Seconds is a science fictional variation on the medieval story of Faust, the alchemist who made a deal with the Devil to restore his youth, only instead of a diabolical agency the modern-day Faust must contend with a faceless corporation that uses technology to perform its restorative magic. Scenarist Lewis John Carlino deftly adapted the plot of David Ely's paranoia-drenched novel in his screenplay, which was then lovingly rendered onto the screen by director Frankenheimer and veteran Hollywood cinematographer James Wong Howe. Frankenheimer's style utilizes low angles, extreme close-ups, distorted wide angle images and moving camera to evoke a surreal universe of paranoia and fear. There is a curious mixture of documentary stylistics in scenes shot on location at a meat packing plant and even an actual plastic surgery operation, with distorted Expressionist sets that hark back to *The Cabinet of Dr. Caligari* and other German classics to create a nightmarish, hallucinatory mindscape. The film contains one of Rock Hudson's most subtle and powerful dramatic performances. He reportedly prepared for the role by carefully studying the mannerisms of co-star John Randolph in order to portray an older man in a younger man's body, and is particularly effective in the climactic scenes in which he struggles helplessly as he is led like a lamb to the slaughter.

In the film, Hamilton literally signs a Faustian contract with the modern equivalent of diabolic forces in order to be transformed into his doppelganger. Advertising art for the film featured a close-up of Hudson's face grotesquely swathed in bandages as he undergoes the transformation to his alternate self. His name, his signature, even his teeth have been changed by the seemingly omniscient Company, but the Hamilton persona still persists inside the artificial shell of Wilson. It is the re-emergence of his former personality, a merging of the original self with the double, that causes the annihilation of both Wilson and Hamilton.

The 1960s space oddity *Journey to the Far Side of the Sun* (a.k.a. *Doppelganger*, 1969) posited another mind-bending science fiction variation on the theme: an entire planet of doppelgangers. In the year 2069 an unmanned solar probe launched by the European Space Exploration Council, or EUROSEC, detects an Earth-like planet in orbit on the opposite side of the sun. EUROSEC scientist Dr. Kurt Hassler (Herbert Lom) has been spying for a hostile eastern power and passing data about the discovery to them until his treachery is discovered and he is killed by security forces. The head of the European space consortium, Jason Webb (Patrick Wymark) hastily organizes an expedition to the newly-discovered world in collaboration with NASA administrator David Poulson (Ed Bishop). An American astronaut, Col. Glenn Ross (Roy Thinnes), and a British astrophysicist, Dr. John Kane (Ian Hendry), are selected for the mission.

The spacefarers are scheduled to reach the planet in three weeks and return three weeks later. Traveling in their ship, the *Phoenix*, they make planetfall as planned and descend to the surface in a landing craft that is severely damaged by an electrical storm and crash-lands. The astronauts are located and brought back to EUROSEC headquarters for debriefing, but Kane dies from his injuries in the interim. Under questioning, Ross cannot account for the fact that they seem to have returned to Earth after only three weeks, but insists that they did not abort the mission prematurely. The answer to this riddle is that the world on the far side of the Sun is a reverse mirror image of Earth, and that they are not dealing with the real Col. Ross, but with his doppelganger from the other planet. To support this theory, Ross displays a watch that runs counterclockwise and is able to read text that is mirror-

Astronauts Dr. John Kane (Ian Hendry, left) and Col. Glenn Ross (Roy Thinnes) prepare to blast off on their *Journey to the Far Side of the Sun* **(a.k.a.** *Doppelganger,* **1969).**

image reversed. Furthermore, X-rays from Kane's autopsy reveal that his internal organs are reversed onto the other side of his body.

In order to recover more data, EUROSEC plans to retrieve the flight recorder from the *Phoenix*, which is still in Earth orbit. They build a new spacecraft, which Ross insists on christening the *Doppelganger*, and blasts off to rendezvous with the *Phoenix*, but a technical glitch damages the shuttlecraft during the docking procedure and he is forced to return to Earth. Ross attempts to land the damaged spacecraft under manual control, but the *Doppelganger* crash-lands at the space center, vaporizing Ross and destroying the facility and all of its records of the mission.

Made during the heyday of the Apollo Moon landings and a year after the release of Stanley Kubrick's ground-breaking SF epic *2001: A Space Odyssey*, *Journey to the Far Side of the Sun* exploits the contemporaneous enthusiasm for space exploration. Written and produced by the husband and wife team of Gerry and Sylvia Anderson, who were responsible for "Supermarionation" TV puppet shows like *Thunderbirds,* the film contains impressive 60s-era model work and competent special effects. On the minus side, the screenplay starts with an intriguing idea but never explains how the alternate Earth came into existence, or explicates the fate of the original Colonel Ross on the other planet. Robert Parrish's direction of the actors is wooden and uninspired, and Patrick Wymark's delivery of dialogue is especially irritating. The distinguished British actor Herbert Lom, who had starred as circus twins in the 1947 crime melodrama *Dual Alibi*, has a throwaway part with very little screen time, while Roy Thinnes, star of the sci-fi TV series *The Invaders*, is cold and stiff in his role as Colonel Ross.

This was the first non–German film, however, to self-consciously reference the legend of the doppelganger, which was the movie's alternate title. In a discussion on the genesis of the film's screenplay, co-scripter Gerry Anderson explained the concept as "a German word which means 'a copy of oneself,' and the legend goes that if you meet your doppelganger, it is the point of your death. Following that legend, clearly, I had to steer the film so that I could end it illustrating the meaning of that word."[4] While the treatment of the theme is intriguing, the concept of the doppelganger planet could have been more clearly developed. It remains unclear as to whether the alternate Earth had always existed in opposition to our planet's orbit, or if it just popped into existence out of nowhere.

The exploration of another mysterious planet was the basis for Russian director Andrei Tarkovsky's space saga *Solaris* (1972). Based on a novel by the acclaimed Polish science fiction writer Stanislaw Lem, the film takes place sometime in the future when humankind has achieved interstellar flight and has constructed a space station in orbit around the planet of Solaris in another star system. Solaris is a waterworld entirely covered by a vast ocean, and scientists believe that the planet is a sentient being and are trying to communicate with its alien intelligence. The scientific team has sent reports back to Earth concerning anomalous events occurring on the planet, and psychologist Chris Kelvin (Donatas Banionis) is assigned to travel to the space station to investigate. Kelvin sadly bids farewell to his dying father (Nikolai Grinko), who he is certain he will never see again because of the long duration space flight he must endure.

Arriving at the station, Kelvin finds everything in a state of disarray due to psychological breakdowns among the three man crew. The team leader, Dr. Gibarian (Sos Sargsyan), has committed suicide and cyberneticist Dr. Snauth (Yuri Yarvet) and biologist

Natalia Bondarchuk as the alien doppelganger of Hari in Andrei Tarkovsky's *Solaris* (1972).

Dr. Sartorius (Anatoli Solintsin) are suffering from mental problems and speak cryptically of seeing "guests" aboard the station. Kelvin sinks into an uneasy sleep and awakens to find the doppelganger of his dead wife Hari (Natalya Bondarchuk) beside him in bed. The double has no knowledge of the original Hari having committed suicide years earlier, and is confused about what has happened and why she is there. Kelvin is so terrified of the revenant that he launches her out of the station in a space capsule.

The scientists tell Kelvin that the guests are a "materialization of your memory," given human form by the enigmatic intelligence of Solaris, and that the alien force is capable of creating "an unlimited number of duplicates." Sure enough, that night another duplicate of Hari reappears in Kelvin's quarters, but this time he tries to accept her. She becomes a fourth member of the crew until Sartorius reveals that the real Hari committed suicide ten years earlier and that she is not a human being. Upset by these revelations, Hari drinks liquid oxygen in an effort to kill herself, but revives a short time later.

Kelvin begins to suffer his own mental breakdown, becomes physically ill and sleeps for an extended period. When he awakens, he finds that Hari's doppelganger has been destroyed at her own request by Snauth and Sartorius using a device called "the annihilator," and that they have decided it is time for Kelvin to return to Earth. In the last reel, Kelvin seems to be back at his father's house, as seen in the beginning of the film. As his father comes out to greet him, the camera pulls back to an extreme long shot to reveal that in reality he is on a newly formed island on the surface of Solaris, in an environment telepathically derived from his memory, and that his father is yet another doppelganger created by the planetary intelligence..

One of the most critically acclaimed science fiction films in cinema history, *Solaris* was awarded the Grand Prix prize at the 1972 Cannes Film Festival and nominated for the Palme d'Or. But like much of European cinema, compared with Hollywood standards of moviemaking, the film is slow-paced, talky, overlong, dull and pretentious. The screenplay by Tarkovsky and Fridrikh Gorenshtein takes much of the focus away from the novel's theme of the futility of communicating with an enigmatic alien intelligence and instead becomes merely a dramatic study of a failed marital relationship. There are long stretches of dialogue that digress into abstract philosophical discussions and pointless character backstory. On the plus side, the curvilinear space station sets are at once pleasing to the eye and claustrophobic and the visuals are smoothly photographed by cameraman Vadim Yusov, although special effects are minimal. Donatas Banionis plays the protagonist Kelvin as an affable everyman, but Natalya Bondarchuk's performance as the wraith-like, dead-alive Hari dominates much of the film. The most intriguing character of the piece is Solaris itself, a hypnotically swirling mass of living fluid that could have been afforded much more screen time.

Solaris contains one of the most intriguing treatments of the doppelganger theme in the science fiction film. As in *Forbidden Planet*, the film's doppelgangers (Hari and Kelvin's father) are the product of an interface between humans and a mysterious extraterrestrial intelligence that reads their thoughts and manifests them in the real world. In this case, however, the doubles are replicas of dead people, thereby combining the concept of the alien doppelganger with that of the ghost. The hapless Hari, who is actually nothing more than the memory of the personality of Kelvin's deceased wife, is doomed to re-enact the same suicidal impulses over and over again until Kelvin goes mad from guilt. It is not clear why the planetary intelligence keeps producing, "an unlimited number of duplicates," but the implication is that Solaris is probing the minds and emotions of the cosmonauts by creating the "guests" that the humans are forced to interact with. *Solaris* was remade by director Steven Soderbergh in 2002 starring George Clooney that follows Tartovsky's version closely but is inferior to the original in most respects.

Novelist Ira Levin, who had penned the enormously successful supernatural chiller *Rosemary's Baby* (1967), which became a movie mega-hit in its 1968 adaptation, followed it up with a similarly-themed novel *The Stepford Wives* in 1972. The 1975 screen version stars Katherine Ross as Joanna Eberhart, a New York City mother of two whose husband Walter (Peter Masterson) decides to remove his family from the urban blight of the big city. They relocate to the Connecticut suburb of Stepford, but Joanna, who is an aspiring photographer, is unhappy with her new environment, finding suburban life dull and unfulfilling. The other women in town seem oddly detached and she feels even more isolated when her husband starts spending increasing amounts of time at Stepford's exclusive Men's Association. One day Joanna observes her neighbor Carol (Nanette Newman) get into a minor car accident that leaves Carol oddly disoriented, performing repetitive gestures and mechanically repeating phrases before she is quickly hustled off in an ambulance.

Joanna befriends the only two other normal wives in town, the vivacious Bobbie Markowe (Paula Prentiss) and the glamorous Charmaine Wimperis (Tina Louise). The three of them try to organize a woman's consciousness-raising group in Stepford, but the other wives are totally uninterested and prefer to discuss detergents, oven cleaners and other domestic concerns. They further observe that the Stepford wives seem like zombies who are totally subservient to their husbands. Joanna is further put off by the president of the Men's Association, scientist Dale "Diz" Coba (Patrick O'Neal). One night he visits their home with the other husbands, who draw her likeness in great detail and make recordings of her voice.

Things really get scary when Charmaine returns from a weekend trip transformed into one of the zombified wives, and soon afterward the same thing happens to Bobbie. Terrified that she will also lose her individuality, Joanna consults sympathetic psychiatrist Dr. Fancher (Carol Eve Rossen) and confides to her that she thinks the husbands are in on some kind of conspiracy to turn the Stepford women into mindless submissives, and fears she will wind up, "like one of those robots in Disneyland." Dr. Fancher urges her to leave Stepford immediately, but when she returns home to pick up her kids she finds them missing and Walter is uncommunicative as to their whereabouts.

Thinking that her children are at her friend Bobbie's, she goes to her home but they aren't there. She confronts Bobbie and becomes infuriated by her friend's mindless demeanor and winds up stabbing her in the abdomen with a kitchen knife. Bobbie does not bleed or feel pain, but instead begins performing meaningless, repetitive tasks. Realizing that her friend has been replaced by a robot replica, Joanna risks sneaking into the mansion that houses the Men's Association in a desperate attempt to find her children. Instead, she encounters Diz Coba, who leads her into a room that is an exact duplicate of her bedroom at home. Her android doppelganger is waiting inside, a version of herself with larger breasts and black, reptilian eyes that rises to strangle her to death with a nylon stocking. In the last scene Joanna's replacement is shown blandly shopping in a supermarket with the other female automatons.

The plot of *The Stepford Wives* bears a resemblance to Levin's earlier novel *Rosemary's Baby*. In both books, and their film adaptations, a young wife is betrayed by her husband who has joined a mysterious cabal that seeks to manipulate her for their own nefarious purposes. Screenwriter William Goldman and director Bryan Forbes construct a taut thriller that slowly builds to a terrifying climax. The film was shot on location in the Connecticut towns of Darien, Westport and Fairfield, and like *The Other* the horrific events unfold against a backdrop of bright, cheery colors rather than somber, shadowy tones. Actresses Katherine Ross, Paula Prentiss and Tina Louise all deliver solid performances in this woman-centric thriller that wove Women's Liberation themes into the narrative but some female critics found this aspect of the film degrading. The term "Stepford wife" would enter the American lexicon as a description of a non-liberated, male-dominated suburban housewife, and the film inspired several TV sequels and a ridiculous 2004 comedic remake.

The notion of a "fembot" that is indistinguishable from a human woman goes back to the robot woman in Fritz Lang's *Metropolis*. Although the doppelganger theme in *The Stepford Wives* is largely in the realm of social satire, there is something truly chilling about the idea of the entire adult female population of a small community being reduced to the level of soulless automatons in order to satisfy the sexual whims of their husbands. Male

Bobbie Markowe (Paula Prentiss, left) is revealed to be an android double by Joanna Eberhart (Katherine Ross) in *The Stepford Wives* (1975).

viewers might feel equally degraded by the idea that all men want out of a spouse is someone who will keep quiet, clean the house and stoke their egos in bed. When Joanna asks Diz Coba why the husbands are turning them into androids, he merely replies, "Because we can." Satire aside, the climactic scene in which Joanna's blank-eyed double is revealed is disturbing, and conforms to the folkloric belief that if you meet your doppelganger you will die.

More techno-doubles were being cranked out to replace humans in *Futureworld* (1976), a sequel to Michael Crichton's sci-fi sleeper hit *Westworld* (1973). The earlier film, set sometime in the near future, featured a hi-tech resort called Delos, an island where androids cater to the fantasies of tourists in three historical domains: Roman World, Medieval World and the titular Westworld. Tourists fight faux duels with gladiators, knights and cowboys and enjoy sexual escapades with the machines within these "worlds." The iconic Yul Brynner reprised his role from the classic western *The Magnificent Seven* as a robot version of the Gunfighter in Black character who goes on a killing spree when all of the robots in Delos go haywire due to a programming glitch and become homicidal.

Futureworld is set two years after the events of the earlier film, when Delos has been reopened to the public after a massive overhaul. The Westworld theme park has been closed down and replaced with Futureworld, a new park where tourists experience bogus space-

Chuck Browning (Peter Fonda) meets robot Clark (James M. Connor, left) in *Futureworld* (1976).

flight, skiing on Mars, exploring the caves of Venus and other off-world delights. Newspaper reporter Chuck Browning (Peter Fonda) and TV newscaster Tracy Ballard (Blythe Danner) are invited by Dr. Duffy (Arthur Hill), head of the Delos Corporation, to tour the resort in the hope that they will generate positive reviews. Before he departs for the island, however, Browning is contacted by a mysterious man named Frenchy (Ed Geldard), who passes him an envelope containing newspaper clippings about prominent visitors to Delos before he is murdered.

Once they arrive on Delos, Browning and Tracy opt to explore the Futureworld section of the resort. After a simulated space flight they relax in a lounge where tourists are encouraged to have sex with the androids who are, "programmed for your pleasure." Dr. Duffy takes the journalists on a behind the scenes tour of the park's central control room, which is completely staffed by robots, and where they are introduced to the resort's head scientist, Dr. Schneider (John Ryan). That night Browning and Tracy are drugged and taken to Schneider's lab to be cloned, along with two other guests, Russian General Karnovsky (Bert Conroy) and Japanese politician Mr. Takaguchi (John Fujioka). After the procedures have been completed, the guests are returned to their rooms, unaware of what has happened to them.

The next day the journalists begin snooping around the resort's underground passageways and eventually encounter Harry (Stuart Margolin), a mechanic who lives inside the facility with his robot buddy Clark (James M. Connor). Browning shows him Frenchy's picture, and Harry recognizes him as a fellow mechanic at Delos. Before they can get any more information, however, they are interrupted by security guards and returned to their rooms. On the following day, as Tracy is testing out a machine that makes video recordings of her dreams, Browning goes back to see Harry. Together they gain access to Delos's secret research and development area, where they observe the clones of the Russian general, the Japanese politician, Tracy and Browning being programmed to kill their originals. Browning realizes that Frenchy's newsclippings about prominent visitors to the resort indicate that the Delos scientists are replacing world leaders with their manufactured clones.

The two reporters and Harry plan to leave the island the next day, but Dr. Duffy is waiting at Browning and Tracy's hotel room and holds Browning at gunpoint. The scientist explains that the world leaders have been duplicated and replaced with clones not only to ensure a positive business climate for Delos, but also to control irrational humanity and keep it from destroying itself. Duffy and Browning struggle and Duffy is shot and turns out to be an android dupe. In the meantime Tracy encounters her double in the ruins of Westworld and the two engage in a pistol duel. "I have your mind," the doppelganger tells her, "what you think, I think, what you know I know. There can be only one of us." They draw and one of them is destroyed, but it is unclear which one. As Harry is leaving for the plane, Browning's double shows up and stabs him to death, and then goes after his original. The clone chases Browning through the complex until the duplicate is thrown to its death. He meets up with Tracy and figures out she is the original by kissing her, and the couple leaves the island after having phoned in the story in to their news bureau, foiling Delos's insidious duplication scheme.

While it's something of a comedown from *Westworld*, the sequel is nevertheless a competent thriller ably lensed by director Richard T. Heffron, but the film's main problem is in the loopy screenplay by Mayo Simon and George Schenck. For instance, the Delos scientists specialize in robotics, yet they are practicing cloning, a discipline within the realm of biology, as producing and programming cybernetic machines is a far cry from duplicating living beings. The film's low point is Tracy's wholly gratuitous sequence in the dream recording machine, in which she is shown cavorting in an erotic fantasy with the Gunfighter in Black filmed in ludicrous slow motion, which is nothing but a way to sneak Yul Brynner's character into the sequel. Principals Peter Fonda and Blythe Danner deliver lukewarm performances, and although the film makes good use of the Kennedy Space Center location in Houston in the early scenes, much of the film takes place against an industrial backdrop that looks as if it was shot in a napkin factory in Toledo.

By the 1970s the concept of cloning, which was on its way to becoming scientific reality, had permeated into popular culture and had inspired several low-budget movies and telefilms that exploited the sensational aspects of human cloning, such as *Clones* (1973), *Parts—The Clonus Horror* (1978) and *The Clone Master* (1978). *Futureworld*, however, was the first treatment of the theme released by the major studios, having been produced at American International and distributed by MGM, but the film blurs the line between androids and clones. The process of creating the cloned duplicates is obscure; the Delos scientists are shown taking precise measurements of the guests they intend to replicate and the doppelgangers are completed and good to go in a couple of days. As in legend and folklore, the doppelganger aims to destroy the original person as Browning and Tracy have to fight for their lives against their sinister doubles. Telepathy between clones in a manner similar to that attributed to identical twins, was a novel concept that would later reappear in *The Island* (2005).

Another nefarious conspiracy involving clones and world leaders was presented in

The Boys from Brazil (1978), which was based on a novel by *The Stepford Wives*'s Ira Levin. This one is being hatched by a group of Nazis in South America masterminded by the notorious Josef Mengele (Gregory Peck), dubbed the "Angel of Death" for the hideous experiments he conducted at the Auschwitz concentration camp. As the film opens, American wannabe Nazi hunter Barry Kohler (Steve Guttenberg) is staking out a meeting of a Nazi society called the Comrades Organization that is being convened in a mansion in Paraguay. Kohler bugs the place and learns that the Organization has plans to assassinate 94 middle-aged civil servants who are scattered across North America and Western Europe, and afterwards relays this puzzling information to senior Nazi hunter Ezra Lieberman (Laurence Olivier). During the long-distance call, however, Kohler is killed by Nazi thugs and Lieberman, convinced that something important is going on, begins to investigate.

Mengele's enigmatic plan goes into operation as postal worker Emil Doring is murdered in West Germany. Interviewing Doring's widow, Lieberman learns nothing but encounters the murdered man's obnoxious 14-year-old son Erich (Jeremy Black). In the meantime, other suspicious killings have occurred in London and Massachusetts and Lieberman dispatches his young assistant David Bennett (John Rubenstein) to England to investigate the death of John Harrington (Michael Gough), while he travels to the States. Interviewing the family of the victim, Jack Curry, Lieberman is startled to see that the deceased's son, Jack Jr., is Erich Doring's bratty twin (Black). He learns from Curry's widow that their son was adopted from an agency run by Nazi war criminal Frieda Maloney (*The Other*'s Uta Hagen), who is serving time in prison. Calling Lieberman from London, Bennett reports meeting a third son, Simon Harrington (Black), another 14-year-old who looks exactly like the other two.

Lieberman visits Frieda in prison, where she tells him that she was set up in an adoption agency by the Comrades Organization to place 94 babies in specific households in which the father was a low-level civil servant and 20 years older than his wife. All of the babies were male, with black hair and blue eyes, and all were from Brazil. She can only remember the name of one couple, the Wheelocks of Pennsylvania.

Lieberman's investigations are causing the Comrades to get cold feet about the operation. The head of the Organization, Eduard Siebert (James Mason) visits Mengele in Paraguay to tell him that he has canceled all further assassinations in order to avoid any further publicity. Mengele is furious and vows to continue the killings himself. In the meantime, trying to get a handle on what the Nazis are up to, Lieberman pays a visit to a biologist friend, Dr. Bruckner, who explains that Erich Doring, Jack Curry, Jr., and Simon Harrington are all clones of the same individual. In a flash of insight Lieberman realizes what the Organization is up to. Mengele has created 94 clones of Adolf Hitler from samples of his DNA and has attempted to duplicate the circumstances of the Fuhrer's upbringing by placing the clones in a similar home environment. Hitler's father had died when the boy was 14, hence the series of assassinations.

Both Mengele and Lieberman converge on the Wheelock farm in rural Pennsylvania, but Mengele gets there first and kills foster father Henry Wheelock (John Dehner). When Lieberman arrives, the doctor and the Nazi hunter struggle and Lieberman is shot but manages to release the farmer's pack of Dobermans, who pin Mengele down. Just then Bobby Wheelock (Black) arrives on the scene and tries to figure out what's going on. Bobby has trained the dogs to attack by using the word "action" and desist when he says "cut," and when he discovers the body of his father he sics the Dobermans on Mengele and watches with sadistic pleasure as the dogs tear him to pieces. In the aftermath, as Lieberman is recovering in the hospital, Bennett visits him and insists that all of the boys from Brazil must be eliminated, but Lieberman, citing humanitarian concerns, burns the list of the 94 clones to ensure that this doesn't happen.

Ira Levin's intriguing plotline, as adapted by screenwriter Heywood Gould, unfolds as a science fiction mystery story under the steady direction of Franklin Schaffner, who had previously directed the doppelganger espionage thriller *The Double Man* (1967). Sporting a cast of seasoned actors that includes Michael Gough, Uta Hagen and James Mason, the film's biggest problem, however, lies with its two stars. Gregory Peck is woefully miscast as the Nazi "Angel of Death" Mengele and delivers his lines with an almost laughable approximation of a German accent, while the great Laurence Olivier, who had played a Mengele-like Nazi character in *Marathon Man* (1976), adopts a high-pitched Yiddish dialect that is highly irritating and frequently obscures the intelligibility of his dialogue.

Perhaps the most memorable characters in *The Boys from Brazil* are the boys themselves. As portrayed by Jeremy Black, these budding Fuhrers project the sinister psychopathology of the original, and the notion of nearly a hundred Hitler clones secretly growing toward maturity is disquieting. The idea that Mengele and the Comrades could replicate the environmental and societal factors that could mold the clones into full-fledged Nazi dictators is highly implausible. The way that these Hitler doppelgangers keep popping up in different locations lends their presence a feeling of the uncanny, and their very existence is the film's central mystery.

The year 1978 also saw the release of director Philip Kaufman's remake of *Invasion of the Body Snatchers*. The updated version takes place in San Francisco during the rainy winter months, where alien spores have settled on the city's vegetation and are producing strange flowering growths. Health Department worker Elizabeth Driscoll (Brooke Adams) takes one of the flowers home with her to show her boyfriend Geoffrey Howell (Art Hindle) what she believes to be a new species of plant life. The next morning Geoffrey seems changed and indifferent to her, as if he is another person. She confides her feelings to coworker Matthew Bennell (Donald Sutherland), who advises her to consult pop psychologist Dr. David Kibner (Leonard Nimoy), whose book party he is attending that night.

At the party a woman becomes hysterical, declaring that her husband is no longer her husband and Kibner attempts to soothe her with a verbal stream of New Age psychobabble. When Elizabeth explains her misgivings about her partner Geoffrey, he merely suggests that she is experiencing doubts about the relationship, but admits that there seems to be an "hallucinatory flu" of similar cases plaguing the city. Soon afterward Matthew's friend Jack Bellicec (Jeff Goldblum) and his wife Nancy (Veronica Cartwright), who operate a bath house in the city, discover a half-formed "blank" of Jack on one of the beds, and call Matthew over to investigate. The sight of the body convinces Matthew that the outbreak of doppelgangers is a real phenomenon, and he races to Elizabeth's house where he finds another blank growing in her garden. He takes Elizabeth, who is in a semi-comatose state, to his house and calls the police, but they find that both of the blanks have mysteriously disappeared.

Matthew, Elizabeth, Jack and Nancy are convinced that the population of San Fran is in the process of being replaced by doppelgangers while they sleep. They take refuge in

Matthew's home where he is almost replicated by one of the pods when he falls asleep. After this failed attempt the Pod People attack the house, but the four of them manage to escape and the two couples split up to avoid the body snatchers. Matthew and Elizabeth hide out in the Health Department building where they work, and from this vantage point they observe the doppelgangers distributing the pods to various cities and towns in the Bay Area. They are soon discovered by Jack and Dr. Kibner, who have been assimilated by the pods, and their former friends explain that they are about to enter a new world void of human emotion when they succumb to sleep and their bodies and minds are taken over by the aliens. Because they have taken a stimulant drug, however, the couple overcome their captors and flee out into the street.

Pursued through the darkened streets of the city by the pod people, Matthew and Elizabeth make their way to the waterfront, where they see pods being loaded onto cargo ships to be transported around the world. Leaving Elizabeth in a hiding place, Matthew discovers a huge warehouse where the pods are being cultivated and sets it on fire, incinerating many of the pods. When he returns, however, he finds that she has fallen asleep and her body has become a desiccated husk, whereupon her naked double arises to confront him. He flees once more, but the next day he encounters Nancy, who has not yet been taken over, and shockingly reveals that he has become one of the pod people by uttering an inhuman shriek and pointing her out to the others.

Kaufman's approach to the material is more measured than Don Siegel's roller coaster ride, and the screenplay by W.D. Richter unfolds the narrative at a more leisurely pace. Transposing the action from a small town to a major city jacks up the fear factor as an entire metropolis is overwhelmed by the pod invasion. Even prosaic garbage trucks become instruments of evil as they make their rounds through the city picking up bags full of dried-out human remains. Unlike the Siegel version, special effects are used to graphically depict the transformation from human to pod person. The film was shot almost entirely on location using San Francisco landmarks such as Union Square Park, Alamo Square, Chinatown and City Hall Park, and the Health Department Building where Matthew and Elizabeth work. Kaufman renders San Fran not in the bright, sunny tones Hitchcock used in *Vertigo*, but as a rainy, gloomy landscape that conceals an evil secret.

Principals Donald Sutherland, Brooke Adams, Jeff Goldblum and Veronica Cartwright make for a quirky repertory company that performs their roles with a touch of humor against a New Age 1970s backdrop. Leonard Nimoy, who had plenty of practice playing an unemotional alien in his role on TV's *Star Trek*, is perfectly cast as a similarly unemotional pod person. Director Don Siegel has a cameo as a cab driver and Kevin McCarthy appears as a wild-eyed doomsayer proclaiming the invasion in a send-up of the original movie. Despite the downbeat ending, the film proved to be a critical and popular success and is considered one of the most effective remakes in film history.

The film posits an entire city populated by alien doppelgangers, mindless hordes that chase the characters through the nighted streets in a frenzy. In a brief prologue at the beginning of the film the aliens are depicted as gelatinous creatures rising into the atmosphere of their home world as they begin their journey to Earth. They descend onto our planet inside raindrops that are absorbed by plant life and are transformed into sinister flowers. Because the audience is shown the reality of the invasion from the beginning, there is no suspense as to the situation being a delusion or "hallucinatory flu." Unlike the 50s version, the remake shows the destruction of the original person as the pods absorb their life force and turn them into desiccated husks that are thrown into the garbage.

John W. Campbell's classic pulp novella *Who Goes There?* featured a shape-shifting extraterrestrial xenomorph discovered by a scientific team in the Arctic. The story was first lensed by Howard Hawks as *The Thing from Another World* in 1951, but the 50s version of the Campbell story dispensed with the notion of an alien shape-shifter that could mimic humans and form itself into their doppelgangers and simply made the alien being into a vampire from outer space. In 1982 cult director John Carpenter helmed a remake that followed the plotline of the original more closely.

The locale has been shifted to the Antarctic, where, as the film opens, a helicopter from a Norwegian research camp is inexplicably hunting a sled dog through the snow toward an American scientific outpost. The chopper is accidentally destroyed during landing and the pilot is killed, but the passenger keeps trying to shoot the dog, wounding one of the Americans before he is shot dead by the American station commander Garry (Donald Moffat). An American helicopter is promptly dispatched to the Norwegian base flown by hard-drinking pilot R.J. MacReady (Kurt Russell) with base physician Dr. Copper (Richard Dysart) on board to investigate, while the dog is taken into the facility by husky wrangler Clark (Richard Masur).

MacReady and Dr. Copper find the Norwegian outpost a charred, deserted ruin littered with corpses. They bring one of the bodies, a horribly deformed corpse that looks like it has two faces melted together, back to their base along with a number of videotapes made by the Norwegian expedition. After they return, Clark puts the Malamute into the kennel with the other dogs, but it turns into a bloody monstrosity that kills off the dogs before it is incinerated with a flamethrower. The team's biologist, Blair (Wilfred Brimley) performs an autopsy on the two-faced corpse that leads to the conjecture that they are dealing with an organism that perfectly imitates and absorbs other life forms. Playing back videotapes, they learn that the Norwegians had excavated a UFO that had been buried under the Antarctic ice for 100,000 years. They also find out that the Norwegians had discovered the craft's occupant, chipped it out of the ice, and brought it back to their base for analysis. After being thawed out, the alien creature was restored to life and wrecked havoc at the Norwegian outpost.

The Americans realize that they are dealing with a shape-shifting alien that has entered their base in the form of the Malamute. Because the unsuspecting humans had let the dog roam freely around the base, it could have absorbed and replaced any of the men. Blair calculates that there is a 75 percent possibility that at least one of the team members has been infected, and that the entire population of the world would be absorbed and replicated in a matter of months after first contact. Crazed by this dire knowledge, Blair sabotages the helicopter and smashes the radio to isolate the base and prevent the alien from escaping, whereupon he is kept isolated from the others in an equipment shed.

Despite their best efforts, several members of the team are found to be doppelgangers and metamorphose into revolting monsters before being dispatched by flamethrowers. The remaining men descend into paranoia and turn on each other, and when Commander Garry becomes suspect, MacReady assumes de facto authority over the group. Pondering the dilemma of "how do we know who's human?" MacReady hits on a solution. Knowing that each separate part of the creature is alive, he proposes that they all give a blood sample into which a heated wire will be inserted into the sample; if the blood moves away from the wire, that person is an alien. When the test is administered, all of the men turn out to be human except Palmer (David Clennon), who transforms into one of the things before being flamed out.

Unfortunately, it turns out that Blair has been assimilated and another man, Childs (Keith David) is missing. Soon afterward the base's electrical generator is destroyed and MacReady realizes that the alien intends to let them all freeze to death in the Antarctic cold while it will survive until a relief mission arrives in the spring. Knowing that they are all dead men, MacReady orders the dynamiting of the base, which will hopefully kill off any of the remaining creatures. After the blast goes off only MacReady is left alive, but Childs mysteriously reappears. The film ends with the two men sitting in the burning ruins of the camp, and the issue of whether or not the alien has survived is left unresolved.

For all of Carpenter's skill as a horror director, *The Thing* fails to generate much suspense, but instead relies on lurid special effects sequences for their shock value. Part of the problem lies in the low key performances of its all-male cast, including action hero Kurt Russell and character actor Wilfred Brimley, who exhibit little in the way of characterization. The exteriors, shot in northern British Columbia, are snowy and picturesque but fail to accentuate the supposedly icebound isolation of the men during the harsh Antarctic winter. Russell traipses around outdoors wearing nothing but a bomber jacket in what is purportedly 40 to 100 degrees below zero weather. The film's real stars are the special effects created by F/X wizards Rob Bottin and Stan Winston that are truly nightmarish, including a bloody mass of snarling dog flesh and a man-headed spider thing. These gruesome creature creations pleased fans of gore and violence, but the film sometimes seems like a group of disjointed effects sequences in search of a movie. By not showing the finding of the buried saucer and the thawing out of the creature directly, two of the story's most dramatic scenes are deleted. The film's ambiguous ending fails to provide dramatic closure and concludes the action too abruptly.

Carpenter's version of *The Thing*, written by Bill Lancaster (the son of screen star Burt Lancaster), follows the plot of the Campbell story closely. Taking a cue from earlier genre films, the alien beings are able to form themselves into doppelgangers of human beings. The film also drew inspiration from Ridley Scott's 1979 sci-fi megahit *Alien*, which also featured a shape-shifting extraterrestrial xenomorph killing off humans within a confined space. Because the Thing appears in so many guises, it's not clear exactly what its original form is; in the Campbell novella the creature frozen in the ice has three eyes and snakelike tentacles for hair. Note that the xenomorph is not only able to mimic the forms of the men perfectly, but it is also able to copy their memories and mannerisms as well, although it is not clear how this is accomplished.

Decades later, producers Marc Abraham and Eric Newman hit on creating a prequel to Carpenter's movie, set in 1982, that would depict the events that occurred at the Norwegian camp before the Americans became involved. Scenarist Eric Heisserer was assigned to "reverse engineer" the narrative from the materials that had appeared in the earlier film. The prequel, also titled *The Thing*, was directed by Matthijs van Heijninger, Jr., and released by Universal in 2011.

The film begins with the discovery of a massive flying saucer excavated from underneath the Antarctic ice by a Norwegian research team at Thule Station. The head scientist on the team, Dr. Sander Halvorson (Ulrich Thomsen), and his assistant, American scientist Adam Finch (Eric Christian Olsen), ask for assistance in evaluating the find, so American paleontologist Kate Lloyd (Mary Elizabeth Winstead) is flown into Thule by helicopter pilot Sam Carter (Joel Edgerton), along with co-pilot Derek Jameson (Adewale Akinnuoye-Agbaje) and crew chief Griggs (Paul Braunstein).

After viewing the crash site, the Americans are informed that an alien being was found near the crashed saucer and has been transported to the station while still frozen inside a block of ice. That night, as the scientists celebrate their discoveries, the alien breaks out of its icy coffin and escapes. When the team catches up with the alien they find it has partially assimilated one of the scientists, Henrik (Jo Adrian Haavind), and they incinerate the Thing with flamethrowers. An examination of the remains reveals that Henrik's body was contained inside the alien's body in a kind of amniotic sac, and the creature's cells had been replicating his own human cells. This means that any one of them may be an alien doppelganger in human guise.

The next day, as Derek, Carter and Griggs prepare to evacuate an ailing team member, Kate discovers blood in a shower stall along with small bits of metal that turn out to be dental fillings. She theorizes that the Thing can copy and assimilate living tissue, but not inorganic matter, and fearing that one of the crew has been transformed and is aboard the helicopter, she rushes outside and motions for it to land. Unfortunately, Griggs turns into the creature and attacks, causing the chopper to crash and burn. When Kate returns to the shower stall, she finds that someone has cleaned up all the blood.

Mass paranoia ensues as the scientists try to figure out who's human and who's not. Remembering the metal dental filings that could not be reproduced by the Thing, Kate comes up with a partial humanity test. Each team member is compelled to say "ahh" and their mouths examined for metal fillings, but the test doesn't apply to those who have porcelain dental work or excellent oral hygiene. After several team members are shown to be human, they know that the creature is still among them when the Thing manifests itself as a grotesque being breaking out of its human guise into a mass of teeth and writhing tentacles.

In the end Thule Station is engulfed in flames and Kate and Carter pursue Sanders, who they suspect of having been infected, back to the UFO, thinking the alien will try to escape in the craft. The machine sweeps Kate deep into the mechanism of the saucer, where she encounters a grotesque monstrosity still wearing Sanders's face and blasts it with the flamethrower, which causes the machine to shut down. Carter rejoins Kate and they contemplate trying to make it to a Russian outpost in their Snowcat vehicle until Kate notices that Carter is minus the earring he always wears and, realizing he is the Thing, incinerates him. The film ends ambiguously with Kate sitting in the vehicle trying to figure out her next move. In an epilogue shown over the closing credits, two of the remaining Norwegians are shown hunting down a Malamute dog, which is really the Thing, in a helicopter as the movie cycles back into the opening sequence of the 1982 film.

This unnecessary prequel does little to improve on the earlier version. The special effects have been ramped up to 21st-century standards using CGI techniques, but Matthijs van Heijningen's direction is competent but flat and uninspired and marred by the overuse of hand-held camera. Lead actress Mary Elizabeth Winstead attempts to play a character that is at once a vulnerable female and an aggressive leader, and fails on both counts. The rest of the cast is equally uninspired, and like the earlier version, the film relies too much on effects at the expense of the human element. The worst fault of Eric Heisserer's screenplay is the ambiguous ending that leaves the fate of the main character unresolved but suggests that she failed to survive the ordeal. Campbell's method of separating the humans from the doppelgangers by testing their blood, which was used in the '82 version, has been discarded and replaced by the silliness of examining the team's dental work.

Carpenter's version of *The Thing* was released during the "sci-fi summer" of 1982, along with a gaggle of high profile genre entries that included *Blade Runner, The Road Warrior, Tron* and Steven Spielberg's superhit *E.T.—The Extraterrestrial. The Thing* was crushed by the box-office competition, but two years later Carpenter would direct another movie featuring an alien doppelganger that was the diametrical opposite of the horrifying extraterrestrials depicted in the earlier film, entitled *Starman* (1984).

Starman begins with a prologue showing the unmanned Voyager spacecraft launched from Earth in 1977 leaving the solar system and traveling to a planet orbiting another star. In response, an alien ship leaves the planet bound for Earth to establish contact with humankind. When the alien ship reaches our planet, however, it is shot down by the U.S. military and crash-lands in a rural area of Wisconsin in the vicinity of Ashland. A small blue light issues forth from the downed ship and floats to the nearby home of Jenny Hayden (Karen Allen).

Jenny is grieving after the recent loss of her husband, Scott (Jeff Bridges), and has been watching home movies of him on her projector before going to sleep. The blue light enters her home and roams about the habitation to familiarize itself with Earth life and culture. After scanning Scott's features from a photograph, it finds a lock of Scott's hair inside a scrapbook and uses the DNA contained in the hair to fashion itself into Scott's double. Waking from sleep, Jenny is horrified when confronted by the simulacrum of Scott, but the Starman explains that his spaceship has been destroyed and that he needs to rendezvous with a rescue ship that will land in Barringer Crater, located just outside Winslow, Arizona, in three days or he will perish.

The rest of the film unfolds as a road movie as Jenny reluctantly accompanies Starman on a cross-country trip from Wisconsin to Arizona. They are pursued by a team of U.S. government saucer busters led by NSA director George Fox (Richard Jaekel) and SETI scientist Mark Shermin (Charles Martin Smith). Their objective is to capture Starman and dissect him, a goal that does not sit well with Shermin. As they flee across several states, Jenny is at first an unwilling hostage, but one night at a diner rest stop she watches Starman use his powers to restore a deer that a hunter has killed to life, and finds the act endearing. Soon afterward he must perform the same magic on Jenny when she is badly wounded by a policeman's bullets.

During the final phase of their journey they are riding in a boxcar together and make love. In the aftermath, Starman tells her that he has given her a baby even though she was previously infertile. It will be a male child, a human/alien hybrid that will grow up to be a great teacher. In the meantime, the agency has computed the trajectory of the alien's ship before it was shot down and knows the landing location was to be in Arizona's Barringer Crater, the site of an ancient meteoric impact. As Starman and Jenny near their destination they are apprehended by Shermin and some local police, but Jenny convinces him to let them go as Starman is clearly on his last legs and will die if he doesn't reach the ship.

They finally reach the crater as Fox sends a squadron of helicopters after them, intending to capture the alien dead or alive. At that moment an enormous spherical ship of gleaming metal descends on the crater, scattering the copters like flies. Starman and Jenny share a tearful goodbye and the alien gives her a small metal sphere that will be a gift to their son and ascends into the heavens in the spaceship.

Starman is perhaps John Carpenter's finest film, a heartwarming love story that is quite unlike the main body of the director's oeuvre of horror thrillers. The film strikes just the right balance between science fiction, romance and comedy along with religious overtones. Jeff Bridges's performance as the extraterrestrial visitor is nothing short of brilliant and would earn him an Academy Award nomination for Best Actor. He portrays this stranger in a strange land with humor and dignity, using herky-jerky head movements that connote his curiosity and otherness. Karen Allen's supporting performance as Starman's reluctant accomplice is almost as impressive, and Charles Martin Smith shines in his role as the SETI scientist with a heart of gold. Composer Jack Nitzsche received a Golden Globe Award nomination for his rousing orchestral score for the film.

This is perhaps the only instance in which an alien body snatcher is represented in a positive light. The Starman is a benign doppelganger, a seemingly bodiless intelligence who assumes Scott's appearance via "symbiotic transformation" in order to appeal to Jenny, or as he puts it in his peculiar syntax, "I look like Scott so you will not be a little bit jumpy." Both alien technology and cloning are utilized to create Scott's double. In reality he is a Jesus-like figure who descends from the heavens and has the healing power to restore life to the dead. Starman resembles similar alien Christs such as the saintly Klaatu in *The Day the Earth Stood Still* (1951) and the cute and cuddly E.T. in *E.T.—The Extraterrestrial*. He hails from a heavenly, utopian world where there is no war, hunger or mass suffering. Note that the Voyager spacecraft was also responsible for bringing aliens into contact with humankind in *Star Trek: The Motion Picture* (1978).

Time travel doppelgangers abounded in Robert Zemeckis's popular sci-fi comedy *Back to the Future* series of films. Unlike some time travel tales, in which the past, present and future are immutable and unchangeable, the series posits a temporal continuum that is plastic and subject to change, and having direct interaction with one's former selves can result in unforeseen consequences.

The protagonist in all three films is one Marty McFly (Michael J. Fox), a young, aspiring guitar player growing up in the suburban community of Hill Valley, California. The first entry in the series, *Back to the Future* (1985), takes place in 1985, where Marty hangs out with his zany inventor pal Dr. Emmet Brown (Christopher Lloyd), who shows him a time machine he has invented that is fitted inside a DeLorean sports car. The Doc explains that the machine is powered by plutonium he has pilfered from a group of Libyan terrorists, but as they are testing the device the Libyans show up and shoot Doc to death. While escaping in the DeLorean, Marty accidentally activates the time machine and is propelled 30 years into the past to the year 1955.

Through a series of comic misadventures, Marty becomes involved with the past selves of his father, George (Crispin Glover), and his mother, Lorraine (Lea Thompson), and runs afoul of high school bully Biff Tannen (Thomas F. Wilson) and his gang of reprobates. Marty must ensure that George and Lorraine get married or he will cease to exist. Trying to return to his own time, he contacts the younger version of Doc Brown, who informs him that, absent the DeLorean's plutonium fuel they will have to harness the electricity of a lightning storm to power the time machine back to the future. Marty warns the Doc about what will happen to him in 1985, but the scientist is reluctant to do anything that will alter events in the future.

That night, at the Hill Valley High School dance, Marty's plan to bring George and Lorraine together comes to fruition, while Marty jams with the band onstage and delivers a blistering electric guitar solo. His mission accomplished, he joins Doc, who has wired up the DeLorean to a lightning rod in the town square. A bolt of electricity from the lightning storm provides enough power to send the DeLorean back to 1985. Marty arrives at the moment Doc is shot, and briefly observes his 1985 self running for the DeLorean to escape the Libyans. Checking on Doc Brown, he discovers that he is not dead, having heeded Marty's warning and protected himself with a bulletproof vest. He takes possession of the time machine, while Marty is reunited with his girlfriend, Jennifer (Claudia Wells), but before long Doc shows up and insists they must travel forward in time to 2015 to fix some problems that have arisen in the future. The film ends with the three of them getting into the DeLorean and embarking on another time travel adventure.

While the first film only provided a glimpse of Marty's time paradox doppelganger, in the sequel, *Back to the Future Part II* (1989), all of the major characters encounter their doubles through time travel. The narrative picks up where it left off at the end of the first movie, with Marty, his girlfriend Jennifer (played here by Elizabeth Shue) getting into Doc Brown's DeLorean time machine to straighten out problems that have arisen in the year 2015. Slipping through a time warp, they arrive in a futuristic Hill Valley replete with flying cars, weather control, holograms, antigravity hoverboards, fusion power and other technological marvels. Explaining that "no one should know too much about their future," Doc uses an electronic device to render Jennifer unconscious and conceals her in an alley. Having tooled around the time stream, Doc knows that Marty's son, Marty Junior, is about to be pressured into participating in a robbery that will land him in prison, and wants Marty to stand in for his son, who is as alike as a twin, and prevent this dire event from occurring. Before sending him out on this mission, Doc tells him, "don't interact with anyone, try not to look at anything," for fear of creating further time paradoxes.

The wimpy Marty Jr. is being harassed by bully Griff Tannen (Thomas F. Wilson), who is the grandson of Biff from the first movie, into committing the robbery, but gets knocked out during Griff's physical intimidation and replaced by his doppelganger, Marty. Marty defies Griff and his gang and is chased through the town square on hoverboards until the gang smashes up some property and gets arrested. Having saved his son from a terrible fate, Marty spies a sports almanac for the years 1950–2000 in a store window and buys it, thinking he will make some money from knowing the outcome of sports events. When he rejoins Doc Brown, however, the scientist forbids Marty from taking the almanac back to 1985 with him and forces him to discard it. Unknown to them, Biff Tannen, who is now an old man in 2015, has eavesdropped on their conversation and retrieves the almanac.

Before they can return to 1985, however, the police discover Jennifer's unconscious body and return her to her 2015 residence, where she awakens and is disoriented when she finds herself inside the futuristic house. She hides from the McFly family and when she tries to slip out the front door she encounters her 2015 self, which causes them both to faint. In the meantime, Marty and Doc have followed her to the McFly home and are in turn followed by Biff. While they are ministering to Jennifer, Biff steals the time machine with the almanac in it, travels back to 1955 and gives the almanac to 1955 Biff so he can bet on sports events and make a fortune. He then travels forward to 2015 and exits the DeLorean, with no one the wiser.

Marty and Doc load the unconscious Jennifer into the time machine and travel back to 1985, but find Hill Valley changed beyond recognition because Biff has used the information in the almanac to make a fortune and is now a crime boss who rules the town. In this alternate reality 1985, Marty's father died years ago, his mother is now married to Biff, and Doc Brown has been committed to an insane asylum. Marty is now Biff's son, and confronts his "father" inside Biff's palatial casino, where he learns that he obtained the almanac from his future self on November 12, 1955. Biff tries to murder Marty, who escapes into Doc's flying DeLorean as the pair head back to 1955 to put things right.

November 12 happens to be the night of the big dance at Hill Valley High from the first movie. Marty is charged with the task of retrieving the almanac from Biff, but cautions him that "you must be very careful not to run into your other self." Doc heeds his own advice when he encounters his 1955 self and conceals his identity from his double. Meanwhile, Marty manages to get hold of the almanac and is pursued by Biff and his gang as his time traveling doppelganger from the first movie performs his guitar solo onstage. The almanac changes hands several times before Marty finally obtains it when Biff gets into a car accident. Marty burns the almanac to ashes, thereby transforming the 1985 alternate

Marty McFly (Michael J. Fox) must be careful not to make contact with his time-traveling doppelganger in *Back to the Future Part II* (1989).

reality back to normalcy, but before he can return to his own time the DeLorean is struck by lightning and disappears, stranding him in 1955. In a build-up to the next movie in the series, a letter is delivered to Marty indicating that Doc is alive and well, having been transported back through time to 1885.

The *Back to the Future* series proved to be enormously successful at the box office, thanks to the brisk direction of Robert Zemeckis, the effervescent screen persona of star Michael J. Fox, the comic genius of co-star Christopher Lloyd and the fine performances of the supporting players. The plot of *Back to the Future II*, penned by Zemeckis and Bob Gale, is the most complex of the three movies in the series, playing off the notions of mind-boggling time paradoxes and alternate realities within the realms of the real-world 1985, the futureworld of 2015, the alternate universe of 1985 and the 1955 of the first movie. Although the 2015 future pictured in the film in no way resembled the real world of 2015, the film portrayed the future in a positive light as opposed to the dystopias depicted in many science fiction films. Special effects consortium Industrial Light & Magic employed novel film techniques such as the VistaGlide motion control camera system and digital compositing that seamlessly allowed the actors and their doppelgangers to be depicted onscreen at the same time.

One of the film's most intriguing aspects is the depiction of time travel doppelgangers, where different versions of the same person can exist in the same temporal frame via time travel. Thus, Marty has numerous doubles in the film, including his 2015 self, his lookalike son Marty Jr., and his time traveling self from the first movie. Villain Biff Tannen appears as his 2015 self, his 1955 self, and as his grandson, Griff. Jennifer and Doc Brown also encounter their time travel doubles. Except for the two versions of Biff, the other characters have minimal contact with their doppelgangers, lest they create paradoxes in the time stream that alter reality in negative ways. This idea is an update of the folkloric belief that encountering one's double is highly unlucky or can lead to the annihilation of the self. The third movie in the series, *Back to the Future Part III* (1990), involves Marty's and Doc's adventures in the old west, and ties up the loose ends of the previous films. It features doppelgangers in the form of Marty's great grandparents Seamus and Maggie McFly and Biff's ancestor, Buford "Mad Dog" Tannen, but does not delve into the time paradox aspect of the doubles.

Jack Finney's seminal novel of alien invasion got a third go round in director Abel Ferrara's adaptation, titled *Body Snatchers* (1993). The action has been moved away from the California locales of the novel and the previous screen versions to a U.S. Army base in Alabama, where Environmental Protection Agency agent Steve Malone (Terry Kinney) has been assigned to assess the possible effects of chemical pollution on the surrounding ecosystem caused by the storage of chemical warfare weapons at the base. Accompanying him are his second wife, Carol (Meg Tilly), their son Andy (Reilly Murphy) and his daughter by the previous marriage Marti (Gabrielle Anwar), who are going to spend their summer at the base during his inspection.

Once the family is billeted at the base, Marti takes up with the commander's daughter Jenn Platt (Christine Elise), an Army brat and rebellious kindred spirit. Andy is placed in day care, but becomes distressed by the conformity of the other kids and runs away. He is brought home by Tim Young (Billy Wirth), a helicopter pilot who Marti takes an immediate liking to. In the meantime, Steve confers with the base's medical officer, Major Collins (Forest Whitaker), who questions him about an outbreak of narcophobia, or fear of sleep, that is going around the base, and it's possible relationship to chemical pollution. That night, as Marti and Tim go out on a date, a troop of soldiers is shown picking up slimy green pods from the bottom of a nearby river.

During that same evening, Andy wakes up during the night and enters his parent's bedrooms to find the dried-out husk of his mother's skin lying on the floor and is further terrified when his mother's double emerges from a closet totally naked. The child insists that his mother is no longer his mother, but no one will believe him. The next night Marti is almost taken over by the pods when she dozes off while taking a bath, and Steve likewise narrowly avoids becoming a pod person. As Steve, Marti and Andy flee for their lives, the pseudo-Carol taunts them by saying, "Where you gonna go, where you gonna run, where you gonna hide? Nowhere, 'cause there's no one like you left."

The pod people are in the process of taking over the base and pursue the remaining human family members until Steve, Marti and Andy take refuge in a warehouse. Steve leaves Andy and Marti in their hiding place and goes to Major Collins's office to get a handle on what's going on. His visit is interrupted by a group of the Pod People led by the base commander, General Platt (R. Lee Ermey) as Steve watches from concealment. The General tries to soothe Collins with the usual Pod talk about how wonderful things will be once he has surrendered his humanity and individuality. He also explains that the Pods are alien life forms from outer space who are destined to take over planet Earth. Collins blows his brains out with a revolver rather than submit to the Pod People's agenda.

When Steve returns to the warehouse to lead his children to safety, Marti figures out that their father has been replicated, but Tim arrives and shoots Steve, who decomposes into a slimy lump of protoplasm. As Tim tries to commandeer a chopper he is separated from Andy and Marty, who are taken to the base infirmary where people are being turned into Pods in assembly-line fashion. Marti's conversion into her alien double is almost complete when she is rescued by Tim, and they are joined by Andy on their way to the aircraft hanger, but soon after takeoff Andy, who has been turned into one of the Pods, attacks him in an effort to get the helicopter to crash. The child is thrown out of the chopper to his death, and Tim and Marti manage to make it to a military base in Atlanta and the film's ambiguous ending.

Easily the least impressive of the three versions of the Finney novel, *Body Snatchers* is also the least faithful to the book. The locale has been changed and all of the original characters have been replaced. The first half of the film seems more like a drama about the problems of a dysfunctional family but the narrative manages to hit its sci-fi-horror stride in the second half. There are some truly horrific moments, such as Andy's mother emerging from the closet stark naked, the creepy Pod transformation scenes, and the child being ejected from the helicopter, but the acting and direction seem otherwise uninspired, with the exception of Meg Tilly's coolly evil Pod persona and future Oscar winner Forest Whitaker's histrionic performance as the suicidal Major Collins. The movie's distributor, Warner Brothers, gave the film a very limited release, consigning it to box-office oblivion.

As in the other versions of *Body Snatchers*, the suspense lies in not knowing who is human and who is a doppelganger. The scenes that depict the original people being replicated by the Pods are more graphic and are shown in greater detail than in the earlier versions. Tendrils worm their way inside the nose and mouth of the victim while a human form is shown growing inside the Pod, which seems like an obscene travesty of a womb. The alien origin of the Pods is obscured to the point that it is unclear until late in the film that they are not a product of toxic chemical contamination but are extraterrestrial in nature. The film's ambiguous ending makes it unclear whether the entire world has been subdued by the Pod doubles of humanity. A fourth version of Finney's work, entitled *The Invasion* was released in 2007 that dispenses with the doppelganger theme entirely in favor of having humans taken over by a plague of fungal spores from outer space.

In the wake of the *Back to the Future* series and James Cameron's groundbreaking sci-fi actioner *Terminator* 2 (1991), time travel science fiction adventures starring action stars became a hot ticket in the 1990s. *Timecop* (1994) starred Belgian martial arts star Jean-Claude Van Damme (a.k.a the "Muscles from Brussels") as the titular temporal policeman. The film begins in 1994, when time travel has become a technological reality and a clandestine government agency called the Time Enforcement Commission (TEC) is being set up to monitor anomalies in the time stream due to criminal misuse of this new technology. The fledgling agency is placed under the jurisdiction of U.S. Senator Aaron McComb (Ron Silver). Max Walker (Van Damme) is a cop who has just joined TEC is at home with his wife, Melissa (Mia Sara), when they are attacked by a team of vicious thugs who set off a bomb that blows up the house and kills Melissa, while Walker is beaten within an inch of his life but survives to join the fledgling time travel police force.

In 2004, ten years after these events, the TEC is a fully functioning organization under the direction of Commissioner Eugene Matuzak (Bruce McGill) and Walker is a seasoned temporal enforcer. Walker is sent back to 1929 to prevent renegade agent Lyle Atwood (Jason Schombing) from manipulating the stock market, but while apprehending Atwood he learns that the former agent is acting on behalf of Senator McComb, who needs money to continue his 2004 presidential campaign. Rather than turn state's evidence against McComb, who has threatened his family, Atwood chooses to jump out of his office window to his death.

On his next assignment, Walker is sent back to 1994 with his new partner, rookie Sarah Fielding (Gloria Reuben) to investigate McComb's suspicious dealings with Jack Parker (Kevin McNulty), whose company has developed a revolutionary computer chip. They witness a meeting where McComb is hesitant to invest in the new technology firm, but in the middle of negotiations the 2004 version of McComb materializes along with several members of his goon squad. Knowing the firm's tech stock will make a fortune in the future, the 2004 McComb makes his 1994 counterpart, who is a much more passive version of himself, purchase the company. He also explains that the two McCombs must never come into physical contact with one another because, "the same matter cannot occupy the same space at the same time." When Walker attempts to intervene in the transaction, the 2004 McComb kills Parker and his partner Fielding turns on him, but is herself gravely wounded.

Walker manages to escape back to 2004, where he finds everything changed. McComb is in the process of disbanding the TEC, and Matuzak, no longer recognizes him. Playing on his boss's contempt for McComb, he convinces Matuzak to send him back to 1994 once more to restore order and thwart McComb's scheme to become president by getting agent Fielding to testify against him. After doing the time warp to '94, Walker locates Fielding in a hospital, and after she agrees to testify she is killed by one of McComb's agents, but while he is there he happens to catch a glimpse of Melissa and resolves to prevent her death, which is due to occur that night.

Carefully avoiding his 1994 self, he approaches Melissa and tells her he is from the future and arranges to be at their house that evening. As before, McComb's men show up, but this time the two Walkers are there to fight them off, although the '04 Walker must hide his actions from his past self. After the hoods have all been disposed of, the future Walker squares off against the future version of McComb, who has taken Melissa hostage and threatens to explode a bomb. Unexpectedly, the '94 McComb, who has been summoned to the house by a phone call from Walker, enters the room, and Walker pushes the two versions of McComb together. Since the same matter cannot co-exist with itself at the same time, the two McCombs fuse into a writhing mass of protoplasm that disappears into nothingness. The future Walker saves Melissa from the bomb and returns to his own time to find his wife alive and well, along with their nine-year-old son.

Based on a Dark Horse Comics graphic novel written by Mark Verheiden and Mike Richardson and adapted for the screen by the authors, *Timecop* is a fast-paced science fiction thriller that unfolds smoothly under the able direction of Peter Hyams, who had handled similar material well in *Outland* (1981). The film's time machine is a fun invention that consists of a rocket sled-like device mounted on rails that aims at a solid wall before propelling the time travelers into the past (time travel past 2004 isn't possible because "the future doesn't exist yet"). When the passengers reach their destination, however, the machine is nowhere to be seen and the characters seem to pop into reality through an elastic bubble. *Timecop* is considered Van Damme's best effort, but a number of critics thought it compared unfavorably with Arnold Schwarzenegger's similarly-themed time travel thriller *Terminator 2*. Ron Silver very nearly steals the show in his dual role as twin selves from different times.

Timecop presents the most plausible scientific rationale for the belief that it is perilous to encounter one's doppelganger because "the same matter cannot occupy the same space at the same time." The merging of the two Senator McCombs, depicted using computer generated special effects, is the climactic sequence of the film. As in *Back to the Future Part II*, the time roving doubles must avoid direct contact with each other as much as possible to avoid creating temporal anomalies, and while Walker observes this rule, McComb comes to grief violating it. The interplay between the twin McCombs seems almost like a comic duet, with the older self dominating the younger, who comes off as less sinister and a bit of a dim bulb as well. *Timecop* also started a trend toward the doppelganger being a feature of sci-fi adventure vehicles for action stars such as Arnold Schwarzenegger, Keanu Reeves, Bruce Willis, Tom Cruise and Jet Li.

In 1962, French avant-garde filmmaker Chris Marker produced a short film entitled *La Jetée* (*The Pier*), a tale involving a post-apocalyptic time traveler who meets his doppelganger in an unexpected fashion. In the early 1990s, Universal greenlighted a feature-length adaptation of the film. David Peebles, who had co-written *Blade Runner* (1982), authored a screenplay with his wife Janet that was based on the Marker film but greatly expanded the narrative into feature length. Sci-fi/fantasy director Terry Gilliam, formerly of Britain's Monty Python comedy troupe and director of science-fantasy films such as *Time Bandits* (1981) and *Brazil* (1986), signed on to direct the project, entitled *12 Monkeys* (1995).

The film opens with a title stating, "Five billion people will die from a deadly virus in 1997. The survivors will abandon the surface of the planet." In the year 2035 the remnants

James Cole (Bruce Willis) explores a plague-ridden Philadelphia in *12 Monkeys* (1995).

of human civilization eke out a hellish existence living beneath the surface, which is contaminated by the deadly germ. Humankind's only hope of survival lies in a time travel device invented by future scientists, who intend to send people back in time to prevent the plague from occurring. Violent, antisocial prisoner James Cole (Bruce Willis) is selected to "volunteer" on a mission to go back in time and make contact with a clandestine organization called the "Army of the 12 Monkeys," a group of radical animal rights activists who were responsible for loosing the deadly virus on the world. Cole has been picked "because I remember things," and the thing he remembers most vividly is seeing a man being shot to death as a boy while visiting an airport with his parents. He continues to have recurring dreams about this event, memories that have some hidden significance which enable him to travel to the past more freely.

Unfortunately, "science ain't an exact science with these clowns," and imperfections in the time travel process strand Cole in Baltimore, in the year 1990, six years too early to complete the mission. He is arrested wandering the streets as a vagrant and sent to a mental hospital, where he is diagnosed as a paranoid schizophrenic and placed under the care of clinical psychiatrist Dr. Kathryn Railly (Madeleine Stowe), who is intrigued by his story of being a time traveler from the future. In the asylum he is befriended by fellow inmate Jeffrey Goines (Brad Pitt), a hyperactive nutcase whose father is Nobel-prize winning virologist Dr. Leland Goines (Christopher Plummer).

The mystery around Cole deepens when, after an attempted escape, he is placed in restraints inside a solitary cell and vanishes in a seemingly impossible fashion. He has been summoned back to 2035 where he reports on his time trip to the scientists running the project. Encouraged by his contact with Jeffrey, who is thought to be involved with the 12 Monkeys, he is sent back to 20th-century Baltimore again, and on this occasion he lands in 1996, an opportune time to prevent the plague. He seeks out Dr. Railly and kidnaps her, thinking that she can help him on his quest. At first she is horrified and rebellious, but little by little she begins to bond empathically with Cole and comes to believe his story when he exhibits seemingly precognitive knowledge of events. Cole traces the activist group to Philadelphia, where they make contact with members of the 12 Monkeys and learn that Jeffrey Goines is their leader and is able to send a message back to the future via an elaborate telephone hookup. While slumming around a bad neighborhood in Philly they are attacked by a couple of violent street toughs and Cole winds up beating one of them to death. Now wanted for kidnapping and murder, the police close in, but before they can capture him Cole vanishes mysteriously once more.

The scientists in 2035 decide to send Cole back to 1996 again to finalize the mission, but the time traveler's sanity has been seriously compromised. "The human mind," he muses, "is not meant to exist in two different dimensions." He is sent back anyway and encounters Dr. Railly at the rundown headquarters of the 12 Monkeys in Philadelphia, but this time he has had a psychotic break and is barely functioning. It turns out that Jeffrey Goines and the Monkeys are merely pulling a prank by letting animals out of the city zoo, and the real culprit is Leland Goines's assistant, Dr. Peters (David Mires), who has stolen vials of a deadly bio-engineered virus from his laboratory and intends to fly around the world infecting the human populations of every continent with the disease. Railly takes it upon herself to voicemail the future that they are on the wrong track because the Monkeys are not responsible for the plague that will decimate humankind.

Cole is still wanted by the police, so Railly buys disguises for both of them and makes arrangements to fly to Florida. While they are at the airport, however, Cole is approached by two of his fellow time travelers from 2035 who have been alerted to the situation. They give him a handgun and order him to kill Dr. Peters, who is also at the airport boarding a plane on the first phase of his journey. Cole takes the gun and tries to run through the airport metal detector, setting off the alarm that summons the police, who shoot him to death. Witnessing the shooting is Cole as a boy (Joseph Melito) who sees the event that will haunt him for his entire life, the death of his future self.

Director Gilliam imbues this tragic time travel tale with his signature fantastic visuals, creating a wonderfully dystopian sci-fi ambience in the 2035 scenes and making effective use of dilapidated locations in Baltimore and Philadelphia that conjure a landscape of intense urban blight. Aside from the visuals, Gilliam guides his characters through a complex and at times mind-boggling narrative with aplomb and smooth pacing, coaxing fine performances from action hero Bruce Willis and co-star Madeleine Stowe. Brad Pitt steals every scene he's in as fruitcake activist Jeffrey Goines, and his histrionic, over the top portrayal would earn him an Academy Award nomination for Best Supporting Actor.

The basic thrust of the narrative, taken from *La Jetée*, revolves around the idea of the time paradox doppelganger. Cole is able to travel back to the past because of this vivid event that is indelibly etched into his memory, yet it is this power of remembrance that will ultimately lead to his annihilation. Once again being in the same time and place as one's double is fatal as the folk belief smoothly transitions into a science fiction idiom.

Another sci-fi iteration of the doppelganger theme was to have profound cultural resonance on the cusp of the new millennium. *The Matrix* (1999), conceived and executed by writer/director siblings Andy and Larry Wachowski, ushered in the era of cyberpunk cinema, a science fiction subgenre in which bands of young hacker revolutionaries faced off against machine intelligences after the computer brains have achieved self awareness (an event referred to as the "Singularity" in science fiction parlance) and threaten the existence of humankind.

The narrative centers around Thomas Anderson (Keanu Reeves), a computer programmer by day who dabbles as a hacker at night under the handle "Neo" and sells copies of illegal software to his druggie friends. An anomalous prompt begins appearing on Anderson's home computer that reads, "Wake up, Neo. The Matrix has you." One night at a club he encounters the black-clad female hacker Trinity (Carrie-Anne Moss), who tells him that the notorious criminal hacker Morpheus is seeking him out and that he is in some kind of danger. The next day he is arrested at his job by a group of men in black led by Agent Smith (Hugo Weaving), who interrogates him about his connection with Morpheus and seems to have godlike powers to manipulate reality.

Soon afterward Anderson makes contact with Morpheus (Laurence Fishburne), an imposing figure who informs him that the life he is living is a lie. He offers him a choice of two pills, a red one which will reveal the true nature of reality, and a blue one that will return him to the world of his illusions. He chooses the red one and finds himself inside a womb-like pod with various parts of his body hooked up to cables. Freeing himself from the device, he can see endless vistas of the womb-pods, whereupon a squid-like machine appears and promptly deposits him into a vat of wastewater, where he is fished out and secretly taken aboard Morpheus's hovercraft, the *Nebuchadnezzar*.

Once on board the ship Anderson's body is rehabilitated

Trinity (Carrie-Anne Moss) monitors Neo (Keanu Reeves) as his digital double moves through cyberspace in *The Matrix* (1999).

Neo (Keanu Reeves, left) is able to defy gravity and perform other superhuman feats as he battles Agent Smith (Hugo Weaving) in *The Matrix* (1999).

and Morpheus explains the nature of his situation. Two hundred years ago, in the 21st century, a war between humans and a machine intelligence rendered the Earth uninhabitable, forcing the remnants of humanity to retreat underground. Deprived of solar power by a change in Earth's climate, the machines must harness bio-energy from human bodies bred for this purpose. The world he has lived in all his life is nothing but a digital simulacrum of a late 20th-century city designed to keep their human hosts pacified and distracted by the illusion within a "neural active simulation" of the real world. This artificial reality is called "the Matrix," and Morpheus and his fellow human rebels are dedicated to freeing the slaves from their digital bondage. To further this end they have discovered ways to hack into the Matrix and use it against their oppressors, and Morpheus believes that Anderson is "the One," a cyber-savior who will free humanity from the bondage of the machines.

Morpheus, along with Trinity and the other crew members of the *Nebuchadnezzar*, including Cypher (Joe Pantoliano), Tank (Marcus Chong) and Dozer (Anthony Ray Parker), begin to train Anderson in the ways of the Matrix. Using a plug located in the back of their heads, the rebels can jack into its virtual reality while in the real world their bodies remain in a coma-like sleep. Once inside the Matrix they exist as doubles of themselves, as "a residual self image," Morpheus explains, "a mental projection of your digital self" that is linked to the physical body. "If you die in the Matrix," Anderson asks, "you die here?" "The body cannot live without the mind," Morpheus replies, "your mind makes it real." The Matrix is policed by Agents, sentient hunter-killer programs with extraordinary powers that seek out and exterminate the free humans, but the rebels have developed techniques of their own that enable them to bend physical laws within the simulation.

Martial arts skills are downloaded into Anderson's brain via his skull socket and Morpheus further develops his abilities by coaching him inside a training program. When he is ready, Anderson changes his name to "Neo" and ventures into the Matrix with his companions to consult the Oracle (Gloria Foster), a sentient program with the power of prophecy, to find out if he is the One. Alas, the Oracle proclaims that Neo is not the promised savior, but Neo keeps it to himself. Before they can exit the Matrix (this is accomplished using a phone/modem connection), they are attacked by a squad of agents led by Smith and Morpheus is taken prisoner. Meanwhile, back in the real world, Cypher is conspiring with Agent Smith to betray the rebels. He prevents them from getting out of the Matrix while killing several of his crewmates aboard the *Nebuchadnezzar* and is preparing to do the same to Trinity and Neo by pulling out their head jacks, but is foiled by Tank, who he mistakenly left for dead.

Once they are back in the real world, Neo is obsessed with going back into the Matrix to rescue Morpheus, and Trinity insists on going back with him. Arming themselves to the teeth for their mission, they blast their way into the building where Morpheus in being held and rescue him, and during the rescue Neo exhibits a command of the Matrix that allow him to perform superhuman feats and deal with the Agents on equal terms. Morpheus and Trinity escape from the Matrix but Neo is seemingly killed by Agent Smith's bullets, but he is brought back to life by a kiss from Trinity in the real world. The resurrected Neo, whose powers have now been enhanced by his near death experience, goes *mano a mano* with Agent Smith while the *Nebuchadnezzar* is attacked by squid-like Sentinel machines that rip through the ship's hull with lasers. Neo defeats Smith with his newfound powers and exits the Matrix in time for Morpheus to fire the electromagnetic pulse weapon that destroys the Sentinels. In the aftermath, Neo is shown inside the Matrix taunting the machine masters before soaring into the air like a superhero.

The Matrix proved to be an enormous critical and popular success that also broke new ground in the realm of cinema technology that were devised by F/X wizard John Gaeta. The film employed a technique that came to be called "bullet time" that combined slow motion cinematography with 360 degree camera movement to create the illusion of the characters dodging bullets in flight. This was achieved using an array of super slo-mo cameras placed in a circle around the subject and fired simultaneously. The individual images recorded by the cameras were skillfully edited together using "time slice photography" to create the illusion of movement around the actor. Another innovation involved the use of "wire work," a technique pioneered by Asian action cinema, in which the actors are suspended by an elaborate system of wires to make them seem as if they are levitating or flying through the air. These innovative techniques even beat out George Lucas's *Star Wars* retread *The Phantom Menace* to win an Academy Award in the special effects category and would garner a total of four Oscars.

Thematically, the film's plot derived from a diverse number of sources, including Lewis Carroll's *Alice's Adventures in Wonderland*, Mamoru Oshii's 1995 anime feature *The Ghost in the Shell*, and William Gibson's seminal science fiction novel *Neuromancer*. *The Matrix* was part of a wave of cyberpunk movies that came along at the end of the Millennium such as *The Lawnmower Man* (1992), *Johnny Mnemonic* (1995), *Virtuosity* (1995), *The Thirteenth Floor* (1999), *eXistenZ* (1999) and *Strange Days* (1995). These films exploited anxieties about the so-called "Y2K Bug," a programming glitch that was supposedly poised to crash the world's computer systems on January 1st, 2000, and the potential for abuse of newly invented virtual reality technology.

Critics of science fiction cinema consider *The Matrix* to be a milestone in the history of the genre, and the Wachowski brothers would be hailed as the sci-fi equivalent of the Coen brothers. The film had a deep cultural resonance within American society, but was criticized in certain circles for its glorification of violence and gunplay. For better or worse, the black-clad images of Keanu Reeves, Laurence Fishburne and Carrie Anne-Moss would become iconic symbols of youthful rebellion.

In the filmic reality of *The Matrix* the double is presented as a digital construct, a simulacrum of the body connected with sleep and the world of dreams. While the body sleeps the doppelganger is propelled into a virtual realm where it possesses magical powers. This idea ultimately derives from ancient shamanic and psychic practices having to do with bilocation and out of body experiences. There is also a connection with the phenomenon of "lucid dreaming," in which the dreamer becomes aware he is dreaming and can influence events within the dream, and the name "Morpheus" is a reference to the Greek god of sleep. In an early scene in the film, Anderson quips, "ever get that feeling where you're not sure if you're awake or still dreaming?" The Keanu Reeves character has a dual identity as "Anderson" inside the Matrix and "Neo" in the real world, and although he completely transitions into the Neo identity, he is always referred to as "Mr. Anderson" by Agent Smith. Note that Morpheus, Trinity and the other characters that enter the Matrix do not have this dual identity.

The inevitable sequel, *The Matrix Reloaded*, followed in 2003. The film takes place six months after the original movie as the machines are poised to attack Zion, the underground city of the humans. Defying orders to remain with the Zionites, Neo returns to the Matrix to consult the Oracle, who tells him to seek out the Keymaker (Randall Duk Kim), a rogue program who will give him access to the Source of the Matrix. He also learns that the Keymaker is being held prisoner by the Merovingian (Lambert Wilson), a Gallic mob boss in the Matrix. When the interview is concluded, Neo is attacked by a resurrected Agent Smith, who now has the power to duplicate himself into an infinite number of doppelgangers. In the ensuing battle (referred to as the "Bruiser Brawl" during production), Neo is almost overwhelmed by an army of Smiths before he manages to fly away to safety.

Following the Oracle's instructions, Neo, Morpheus and Trinity re-enter the Matrix to seek out the Merovingian, who is dining at a

Neil and Adrian Rayment pose as the deadly albino twins in *The Matrix Reloaded* (2003).

fancy restaurant. He refuses to give up the Keymaker, who has access to "back doors" that allow instantaneous passage to other areas of the Matrix with his keys. In the ensuing battle Neo is lured through a back door and finds himself transported hundreds of miles from the city, while Morpheus and Trinity face off against the Merovingian's henchmen, the Twins (played by identical siblings Neil and Adrian Rayment). The twins, who wear identical white outfits and sport bleached white dreadlocks, have deadly martial arts prowess as well as the power to de-materialize and re-materialize themselves at will. In the film's most dynamic sequence, Morpheus and Trinity battle both the twins and a group of Agents on a freeway filled with traffic as bullets fly and cars careen off the roadway. Morpheus manages to defeat the twins by blowing up their car and they escape with the Keymaker.

As the Zionites prepare for the onslaught of the machines, Neo goes back into the Matrix with Morpheus and the Keymaker to penetrate the one door that leads to the Source. This involves shutting down electrical power to the building in which the door is housed. When the initial attempt to do this fails, Trinity goes in and succeeds, but is mortally wounded by an Agent. Meanwhile, Neo and Morpheus battle Agent Smith's doppelgangers and the Keymaker manages to unlock the door to the Source, but is killed in the process. Neo goes through the door and encounters the Architect (Helmut Bakaitis), a being who claims to have created the Matrix. He offers Neo a choice between saving Trinity and saving Zion, and he chooses Trinity. Using his powers he saves her but ends up in a coma at the conclusion of the film.

Compared to the first movie, the sequel is overlong and its narrative too convoluted. Audiences who were expecting non-stop superheroics were somewhat let down by the film's slow buildup, lack of inside-the-Matrix action and cliff-hanger ending. Although the Bruiser Brawl and Freeway Chase sequences were top-notch, the rest of the film suffered in comparison by coming off as overly talky and pretentious. The dialogue was replete with pseudo-profundities such as the Oracles proclamation, "We're all here to do what we're all here to do." Regardless of its flaws, however, *The Matrix Reloaded* was an exercise in hi-tech sci-fi entertainment that pioneered the use of "virtual cinematography" using "virtual cameras" to create complex images and "optical flow" algorithms to manipulate them.

The Neo alter ego had progressed into full superman mode as "The One" and was now costumed in dark glasses and a Jesuit's black cassock. His double in the Matrix possesses godlike powers of flight, the manipulation of matter and superhuman strength. His nemesis Agent Smith acquired the ability to create endless doppelgangers of himself, proclaiming that, "the best thing about being me is, there's so many mes." This power of replication almost allows him to overwhelm Neo by sheer numbers. Another set of doppelgangers consists of the Twins, a pair of deadly, white-attired albinos with the power to become phantoms. They speak sparse lines of dialogue like "Can we move along?" and "We are getting aggravated" in droll British accents that are somehow amusing despite their air of menace.

Six months later the third film in the series, *The Matrix Revolutions* (2003) was released to the general disappointment of *Matrix* fans. The third film brought closure to the trilogy, but most of the action took place outside the Matrix as the machines attacked the city of Zion with swarms of hunter-killer Sentinels. Neo spends a fair amount of time trapped in a virtual subway station somewhere outside the Martix where his powers are nullified, and in the machine world on the Earth's surface instead of exercising the superhuman abilities of his doppelganger. *Revolutions* builds to a tragic, highly unsatisfying denouement in which several of the main characters meet their fates.

As the new millennium arrived, cyberpunk cinema went out of vogue, partly because the world had passed through the Y2K "crisis" unscathed and also because the promised glories of virtual reality never arrived. Science fiction films turned their attention to a novel set of ideas and technologies. *The 6th Day* (2000) explored hi-tech aspects of cloning and presented a new take on the sci-fi doppelganger. Set "in the near future, sooner than you think," the film stars Arnold Schwarzenegger as Adam Gibson, who operates the Double X Charter helicopter company with his partner Hank Morgan (Michael Rapaport). Contracted to fly VIP client Michael Drucker (Tony Goldwyn), billionaire head of the biotech firm Replacement Technologies, to a remote mountain for a skiing trip, both Adam and Hank are required to submit to a "vision test" on a strange machine and a blood test for drugs prior to the flight. Unbeknownst to Drucker, however, Hank agrees to fly the charter flight because it is Adam's birthday in order to allow Adam to shop for a present for his daughter.

The next thing Adam knows is waking up from sleep in the back of a taxi at a downtown shopping area. After purchasing an animatronic doll as a present, he returns home and is shocked to find his family celebrating his birthday with his doppelganger. He slinks away from the scene in confusion and is accosted by a team of assassins who try to kill him, including femme fatale Talia (Sarah Wynter) and street punk Wiley (Rod Rowland), but he manages to kill the both of them and escapes. The assassins have been sent by Drucker, who brings the two corpses back to the Replacement Technologies laboratories and proceeds to replace them with clones. This is accomplished through the use of "blanks," incomplete human bodies kept ready for this purpose, which are modified into doubles of the original persons by being infused with a sample of their DNA. Their memories and personalities are then downloaded into the blanks from "syncording" modules that have recorded this information. The process takes about two hours, after which Talia and Wiley have been restored to life in new bodies. Drucker must operate in secret because human cloning is forbidden under the so-called "Sixth Day Laws."

In the meantime, Adam is betrayed to the assassins once more when he tries to go to the police. He escapes again and makes contact with Hank, who is incredulous about Adam's story until they return to Adam's home and he sees the double for himself. Adam gets the idea of killing the doppelganger who has usurped his identity, but cannot bring himself to do it, so they return to Hank's apartment, where Hank is shot to death by another assailant, a man named Tripp (Colin Cunningham). Adam chases down Tripp, who turns out to be an anti-cloning activist who is responsible for murdering Drucker, Hank, and everyone else on the ski junket. Tripp tells him that Replacement Technologies has been secretly cloning people in violation of the Sixth Day Laws, and that everyone he killed has been cloned, including Adam, who Drucker mistakenly thought was flying the helicopter.

When Drucker's goon squad arrives at Hank's, Tripp opts to commit suicide rather than be captured. During the ensuing shootout, Talia is wounded and Adam retrieves her severed thumb, which he uses to gain access to Drucker's lab by using it to fool a thumbprint reader security system. Once inside the building he encounters Dr. Griffin Weir (Robert Duvall), the brilliant scientist who has perfected the illegal cloning techniques. He tells Adam that Drucker died years earlier but has survived by cloning himself many times, and that he must conceal this fact because as a clone he has no legal right to his corporation's assets. Furthermore, Adam must not be seen with his clone or Drucker will exterminate his family. Dr. Weir has a beef with Drucker over cloning issues involving his critically ill wife and gives Adam Drucker's syncording module, whereupon Adam departs. When Drucker arrives on the scene he kills Weir in retribution and sends his thugs to kidnap Adam's family.

Adam teams up with his clone and they devise a plan to infiltrate Drucker's headquarters and rescue their mutual family. He breaks into Replacement Technologies to create a diversion but is captured, and Drucker employs the syncording machine to read his memory and learns that the clone plans to fly onto the building's roof, plant a bomb and fly out with the family. Warned too late, Drucker is unable to prevent this from happening, but proves that the other Adam is the original and he is really the clone. Driven to rage by this revelation, Adam fights back and takes out Talia, Wiley and the others, but Drucker is mortally wounded in the fracas and must clone himself immediately to avoid death. Unfortunately, a stray shot has ruptured the clone tank holding the blanks and the replication process is incomplete, creating a freakish cloned version of Drucker. Just then the bomb planted by the second Adam goes off and Drucker is killed in the explosion as Adam is rescued by a helicopter piloted by his double. In an epilogue, the cloned Adam says farewell to the original as he departs for Argentina to set up a charter business there.

Many critics thought the film compared unfavorably with previous Schwarzenegger science fiction vehicles such as *Terminator 2* (1991) and *Total Recall* (1990), but *The 6th Day* is a competently made sci-fi thriller with an intriguing storyline and flashy visuals. Action director Roger Spottiswoode keeps the gun fights, fist fights, helicopter flights, car chases and explosions moving along briskly while smoothly guiding the viewer through the twists and turns of the film's complex plot. The screenplay by the husband and wife team of Cormac and Marianne Wibberley provides clear exposition of the unusual process of the replication of human clones. Production designers Jim Bissell and John Willett, along with cinematographer Pierre Mignot, create dazzling images of a bright and positive tomorrowland as a backdrop for the action. Schwarzenegger plays Adam Gibson as his usual grimacing action hero screen persona, but also manages to generate audience sympathy for his portrayal of an innocent person drawn into a murderous situation and a mind-bending encounter with his alternate self. Tony Goldwyn plays it cool as the oily corporate villain, while veteran thesp Robert Duvall provides some true acting grit as the scientist who is tenderly caring for his critically ill wife.

One of the film's most memorable scenes is when Adam hides amid the pre-human "blanks" floating inside a gigantic water tank that is used to create the clones. The concept of blanks first appeared in *Invasion of the Body Snatchers*, where they are partially formed templates waiting to be transformed into the doppelgangers of individual human beings. Adam's clone, not the original Adam, is the movie's protagonist, and the replicated Adam suffers a severe bout of existential angst upon learning that he is merely a copy, which leads him to wonder, "Am I really human?" Drucker, Talia and Wiley also exist in doppelganger form when they are killed and resurrected as clones. Wiley even claims he can feel the pain of being killed from his former bodies the way amputees can feel pain in phantom limbs they no longer have. Contrary to the usual narrative of avoiding one's double, Adam's situation is only resolved when he teams up with his twin.

Corporate assassins Talia Ellsworth (Sarah Wynter) and Robert Marshall (Michael Rooker) prepare to "synchord" the memories of Adam Gibson (Arnold Schwarzenegger) prior to cloning in *The 6th Day* (2000).

The trend of pairing action heroes with their doubles continued with *The One* (2001), a vehicle for Hong Kong martial arts star Jet Li. Opening titles inform us that there is not just one universe, but a multitude of them comprising a "multiverse," and that "there is not one you there are many." In one of these alternate realities, dubbed the "Alpha Universe," travel between the various realms has been achieved and is monitored by a police force called the "Multiverse Authority," or MVA. A renegade MVA agent, Gabriel Yulaw (Jet Li) has been traveling through the universes systematically murdering all other versions of himself in the belief that when all of them have been exterminated he will become "The One," a super-being with godlike powers. He has succeeded in killing 123 doubles and absorbing their life energies and has only one more to go to reach his goal when he is collared by MVA agents Rodecker (Delroy Lindo) and Funsch (Jason Statham). Yulaw is sentenced to life imprisonment in the Stygian penal colony in the Hades universe when he escapes using his super powers and travels to our universe to kill doppelganger number 124 and become The One.

His last remaining double is Los Angeles County Sheriff's Department officer Gabe Law (Li), who has been experiencing boosts to his speed and strength that he cannot account for, not knowing that he, too has been absorbing the energies from Yulaw's 123 victims. While he is involved in transporting a prisoner, Yulaw strikes and the twins do battle. Gabe is shot and wounded by Yulaw during the melee, but is prevented from killing him when Roedecker and Funsch suddenly appear and cause Yulaw to flee. Gabe is taken to a hospital where he is attended by his wife, T.K. Law (Carla Gugino), and a group of his fellow officers, and while he is being given an MRI he must remove his wedding ring, which will interfere with the procedure. While undergoing the MRI Yulaw shows up and tries to kill him, but Rodecker and Funsch arrive to do battle with the renegade and both Gabe and Yulaw escape in the confusion.

The two MVA agents decide to split up, with Rodecker, the more experienced of the two going after Yulaw while Funsch pursues Gabe. They must be careful to capture Yulaw alive, however, for if they kill him Gabe might become the One, an event that could have unknown consequences and lead them into a situation where they have to assassinate Gabe as well. Rodecker catches up with Yulaw, but after a fierce battle the agent is killed and Yulaw, impersonating Gabe, takes refuge in Gabe's home. In the meantime, Funsch catches up with the bewildered Gabe and explains what is happening to him. "Each time he kills one of you," he tells Gabe, "the energy divides among the survivors." Gabe can now sense the presence of his double and rushes home to confront him, only to watch in horror as Yulaw murders his wife while he is helpless to prevent it.

From this point on Gabe is consumed with avenging his wife's murder and teams up with Funsch to take him down and even tells the agent to kill him if he dispatches Yulaw. They corner the renegade inside a factory, where the two square off in a martial arts battle royal. Driven by rage, Gabe triumphs over his evil twin, but instead of killing him, he and Funsch manage to shift dimensions back to the Alpha Universe, where he is brought to justice by the MVA. At first the authorities can't tell the difference between the two until Funsch notices the pale band of skin on Gabe's finger from wearing his wedding ring, which was removed for the MRI. Instead of sending Gabe back to our universe, however, Funsch beams him to another where he meets his wife's twin, while Yulaw is sent to the prison world in the Hades universe.

The main problem with *The One* lies in plot elements borrowed from other movies. The notion of "The One" as a kind of martial arts messiah was cribbed from *The Matrix*, along with the ability to dodge bullets in flight. A police force that prevents unauthorized travel between different realms was borrowed from *Timecop*, and a mystical warrior hunting down his rivals and absorbing their life force until only he is left first appeared in Russell Mulcahy's sword and fantasy saga *Highlander*. Clocking in at about 82 minutes of run time sans credits, Hong Kong action director James Hong moves the film along at a blistering pace, squeezing in a seemingly endless series of kung-fu battles, car chases, gunfights and dimensional warps that go by at supersonic speed. Chop-socky sensation Jet Li delivers some stunning martial arts sequences, but leaves something to be desired in the acting department.

Despite its derivate elements, however, Wong and co-scripter Glen Morgan deserve credit for inventing the idea of different versions of an individual existing in multiple universes, with all the alternate selves linked together in their parallel lives. Gabe Law and Gabriel Yulaw represent the standard good and evil twin dichotomy translated into a science fiction idiom. As per usual, existing within the same time/space continuum as one's doppelganger puts the protagonist in mortal danger. Jet Li, guided by the film's fight director Cory Yuen, reportedly used contrasting martial arts styles to express the psychological difference between the twin combatants. The attacker Yulaw uses the aggressive Shin Yi ("shape

Martial arts star Jet Li battles his interdimensional doppelganger in *The One* (2001).

will-fist") style, while Gabe employs the defensive Ba Qua ("8 trigram palms") method that utilizes circular hand movements. The combination of the images of the two Lis during the film's climactic fight sequence is flawlessly composited and beautifully choreographed.

The parade of science fiction doppelgangers continued with *The Island* (2005), a $126 million high concept, high technology production helmed by producer/director Michael Bay. In the far future world of 2019, a colony of humans live an isolated existence completely cut off from the outside world, which has become contaminated by an environmental disaster. The oddly child-like inhabitants of this community have numbers imprinted on their arms and are closely monitored by a cadre of guards and scientists who strictly regulate every aspect of their lives. Periodically, survivors of the devastation are brought into the colony for rehabilitation, while other members are selected by lottery to start a new life on "The Island," a paradise that is the last uncontaminated location in the outside world.

Lincoln Six Echo (Ewan McGregor) and Jordan Two Delta (Scarlet Johansson) are two inhabitants of the colony who feel a closeness to each other that is strictly forbidden by the guards. Lincoln is a bit of a rebellious spirit who is examined by colony scientist Dr. Merrick (Sean Bean) because of a strange recurring dream he keeps having about being thrown off a futuristic-looking yacht and drowned. He is able to draw a picture of the distinctively shaped craft, which he somehow knows is named the "Renovatio." Dr. Merrick decides to keep Lincoln under tighter surveillance, but he still manages to roam through restricted areas of the facility, where he strikes up a friendship with quirky technician James "Mac" McCord (Steve Buscemi). On another one of his forays he discovers a live moth, which suggests that the outside world is not as contaminated as they have been led to believe. Following the moth, he finds his way to an area where he learns the horrible truth that the members of the colony are in reality clones of rich and famous people who are harvested for their organs and body parts when these are needed by their celebrity "sponsors."

Returning to the colony, Lincoln learns that Jordan has been selected to leave for The Island, but convinces her to escape from the facility with him instead. Pursued by Dr. Merrick and the security guards, they manage to find their way to the outside and locate McCord in a nearby Arizona town. The amiable but hapless McCord provides the clones with the location of Lincoln's sponsor, Tom Lincoln, in Los Angeles and buys them train tickets to L.A. before being gunned down by Merrick's assassins. The clones escape and Merrick, desperate to recapture his property to avoid violating anti-cloning laws, enlists the aid of mercenary Albert Laurent (Djimon Hounsou) to track down his errant "products."

Tom Lincoln (Ewan McGregor) confronts his cloned double Lincoln 6 Echo (also Ewan McGregor) in *The Island* (2005).

Reaching L.A., Lincoln and Jordan are dazzled and confused by the mega-city but manage to make contact with Tom Lincoln (McGregor), who is a famous race car driver. Amazed by his lookalike and their strange story, Tom gives them refuge in his home, where Lincoln spies a model of Tom's yacht, the Renovatio, and perceives that he has a telepathic link with his sponsor's mind. While pretending to help the clones, however, Tom, who is seriously ill and has about two years to live, secretly contacts the Merrick Institute and alerts them concerning the whereabouts of his "insurance policy." He takes Lincoln out for a drive in his sports car and delivers him to an abandoned building where Laurent is waiting, but Lincoln fools Laurent into shooting Tom and then assumes his sponsor's identity.

Back at the colony, Merrick learns that an error in the cloning process has resulted in Lincoln having telepathic access to his sponsor's memories, and to avoid this occurring with others he must destroy the last four generations of clones. This to be accomplished via mass winnings of the lottery that will pick out the clones selected for extinction. Meanwhile, Lincoln and Jordan resolve to return to the facility and free its inhabitants by destroying the holographic projectors that conceal their view of the outside world. Lincoln gains entrance to the institute during an appointment for his sponsor to be re-cloned, while Jordan allows herself to be captured and transported back by Laurent. As their plan proceeds, Laurent, appalled by the coming slaughter of the clones and haunted by memories of genocidal wars in his native Africa, changes sides and helps Lincoln and Jordan in their endeavor. Merrick perishes in mortal combat with Lincoln, who destroys the hologram machinery, and the colony gains their freedom as they apprehend the real world for the first time.

Michael Bay, best known for his big budget actioners like *The Rock* (1996) and *Pearl Harbor* (2001) and, later, the *Transformer* movies, crafts a slick piece of science fiction entertainment that contains some serious subtext. The screenplay concocted by Alex Kurtzman, Roberto Orci and Walter F. Parkes, invokes memories of the holocaust by positing a group of humans who are tattooed with numbers on their arms and confined in a virtual concentration camp where they are destined for eventual extermination. In one scene a group of clones is about to be killed in a gas chamber before being rescued by Lincoln. In addition, the film obliquely addresses the moral issue of harvesting embryonic stem cells from aborted fetuses. Bay and his co-producers were sued by the makers of the obscure, low budget sci-fi thriller *Parts—The Clonus Horror* (1979), that shared similar plot elements and the case was reportedly settled out of court for a six figure sum. Principal cast members McGregor, Johansson, Hounsou and Bean acquit themselves well, with character actor Steve Buscemi providing some much needed comic relief. While the movie runs a bit overlong at two hours and 16 minutes, the action sequences are well constructed and the character's situations dire enough to keep the viewer's interest throughout. Unfortunately, the film did poorly in its American release, a failure that was blamed on TV adverts that didn't present a clear picture of what the movie was about.

As the *6th Day*, the clones featured in *The Island* are kept in a kind of suspended animation until decanted and turned into doppelgangers. Scientifically, this idea is far-fetched to the point of fantasy. While all of the characters in the colony are doubles of their sponsors, we are shown only one set of them consisting of Tom Lincoln and his clone Lincoln Six Echo. Supposedly genetically identical, the two have fundamentally different personalities: Tom wears eyeglasses but Lincoln does not; Tom speaks with a Scottish accent and Lincoln uses American idiomatic speech; Tom is snarky, self-centered, cowardly and aggressive

Five. Human Duplicators   195

while Lincoln is soft-spoken, courageous, gentle and self-sacrificing. *The Island* posits the notion of clones possessing a telepathic link with their sponsors in a manner similar to that reported between identical twins, a motif that first appeared in *Futureworld*.

During the 2000s the superhero subgenre of science fiction film achieved a megapopularity. One of the most lucrative of the hero franchises starred the Marvel Comics character Spider-Man. "Spidey," as he was nicknamed, was created when a radioactive spider sank its fangs into physics student Peter Parker, giving him super strength, the ability to climb up walls and spin spider webs from his wrists. The wisecracking superhero began his big screen career in *Spider-Man* (2002), which was followed by *Spider-Man 2* (2004) and *Spider-Man 3* (2007). All three films were directed by Sam Raimi and starred Tobey Maguire in the title role. While Peter Parker's alter ego was Spider-Man, unlike most superheroes he also had a comic book doppelganger named Venom, a super villain who wore a black variant of the Spidey suit and had the same spider powers.

Venom made his screen debut in *Spider-Man 3* when a meteorite hits the Earth in New York's Central Park, releasing a sentient crawling black gunk that attaches itself to the wheel of Parker's motorbike and later slithers into his rented room. Soon afterward, a new villain called the Sandman is created when a criminal named Flint Marko (Thomas Hayden Church) unwittingly falls into an experimental particle accelerator and his body fuses with the sand on the floor of the device, giving him the power to turn into a human sandstorm. After briefly tangling with the Sandman, Parker learns that Marko was responsible for the murder of his beloved Uncle Ben (Cliff Robertson) years earlier. One night as he lays in bed dreaming about taking revenge on Marko for the murder, the alien goo is aroused by his negative thoughts and swarms over his entire body, changing his costume into a black version of the Spider-Man suit.

Parker finds that the black stuff has amped up his spider

The Amazing Spider-Man (Tobey Maguire) squares off against his evil counterpart Venom in *Spider-Man 3* (2007).

powers, but at the same time it brings out the dark side of his emotions. He takes a sample of the space gunk to his mentor, physics professor Dr. Curt Connors (Dylan Baker), whose analysis reveals it to be a "symbiote," a parasitic organism that feeds on and amplifies the negative characteristics of its host, especially aggression. During his next encounter with the Sandman he fights more aggressively, dissolving the villain in a blast of water. Thereafter he takes to secretly wearing the black suit underneath his street clothes. Parker's descent into the dark side continues when he humiliates Eddie Brock (Topher Grace) a rival for his gig as a photographer for the *Daily Bugle* by showing his Spider-Man photos to be faked. The last straw comes when he physically abuses his girlfriend, Mary Jane Watson (Kirsten Dunst), and realizes he must rid himself of the baleful influence of the symbiote.

Retreating to the bell tower of a church, Parker attempts to remove the alien life form from his body, but finds it impossible until the church bell peals and the vibrations weaken the symbiote and it falls from his body and plunges to the church below. Unfortunately, the black stuff falls on Eddie Brock, who happens to be in one of the pews praying for Peter Parker's death. The symbiote gloms onto Brock and transforms him into Venom, a dark counterpart of Spider-man who sports a mouthful of wicked fangs. The newly-formed villain searches out the re-formed Sandman and convinces him to team up so they can get revenge on their mutual foe. Together they kidnap Mary Jane and leave her suspended from a skyscraper in Venom's webs. With the aid of his frenemy Harry Osborn (Jesse Franco), a.k.a. the Green Goblin, Spidey takes on the two super villains.

During the battle Spider-Man remembers that the symbiote was affected by the sound of the church bell and traps Venom inside a cage consisting of metal tubes that, when struck, produce vibrations that separate Brock from the alien suit, but Brock is killed by one of the Goblin's bombs that also destroys the symbiote. Osborne dies protecting Spidey but together they rescue Mary Jane. Parker confronts the Sandman, who reveals that his uncle's death was an accident and is forgiven, whereupon he peacefully floats away.

The brainchild of comics writer Stan Lee and artist Steve Ditko, the Spider-Man character combined the usual superheroics with a healthy dose of youth angst as Peter Parker and his friends struggle with their careers, education and romantic relationships. *Spider-Man 3* delves into these aspects of the character's lives more than the first two films in a convoluted screenplay by Sam and Ivan Raimi and Alvin Sargent that frequently slows down the action in favor of drawn-out dramatic and romantic interludes. In addition, Kirsten Dunst gets to belt out a couple of musical numbers, while Tobey Maguire performs some ridiculous dance routines. Despite these flaws, the film proved to be the highest grossing entry in the trilogy, but would be the last Spider-Man film of the decade. The franchise was later rebooted with *The Amazing Spider-Man* in 2012 with an all-new cast and production team.

The film's advertising tag line read, "The Greatest Battle Lies Within," referring to the inner struggle between Spider-Man and his black-suited doppelganger. Parker must overcome the seductive but negative alien force that is drawing him toward the dark side, and only does so with the aid of sonic vibrations from the church bell that symbolizes spiritual rightness. Later on, when Eddie Brock assumes the persona of Venom, Spider-Man is forced to enter into mortal combat with his evil double until only one of the spider-men remains alive. Once again it is an alien life form that creates the film's doppelganger.

James Cameron's $300 million sci-fi blockbuster *Avatar* (2009) broke box office records and went on to become the highest-grossing film of all time and the first movie to earn more than $2 billion. A technological triumph, *Avatar* pioneered the use of motion capture techniques combined with stereoscopic filming and digital animation to usher in a brave new world of 3-D cinema.

Avatar takes place in the middle of the 21st century, when Earth's resources have been depleted and the planet must rely on mining a rare element with superconducting properties called unobtainium on the distant world of Pandora to solve its energy crisis. Pandora is a tropical world with a poisonous atmosphere, inhabited by strange beasts and a race of ten foot-tall blue-skinned humanoids called the Na'vi. The indigenous population is hostile to the invasion and exploration of their domain by the off-world "Sky People," so the earthlings have created human/alien hybrid beings called *avatars* to win the hearts and minds of the natives.

The film begins with a dream sequence in which the protagonist Jake Sully (Sam Worthington), a paraplegic ex-Marine, wakens from a dream of flying to find he has completed the six-year interstellar journey to Pandora. Jake has accepted the job of "avatar driver" offered to him by the Resources Development Administration (RDA) after his identical twin brother Tommy was killed in a holdup. The avatars, remotely controlled bodies grown

Jake Sully (Sam Worthington) contemplates his bio-engineered human-alien hybrid "avatar" in *Avatar* (2009).

from human DNA mixed with that of the natives, are very expensive and are keyed to the specific nervous systems of the drivers. Because Jake's genome is identical to his twin's, the RDA recruited him to take his brother's place, and Jake has accepted in the hope that he will earn enough money to afford an operation that will restore his crippled legs.

Checking into the facility, he meets with the scientist running the avatar program, Dr. Grace Augustine (Sigourney Weaver), who is none too pleased that Jake has replaced his brother, a scientist who trained for years for the mission. Despite her misgivings, Parker Selfridge (Giovanni Ribisi), head of the RDA mining operation, orders her to accept him as a security guard. Jake is shown his avatar, whose facial features resemble his own, floating in a tank awaiting activation. He also meets a fellow newbie avatar driver, exobiologist Dr. Norm Spellman (Joel David Moore).

The next day Jake and Norm are hooked up to their avatars via a coffin-like link machine that transfers their consciousness into their avatar bodies while they are in a state of dreaming REM (rapid eye movement) sleep inside the link chamber. No longer crippled inside his new body, Jake is intoxicated by the experience. On his first mission into the Pandoran jungle, however, he is attacked by a carnivorous beast and separated from Grace, Norm and the others. Forced to fend for himself in the alien environment, he is rescued from a pack of fierce dog-like creatures by Neytiri (Zoe Saldana), a Na'vi woman who has witnessed Jake being anointed by a sacred floating seed that she takes as an omen from the Na'vi deity Eywa. Neytiri introduces Jake to her tribe, the Omaticaya, where the clan's shaman Mo'at (C.C.H. Pounder) orders them to accept him on the basis of the omen.

Back at the base, the formidable head of RDA's paramilitary security force, Colonel Miles Quaritch (Stephen Lang), recruits Jake to secretly spy on the Omaticaya so he can learn their weaknesses. At first Jake goes along with Quaritch's scheme, but as he is drawn into the everyday life of the tribe, he becomes more and more sympathetic to the Na'vi. When the largest unobtanium deposit on Pandora is located underneath Hometree, an enormous ancient tree that is home to the Omaticaya clan, Parker and Quartich plan to burn the tree down. In response, Grace relocates her operation to a mobile link facility located high in the mountains, where she hopes to negotiate the peaceful relocation of the tribe to a new home. By this time Jake's identity has been shifted into his avatar body and his allegiance is now completely with the Na'vi. He mates with Neytiri and is initiated as a full member of the Omaticaya clan.

Unfortunately, Grace and Jake are unable to convince the tribe to move to another location and Quartich and his troops engage in a one-sided battle pitting his hi-tech military against the primitive forces of the Na'vi. A slaughter ensues in which Hometree is destroyed and Quartich neutralizes Jake and Grace by locating the mobile link facility and severing the connection, rendering their avatar bodies lifeless. The two traitors are returned to the base, but Grace engineers an escape with the aid of renegade helicopter pilot Trudy Chacon (Michelle Rodriguez) who agrees to fly another mobile link unit to an undisclosed location. Grace is mortally wounded during the escape and Jake, reunited with his avatar using the new link, attempts to save her life by transferring her consciousness permanently into her avatar body at the Tree of Souls, the tribe's sacred site that holds the entire racial memory of the Omaticaya, but the ritual fails and Grace dies.

A full-scale war ensues as Jake rallies the other Na'vi tribes to attack the humans and Quartich responds by bringing all of his military forces to bear on the army of the united tribes. The humans are defeated when the planetary awareness of Pandora, aroused by the interloper's desecration of the planet, sends an army of jungle beasts against them. During the battle, however, Quartich manages to locate the mobile link and attacks Jake while wearing a robotic exoskeleton AMP suit that provides him with superior strength and agility. He goes after Jake's human body while it lies helpless inside the link chamber and almost succeeds in asphyxiating him in Pandora's lethal atmosphere before he is killed by Neytiri's poison arrows. In the aftermath, the defeated humans are forced to return to Earth and Jake's consciousness is permanently transferred into his avatar body at the Tree of Souls.

Avatar set box-office records and was nominated for Academy Awards for Best Picture and Best Director but only won Oscars in the technical categories of Best Cinematography, Best Visual Effects and Best Art Direction. Director Cameron, who had ushered in a breakthrough in movie effects using computer generated imagery in *Terminator 2* (1991), further revolutionized the science of film-making with *Avatar*'s groundbreaking stereoscopic camera and motion capture imagery. Smoothly directed and brilliantly executed by Cameron and his technical team, the film is a milestone in the history of science fiction cinema. Cameron's screenplay, however, seems to have drawn many of its narrative elements from Frank Herbert's classic science fiction epic, *Dune*. Both plots feature an off-world hero forced to fend for himself on a hostile world who is adopted by an indigenous tribe of warriors, marries a native woman and becomes a messianic figure leading a revolt against his adopted planet's oppressive conquerors. Like *Dune*, the film also carries a serious ecological message.

The avatar concept has certain similarities with the digital doppelgangers depicted in the *Matrix* movies. In both films the protagonist uses a machine that links the protagonist to an alternate version of themselves while their bodies lie inert in a dreaming state. Their doubles can then perform superhuman feats while inhabiting a fantastic alternate reality. In *Avatar*, Jake Sully comes to prefer his existence in a bio-engineered artificial body to his life as a cripple in the human world as actor Sam Worthington becomes increasingly upstaged by his motion-captured, computer-generated onscreen alter ego. The film connects the double with shamanic dream states as recorded in the folklore of pre-industrial cultures and with the present-day phenomenon of "lucid dreaming." The motif of Jake having to replace his identical twin brother as an avatar driver is another reference to the doppelganger concept.

Imagine a world in which everyone has a doppelganger, which is the premise of the tech-noir thriller *Surrogates* (2009). In the year 2025 the science of robotics has advanced to the point where most everyone has an android double or "surrogate." This allows everyone to live their lives vicariously through their "surreys," who are younger and more physically attractive than their "operators," who lead a homebound existence propped up in the "stim chairs" that electronically transmit their consciousness into their surrogates. Each surrogate is coded to its operator's individual neural signature. Not everyone is so enchanted with this arrangement, however, and there are surrogacy free zones that only human beings are allowed to inhabit.

One night in Boston the surrogate of Jarid Canter (James Francis Ginty), the son of Dr. Lionel Canter (James Cromwell), is destroyed by an assassin wielding a pulse weapon and the boy is later found dead in his stim chair. FBI agent Tom Greer (Bruce Willis) and his partner Jennifer Peters (Radha Mitchell) are called in to investigate the illegal weapon that caused the death of both surrogate and operator, a situation that could mean the end of surrogacy itself. After meeting with Dr. Canter, who has become an eccentric recluse, Greer and Peters trace the weapon to Miles Strickland (Jack Noseworthy), a "meatbag" human anarchist with uncertain motives. Greer leads a tactical squad of surrogate cops in an effort to collar Strickland, who uses the weapon to disable them and flees into the Dread Reservation, Boston's surrogacy free zone, pursued by Greer riding aloft in a helicopter. Strickland fries the surrogate chopper pilot and Greer's surrogate is injured when he crash-lands inside the Reservation, but even after losing an arm, Greer's robot double pursues his quarry with superhuman strength and agility. When he catches up with Strickland, though, his surrogate is destroyed by a human mob and Strickland takes refuge with the commune's charismatic leader, The Prophet (Ving Rhames).

Deprived of his surrey and having broken FBI policy by entering the Dread Reservation, Greer is suspended from the bureau by his superior, Andrew Stone (Boris Kodjoe). Oddly, Greer resists getting a new surrogate even though he must endure the hard looks of androids on the street who look down on him as a meatbag, and the scorn of his estranged wife Maggie (Rosamund Pike). Still obsessed with finding the weapon even though he has been taken off the case, Greer infiltrates the Dread Reservation only to find that Strickland has died, probably at the hands of the Prophet, who has taken possession of the device. Greer then consults with contacts in the army, who inform him that the weapon was developed by Virtual Self Industries (VSI), the company that manufactures the surrogates, but was canceled after a preliminary evaluation.

That night the real Jennifer Peters is murdered by an unknown assailant who then commandeers her surrogate. Further digging around by Greer reveals that Stone gave the weapon to Strickland in an attempt to kill Dr. Canter but instead he mistakenly killed Jarid Canter, who was illegally using one of his father's surreys at the time. Back at the Reservation, the Prophet suddenly orders the weapon to be given to Peters's surrogate as Stone, desperate to get the weapon back, orders his men to attack the Reservation and retrieve it. During the battle a stray bullet hits the Prophet and reveals him to be a surrogate.

In the meantime, Greer pays a visit to Canter, who has been running both the Prophet and his partner's surrogates in a bid to use the weapon to exterminate all surrogates and their operators in order to end surrogacy, which he now considers to be evil. Manipulating "Peters," he kills Stone, who was working for VSI, and prepares to download the effects of the weapon into the entire surrogacy network before taking poison to prevent Greer from stopping him. Greer then takes control of Peters's surrogate and manages to buffer the effects of the weapon so that only the surrogates are destroyed. As the weapon's effects course through the system, all of the androids are disabled and their operators stumble out into the streets to greet a brave new world without their surrogates.

Following Hollywood's trend of adapting graphic novels for the screen, *Surrogates* was derived from the 2005–2006 comic book series *The Surrogates* by Robert Venditi. Adapted for the screen by John Brancanto and Michael Ferris, the plot unfolds as a tech-noir murder mystery that melds the detective genre with science fiction. Director Jonathan Mostow keeps the action flowing along smoothly and keeps the interpersonal scenes interesting during the film's fast-paced, eighty-odd minute running time. Middle-aged action hero Bruce Willis shambles through a low-key performance that carries the film, along with a supporting cast consisting of mostly unknowns. Critical consensus rates the film as a competently made but predictably plotted sci-fi thriller, a slick piece of entertainment but an otherwise mediocre programmer.

Like *The Matrix* and *Avatar, Surrogates* posits a technological means whereby a person's consciousness can be projected outside their body and into a doppelganger with special powers and abilities. Greer's surrogate is able to perform the kind of superhuman feats in the real world that the *Matrix* characters can only accomplish in a virtual reality simulation. Willis's android double is played by a younger actor, *90210* heartthrob Trevor Donovan, who is cleverly made up to resemble a younger version of Willis, but one's surrogate double could be of a different age, race or sex than their operator. When they are not in use, the androids stand motionless inside of a cage-like receptacle until their operators reactivate them. The notion of the robot double taps into a rich vein of sci-fi cinema that ultimately goes back to *Metropolis* and continues through *The Human Duplicators, Futureworld* and *The Stepford Wives*.

"The Moon," as science fiction writer Robert Heinlein once stated, "is a harsh mistress," and the isolated lunar environment provides the backdrop to the British sci-fi thriller *Moon* (2009). The film takes place in the year 2035, when an energy shortage on Earth has led to the establishment of lunar facilities to mine rocks containing the fuel helium-3 for use in nuclear fusion reactors. The energy consortium Lunar Industries Ltd. operates Sarang Station, an automated mining operation located on the Moon's far side. Massive harvester vehicles churn up rocks on the lunar surface containing the helium-3 material, which is then loaded into canisters and shot back to Earth using a rail gun device.

While Sarang Station is almost fully automated, it is manned by a single human operator, Sam Bell (Sam Rockwell), who troubleshoots when problems arise with the machines. Sam is two weeks shy of completing his three-year stint at the station and is looking forward to returning to Earth. He lives in total isolation, his only companion an intelligent computer, GERTY 3000 (voiced by Kevin Spacey), that looks after his every need. Due to spotty communications on the Moon's far side, he is only able to receive occasional video messages from his wife, Eve (Kaya Scodelario) and his three-year-old daughter, Tess, and has sporadic contact with the mining company. For recreation he tends to a small garden, works on a scale model project and watches reruns of television sitcoms. Lately, though, he has been having strange dreams and sees a hallucination of a teenage girl that startles him into accidentally burning his hand.

One day there is a problem with one of the harvesters, and Sam has to go outside the station in a lunar rover to repair it, but the vehicle crashes and traps him inside. He awakens inside the station's infirmary, where GERTY informs him he has sustained a head injury and suffered amnesia about the accident. Following a vague intuition that something isn't right, Sam tricks GERTY into letting him go outside, where he rides a second rover out to the scene of the accident and discovers a duplicate Sam inside the crashed vehicle.

Sam 2 brings Sam 1 back to the Station in time to save his life, and when he recovers the two Sams try to puzzle out the mystery of their dual existence. They eventually find out that they are both clones of the original Sam Bell and discover a secret chamber containing a multitude of Sam Bell clones lying in suspended animation in a gigantic hibernation chamber. The grim truth is that it is easier and cheaper for the company to replace a clone every three years than to send human astronauts to the station. The clones have a three-year lifespan and are disposed of at the end of their tenure in an incineration chamber disguised as a spacecraft that is supposed to take them back to Earth. To test the theory, Sam 1 drives one of the rovers outside the perimeter of the station, where he is able to put in a call to his home on Earth. A teenage girl answers the phone who identifies herself as his daughter, Tess (Dominique McElligott), and he is told that his wife died many years ago before he hears the voice of the original Sam Bell calling her from another room and hangs up.

GERTY informs the Sams that the company is sending a team to the station to repair the damaged harvester, and they realize that if the two clones are discovered together the company will kill them both. By this time Sam 1 is nearing the end of his shelf life and is deteriorating rapidly, so he agrees to sacrifice himself by being placed back in the crashed rover so that the company will suspect nothing. Sam 2 then reboots GERTY, wiping out the machine's memory of recent events and then returns to Earth inside one of the helium-3 canisters. A brief epilogue on the sound track tells us that Sam 2 has given legal testimony against Lunar Industries, which is now being investigated for illegal use of clones.

This neat little exercise in "hard" science fiction had a limited release but drew critical acclaim. The film's scenario of mining the Moon for helium-3 fuel for fusion reactors has been proposed by NASA scientists and astronauts and has a scientific plausibility that may one day be realized. Director Duncan Jones deserves kudos for creating realistic sets that invoke the sci-fi architecture of Kubrick's *2001* on a minuscule budget of $5 million. The Moon is depicted as a horribly desolate, claustrophobia-inducing landscape that could easily drive an isolated human to madness. Sam Rockwell's riveting performance in a dual role as the two Sams must carry the film in what is essentially a one-man show, aided only by the soothing tones of Kevin Spacey as the voice of GERTY. While it tends to be slow and densely plotted at times, *Moon* has a mysterious, haunting quality.

Like *The 6th Day* and *The Island*, *Moon* explores the angst of clones who don't know they're clones and are treated as mere products of immoral corporate enterprise that are to be exploited to the max for profit. All of these films portray clones as fully-grown adult humans who can be decanted and turned into doppelgangers at will, which is a fantasy version of genetic science. This science fiction take on cloning also ignores the fact that clones are usually imperfect copies of their originals. Dolly the sheep, for instance, suffered from many genetic disorders and had to be euthanized before completing the animal's normal life span. In *Moon*, however, the genetic defects are deliberately introduced into the cloning process. The film's two Sams are quite different in temperament; Sam 1 is slovenly, quirky and eccentric, while Sam 2 is neat, quiet and severe. The "original" Sam Bell leads a normal life back on Earth and is presumably ignorant about what the company has done with his clones, but Sam 1 seems to have a telepathic link with his progenitor as he catches hallucinatory glimpses of his teenage daughter. Once more doppelgangers being in temporal and spatial proximity to each other puts them both in mortal peril.

The redoubtable Bruce Willis was back with yet another science fiction doppelganger tale in *Looper* (2012). The film's protagonist is simply called Joe (Joseph Gordon-Levitt), a 25-year-old drug-addicted stone killer who works for a Kansas City crime syndicate in 2044. Thirty years in the future, in 2074, time travel has been invented but has been outlawed and is used only by criminals. Because the disposal of dead bodies has become impossible in 2074, the victims are sent back to 2044 to be disposed of. Joe is a "looper," a mob assassin who shoots them as soon as they materialize from the future and gets rid of the corpses. In order to ensure that there is no connection between the loopers and the syndicate, the assassins are compelled to murder their own future selves, who are sent back with their faces covered and gold bars strapped to their bodies as payment. This arrangement is called "closing the loop." The looper operation is overseen by Abe Mitchell (Jeff Daniels), a mob boss from 2074, who makes sure that all loose ends are neatly tied up.

Joe's friend and fellow looper Seth (Paul Dano) is one of about ten percent of the population possessing a mutation that gives them the power of telekinesis (TK) whereby they can move small objects by mental power alone. One night Seth shows up at Joe's pad in a frantic state, begging Joe to hide him from Mitchell's goons. It seems that he has "let his loop run" by refusing to kill his future self and allowing him to escape. He also warns Joe about a mysterious individual known only as "the Rainmaker," who is taking over the five worldwide crime syndicates in the future and closing all the loops. Joe reluctantly hides Seth inside a hidden chamber in his apartment, but is brought before Mitchell who convinces him to betray his friend.

Joe's next assignment is to close his own loop. His older self (played by Bruce Willis) materializes at the killing spot but unlike the other victims his face is exposed. Using some fancy moves, Old Joe manages to knock Young Joe out and escapes. When Young Joe comes to, he realizes he has let his loop run and returns to his apartment to retrieve the loot he has amassed from his killings, but is attacked by Mitchell's men and falls off a fire escape. At this point the film cuts to an alternative timeline in which Young Joe kills Old Joe and closes his loop. Safe for the next 30 years, Joe emigrates to Shanghai, where he continues to work as an assassin and gradually morphs into the older version of himself. He marries an Asian woman (Summer Qing) and they live an idyllic life until the 30 years are up and three hired killers arrive to fulfill the terms of the contract. His wife is killed during the home invasion but Joe manages to overcome the assassins, commandeers their time machine and travels back to 2044 to change history and save his wife.

Joe returns to the scene of his attempted assassination and drags Young Joe to safety, and the next day the two Joes meet at a diner to plan a strategy. The elder Joe explains that they must take out the Rainmaker in order to save his wife and prevent themselves from being killed. Old Joe has data sheets on three children who were born on the Rainmaker's birthday and proposes they team up to eliminate all of the kids, which will prevent the Rainmaker from reaching adulthood. Joe the younger takes one of the addresses but Mitchell's gang shows up at the diner and the two Joes are separated. Young Joe, following the info on his portion of the document, makes his way to the farmhouse of Sara (Emily Blunt), a young widow and her ten year-old son Cid (Pierce Gagnon). Sara gives him refuge when she realizes that Joe will protect Cid from his older self, who will eventually come looking for the child.

One day Jessie (Garret Dillahunt), one of Mitchell's hired guns, shows up at the farm looking for Joe, but when he menaces Sara, Cid comes to the rescue and demonstrates that he has major-league telekinetic powers by destroying the gunman. It is clear that Cid will grow up to be the rainmaker, and when Old Joe arrives to kill the boy Sara and Joe flee into a nearby field, where the elder Joe gets Cid in his sights. When Sara steps into the line of fire to shield her son, Young Joe is too far away to help. Realizing that the boy will become the Rainmaker if he sees his mother murdered before his eyes, Young Joe turns his gun on himself, his suicide causing Old Joe to vanish into non-existence while saving the mother and son.

A hard-edged exercise in future noir, *Looper* offers plenty of urban grit in the first half, but softens its tone and slows down when Young Joe arrives at the farm. The basic problems with writer/director Rian Johnson's screenplay are the film's protagonist and the overly complex narrative. While Young Joe becomes a surrogate husband and father in the film's second half, it's hard to sympathize with a junkie mob assassin, or with Old Joe as a child murderer. The time travel aspect of the plot is overly complicated and frequently hard to follow. Bruce Willis and Joseph Gordon-Levitt are merely adequate in their morally ambiguous lead roles, but Jeff Daniels is more effective playing the malevolent but businesslike crime boss Mitchell and Emily Blunt delivers a thoughtful portrayal of Sara as a mixture of toughness and feminine vulnerability. The most memorable performance in the film is arguably that of young Pierce Gagnon as Cid, whose telekinetic powers and tormented past set him apart from humanity and make him into a brooding child with a malevolent personality seething just below the surface.

Young Joe and Old Joe constitute a pair of temporal paradox doppelgangers, but unlike the time-traveling doubles in *Back to the Future Part II* or *Timecop* they are able to exist in the same space-time continuum and even work together without creating catastrophic effects on the time stream. Ultimately, however, the conflict between the two Joes leads to the annihilation of both selves. Gordon-Levitt was reportedly fitted with facial prosthetics that made the actor resemble Bruce Willis more closely.

In *Oblivion* (2013) it is the year 2077, when the Earth has been devastated after a war with an alien race called the Scavengers that has destroyed the Moon and caused geological cataclysms. Humankind countered with nuclear weapons that defeated the aliens but contaminated the planet with radiation. New York City is now a vast wasteland littered with the ruins

Assassin Joseph Gordon-Levitt (top) and his time-traveling older self Bruce Willis are featured in this poster for the sci-fi thriller *Looper* (2012).

of famous landmarks. The remaining human population has been evacuated to Titan, a moon orbiting Saturn, and enormous "hydro rigs" hover above the oceans, extracting energy from seawater for the Titan colony and transmitting it to the "Tet," a humongous orbiting space station that resembles an inverted pyramid.

Jack Harper, a.k.a. "Tech 48" (Tom Cruise), and his lover Victoria "Vika" Olsen (Andrea Riseborough) live together in a beautiful futuristic house suspended high above the surface called the Tower. Both of them have been subjected to a "mandatory memory wipe" making them unable to remember anything that happened before the war, but Jack has fragmentary memories of being with a strangely familiar woman on top of the Empire State Building during pre-war times. Jack's job is to repair the combat drones that guard the hydro rigs and are periodically damaged by remnant guerrilla bands of Scavengers, called "Scavs." He is aided by Vika, who monitors his movements and directs him to downed drones with the aid of Sally (Melissa Leo), a mission controller in the Tet. Jack flits around the ruined city in a neat little flying machine called a "bubble ship" seeking the malfunctioning drones while avoiding the Scavs.

Jack takes time off from his maintenance duties at a secret lake house he has built within the forbidden "Radiation Zone" which, oddly, is green and uncontaminated. After discovering that the Scavs are beaming a signal into space, he is vectored to the site of a spacecraft that has crash-landed on Earth, where he discovers that it is not an alien ship, but a pre-war human spaceship called the *Odyssey*. Inside one of the ship's life pods he discovers the sole survivor of the wreck, who is the woman he has seen in his memories. He transports the pod back to the tower and revives the woman, who turns out to be an astronaut named Julia Rosakova (Olga Kurylenko). Vika is none too pleased to have another woman around as competition for Jack's affections, and is further incensed when Jack and Olga fly back to the crash site the next day to retrieve the *Odyssey*'s flight recorder.

While in the process of making the retrieval they are attacked and taken prisoner by the Scavs, who turn out to be the remnants of humanity still living on Earth and not the aliens he has been led to believe. Their leader, the charismatic Malcolm Beech (Morgan Freeman) explains that the Tet and the hydro-rigs are in reality alien vessels, and that mankind lost the war with the invaders. Beech initiated the process of bringing down the *Odyssey* in order to acquire the ships fuel cells, which can be converted to nuclear weapons, and proposes that Jack reprogram a captured drone, arm it with the nuclear bombs and send it back to the Tet to blow it up. Jack refuses, but Beech lets him and Julia go anyway, hoping he will come around eventually.

As Jack's memories return he realizes that Julia is his wife and that they were married before the war. When they return to the Tower, however, Vika refuses to admit them and reports to Sally that Jack is being insubordinate. Sally responds by activating a secret drone hidden within the tower that kills Vika before it is taken out by Julia firing weapons within the bubble ship. Jack and Julia flee from the Tower with three drones in hot pursuit, and in the aerial battle Jack's aircraft is shot down and destroyed., but soon afterward he watches a second aircraft land to repair one of the downed drones and is shocked to encounter his own doppelganger, who is designated as "Tech-52." Jack fights with his double and overcomes him, but Julia is seriously wounded during the battle, so Jack takes Tech-52's aircraft and heads back to the Tower to retrieve a lifesaving medikit. When he arrives he finds a double of Vika waiting for him as if nothing has happened, but ignores her and returns to save Julia's life.

Jack transports Julia to his secret lakeside abode to recuperate before rejoining Beech at the Scav's secret lair. He agrees to implement Beech's plan and is told he is one of thousands of clones the aliens made of the original Jack Harper that were used to exterminate humans, but that the original Harper was a hero astronaut. While he is repairing the captured drone, however, another group of drones attacks the Scav base, damages their drone beyond repair and mortally wounds Beech. Jack and the dying Beech devise a new plan to transport the fuel cell bombs into the Tet concealed inside the bubble ship.

As Jack and Beech fly to the Tet, Jack plays back the *Odyssey*'s flight recorder and learns that he and Vika were both astronauts on a mission to Saturn when they were ordered to rendezvous with the Tet when it first reached Earth. It was Jack who detached the hibernation chamber module containing Julia's life pod from the main body of their spaceship before being captured and cloned by the aliens. As the bubble ship proceeds inside the Tet, Jack sees seemingly endless numbers of Jack Harper clones held in suspended animation inside row after row of transparent cells. Once they are far enough inside the Tet, they detonate the nukes and destroy it, ending the alien's domination of the Earth. In an epilogue set three years later, Jack's remaining clone, Tech-52, has regained all of his memories and finds his way to a reunion with Julia at the lakeside retreat.

The best thing about *Oblivion* is the film's dazzling science fiction visual style that lends it a sleek futuristic look that is easy on the eyes. Producer/director Joseph Kosinski developed the idea from his unpublished novel illustrated with concept art by Andre Wallin. Working with art director Kevin Ishioka, model maker Daniel Simon and the technicians from effects shops Digital Domain and Pixomondo, Kosinski crafts a sleek sci-fi thriller that departs from the dark, dystopian domains that typify much of the genre. Cinematographer Claudio Miranda shot the movie in Sony's proprietary 4K format using their state of the art CineAlta F65 camera, resulting in visuals captured in stunning high resolution. Instead of employing standard blue screens for compositing images, front projection on a massive white reflective screen that surrounded the Tower set provided the illusion of skyscapes at a great height. Much of the exterior work was filmed in Iceland, whose barren landscape and black volcanic soil conjured the stark remains of a broken planet.

Action hero Tom Cruise dominates the film in his starring role as the astronaut turned maintenance man Jack Harper, with able assists from fellow cast members Morgan Freeman, Andrea Riseborough and Olga Kurylenko, but *Oblivion* is clearly not an actor's film, as the human characters are frequently dwarfed into insignificance by their futuristic surroundings. The plot combines the science fiction themes of a post-apocalyptic world and an alien invasion, with mixed results. The alien invaders are never pictured onscreen, for instance, which reduces the feeling of their menace. There are other holes in the plot, such as how Jack manages to build his dream house undetected while his time is so tightly controlled.

Once again the film's doppelgangers are clones unaware of their true nature who are being exploited by hi-tech slave masters with a hidden agenda, although in this instance their manipulators are alien, not human. As in *Moon*, the protagonist is confronted with a veritable army of doppelgangers, all of whom share his memories and personality. Much of the film has a dreamlike ambience that conjures the fantastic realm of the double. The film's bittersweet ending provides one of the few instances in movie history in which the double is seen in a positive, rather than a negative light.

The Australian science fiction thriller *Predestination* (2013) took the idea of the time paradox doppelganger to a whole new level. In the film, after time travel is invented in 1981, a secret governmental organization called the Temporal Agency is established with the goal of preventing terrorist acts from occurring in the past. One of their prime targets is the so-called "Fizzle Bomber," who was responsible for a string of bombings that caused mass casualties in the 1970s. The film opens in 1975 as Temporal Agent Doe tries to defuse one of the Bomber's devices in the basement of an office building and is severely burned in the process. Another agent suddenly appears to transport Doe to the future, where his burns are treated and he undergoes facial reconstruction surgery that drastically alters his appearance.

When he recovers, Agent Doe (Ethan Hawke) is sent back to 1970 in another assignment, where he has taken a job as a bartender in a New York City dive. One night an oddly androgynous individual walks into the bar and strikes up a conversation with the barkeep. He introduces himself as John (played by actress Sarah Snook in male drag), a writer of true confession magazine articles using the nom de plume of "The Unmarried Mother." A hard-bitten, cynical individual, John proceeds to tell his bizarre life story to Doe as it unfolds on the screen in flashback. It seems that "John" was born as "Jane" and taken to an orphanage soon after birth by a mysterious man who is presumably her father. Jane grew up to be an intelligent girl, but is an introvert with anti-social tendencies and as a result is never adopted. Having no family, she became a rebellious, bitter person with no emotional connection to others.

Upon reaching adulthood, Jane applied for a job at SpaceCorp, an outfit that provides women to keep lonely astronauts happy in outer space, but she is rejected due to an unspecified physical condition. Soon afterward she met a man who is handsome, rich and kind (whose face is not shown to the audience) and fell in love. Her happiness is short lived, however, as her lover simply walked away one night and left her, and she later finds that she is pregnant with his child. The baby girl was delivered via Caesarian section and was kidnapped soon after birth by a mysterious man. To compound her misery, during the C-section the doctors discovered that Jane was a hermaphrodite with two sets of sexual organs. The doctors were forced to perform a hysterectomy during the operation, and Jane underwent sexual reassignment surgery and became John. Since that time John has been consumed with the idea of taking revenge on the man who was responsible for her plight.

When John's tale of woe is ended, Agent Doe offers to take her back to that night in 1963 when she was betrayed so she can exact vengeance on her lover. Using a time travel device that looks like an ordinary violin case, they return to that fateful night and Doe leaves John to seek out the man she wants to kill, but unexpectedly John runs into Jane and realizes that he is in actuality the man who fell in love with her. After the romance has run its course, Doe steals their baby, which is the infant Jane, and time travels back to 1945 to place it in the orphanage. Because Jane, John and the baby are one and the same person it creates a "predestination paradox," embodied in an individual who is free from any history or ancestry and is therefore outside of time.

Creating an agent who embodies this paradox has been the goal of the Agency all along, and John is recruited as an agent by the timecops. Doe then goes back in time to 1975 to help the agent burned while trying to defuse the bomb in the film's opening sequence (who turns out to be John). When John goes back to the future he undergoes plastic surgery that turns him into Agent Doe, meaning that Jane, John and Agent Doe are all the same person. Doe is sent back to 1975 once more for another crack at the Fizzle Bomber, who is revealed as a doppelganger of his future self who has gone psychotic from the effects of too much time travel. This means that Jane, John, Doe and the Fizzle Bomber are all temporal aspects of the same person. The bomber tries to convince Doe that the lives he has taken will ultimately save more people than are lost as the time stream unfolds and begs the Agent not to kill him, but Doe fulfills his mission, thereby being responsible for his own conception and death.

This convoluted exercise in time paradox confusion was written and directed by Australia's Spierig Brothers, who had previously produced the science fiction vampire film *Daybreakers*. Adapted from sci-fi luminary Robert Heinlein's story "All You Zombies," the twists and turns of the plot are difficult to follow and the plot ultimately requires multiple viewings to become comprehensible. There are logical holes in the narrative, such as the fact that John and Jane, who are nearly as alike as identical twins, somehow never notice their resemblance to each other when they become lovers. If one is able to keep track of all the intricacies of the time travel paradoxes, *Predestination* is a clever and absorbing science fiction thriller. It's basically a two actor show, starring Ethan Hawke and Sarah Snook, who both play multiple roles. Special effects are minimal and the film must rely instead on the mind-bending concepts of its story.

Like *Back to the Future Part II*, *Timecop*, *12 Monkeys* and *Looper*, *Predestination* presents its doppelgangers as individuals caught in a web of temporal paradox. *Predestination* goes much further than any of the other films, however, in that all four of the main characters are aspects of the same person. While this arrangement might seem clever on paper, on the screen actors Ethan Hawke and Sarah Snook hardly resemble each other, which makes the idea that they're all the same person less than credible. Like *Dr. Jekyll and Sister Hyde*, there is a gender-bending duality to one pair of doubles.

Ethan Hawke is a time-travelling secret agent with multiple identities in *Predestination* (2013).

An organization that manufactures doppelgangers on demand in a near future society is the premise of the British/Irish/Dutch co-production *Identicals* (a.k.a. *Brand New-U*, 2015). The plot centers around film editor Slater Brennan (Lachlan Nieboer) and his girlfriend Nadia Seville (Nora-Jane Noone), who seem like a happy couple until Nadia is abducted from Slater's house by armed men. Right after the kidnapping Slater receives a phone call directing him to contact the Brand New-U corporation if he wants to find Nadia. When he returns to his apartment, he finds a corpse that is a double of Nadia has been placed there and he flees before the police arrive to arrest him for the murder of his lover.

The next day he visits the offices of Brand New-U, and confers with a Manager (Michelle Asante) who tells him that the outfit is in the business of "identity cloning," a service that provides new and improved lives for their clients. This is accomplished by identifying a "life donor" who will be eliminated and replaced by the client, whose "death" will be simulated by planting a lookalike corpse. The Manager tells Slater that Nadia is currently going through this process, and he agrees to a Brand New-U identity swap in the hope of somehow finding her.

Slater undergoes plastic surgery and psychological testing and is duly installed in a new identity, although he is warned that he must take nothing of his old life with him, and that his new life is the property of the company. He is provided with a group of bogus "friends," with whom he doesn't get along, and his existence seems shallow and empty. One day he encounters a woman who is a ringer for Nadia and begins a relationship with her, but this is forbidden by the company, who use drones to provide constant surveillance of their clients. Slater and Nadia are accosted by a group of men dressed as Santa Claus, who hustle them into a car and threaten them. One of the Santas removes his disguise and reveals himself to be Slater's double, who tells him that he will need a "lifespace adjustment" and will be obliged to eliminate the next life donor himself. He is then forced out of the car, which drives away with Nadia inside.

Provided with a second new identity, Slater is moved to a high-rise apartment in which a pair of powerful binoculars has already been set up on a tripod for him. Through the binoculars he observes a woman in a nearby apartment who is Nadia's double, except that she now has long blonde hair. Soon afterward, Slater is visited by a gun dealer (Tony Way), who provides him with an assortment of firearms, weapons ostensibly to be used to dispatch his life donor. Slater visits the blonde version of Nadia in her apartment and makes love to her, and after the lovemaking she abruptly leaves to summon his double. The doppelgangers confront each other in her apartment, where his double taunts him by asking, "can you be the stronger Slater?" He menaces Slater with a straight razor before Slater pulls out a gun and shoots his double to death.

Identicals steals its basic premise from John Frankenheimer's *Seconds*, whose plot also featured a shadowy corporation that arranges for its clients to assume new identities. As in *Seconds*, a dead body is substituted for the client at a bogus death scene, connections with the client's former life are forbidden and the client is provided with a group of phony friends to smooth their transition to a new life. Writer/director Simon Pummell offers up glossy art house visuals, but his screenplay is frequently confusing to the point of incoherence. It is never explained, for instance, why it is necessary to kidnap Nadia at gunpoint if she has already consented to the new life process, or how such an organization as Brand New-U can operate in the open while it perpetrates homicides and other seemingly criminal practices. In Pummell's futureworld an ominous sterility lurks behind the glittering façade of mega buildings, and the actors are frequently framed against screens depicting icons and scrolling alphanumerics that are images presumably generated by the ubiquitous drones that keep them under constant surveillance.

In an interview about the film, Pummell explained that the movie's doppelgangers represent "data doubles," that are a by-product of the digital domain of the internet. The actor's faces are constantly being scanned in what is meant as a metaphor for the net scans, medical scans, airport scans, etcetera that are an integral part of 21st-century life. Nadia's blonde-haired double is cold and distant, and Slater's is sadistic and murderous. And as is frequently the case, the protagonist is forced to confront his doppelganger face to face in a struggle that only one can win.

The aliens, clones, time travelers and robots of science fiction provide fertile ground in which to develop the doppelganger myth. It's a sure thing that the most popular genre in the history of the cinema will continue to produce human duplicators well into the future.

Chapter Six

Conclusion
Double Impact

The theme of the uncanny double continues to have resonance through the centuries, stretching back to the beginnings of literature itself. There is something compelling about having a close encounter with one's alternate self, the most intimate type of ghost imaginable. The idea of the double has its origins in mystical experiences derived from prehistoric shamanic traditions, and continues to be part of human experience today. As Freud pointed out, the doppelganger conjures feelings of the uncanny when one encounters the apparition of oneself. In film, as in folklore, this confrontation often leads to the annihilation of one or both selves.

While the doppelganger also appears in historical, comic and dramatic works, it is most at home in the dark genres of mystery, horror and science fiction, where it inspires feelings of both awe and dread. The motif of the double appears in the works of some of the most acclaimed directors in film history. This list includes Fritz Lang (*Metropolis*), Robert Weine (*The Student of Prague*), Rouben Mamoulian (*Dr. Jekyll and Mr. Hyde*), Robert Siodmak (*The Dark Mirror*), Billy Wilder (*Fedora*), John Frankenheimer (*Seconds*), Don Siegel (*Invasion of the Body Snatchers*), Jack Arnold (*It Came from Outer Space*), Brian de Palma (*Sisters, Obsession*), Mario Bava (*Black Sunday*), Terry Gilliam (*12 Monkeys*), Roger Corman (*The Masque of the Red Death*), Roman Polanski (*The Tenant*), David Cronenberg (*Dead Ringers*), John Woo (*Face/Off*) James Cameron (*Avatar*), and Andrei Tartovsky (*Solaris*). The great Alfred Hitchcock seems to have been mightily obsessed with the doppelganger, a theme that appears in some of his finest works, such as *Rebecca, Shadow of a Doubt, Strangers on a Train, North by Northwest, Vertigo* and *Psycho*. In the process, these filmmakers have adapted classic literary works by Fyodor Dostoyevsky, Edgar Allan Poe, Robert Louis Stevenson, and Nikolai Gogol, as well as the works of popular modern authors such as Jack Finney, Patricia Highsmith, Ira Levin and Stephen King, for the big screen.

Performances by some of film's most gifted actors have enlivened these uncanny tales, distinguished names such as Albert Dekker (*Among the Living*), Boris Karloff (*The Black Room, The Haunted Strangler*), Jeff Bridges (*Starman*), Olivia de Havilland (*The Dark Mirror*), Jeremy Irons (*Dead Ringers*), Laurence Olivier (*Rebecca, The Boys from Brazil*), Henry Fonda (*The Wrong Man*), Mickey Rourke (*Angel Heart*), Nicolas Cage (*Face/Off*), Fredric March (*Dr. Jekyll and Mr. Hyde*), Bette Davis (*Dead Ringer*) and Barbara Steele (*Black Sunday*), among others.

Films on the doppelganger theme include a number of motion picture classics and seminal works in movie history. At the top of the list are some of Hitchcock's most famous thrillers. *Rebecca* won the Academy Award for Best Picture, while *Vertigo* is widely considered the greatest romantic thriller of them all by critics and film historians. Hitch's *Psycho* had a powerful transformative effect on both the crime melodrama and the horror movie, an influence that is still being felt today. Stuart Heisler's *Among the Living* was one of the very first films noir that introduced the German Expressionist style into the mystery genre. In the realm of the horror film the 1913 version of *The Student of Prague* was the first feature-length horror film in cinema history. Rouben Mamoulian's *Dr. Jekyll and Mr. Hyde* utilized novel filmic techniques during the early sound period and won an Oscar for its star, Fredric March, while Mario Bava's gothic masterpiece *Black Sunday* had an enormous influence on the horror movies of the 1960s and 70s.

But the doppelganger theme arguably had the most profound effect on the science fiction film, where it featured prominently in some of its greatest works. Fritz Lang's *Metropolis* was the first sci-fi blockbuster and a seminal film in the history of the genre. Don Siegel's *Invasion of the Body Snatchers* and Fred MacLeod Wilcox's *Forbidden Planet* are considered two of the most important and artistic films of the 1950s sci-fi cycle. Andrei Tartovsky's *Solaris* won wide critical acclaim, especially in European circles. *The Matrix* and its sequels were enormously popular, pioneered new techniques in special effects technology, and led to further science fiction excursions by the Wachovski brothers. James Cameron's *Avatar* led to the 3-D revolution while becoming the most popular film of all time.

In addition to these screen classics are a number of well made, intriguing and entertaining movies that feature the doppelganger, such as *Obsession, The Big Clock, Warning Shadows, The 6th Day, Dual Alibi, The Other, The Stepford Wives, The Picture of Dorian Gray, Oblivion, Enemy, The Haunted Strangler, I Married a Monster from Outer Space, The Scar, The Masque of the Red Death, Predestination, The Island, The Changeling, Strange Impersonation* and *The Man Who Haunted Himself*. Then there are oddities and guilty pleasures like *Doppelganger: The Evil Within, Dead Men Walk, The Human Duplicators, Nightmare Castle, Fight Club, Bowery at Midnight, The Purple Monster Strikes, The Dark Half, Dr. Jekyll and Sister Hyde, The Manster* and *Futureworld*.

Doppelgangers appear in a wide variety of forms in these films. In the noir and mystery genres they are criminals who alter their features to become another's double in films like *Strange Impersonation, The Man with My Face, The Double Man, Fedora, Angel Heart* and *Face/Off*. There are pairs of good and evil identical twins in *Among the Living, The Dark Mirror* and *Dead Ringer*, and cases where both twins have gone bad in *Dual Alibi, The Krays* and *Legend*. Sometimes no explanation at all is offered for the existence of a doppelganger, such as in *The Scar, The Man Who Haunted Himself, The Double* and *Enemy*. A number of Hitchcock's thrillers feature doppelgangers who are two individuals or pairs of individuals linked by fate, criminality or murder as in *Shadow of a Doubt, The Wrong Man, Strangers on a Train, Frenzy* and *Family Plot*.

In the horror genre, the doppelganger also assumes a multitude of forms. The most numerous of these are found in the many screen adaptations of *Dr. Jekyll and Mr. Hyde* and its derivatives, in which the titular physician is transmogrified into his evil opposite number. As in the mystery film, there are pairs of good and evil twins such as those in *The Black Room, Bowery at Midnight* and *Sisters*. The double is associated with such denizens of the realm of horror as ghosts (*Nightmare Castle, The Other, The Changeling*), vampires (*Dead Men Walk, Twins of Evil*) and witches (*Black Sunday, The Long Hair of Death*). Unborn twins menaced their living brethren in *The Dark Half* and *The Unborn*, while the Devil was involved with the double in *The Student of Prague* and *The Masque of the Red Death*.

The science fiction film offers an even more varied selection of doppelgangers: robots in *Metropolis*, *The Perfect Woman*, *The Stepford Wives* and *Surrogates*; aliens in *The Purple Monster Strikes*, *It Came from Outer Space*, *Invasion of the Body Snatchers*, *I Married a Monster from Outer Space*, *The Day Mars Invaded Earth*, *Solaris*, *Starman* and *Spider-Man 3*; clones in *Futureworld*, *The Boys from Brazil*, *The 6th Day*, *The Island* and *Oblivion*. Time travelers had close encounters with their temporal doubles in *Back to the Future Part II*, *Timecop*, *12 Monkeys*, *Looper* and *Predestination*. Doppelgangers were offered for sale in *Seconds* and *Identicals*, while humans projected their consciousness into alternative selves in *The Matrix*, *Surrogates* and *Avatar*.

One type of doppelganger that cuts across genre lines is the invisible or unseen variety. This appears in films where the protagonist searches for what is in actuality a hidden aspect of the self. Examples include such diverse works as *The Big Clock*, *Forbidden Planet* and *Angel Heart*.

Film, as critics and cinema theorists have pointed out, is a realm of doubles. Ghost images of the actors are captured and duplicated, and their likenesses compelled to go through their preordained motions for our amusement. The doppelganger can also be viewed as a metaphor for the psychological process of experiencing cinema itself. While the audience is watching a film they are simultaneously in two places at once, sitting in a darkened theater and vicariously experiencing the actions of our larger than life alternate selves on the screen. As in Arthur Robinson's German Expressionist classic *Warning Shadows*, the audience merges with the shadowplay doubles that act out their passions, their foibles and ultimately, their nobility. In other words, all of us have doppelgangers when we go to the movies.

Filmography

Among the Living (1941) Director: Stuart Heisler. Producer: Sol C. Siegel. Screenplay: Lester Cole. Garrett Ford. Cast: Albert Dekker, Susan Hayward, Harry Carey, Frances Farmer, Ernest Whitman, Maude Eburn, Jean Phillips. USA (Paramount) B&W. 68m. DVD: Paramount Home Video.

Angel Heart (1987) Director/Screenplay: Alan Parker. Producers: Alan Marshall, Elliot Kassner. Cast: Mickey Rourke, Robert De Niro, Lisa Bonet, Charlotte Rampling, Brownie McGhee, Kathleen Wilhoite. USA (Tristar), Color. 113m. DVD: Lions Gate.

Avatar (2009) Director/Producer/Screenplay: James Cameron. Producer: Jon Landau. Cast: Sam Worthington, Zoe Saldana, Sigourney Weaver, Stephen Lang, Michelle Rodriguez. USA (20th Century Fox). Color. 3-D. 161m. DVD: 20th Century Fox Home Entertainment.

Back to the Future Part II (1985) Director: Robert Zemeckis. Producers: Neil Canton, Bob Gale. Cast: Michael J. Fox, Christopher Lloyd, Lea Thompson, Thomas F. Wilson, Elisabeth Shue. USA (Universal). Color. 108m. DVD: Universal Home Entertainment.

The Big Clock (1948) Director: John Farrow. Producer: Richard Maibum. Screenplay: Jonathan Latimer. Cast: Ray Milland, Charles Laughton, Maureen O'Sullivan, Elsa Lanchester, George Macready, Rita Johnson.USA (Paramount) B&W. 95m. DVD: Universal Home Entertainment.

The Black Room (1935) Director: Roy William Neill. Producer: Robert North. Screenplay: Henry Myers, Arthur Strawn. Cast: Boris Karloff, Marian Marsh, Robert Allen, Thurston Hall, Katherine DeMille. USA (Columbia). B&W. 70m. DVD: Sony Pictures Home Entertainment.

Black Sunday (1960) Director: Mario Bava. Producer: Massimo De Rita. Screenplay: Ennio De Concini, Mario Serandrei. Based on *Vij* by Nikolai Gogol. Cast: Barbara Steele, John Richardson, Ivo Garrani, Arturo Dominice. Italy. (Unidis/American International). B&W. 87m. DVD: Kino on Video.

Body Snatchers (1993) Director: Abel Ferara. Producer: Robert H. Solo. Screenplay: Stuart Gordon, Dennis Paoli, Nicholas St. John, from the novel by Jack Finney, Cast: Gabrielle Anwar, Terry Kinney, Billy Wirth, Forest Whittaker, Meg Tilly. USA (Warner Bros.). Color. 87m. DVD: Warner Home Entertainment.

Bowery at Midnight (1942) Director: Wallace Fox. Producers: Sam Katzman, Jack Dietz. Screenplay: Gerard Schnitzer. Cast: Bela Lugosi, Wanda McKay, Tom Neal, John Archer. USA (Monogram), B&W, 61m. DVD: Troma Team Video.

The Boys from Brazil (1978) Director: Franklin J. Schaffner. Producers: Martin Richards, Stanley O'Toole. Screenplay: Heywood Gould, from the novel by Ira Levin. Cast: Gregory Peck, Laurence Olivier, James Mason, Lilli Palmer, Uta Hagen, Steve Gutenberg, Michael Gough. USA (ITA Entertainment). Color. 123m. DVD: Lions Gate.

"The Case of Mr. Pelham" (1955) Director/Producer: Alfred Hitchcock. Screenplay: Francis Cockrell, from a story by Anthony Armstrong. Cast: Tom Ewell, Raymond Bailey, Kirby Smith, Kay Stewart, John Compton, Norman Willis. USA (CBS-TV). B&W. 23m. DVD: Universal Home Entertainment (in *Alfred Hitchcock Presents*, Vol. 1)

The Changeling (1980) Director: Peter Medak. Producer: Joel B. Michaels, Garth H. Drabinsky. Screenplay: Russell Hunter, William Gray, Diana Maddox. Cast: George C. Scott, Trish Van Devere, Melvyn Douglas, John Colicos, Jean Marsh, Helen Burns. Canada. (Associated Film Distributors). Color. 107m. DVD: HBO Home Video.

The Dark Half (1993) Director/Producer/Screenplay: George A, Romero Producers: Declan Baldwin, Christine Forrest. Screenplay: Paul Hunt, Nick McCarthy, from the novel by Stephen King. Cast: Timothy Bottoms, Amy Madigan, Julie Harris, Michael Rooker. USA (Orion Pictures). Color. 121m. DVD: MGM Home Entertainment.

The Dark Mirror (1946) Director: Robert Siodmak. Producer/Screenplay: Nunnally Johnson. Cast: Olivia De Havilland, Lew Ayres, Thomas Mitchell, Dick Long, Charles Evans, Gary Owen. USA (Universal). B&W. 85m. DVD: Universal Home Entertainment.

The Day Mars Invaded Earth (1962) Director/Producer: Maury Dexter. Screenplay: Harry Spalding. Cast: Kent Taylor, Marie Windsor, William Mims, Betty Beal, Lowell Brown, Gregg Shank. USA (20th Century Fox). B&W. 70m. DVD: 20th Century Fox Home Entertainment.

Dead Men Walk (1943) Director: Sam Newfield. Producer: Sigmund Neufeld. Screenplay: Fred Myton. Cast: George Zucco, Dwight Frye, Mary Carlisle, Fern Emmett, Robert Strange, Hal Price, Sam Flint. USA (PRC). B&W. 63m. DVD: Vintage Home Entertainment.

Dead Ringer (1964) Director: Paul Henreid. Producer: William H. Wright. Screenplay: Rian James, Albert Beich, Oscar Millard. Cast: Bette Davis, Karl Malden, Peter Lawford, Philip Carey, Jean Jagen. USA (Warner Bros.). B&W. 115m. Color DVD: Warner Home Entertainment.

Dead Ringers (1988) Director/Producer/Screenplay: David Cronenberg. Producer: Marc Boyman. Cast: Jeremy Irons, Genevieve Bujold, Stephen Lack, Barbara Gordon. Canada (20th Century-Fox). Color. 113m. DVD: Warner Home Entertainment.

Dr. Jekyll and Mr. Hyde (1920) Director: John S. Robertson. Producers: Adolf Zukor, Jesse L. Lasky. Screenplay: Thomas Russell Sullivan, Clara Beranger, from the story by Robert Louis Stevenson. Cast: John Barrymore, Martha Mansfield, Charles W. Lane, Nita Naldi. USA (Paramount). B&W. Silent. 80m. DVD: Alpha Video.

Dr. Jekyll and Mr. Hyde (1931) Director/Producer: Rouben Mamoulian. Screenplay: Samuel Hoffenstein, Percy Heath, from the story by Robert Louis Stevenson. Cast: Fredric March, Miriam Hopkins, Rose Hobart, Holmes Herbert, Halliwell Hobbes, Edward Norton, Tempe Piggott. USA (Paramont). B&W. 96m. DVD: Warner Home Entertainment.

Dr. Jekyll and Mr. Hyde (1941) Director/Producer: Victor Fleming. Screenplay: John Lee Mahin, from the story by Robert Louis Stevenson. Cast: Spencer Tracy, Ingrid Bergman, Lana Turner, Donald Crisp, Ian Hunter, Barton MacLaine, C. Aubrey Smith. USA (MGM). B&W. 113m. DVD: Warner Home Entertainment.

Dr. Jekyll and Sister Hyde (1971) Director: Roy Ward Baker. Producer: Albert Fennell. Producer/Screenplay: Brian Clemens. Cast: Ralph Bates, Martine Beswick, Gerald Sim, Lewis Fiander, Susan Broderick, Ivor Dean, Tony Calvin. UK (Hammer/Anglo-EMI). Color. 97m. DVD: Starz/Anchor Bay.

Doppelganger: The Evil Within (1992) Director/Screenplay: Avi Nesher. Producer: Donald P. Borchers. Cast: Drew Barrymore, George Newbern, Sally Kellerman, George Maharis, Dennis Christopher. USA. (ITC Entertainment). Color. 104m. DVD: Lions Gate.

The Double (2013) Director/Screenplay: Richard Ayoade. Producers: Robin C. Fox, Amina Dasmal. Screenplay: Avi Korine, from the novel by Fyodor Dostoyevsky. Cast: Jesse Eisenberg, Mia Wasikowska, Wallace Shawn, Noah Taylor, James Fox. UK (Studio Canal). Color. 93m. DVD: Magnolia Home Entertainment.

The Double Man (1967) Director: Franklin Schaffner. Producer: Hal E. Chester. Screenplay: Alfred Hayes, Frank Tarloff. Cast: Yul Brynner, Britt Ekland, Clive Revill, Anton Diffring, Lloyd Nolan. UK (Warner Bros.). Color. 105m. DVD: Warner Home Entertainment.

Double Take (2009) Director/Screenplay: Johan Grimonprez. Producers: Nicole Gerhards, Emmy Oost, Hanneke M. van der Tas, Denis Vaslin. Screenplay: Tom McCarthy. Cast: Ron Burrage, Mark Perry, Delfine Balfort. Belgium/Germany/Netherlands. (Zap-O-Matic). Color. 80m. DVD: Kino on Video.

Double Vision (1992) Director: Robert Knights, Producers: Steve Walsh, Lance O'Connor. Screenplay: Tony Grisoni. Cast: Kim Cattrall, Gale Hansen, Macha Meril, Naveen Andrews, Christopher Lee. Canada/France/UK Germany (Republic Pictures.), Color. 92m. DVD: Delta Home Entertainment.

Dual Alibi (1947) Director: Alfred Travers. Producer: Louis H. Jackson. Screenplay: Renalt Capes, Vivienne Ades, Stephen Clarkson, Alfred Travers. Cast: Herbert Lom, Phyllis Dixey, Terrence De Marney, Ronald Frankau. UK (Pathe). B&W. 81m. DVD: Unavailable.

Enemy (2013) Director: Denis Villeneuve. Producers: M.A. Faura, Niv Fichman. Screenplay: Javier Gullon. Cast: Jake Gyllenhaal, Melanie Laurent, Sarah Gadon, Isabella Rossellini. Canada/Spain (El/Alfa/A24) Color. 90m. DVD: A24 Films/eOne Entertainment.

Face/Off (1997) Director: John Woo. Producers: David Permut, Barrie M. Osborne, Terence Chang, Christopher Godsick, Screenplay: Mike Werb, Michael Colleary. Cast: John Travolta, Nicolas Cage, Joan Allen, Gina Gershon, Allesandro Nivola. USA (Paramount-Touchstone) Color. 139m. DVD: Paramount Home Video.

Family Plot (1976) Director/Producer: Alfred Hitchcock. Screenplay: Ernest Lehman. Cast: Barbara Harris, Bruce Dern, William Devane, Karen Black, Cathleen Nesbitt. USA (Universal). Color. 121m. DVD: Universal Home Entertainment.

Fedora (1978) Director/Producer/Screenplay: Billy Wilder. Screenplay: I.A.L. Diamond, based on the novella by Tom Tryon. Cast: William Holden, Hildegard Knef, Jose Ferrer, Frances Sternhagen, Stephen Collins. Germany/France (United Artists). Color. 114m. DVD: Olive Films.

Fight Club (1999) Director: David Fincher. Producers: Art Linson, Cean Chaffin, Ross Grayson Bell. Screenplay: Jim Uhls, from the novel by Chuck Palahniuk. Cast: Brad Pitt, Edward Norton, Helena Bonham Carter, Meat Loaf Aday, Jared Leto. USA (Fox 2000/Regency/Linson Films)., Color. 139m. DVD: 20th Century Fox Home Entertainment.

Forbidden Planet (1956) Director: Fred McLeod Wilcox. Producer: Nicholas Nayfack. Screenplay: Cyril Hume. Cast: Leslie Nielsen, Walter Pidgeon, Anne Francis, Warren Stevens. USA (MGM). 98m. Color. DVD: Warner Home Video.

The Forest (2015) Director: Jason Zada. Producers: Tory Metzger, David S. Goyer, David Linde. Screenplay: Ben Ketai, Sarah Cornwell, Nick Antosca. Cast: Natalie Dormer, Taylor Kinney, Yukiyoshi Ozawa, Eoin Macken, Stephanie Vogt, Rina Takasaki, USA (Gramercy/Icon). Color. 93m. DVD: Universal Home Entertainment.

The Four Sided Triangle (1953) Director: Terrence Fisher. Producers: Michael Carreras, Alexander Paul. Screenplay: Paul Tabori, William F. Temple. Cast: Stephen Murray, Barbara Payton, James Hayter, John Van Eyssen, Kynaston Reeves. UK (Hammer/Astor). B&W. 81m. DVD: Starz/Anchor Bay.

Frenzy (1972) Director/Producer: Alfred Hitchcock. Screenplay: Anthony Shaffer. Cast: John Finch, Alec McCowan, Barry Foster, Billie Whitelaw, Barbara Leigh-Hunt, Bernard Cribbins. UK (Universal). Color. 116m. DVD: Universal Home Entertainment.

Futureworld (1976) Director: Richard T. Heffron. Producers: Paul N. Lazarus, James T. Aubrey, Samuel Z. Arkoff. Screenplay: Mayo Simon, George Schenck. Cast: Peter Fonda, Blythe Danner, Yul Brynner, Arthur Hill, John Ryan, Ed Geldard, James M. Connor. USA (American International). Color. 104m. DVD: MGM Home Entertainment.

The Haunted Strangler (1958) Director: Robert Day. Producer: John Croydon. Screenplay: Jan Read, John C. Cooper. Cast: Boris Karloff, Anthony Dawson, Elizabeth Allen, Jean Kent. UK (Anglo-Amalgamated), B&W. 81m. DVD: Image Entertainment.

Hollow Triumph (a.k.a. *The Scar*, 1948) Director: Steve Sekely. Producer: Paul Henreid. Screenplay: Daniel Fuchs. Cast: Paul Henreid, Joan Bennett, Eduard Franz, Leslie Brooks, John Qualen. USA (Eagle-Lion). B&W. 83m. DVD: Synergy Entertainment.

The Human Duplicators (1965) Director/Producer: Hugo Grimaldi. Producer/Screenplay: Arthur C. Pierce. Cast: George Macready, George Nader, Richard Kiel, Barbara Nichols, Hugh Beaumont, Richard Arlen. USA (Woolner Bros./Allied Artists). Color. 80m. DVD: Live Home Video.

I Married a Monster from Outer Space (1958) Director/Producer: Gene Fowler, Jr. Screenplay: Louis Vittes. Cast: Tom Tryon, Gloria Talbot, Ken Lynch, Robert Ivers, Chuck Wassil. USA (Paramount). B&W. 78m. DVD: Warner Home Video.

Identicals (a.k.a. *Brand New-U2*, 2015) Director/Screenplay: Simon Pummell. Producers: Janina Marmot, Conor Barry, John Keville, Reiner Selen. Cast: Lachlan Nieboer, Nora-Jane Noone,

Nick Blood, Tony Way. UK/Ireland/Netherlands, (The Match Factory). Color. 100m. DVD: Sony Pictures Home Entertainment.

Invasion of the Body Snatchers (1956) Director: Don Siegel. Producer: Walter Wanger. Screenplay: Daniel Mainwaring, from the novel by Jack Finney. Cast: Kevin McCarthy, Dana Wynter, Larry Gates, King Donovan, Carolyn Jones. USA (Allied Artists). B&W 80m. DVD: Paramount Home Video.

Invasion of the Body Snatchers (1978) Director: Philip Kaufman. Producer: Robert H. Solo. Screenplay: W.D. Richter, from the novel by Jack Finney. Cast: Donald Sutherland, Brooke Adams, Leonard Nimoy, Veronica Cartwright, Jeff Goldblum. USA (United Artists). Color. 115m. DVD: MGM Home Entertainment.

The Island (2005) Director/ Producer: Michael Bay. Producers: Walter F. Parkes, Ian Bryce. Screenplay: Caspian Tredwell-Owen, Alex Kurtzman, Roberto Orci. Cast: Ewan McGregor, Scarlet Johansson, Djimon Hounsou, Sean Bean, Steve Buscemi, Michael Clarke Duncan. USA (Warner Bros.). Color, 136m. DVD: Dream Works Home Entertainment.

It Came from Outer Space (1953) Director: Jack Arnold. Producer: William Alland. Screenplay: Harry Essex. Cast: Richard Carlson, Barbara Rush, Charles Drake, Joe Sawyer, Russell Johnson. USA (Universal). B&W. 3-D. 81m. DVD: Universal Home Entertainment.

Der Januskopf (*The Janus Head*, 1920) Director: F.W. Murnau. Producer: Erich Pommer. Screenplay: Hans Janowitz. Cast: Conrad Veidt, Bela Lugosi, Magnus Stifter, Margarete Schlegal, Willy Kaiser-Heyl. Germany (Decla-Bioscop). B&W. Silent. Running Time Unknown. DVD: Unavailable.

Journey to the Far Side of the Sun (a.k.a. *Doppelganger*, 1969) Director: Robert Parrish. Producers/ Screenplay: Gerry Anderson, Sylvia Anderson. Screenplay: Tony Williamson. Cast: Roy Thinnes, Herbert Lom, Ian Hendry, Lynn Loring, Patrick Wymark. UK (Rank/Universal). Color. 101m. DVD: Universal Home Entertainment.

The Krays (1990) Director: Peter Medak. Producers: Dominic Anciano, Ray Burdis. Screenplay: Philip Ridley. Cast: Martin Kemp, Gary Kemp, Billie Whitelaw, Tom Bell, Kate Hardie. UK (Rank). Color. 119m. DVD: Universal Home Entertainment.

Legend (2015) Director/Screenplay: Brian Helgeland. Producers: Chris Clark, Quentin Curtis, Brian Oliver. Cast: Tom Hardy, Emily Browning, David Thewlis, Christopher Eccleston, Chazz Palminteri. UK (Universal). Color. 131m. DVD: Universal Home Entertainment.

The Long Hair of Death (1964) Director/Screenplay: Antonio Margheriti. Producer: Felice Testa Gay. Screenplay: Tonino Valerii. Cast: Barbara Steele, George Ardisson, Halina Zalewska. Italy (U.N.I.D.I.S.). B&W. 100m. DVD: RaroVideo.

Looper (2012) Director/Screenplay: Rian Johnson. Producers: Ram Bergman, James D. Stern. Cast: Bruce Willis, Joseph Gordon-Levitt, Emily Blunt, Pierce Gagnon, Paul Dano, Noah Segan, Piper Perabo, Jeff Daniels. USA (Tristar). Color. 118m. DVD: Sony Pictures Home Entertainment.

The Man with Bogart's Face (1980) Director: Robert Day. Producer/Screenplay: Andrew J. Fenady. Cast: Robert Sacchi, Victor Buono, Franco Nero, Yvonne De Carlo, Herbert Lom, Mike Mazurki, Michelle Phillips, George Raft. USA (20th Century Fox). Color, 106m. DVD: 20th Century Fox Home Entertainment.

The Man with My Face (1951) Director: Edward Montague. Producer: Ed Gardner. Screenplay: Tom McGowan, Edward Montague, Samuel W. Taylor, Vin Bogert. Cast: Barry Nelson, Carole Mathews, Jack Warden, Lynn Ainley, Jim Boles. USA (United Artists). B&W. 79m. DVD: Unavailable.

The Man Who Haunted Himself (1970) Director/Screenplay: Basil Dearden. Producer: Michael Relph. Screenplay: Anthony Armstrong, Michael Relph, Bryan Forbes. Cast: Roger Moore, Hildegarde Neil. UK (Warner-Pathe), Color. 89m. DVD: Lions Gate.

The Manster (1958) Directors: George Breakston, Kenneth G. Crane. Producer/Screenplay: George Breakston. Cast: Peter Dyneley, Jane Hylton, Tetsu Nakamura, Terri Zimmern, Norman Van Hawley, Jerry Ito. USA/Japan (United Artists/Lopert). B&W. 72m. DVD: Mill Creek Entertainment.

The Masque of the Red Death (1964) Director/Producer: Roger Corman. Producer: George

Willoughby. Screenplay: Charles Beaument, R. Wright Campbell, from the story by Edgar Allan Poe. Cast: Vincent Price, Jane Asher, Hazel Court, USA/UK (American International). Color. 90m. DVD: MGM Home Entertainment.

The Matrix (1999) Director/Screenplay: Andy Wachowski, Larry Wachowski. Producer: Joel Silver. Cast: Keanu Reeves, Laurence Fishburne, Carrie-Anne Moss, Hugo Weaving, Joe Pantoliano. USA (Warner Bros.). Color. 136m. DVD: Warner Home Video.

The Matrix Reloaded (2003) Director: /Screenplay: Andy Wachowski, Larry Wachowski. Producer: Joel Silver. Cast: Keanu Reeves, Laurence Fishburne, Carrie-Anne Moss, Hugo Weaving, Neil Rayment, Adrian Rayment, Jada Pinkett Smith. USA (Warner Bros.). Color. 138m. DVD: Warner Home Video.

Metropolis (1927) Director: Fritz Lang. Producer: Erich Pommer. Screenplay: Thea Von Harbou. Cast: Gustav Frolich, Brigitte Helm, Rudolf Klein-Rogge, Alfred Abel, Fritz Rasp, Theodor Loos. Germany (UFA), B&W, Silent. 124m. DVD: Kino on Video.

"Metzengenstein" (in *Spirits of the Dead*, 1968) Director/Screenplay: Roger Vadim. Producers: Raymond Eger, Alberto Grimaldi. Screenplay: Pascal Cousin, Clement Biddlewood, from the story by Edgar Allan Poe. Cast: Jane Fonda, Peter Fonda, James Robertson Justice, Georges Douking. Italy/France (P.E.A./American International/Cocinor). Color. Approx. 40m. DVD: Homevision/Image.

Moon (2009) Director: Duncan Jones. Producers: Stuart Fenegan, Trudie Styler. Screenplay: Nathan Parker. Cast: Sam Rockwell, Kevin Spacey, Dominique McElligott, Kaya Scodelario. UK (Sony Pictures). Color. 97m. DVD: Sony Pictures Home Video.

Nightmare Castle (*Amanti d'oltretomba*, 1965) Director/Screenplay: Mario Caiano. Producer: Carlo Caiano. Screenplay: Fabio De Agostini. Cast: Barbara Steele, Paul Muller, Helga Line, Marino Masse, Rik Battaglia. Italy. (Emmeci). B&W. 97m. DVD: St. Clair Vision.

North by Northwest (1959) Director/Producer: Alfred Hitchcock. Producer: Herbert Coleman. Screenplay: Ernest Lehman. Cast: Cary Grant, Eva Marie Saint, James Mason, Martin Landau, Leo G. Carroll. USA (MGM). Color.136m. DVD: Warner Home Video.

Oblivion (2013) Director/Producer: Joseph Kosinski. Producers: Peter Chermin, Dylan Clark, Barry Levine, Duncan Henderson. Screenplay: Karl Gajdusek, Micheal deBruyn, Cast: Tom Cruise, Morgan Freeman, Olga Kurylenko, Andrea Riseborough. USA (Universal). Color. 124m. DVD: Universal Home Entertainment.

Obsession (1976) Director: Brian De Palma. Producer: George Litto. Screenplay: Paul Schrader. Cast: Cliff Robertson, John Lithgow, Genevieve Bujold, Stocker Fontelieu. USA (Columbia). Color. 98m. DVD: Sony Pictures Home Video.

The One (2001) Director/Producer/Screenplay: James Wong. Producers: Steve Chasman, Glen Morgan, Charles Newirth, Todd Garner, Lata Ryan, Tom Sherak, Greg Silverman, Happy Walters. Screenplay: Glen Morgan. Cast: Jet Li, Delroy Lindo, Carla Gugino, Jason Statham, James Morrison. USA (Columbia). Color. 87m. DVD: Columbia.

The Other (1972) Director/Producer: Robert Mulligan. Producer/Screenplay: Tom Tryon, from his novel. Cast: Chris Udvarnoky, Martin Udvarnoky, Uta Hagen Diana Muldaur, John Ritter. USA (20th Century Fox). Color. 108m. DVD: 20th Century Fox Home Entertainment.

The Perfect Woman (1949) Director: Bernard Knowles. Producer: Alfred Black, George Black. Screenplay: George Black, Bernard Knowles. Cast: Patricia Roc, Stanley Holloway, Nigel Patrick, Miles Malleson. UK (General Film Distributors). B&W. 88m. DVD: Onyx Media International.

The Picture of Dorian Gray (1945) Director/Screenplay: Albert Lewin. Producer: Pandro S. Berman. Cast: Hurd Hatfield, George Sanders, Angela Lansbury, Donna Reed, Peter Lawford, Bernard Gorcey. USA (MGM). B&W/Color. 110m. DVD: Warner Home Entertainment.

Predestination (2013) Director/Producer/Screenplay: Michael Spierig, Peter Spierig. Producers: Paddy McDonald, Tim McGrahan. Cast: Ethan Hawke, Sarah Snook, Noah Taylor, Christopher Kirby, Madeleine West. Australia (Pinnacle/Stage 6). Color. 97m. DVD: Sony Pictures Home Entertainment.

Psycho (1960) Director/Producer: Alfred Hitchcock. Screenplay: Joseph Stefano. Cast: Anthony Perkins, Janet Leigh, John Gavin, Martin Balsam, Vera Miles, Simon Oakland. USA (Paramount). B&W. 109m. DVD: Universal Home Entertainment.

The Purple Monster Strikes (1945) Directors: Spencer Gordon Bennet, Fred C. Brannon. Producer: Ronald Davidson. Screenplay: Royal Cole, Albert DeMond, Basil Dickey, Lynn Perkins, Joseph Poland, Barney Sarecky. Cast: Dennis Moore, Linda Stirling, Toy Barcroft, James Craven, Mary Moore. USA (Republic Pictures). B&W. Serial. 15 Chapters, 209m. DVD: Metric Collectibles.

Raising Cain (1992) Director/Screenplay: Brian De Palma. Producer: Gale Anne Hurd. Cast: John Lithgow, Lolita Davidovich, Steven Bauer, Frances Sternhagen, Gregg Henry. USA (Universal). Color. 91m. DVD: Universal Home Entertainment.

Rebecca (1940) Director: Alfred Hitchcock. Producer: David O. Selznick. Screenplay: Robert E. Sherwood, Joan Harrison. Cast: Joan Fontaine, Laurence Olivier, George Sanders, Judith Anderson, Nigel Bruce, Leo G. Carroll. USA (Selznick Studios). B&W. 130m. DVD: MGM/UA Home Entertainment.

Shadow of a Doubt (1943) Director: Alfred Hitchcock, Producer: Jack H. Skirball. Screenplay: Thornton Wilder, Sally Benson, Alma Reville. Cast: Theresa Wright, Joseph Cotton, Macdonald Carey, Henry Travers, Patricia Collinge. USA (Universal). B&W. 108m. DVD: Universal Home Entertainment.

Seconds (1966) Director: John Frankenheimer. Producer: Edward Lewis. Screenplay: Lewis Carlino. Cast: Rock Hudson, John Randolph, Salome Jens, Will Geer, Jeff Corey. USA (Paramount), B&W. 106m. DVD: Paramount Home Video.

Sisters (1973) Director/Screenplay: Brian De Palma. Producer: Edward R. Pressman. Screenplay: Louisa Rose. Cast: Margot Kidder, Jennifer Salt, Charles Durning, William Finley. USA (American International). Color. 92m. DVD: The Criterion Collection.

The Sixth Day (2000) Director: Roger Spottiswoode. Producers: Mike Medavoy, Arnold Schwarzenegger, Jon Davison. Screenplay: Cormac Wibberley, Marianne Wibberley. Cast: Arnold Schwarzenegger, Robert Duvall, Tony Goldwyn, Michael Rooker, Sarah Wynter. USA (Columbia), Color 124m. DVD: Columbia Tristar Home Entertainment.

Solaris (1972) Director/Screenplay: Andrei Tarkovsky. Producer: Viacheslav Tarasov. Screenplay: Fridrikh Gorenshtein, from the novel by Stanislaw Lem. Cast: Natalya Bondarchuk, Donatas Banionis, Juri Jarvet, Nickolai Grinko. USSR (Mosfilm). Color. 166m. DVD: The Criterion Collection.

Spider-Man 3 (2007) Director/Screenplay: Sam Raimi. Producers: Laura Ziskin, Ivan Raimi, Grant Curtis. Cast: Tobey Maguire, Kirsten Dunst, James Franco, Thomas Hayden Church, Topher Grace. USA (Columbia). Color 119m. DVD: Sony Pictures Home Entertainment.

Starman (1984) Director: John Carpenter. Producer: Larry J. Franco, Michael Douglas. Screenplay: Bruce A. Evans, Raymond Gideon, Dean Riesner. Cast: Jeff Bridges, Karen Allen, Charles Martin Smith, Richard Jaeckel, Robert Phalen. USA (Columbia). Color. 115m. DVD: Sony Pictures Home Entertainment.

The Stepford Wives (1975) Director: Bryan Forbes. Producer: Edgar J. Scherick. Screenplay: William Goldman. Cast: Katherine Ross, Paula Prentiss, Peter Masterson, Nanette Newman, Tina Louise, Patrick O'Neal. USA (Columbia). Color. 115m. DVD: Anchor Bay Entertainment.

Strange Impersonation (1946) Director: Anthony Mann. Producer: William Wilder. Screenplay: Mindret Lord. Cast: Brenda Marshall, William Gargan, Hillary Brooke, H.B. Warner, Ruth Ford, Lyle Talbot. USA (Republic Pictures). B&W. 68m. DVD: Kino on Video.

Strangers on a Train (1951) Director/Producer: Alfred Hitchcock. Screenplay: Raymond Chandler, Czenzi Ormonde, from the novel by Patricia Highsmith. Cast: Robert Walker, Farley Granger, Ruth Roman, Laura Elliott, Leo G. Carroll, Patricia Hitchcock. USA (Warner Bros./First National). B&W. 101m. DVD: Warner Home Video.

The Student of Prague (*Der Student von Prag*, 1913) Director: Stellan Rye. Screenplay: Hanns Heinz Ewers. Cast: Paul Wegener, John Gottowt, Grete BergerLyda Salmanova, Lothar Korner. Germany (Bioscop). B&W. Silent. 41m. DVD: Alpha Video.

The Student of Prague (*Der Student von Prag*, 1926) Director/Screenplay: Henrik Galeen. Screenplay: Hanns Heinz Ewers. Cast: Conrad Veidt, Werner Krauss, Eliza La Porta, Agnes Esterhazy, Fritz Alberti, Ferdinand von Alten. Germany (Sokol-Film). B&W. Silent. 91m. DVD: Alpha Video.

The Student of Prague (*Der Student von Prag*, 1935) Director: Arthur Robison. Screenplay: Hanns Heinz Ewers, Henrik Galeen. Cast: Anton Wolbrook, Theodor Loos, Dorothea Wieck, Erich Fielder. Germany (Cine-Allianz Tonfilmproduktions). B&W. 87m. DVD: Unavailable.

Surrogates (2009) Director: Jonathan Mostow. Producers: David Hoberman, Tod Lieberman, Max Handelman. Screenplay: John Brancanto, Michael Ferris. Cast: Bruce Willis, Radha Mitchell, Rosamund Pike, Boris Kodjoe, Ving Rhames, James Cromwell. USA (Walt Disney Studios). Color. 89m. DVD: Walt Disney Home Entertainment.

The Tenant (1976) Director/Screenplay: Roman Polanski. Producer: Hercules Bellville. Screenplay: Gerard Brach. Cast: Roman Polanski, Isabelle Adjani, Melvyn Douglas, Shelly Winters, Lila Kedrova. USA (Paramount). Color. 125m. DVD: Paramount Home Video.

The Thing (1982) Director: John Carpenter. Producers: David Foster, Lawrence Turman. Screenplay: Bill Lancaster, based on *Who Goes There?* by John Campbell, Jr. Cast: Kurt Russell, A. Wilfred Brimley, T.K. Carter, David Clennon, Keith David. USA (Universal). Color. 109m. DVD: Universal Home Entertainment.

The Thing (2011) Director: Matthijs van Heijningen Jr. Producers: Marc Abraham, Eric Newman. Screenplay: Eric Heisserer. Cast: Mary Elizabeth Winstead, Joel Edgerton, Ukrich Thomsen, Adewale Akinnuoye-Agbaje, Eric Christian Olsen. USA (Universal). Color. 103m. DVD: Universal Home Entertainment.

Timecop (1994) Director: Peter Hyams. Producers: Moshe Damant, Robert Taper, Sam Raimi. Screenplay: Mark Verheiden. Cast: Jean-Claude Van Damme, Mia Sara, Ron Silver, Gloria Reuben, Bruce McGill. USA (MCA), Color. 99m. DVD: Universal Home Entertainment.

12 Monkeys (1995) Director: Terry Gilliam. Producer: Charles Rowen. Screenplay: David Peoples, Janret Peoples. Cast: Bruce Willis, Madeleine Stowe, Brad Pitt, Christopher Plummer. USA (Universal). Color. 130m. DVD: Universal Home Entertainment.

Twin Dragons (1992) Directors: Ringo Lam, Tsui Hark. Producers: Teddy Robin Kwan, Ng See-Yuen. Cast: Screenplay: Barry Wong, Tsui Hark, Joe Cheung, Wong Yik, Teddy Robin Kwan. Cast: Jackie Chan, Maggie Cheung, Teddy Robin, Nina Li Chi. Hong Kong. (Golden Harvest,/Media Asia), Color. 104m. DVD: Dimension Films.

Twins of Evil (1971) Director: John Hough. Producers: Michael Style, Harry Fine. Screenplay: Tudor Gates. Cast: Peter Cushing, Dennis Price, Mary Collinson, Madeleine Collinson, Damien Thomas. UK (Hammer/Rank/Universal). Color. 87m. DVD: Synapse Films.

The Two Faces of Dr. Jekyll (1960) Director: Terrence Fisher. Producer: Michael Carreras. Screenplay: Wolf Mankowitz. Cast: Paul Massie, Dawn Addams, Christopher Lee, David Kossoff, Francis de Wolff. UK (Hammer/Columbia). Color. 88m. DVD: Mill Creek Entertainment.

The Unborn (2009) Director/Screenplay: David S. Goyer. Producers: Michael Bay, Andrew Form, Brad Fuller. Cast: Odette Yustman, Gary Oldman, Meagan Good, Cam Gigandet, James Remar. USA (Rogue/Universal). Color. 87m. DVD: Rogue Pictures.

Vertigo (1958) Director/Producer: Alfred Hitchcock. Screenplay: Alec Coppel, Samuel Taylor. Cast: James Stewart, Kim Novak, Barbara Bel Geddes, Tom Helmore. USA (Paramount). Color. 120m. DVD: Universal Home Entertainment.

Warning Shadows (*Schatten*, 1923) Director/Screenplay: Arthur Robison. Producers: Enrico Dieckmann, Willy Siebold. Screenplay: Rudolf Schneider. Cast: Alexander Granach, Fritz Kortner, Ruth Weyher, Gustav von Wangenheim, Fritz Rasp. Germany (Pan-Film der Dafu-film-Verleih). B&W. Silent. 90m. DVD: Kino on Video.

"William Wilson" (in *Spirits of the Dead*, 1968) Director/Screenplay: Louis Malle. Producers: Raymond Eger, Alberto Grimaldi. Screenplay: Clement Biddlewood, Daniel Boulanger. Cast: Alain Delon, Brigitte Bardot, Katia Christine, Renzo Palmer. Italy/France (P.E.A./American International/Cocinor). Color. Approx. 40m. DVD: Homevision/Image.

The Woman in White (1948) Director: Peter Godfrey. Producer: Henry Blanke. Screenplay: Stephen Morehouse Avery, from the novel by Wilkie Collins. Cast: Gig Young, Alexis Smith, Eleanor Parker, Sydney Greenstreet, John Emery, John Abbott. USA (Warner Brothers). B&W. 109m. DVD: Warner Home Video.

The Wrong Man (1957) Director/Producer: Alfred Hitchcock. Screenplay: Maxwell Anderson, Angus McPhail. Cast: Henry Fonda, Vera Miles, Anthony Quayle. Harold J. Stone, Charles Cooper, Nehemiah Persoff. USA (Warner Bros.). 105m. B&W. DVD: Warner Home Video.

Chapter Notes

Chapter One

1. Keneva Kunz, trans., *The Vinland Sagas: The Saga of the Greenlanders* and *Eirik the Red's Saga* (London: Penguin Classics, 2008), 36–37.
2. Quoted in Otto Rank, *The Double: A Psychoanalytic Study*, trans. Harry Tucker, Jr. (New York: New American Library, 1979), 8.
3. Quoted in Donald Spoto, *The Dark Side of Genius: The Life of Alfred Hitchcock* (New York: Ballantine Books, 1983), 341.
4. Percy Shelley, *Prometheus Unbound* (New Haven: Yale University Press 1968), 61.
5. Oliver Sacks, *Hallucinations* (New York: Alfred A. Knopf, 2012), 263.
6. Ibid., 265.
7. Ibid., 266–267.
8. Ibid., 268.
9. Carlos Castaneda, *Tales of Power* (New York: Pocket Books, 1974), 46.
10. Ibid., 77.
11. Ibid., 63–64.
12. John Glatt, *Evil Twins* (New York: St. Martin's, 1999), xiii–xiv.
13. "Woman Who Freaked Out After Meeting Doppelganger Meets Second One in Italy," www.abcnews.go.com/International/woman-freaked-meeting-doppelganger-meets-2nd-Italy/story?id=31697423.

Chapter Two

1. Ralph Nelson, trans., *Popul Vuh: The Great Mythological Book of the Ancient Maya* (Boston: Houghton Mifflin, 1976), 9.
2. E.T.A. Hoffman, *The Best Tales of Hoffman*, ed. and introd. E.F. Bleiler (Toronto: Dover Publishing/General Publishing Co., 1967), xxx–xxxi.
3. Ibid., xxxi.
4. Ibid., 122.
5. Mary Shelley, *Frankenstein*, in *Three Gothic Novels* (London: The Penguin English Library, 1976), 356.
6. James Hogg, *The Private Memoirs and Confessions of a Justified Sinner* (New York: New York Review Books, 2002), 111.
7. Ibid., 118.
8. "William Wilson," in *Edgar Allan Poe, The Fall of the House of Usher and Other Writings* (London: Penguin Classics, 1986), 178.
9. Ibid., 176.
10. Guy De Maupassant, "The Horla," in Leslie Shepard, ed., *The Dracula Book of Great Vampire Stories* (Secaucus, NJ: The Citadel Press, 1977), 95.
11. Ibid., 91.
12. Robert Louis Stevenson, *The Strange Case of Dr. Jekyll and Mr. Hyde* (London: Penguin Books, 2002), 40.
13. Ibid., 43.
14. Ibid., 34.
15. Ibid., 82.
16. Oscar Wilde, *The Picture of Dorian Gray* (London: Penguin Modern Classics, 1982), 144.
17. Ibid., 247.
18. Ibid., 11.
19. Ibid., 44.
20. Stephen King, *Danse Macabre* (New York: Berkley Books, 1983), 306
21. Jack Finney, *Invasion of the Body Snatchers* (New York: Fireside Books, 1989), 69.

Chapter Three

1. Robert Porfirio in Alain Silver and Elizabeth Ward, eds., *Film Noir: An Encyclopedic Reference to the American Style* (Woodstock, NY: Overlook, 1979), 11.
2. Spoto, *The Dark Side of Genius*, 351.
3. Patricia Highsmith, *Strangers on a Train* (New York: Harper and Brothers, 1950), 163.
4. Spoto, *The Dark Side of Genius*, 277.
5. Ibid., 348–349.
6. Ibid., 458.
7. Ibid., 405
8. Glatt, *Evil Twins*, 225.

Chapter Four

1. Lotte H. Eisner, *The Haunted Screen* (Berkeley: University of California Press, 1973), 40.
2. Siegfried Kracauer, *From Caligari to Hitler* (Princeton: Princeton University Press, 1947), 29.
3. Eisner, *The Haunted Screen*, 40.
4. Carlos Clarens, *An Illustrated History of the Horror Film* (New York: Capricorn Books, 1967), 40.
5. Ibid., 83.
6. Zack Davisson, *Yurei: The Japanese Ghost* (Seattle: Chin Music Press, 2015), 133.

Chapter Five

1. Peter Bogdanovich, *Who the Devil Made It?* (New York: Alfred A. Knopf, 1997), 178.
2. John Baxter, *Science Fiction in the Cinema* (New York: Paperback Library, 1970), 117
3. Ibid., 140.
4. "Doppelganger," https://en.wikipedia.org/wiki/Doppelg%C3%A4nger_(1969_film).

Bibliography

Ackerman, Forrest J., ed. *Science Fiction Classics: The Stories that Morphed Into Movies*. New York: TV Books, 1999.

Baxter, John. *Science Fiction in the Cinema*. New York: Paperback Library, 1970.

Bogdanovich, Peter. *Who the Devil Made It?* New York: Alfred A. Knopf, 1997.

Butler, Ivan. *Horror in the Cinema*. New York: A.S. Barnes, 1970.

Castaneda, Carlos. *Tales of Power*. New York: Pocket Books, 1974.

Clarens, Carlos. *An Illustrated History of the Horror Film*. New York: Capricorn Books, 1967.

Davisson, Zack. *Yurei: The Japanese Ghost*. Seattle: Chin Music Press, 2015.

Dostoyevsky, Fyodor. *The Double* and *The Gambler*. Richard Pevear and Larissa Volokhonsky, trans. New York: Vintage Books, 2007.

Eisner, Lotte H. *The Haunted Screen*. Berkeley: University of California Press, 1973.

Elsaesser, Thomas. *Metropolis*. London: BFI Publishing, 2000.

Everman, Welch. *Cult Science Fiction Films*. New York: Citadel, 1995.

Finney, Jack. *Invasion of the Body Snatchers*. New York: Fireside Books, 1989.

George, Andrew, trans. *The Epic of Gilgamesh*. London: Penguin Classics, 2003.

Glatt, John. *Evil Twins*. New York: St. Martin's, 1999.

Highsmith, Patricia. *Strangers on a Train*. New York: Harper and Brothers, 1950.

Hoffman, E.T.A. *The Best Tales of Hoffman*, ed. and introd. E.F. Bleiler. Toronto: Dover Publishing/General Publishing Co., 1967.

_____. *The Devil's Elixir*. London: Forgotten Books, 2012.

Hogg, James. *The Private Memoirs and Confessions of a Justified Sinner*. New York: New York Review Books, 2002.

King, Stephen. *Danse Macabre*. New York: Berkley Books, 1983.

Kracauer, Siegfried. *From Caligari to Hitler*. Princeton: Princeton University Press, 1947.

Kunz, Keneva, trans. *The Vinland Sagas: The Saga of the Greenlanders and Eirik the Red's Saga*. London: Penguin Classics, 2008.

Nelson, Ralph, trans. *Popul Vuh: The Great Mythological Book of the Ancient Maya*. Boston: Houghton Mifflin, 1976.

Poe, Edgar Allan. *The Fall of the House of Usher and Other Writings*. London: Penguin Classics, 1986.

Sacks, Oliver. *Hallucinations*. New York: Alfred A. Knopf, 2012.

Shelley, Mary. *Frankenstein*, in *Three Gothic Novels*. London: The Penguin English Library, 1976.

Shelley, Percy. *Prometheus Unbound*. New Haven: Yale University Press, 1968.

Shepard, Leslie, ed. *The Dracula Book of Great Vampire Stories*. Secaucus, NJ: The Citadel Press, 1977.

Silver, Alain, and Elizabeth Ward, eds. *Film Noir: An Encyclopedic Reference to the American Style*. Woodstock, NY: Overlook, 1979.

Spoto, Donald. *The Dark Side of Genius: The Life of Alfred Hitchcock*. New York: Ballantine Books, 1983.

Stanley John. *Creature Features: The Science Fiction, Fantasy and Horror Movie Guide*. New York: Boulevard, 1997.

Stevenson, Robert Louis. *The Strange Case of Dr. Jekyll and Mr. Hyde*. London: Penguin Books, 2002.

Von Gunden, Kenneth, and Stuart H. Stock. *Twenty all Time Great Science Fiction Films*. New York: Arlington House, 1982.

Weldon, Michael. *The Psychotronic Encyclopedia of Film*. New York: Ballantine Books, 1983.

Wilde, Oscar. *The Picture of Dorian Gray*. London: Penguin Modern Classics, 1982.

Index

Abbott, John 39, 40
ABC News 10
Abel, Alfred 137
Academy Award 42, 77, 91, 94, 101, 174, 182, 185, 199, 212
Adams, Brooke 168, 169
Addams, Dawn 104, 106
Adjani, Isabelle 121
The Adventures of Sherlock Holmes 99
Ainley, Lynne 41
Alfred Hitchcock Presents 58
Algol 137
Alias Nick Beal 36
Alice's Adventures in Wonderland 185
Alien 171
aliens 6, 8, 22, 26–28, 135–136, 139, 140, 143–144, 146, 148–162, 168–174, 177–179, 195–198, 204–206, 210, 213
"All You Zombies" 208
Allen, Elizabeth 102
Allen, Joan 77
Allen, Karen 173–174
Allen, Robert 96
Allen, Woody 68
Alraune 84, 86, 137
Alter Ego 3, 6, 9
Alton, John 38
Amanti d'oltretomba see *Nightmare Castle*
The Amazing Spider-Man 196
Among the Living 9, 30, 31–32, 35, 41, 62, 75, 99, 211, 212
Anderson, Judith 43
Andrews, Naveen 74
Androids 8, 26, 28, 135, 136, 155, 163–166, 199, 200–201
Angel Heart 30, 68–71, 85, 211, 212, 213
Ansky, S. 131
Anwar, Gabrielle 177–178
Aokighara Forest 132
Archer, John 97
Ardisson, George 107–108
Armstrong, Anthony 59, 63
Arnold, Jack 144–145, 211
Asher, Jane 111–112
Asylum 35
"August 25, 1983" 68
Autoscopic double 5

Avatar 8, 196–199, 201, 211, 212, 213
The Avenging Conscience 85
Awakenings 5
Ayoade, Richard 21, 80, 81, 122
Ayres, Lew 32

Back to the Future 174–175, 179
Back to the Future Part II 175–177, 180, 204, 208, 213
Back to the Future Part III 177
Bailey, Raymond 58
Baker, Roy Ward 117
Balestero, Christopher 47–48
Balsam, Martin 53, 55
Banionis, Donatas 160–162
Barcroft, Roy 139–140
Bardot, Brigitte 114
Barfly 70
Barrymore, Drew 129–130
Barrymore, John 24, 89–91, 93, 96, 102
Bates, Ralph 116–117
Batman 9, 126
Bava, Mario 106–107, 108, 116, 211, 212
Baxter, John 145, 152
Bay, Michael 192, 194
Beal, Betty 153
Bean, Sean 193–194
Beaumont, Charles 110
Beaumont, Hugh 154, 155
Beckford, William 14
Bennett, Joan 38, 39
Bennett, Spencer Gordon 140
Bergman, Ingmar 112
Bergman, Ingrid 94
Beswick, Martine 116–117
The Big Clock 30, 36–37, 41, 53, 71, 212, 213
Bilocation 1, 7, 10, 186
The Birds 42, 60
Black, Karen 58
The Black Room 9, 95–96, 99, 103, 211, 212
Black Sunday 106–107, 108, 110, 116, 134, 211, 212
Blade Runner 135, 139, 173, 180
The Blair Witch Project 133
Blatty, William Peter 119
Bleiler, E.F. 15, 16
Bloch, Robert 54, 136
Bluebeard 40

The Body Snatcher (film) 96
"The Body Snatcher" (Stevenson story) 177
Body Snatchers (film) 177–179
The Body Snatchers (Finney novel) 6, 27–28, 135, 146
Bogart, Humphrey 30, 68
Bogdanovich, Peter 139
Boileau, Pierre 51
Boles, Jim 41
Bondarchuk, Natalya 161–162
Bonet, Lisa 70, 71
Borges, Jose Luis 60
Bottin, Rob 171
Bowery at Midnight 97–98, 134. 212
The Boys from Brazil 29, 68, 167–168, 211, 213
Bradbury, Ray 145
Branagh, Kenneth 18
Brand New U see *Identicals*
Brannon, Fred C. 140
Brazil 81, 180
Breakston, George 104
The Bride of Frankenstein 96
Bridges, Jeff 173–174, 211
Brimley, Wilford 170, 171
Broderick, Susan 116
Brooke, Hillary 33, 34
Brooks, Leslie 38
Browning, Emily 73
Brynner, Yul 63, 164, 166
Bujold, Genevieve 65–66, 124–126
Buono, Victor 68
Burke & Hare 116, 117
Burrage, Ron 60
Buscemi, Steve 193–194

The Cabinet of Dr. Caligari 16, 84, 86, 87, 158
Cage, Nicolas 76–77, 211
Cagney, James 71, 95
Caiano, Carlo 109, 110
Call Northside 777 48
Cameron, James 179, 196, 199, 211, 212
Campbell, John W., Jr. 26, 27, 135, 170, 171, 173
Capgras Syndrome 6, 28, 147
Carey, Harry 31
Carlson, Richard 143–145
Carmilla 108, 174
Carpenter, John 27, 170–171, 173–174

225

Carroll, Leo G. 52
Carroll, Lewis 185
Carter, Helena Bonham 78
Cartwright, Veronica 168, 169
Casablanca 39
"The Case of Mr. Pelham" 58–59, 68
Castle of Blood 108
The Castle of Otranto 14
Castor and Pollux 12, 13, 73, 78
Catherine the Great 4
Cattrall, Kim 74
CBS-TV 58
CGI 172
Chamisso 88
Chan, Jackie 75
Chander, Raymond 46
The Changeling 72, 122–124
Cheung, Maggie 75
Christine, Katia 113
The Chronicle of the Gray House 86
Church, Thomas Hayden 195
Cicero 9
Clarens, Carlos 90–95
Clark, Mary Higgins 74
The Clone Master 166
Clones 166
Cloning 135, 142, 166, 174, 188–190, 193–194, 202, 209
Collins, Wilkie 14, 39, 40
Collinson, Madeleine 114–116
Collinson, Mary 114–116
Coppola, Francis Ford 78
Corman, Roger 110–112, 211
The Corsican Brothers 75
Cotton, Joseph 44–45
Court, Hazel 110–112
Court TV 9
Craven, James 139–140
Creature from the Black Lagoon 145
Crime in the Streets 147
Criss Cross 32
Cromwell, James 203, 204
Cronenberg, David 8, 66, 104, 124–125, 211
Crowned Heads 68
Cruise, Tom 180, 205–206
The Curse of Frankenstein 101, 142
Cushing, Peter 114, 116
Cyberpunk 183, 185, 188

D-Day on Mars 140
Daimon 18
Daniels, Jeff 203, 204
Danner, Blythe 165, 166
Dano, Paul 203
The Dark Half 9, 29, 128–129, 134, 212, 213
Dark Horse Comics 180
The Dark Mirror 9, 30, 32–33, 35, 62, 75, 211, 212
Dark Passage 34, 68
The Dark Side of Genius 1, 42, 59
Davidovich, Lolita 126
Davis, Bette 60–62, 211
Day, Robert 102

The Day Mars Invaded Earth 153–154, 213
The Day the Earth Stood Still 143, 174
Daybreakers 208
"The Dead Fiddler" 131
Dead Men Walk 97–99, 134, 212
Dead Ringer 9, 30, 60–62, 75
Dead Ringers 8, 66, 124–126, 134
Dearden, Basil 64
De Carlo, Yvonne 68
De Havilland, Olivia 32–33, 211
Dekker, Albert 31–32, 211
Delon, Alain 21, 113–114
De Marney, Terrence 35
De Maupassant, Guy 3, 6, 14, 21, 22
De Mille, Katherine 95
Demon 132
D'entre des morts 51
De Niro, Robert 5, 68, 70, 71
De Palma, Brian 65, 66, 119, 120, 121, 126, 127, 128, 211
Dern, Bruce 58
Detour 97
Devane, William 58
The Devil 16, 19–20, 25, 68, 70, 71, 83, 84, 85, 86, 88, 112, 115, 132, 139, 158, 213
The Devil's Elixir 4, 15–16, 42
De Wolff, Francis 105
Dexter, Maury 154
Dial M for Murder 42, 48
Dick, Philip K. 135
Diffring, Anton 62, 63
Digital Constructs 136, 186
Dissociative Identity Disorder 9, 127
Ditko, Steve 196
Dixey, Phillis 35
DNA 29, 167, 173, 188, 198
Do Androids Dream of Electric Sheep? 135
Dr. Jekyll and Mr. Hyde (1920) 89–91
Dr. Jekyll and Mr. Hyde (1931) 87, 91–93
Dr. Jekyll and Mr. Hyde (1941) 94–95
Dr. Jekyll and Sister Hyde (1971) 116–117, 208, 212
Donovan, King 146, 147
Doppelganger see *Journey to the Far Side of the Sun*
Doppelganger: The Evil Within 129–130, 212
"The Doppelgangers" (Hoffmann story) 16, 42
Dormer, Natalie 132–133
Dostoyevsky, Fyodor 11, 16, 21, 29, 39, 42, 59, 60, 80, 81, 82, 122, 211
The Double (film) 30, 80–81, 212
The Double (novel) 21, 39, 42, 59, 60, 80, 82, 122
The Double Man 30, 62, 168, 212
Double Take 60
Double Vision 74–75
Douglas, Melvyn 212, 122, 123, 124
Dracula (1931 film) 32, 91, 97, 98, 99, 104
Drake, Charles 148

Dream States 1, 7, 8, 10, 22, 73, 75, 86, 88, 89, 136, 149, 151, 186, 193, 198, 199
Dual Alibi 35, 160, 212
Du Maurier, Daphne 42, 43
Dumas, Alexandre 75
Dune 199
Dunst, Kirsten 196
Durning, Charles 120
Duvall, Robert 188, 189
Dybbuk 130, 131, 132
The Dybbuk 131
Dyneley, Peter 103, 104

Easy Rider 113
Edgerton, Joel 172
Eisenberg, Jesse 21, 80–81
Eisner, Lotte 84, 86
Eklund, Britt 63
Emery, John 39
Enemy 30, 81, 212
The Epic of Gilgamesh 11–12, 18
E.T.—The Extraterrestrial 173, 174
Evil Twins 8, 71
Ewell, Tom 58–59
Ewers, Hanns Heinz 16, 84, 85, 86
Ex Machina 141
Existenz 185
The Exorcist 119, 132
Expressionism 16, 30, 32, 33, 39, 42, 50, 71, 84, 86, 94, 113, 119, 158, 212, 213
Eyes Without a Face 77

Face/Off 30, 34, 76–77, 211
Falling Angel 70
Family Plot 30, 57–58, 59, 212
Farmer, Frances 31
Farrow, John 36, 37
Faust 86, 87
Fedora 29, 30, 41, 66–68, 152, 211, 212
Ferara, Abel 177
Ferrer, Jose 67
Fetch 3, 112
Fight Club (film) 9, 30, 78–79, 81, 119, 212
Fight Club (novel) 79
film noir 30, 31, 32, 33, 39, 40, 44, 46, 48, 61, 66, 68, 71, 74, 97
Finch, John 57
Fincher, David 78, 79, 81, 119
Finney, Jack 6, 27, 28, 135, 146, 147, 177, 178, 179, 211
Fishburne, Laurence 183, 186 97
Fisher, Terrence 106, 142
Fleming, Victor 94, 99
Floating Platform One Does Not Reply 137
The Fly 104
Fonda, Henry 48–49, 211
Fonda, Jane 112–113, 114
Fonda, Peter 112–113, 165–166
Fontaine, Joan 42–44
Forbes, Bryan 163
Forbidden Planet 22, 147–150, 162, 212
Ford, Garrett 32

Index

The Forest 132–133
Foster, Barry 56, 57
The Four Sided Triangle 142–143
Fowler, Gene, Jr. 132
Fox, Michael J. 174–177
Fox, Wallace 97
Francis, Anne 148, 150, 151
Franco, James 196
Franju, George 77
Frankenheimer, John 77, 155, 157, 158, 211
Frankenstein (1931 film) 32, 91, 97, 99, 104, 139
Frankenstein (novel) 5, 17–18, 22, 23, 27, 32, 110
Franz, Eduard 38
Freeman, Morgan 205, 206
Frenzy 9, 30, 37, 42, 56–57, 58, 59, 212
Freud, Sigmund 4, 24, 211
Freund, Karl 87, 91
Frolich, Gustav 137
From Caligari to Hitler 86
Frye, Dwight 97, 99
Futureworld 155, 164–166, 195, 201, 212, 213

Gadon, Sarah 82
Galeen, Henrik 86
Garland, Judy 71
Gargan, William 33
Garrani, Ivo 106
Gaslight 40, 94, 101
Gates, Larry 146
Gavin, John 53–56
Geaney, Niamh 10
Genesis 12
The Ghost in the Shell 185
Gibson, William 185
Gigandet, Cam 131
Gilliam, Terry 81, 180, 182, 211
Gilligan's Island 145
The Girl Can't Help It 59
Glatt, John 8, 81
Goethe, Johan Wolfgang von 4–5, 85
Gogol, Nikolai 107, 211
Goldblum, Jeff 168, 169
The Golem 86
Gone with the Wind 94
Good, Meagan 131
Goodbye Piccadilly, Farewell Leicester Square 57
Goodfellas 74
Gordon Films 101
Gordon-Levitt, Joseph 202, 204
gothic novel 14, 15, 17, 42, 118
Gottowt, John 85
Gough, Michael 167, 168
Goyer, David S. 131, 132, 133
Granach, Alexander 88
Granger, Farley 46–47
Greenstreet, Sydney 39–40
Griffith, D.W. 85
Grimaldi, Hugo 155
Grimonprez, Johan 60
Gugino, Carla 191
Guizzardi, Luise 10

Guttenberg, Steve 167
Gyllenhaal, Jake 81–82

Hagen, Uta 118, 119, 167, 168
Haller, David 110, 112
Haller, Ernest 61
Hallucinations 5
Hammer Films 35, 101, 104, 195, 106, 107, 108, 114, 115, 116, 117, 141, 142, 143
Han, Gina 9
Han, Sunny 9
The Hands of Orlac 86, 137
Harbou, Thea von 138, 139
Hard Copy 9
Hardy, Tom 73–74, 136
Hark, Tsui 75
Harris, Barbara 57
Has, Wojciech Jerzy 20
Hatfield, Hurd 26, 99–101
The Haunted Strangler 9, 101–103, 134, 211, 212
The Haunting 123
Hawke, Ethan 207–208
Hawks, Howard 27, 170
Hays Office 98
Hayward, Susan 31, 32
He Walked by Night 39
Heautoscopic Double 5–6
Heinlein, Robert 201, 208
Heisler, Stuart 31, 32, 212
Helm, Brigitte 137–138
Helmore, Tom 48
Hendry, Ian 158, 159
Henreid, Paul 38–39, 60, 61
Herbert, Frank 199
Hermann, Bernard 51, 52, 120
High Sierra 30
Highsmith, Patricia 4, 42, 46, 211
Hill, Arthur 165
Hitchcock, Alfred 1, 9, 30, 37, 42–60, 62, 63, 64, 65, 66, 77, 79, 96, 114, 119, 120, 121, 122, 127, 169, 211, 212
Hitler, Adolf 29, 79, 86, 167–168
Hjortsberg, William 70
Hobart, Rose 91
Hobbes, Halliwell 91
Hogg, James 18–20, 23
Holden, William 29, 66–67
Hollow Triumph 37–39, 60, 63
Holloway, Stanley 141
Homer 12
Homunculus 137
Hong, James 158
"Hop Frog" 110
Hopkins, Miriam 91, 93
"The Horla" 6, 21–22
Horror of Dracula 101, 104, 142
Hough, John 116
Hounsou, Djimon 193
House of Frankenstein 99
Hudson, Rock 156–158
The Human Duplicators 154–155
Hume, Cyril 151
Hutton, Timothy 128–129
Hyams, Peter 180
Hylton, Jane 104

Hypnogogoc and Hypnopompic Hallucinations 7

I Married a Communist 152
I Married a Monster from Outer Space 68, 151–153, 212, 213
I Wake Up Screaming 30
Identicals 209–210
Idioglossia 8
The Incredible Shrinking Man 145
The Incredible Two-Headed Transplant 104
Industrial Light & Magic 177
Inferno 5
Invaders from Mars 143
The Invasion 28, 179
Invasion of the Body Snatchers (1956) 28, 146–147, 152, 154, 189, 211, 212, 213
Invasion of the Body Snatchers (1978) 168–170
Invasion of the Body Snatchers (novel) see *The Body Snatchers*
Iron Man 2 70
Irons, Jeremy 124–126, 211
The Island 192–195
Italian Gothic 107, 108, 110
It Came from Outer Space 143–146, 152, 211, 213

Jack the Ripper 42, 116, 117
Der Januskopf 87, 91
Jens, Salome 156
La Jetée 180, 182
Johansson, Scarlet 193–194
Johnny Mnemonic 185
Johnson, Nunnally 33
Johnson, Rian 204
Johnson, Rita 36
Johnson, Russell 143, 145
Jones, Carolyn 146, 147
Jones, Duncan 202
Jones, Freddie 64
Journey to the Far Side of the Sun 158–160

Kafka, Franz 81
Karloff, Boris 95–96, 101–103, 211
Karnstein Trilogy 109, 114
Katzman, Sam 97
Kaufman, Philip 28, 168, 169
Keller, Marthe 67
Kellerman, Sally 130
Kemp, Gary 71–72
Kemp, Martin 71–72
Kent, Jean 102
Kidder, Margot 119–121
Kiel, Richard 154–155
The Killing 154
King, Stephen 29, 128, 211
Kinney, Taylor 132
Kinney, Terry 179
Kiss of Death 48
Klein-Rogge, Rudolf 137
Knef, Hildegaard 67
Knights, Robert 74
Kodjoe, Boris 200
Korine, Avi 81

Index

Kortner, Fritz 87–88
Kosinski, Joseph 206
Kracauer, Sigfried 86
Krassner, Milton 32
Krauss, Werner 86
Kray, Reggie 8, 36, 71–74
Kray, Ronnie 8, 36, 71–74
The Krays 8, 71–74, 76, 122, 212
Kurylenko, Olga 205, 206

L.A. Confidential 74
Lack, Stephen 125
The Lady Vanishes 42
Lam, Ringo 75
Lancaster, Bill 171
Lang, Fritz 39, 42, 88, 91, 137, 168, 211, 212
Lang, Stephen 198
Lansbury, Angela 26, 99–100, 101
"The Last Demon" 131
Laurent, Melanie 81
Lawford, Peter 61, 100
The Lawnmower Man 185
Lee, Christopher 74, 105, 106
Lee, Rowland V. 96
Lee, Stan 196
Le Fanu, Sheridan 108, 109, 114
The Legacy of a Spy 63
Legend 8, 71, 73–74, 136, 212
Lehman, Ernest 52, 58
Leigh, Janet 53, 55
Leigh-Hunt, Barbara 56
Lem, Stanislaw 160
Leni, Paul 91
Levin, Ira 28, 119, 162, 167, 168, 211
Lewin, Albert 26, 99, 101
Lewis, Matthew Gregory 14, 15
Lewis, Sheldon 91
Lincoln, Abraham 4
Lindo, Delroy 190
Line, Helga 109
The Lineup 147
Linnaeus, Carl 5
Lithgow, John 65, 125–128
Livy 12
Lloyd, Christopher 174, 177
Le locataire chimerique 122
The Lodger 42
Lom, Herbert 35, 68, 158, 160
The Long Hair of Death 107–108, 110, 134, 212
Looper 202–204, 208, 213
Loos, Theodore 87
Lord, Mindret 34
Louise, Tina 163
LSD 157
Lucas, George 139, 185
Lucian 12
Lucid Dreaming 186
Lugosi, Bela 87, 95, 96–98
I lunghi capelli della morte see *The Long Hair of Death*
Lust for a Vampire 109
Lynch, Ken 152

Macready, George 154, 155
The Mad Genius 96
Madigan, Amy 128

The Magnificent Seven 164
Maguire, Tobey 195–196
Maharis, George 130
Mainwaring, Daniel 147
Malden, Karl 61
The Maltese Falcon 30, 40, 68
The Man from U.N.C.L.E. 62
The Man Who Haunted Himself 30, 59, 63–65, 81, 212
The Man Who Knew Too Much 42, 48
The Man Who Mistook His Wife for a Hat 5
Man in the Dark 34
The Man with Bogart's Face 68
The Man with My Face 34, 41–42, 63, 212
The Manchurian Candidate 155
Mankowitz, Wolf 105
Mann, Anthony 33, 38
Mansfield, Martha 89
The Manster 103–104, 130, 134, 212
Marathon Man 168
March, Fredric 24, 87m 91–94, 95, 211, 212
Marcus Twins 8, 124–125
Margheriti, Antonio 107, 108
Marker, Chris 180
Marsh, Marian 95, 96
Marshall, Brenda 33, 34
Mary Shelley's Frankenstein 18
M.A.S.H. 130
La maschera del demonio (see *Black Sunday*)
Maslin, Janet 67
Mason, James 51, 52, 167, 168
The Masque of the Red Death (film) 110–112
"The Masque of the Red Death" (Poe story) 110, 112
Massie, Paul 104–106
Matheson, Richard 136
Mathews, Carole 41
The Matrix 8, 183–186
The Matrix Reloaded 186–187
Matrix Revolutions 187–188
Maugham, Somerset 95
Maxfield, Harry 63
Mayer, Louis B. 91
Mazurki, Mike 68
McCarthy, Kevin 146–147, 169
McGhee, Brownie 70
McGregor, Ewan 193–194
McKay, Wanda 97, 98
McReady, George 36
Medak, Peter 71, 72, 122, 123
Memoirs of a Sinner 20
Mengele, Josef 29, 167–168
Metempsychosis 113
Metropolis 88, 137–139, 141, 142, 155, 168, 201, 211, 212, 213
"Metzengenstein" (film) 112–113
"Metzengenstein" (Poe story) 112–113
MGM Studios 24, 26, 51, 94, 95, 99
Migraine 5, 6
Miles, Vera 48, 49, 53–55
Milland, Ray 36–37

Mims, William 154
Ministry of Fear 35
mirror images 3, 4, 5, 9, 14, 16, 20, 25, 33, 39, 51, 53, 56, 65, 84, 85, 86, 88, 89, 92, 96, 101,106, 131, 132, 159
Mitchell, Radha 199
Mitchell, Thomas 32
The Monk 14, 15
Monogram Studios 96, 97
Montagne, Edward 41
Moon 201–202, 206
Moore, Dennis 139, 140
Moore, Joel David 198
Moore, Mary 139, 140
Moore, Roger 63–65, 71
Moss, Carrie-Anne 183, 186
Mostow, Jonathan 200
Muldaur, Diana 118, 119
Muller, Paul 109–110
Mulligan, Robert 29, 118, 119
multiple personality disorder 4, 9, 10, 15, 24, 79, 103, 121, 126, 127, 130, 134
The Mummy's Hand 99
Murnau, F.W. 42, 87, 88, 91
Murray, Stephen 142, 143
My Fair Lady 141
Myers, Fredric W. H. 7
The Mysteries of Udolpho 14
Mystery Science Theater 155

Nader, George 154, 155
Nakamura, Tetsu 103
Naldi, Nita 89
Narcejac, Thomas 51
The Narrow Margin 154
NASA 153, 158, 202
Nazis 29, 79, 84, 87, 91, 131, 167, 168
Neal, Tom 97–98
Neil, Hildegard 64
Neill, Roy William 96
Nelson, Barry 41
Nelson, Ralph 14
Nero, Franco 68
Nesher, Avi 130
Neuromancer 185
"A New Year's Eve Adventure" 16, 20, 84
Newbern, George 129
Newfield, Sam 99
Nichols, Barbara 154, 155
Nieboer, Lachlan 209
Nielsen, Leslie 147–151
Night and the City 35
Night Has a Thousand Eyes 36
Night of the Living Dead 128
Nightmare Alley 35
Nightmare Castle 109–110, 111, 134, 212
Nimoy, Leonard 168, 169
No Way Out 37
Nolan, Lloyd 68
Noone, Nora-Jane 209
Norton, Edward 78–80
Nosferatu 86, 87, 88
Novak, Kim 49–50
The Nutcracker 14
"Nutcracker and the King of Mice" 14

Oakland, Simon 53
Oblivion 204–206, 212, 213
Obsession 30, 65–68, 120, 125, 211, 212
Offenbach, Jacques 14
Oldman, Gary 131, 132
Olivier, Laurence 29, 42–44, 167, 168, 211
The One 190–192
O'Neal, Patrick 163
Oshii, Mamoru 185
O'Sullivan, Maureen 36
The Other (film) 9, 68, 118–119, 120, 134, 163, 167, 212
The Other (novel) 29, 118, 119, 152
La Otra 61
out of body experiences 1, 6, 10, 186
Outland 180
Ozawa, Yukioshi 132

Palahniuk, Chuck 79
Palmer, Renzo 113
Pantoliano, Joe 184
Paramount Studios 91, 93, 94
Parker, Alan 68, 69, 70
Parker, Eleanor 39–40
Parrish, Robert 160
Parts—The Clonus Horror 166, 194
Patrick, Nigel 141
Patton 63
The Patty Duke Show 40
Payton, Barbara 142–143
Pearl Harbor 194
Peck, Gregory 29, 167–168
Peebles, David 180
Peeping Tom 119, 127
The Perfect Woman 141, 213
Perkins, Anthony 53–56
Phantasms of the Living 7
Phantom Lady 32
The Phantom of the Opera 35
Phillips, Jean 31
Phillips, Michelle 68
The Picture of Dorian Gray (film) 99–101, 134, 212
The Picture of Dorian Gray (novel) 24–26, 68, 89, 99, 113
Pidgeon, Walter 148–151
Pike, Rosamund 200
Pindar 12
Pitt, Brad 78–79, 181–182
Planet of the Apes 63
Play It Again Sam 68
Plummer, Christopher 181
Plutarch 12
Podmore, Frank 7
Poe, Edgar Allan 3, 11, 14, 20, 42, 110
Polanski, Roman 122–122, 211
Popul Vuh 8, 13–14
Porfirio, Robert 32
The Possession 132
Powell, Michael 127
PRC Studios 96, 97
Predestination 206–208
Preminger, Otto 91
Prentiss, Paula 163, 164
Presley, Elvis 129
Price, Vincent 22, 110–112

The Private Memoirs and Confessions of a Justified Sinner 18–19, 85
Prometheus Unbound 5
Psycho 30, 42, 44, 48, 51, 53–56, 57, 59, 64, 96, 120, 122, 127, 211, 212
Pummell, Simon 209–210
The Purple Monster Strikes 139–140, 212, 213

Quatermass II 142
The Quatermass Xperiment 142

Radcliffe, Anne 14
Raft, George 68, 71
Raimi, Sam 195, 196
Raising Cain 126–128, 134
Rampling, Charlotte 70
Randolph, John 155, 158
Rasp, Fritz 88
Raw Deal 38
Rayment, Adrian 186, 187
Rayment, Neil 186, 187
Rear Window 42, 120
Rebecca (film) 30, 42–44, 58, 78, 79, 211, 212
Rebecca (novel) 42
Reed, Donna 100
Reeves, Keanu 180, 183–188
Reinhardt, Max 84
REM Sleep 8
Remar, James 131
Repulsion 121
Reuben, Gloria 179
Revill, Clive 63
Rhames, Ving 200
Richardson, John 106
Richter, Paul 14
Riseborough, Andrea 205, 206
Ritter, John 119
The Road Warrior 173
Robby the Robot 148, 149, 151
Robertson, Cliff 65–66, 195
Robinson, Arthur 87, 88, 213
Roc, Patricia 141
The Rock 194
Rockwell, Sam 201–202
Roeg, Nicholas 107, 110, 112
Roman, Ruth 46
Romero, George 29, 128, 129
Romulus and Remus 8, 12–13
Rooker, Michael 128, 190
Rosemary's Baby 28, 119, 121, 162, 163
Ross, Katherine 29, 162–164
Rossellini, Isabella 82
Rourke, Mickey 68–71, 211
Rush, Barbara 143, 145
Russell, Kurt 170, 171
Rye, Stellan 85

Saboteur 52
Sacchi, Robert 68
Sacks, Oliver 5–6
The Saga of Eirik the Red 3
The Saint 64
Saldana, Zoe 198
Salt, Jennifer 120
Sanders, George 26, 99, 101

"The Sandman" 16
Sara, Mia 170
Sawyer, Joe 143
The Scar see *Hollow Triumph*
Scarlet Street 39
Schaffner, Franklin J. 63, 168
Schatten see *Warning Shadows*
Schauerfilme 84, 87, 89
Schlemihl, Peter 88
Schrader, Paul 66
Schwarzenegger, Arnold 180, 188–190
Scott, George C. 122–124
Scott, Ridley 107, 139, 171
Seconds 77, 155–158, 209, 211, 213
Sekely, Steve 38
Selznick, David O. 43
Seven Days in May 155
The Seven Year Itch 59
The Seventh Seal 112
Sex and the City 74
Shadow of a Doubt 9, 30, 42–46, 47, 59, 211, 212
Shaffer, Anthony 57
Shakespeare, William 24, 151
Shamanism 1, 7, 186, 198, 199, 211
The Shanghai Gesture 30
Shawn, Wallace 80
Shelley, Mary 11, 17, 18, 23, 29, 32
Shelley, Percy Bysshe 5
Shue, Elisabeth 175
Siebenkas 14
Siegel, Don 28, 147, 169, 211, 212
"Signor Formica" 16
Silver, Ron 179, 180
Sinatra, Frank 71
Singer, Isaac Bashevis 131
Siodmak, Robert 32–33, 91, 211
Sisters 9, 66, 119–121, 126, 134, 211, 212
The Sixth Day 188–190
Sleuth 57
Smith, Alexis 39–40
Smith, Charles Martin 173, 174
Snook, Sarah 207–208
Socrates 18
Solaris (1972) 160–162, 211, 212, 213
The Sorceror's Apprentice 84
Soto No Satsujinki (see *The Manster*)
Spaceways 143
Spacey, Kevin 201
Spellbound 42
Spider-Man 195
Spider-Man 2 195
Spider-Man 3 195–196, 213
Spierig, Michael 208
Spierig, Peter 208
Spiner, Brent 136
Spirits of the Dead 21, 112
Spoto, Donald 1, 42, 46, 47, 59
Spottiswoode, Roger 189
Starman 173–174, 211, 213
Star Trek (original TV Series) 136
Star Trek Nemesis 136
Star Trek: The Motion Picture 174
Stat Trek: The Next Generation 136
Star Wars 139, 185

Statham, Jason 190
Steele, Barbara 106–111, 211
Stefano, Joseph 54
The Stepford Wives 28, 162–164, 167, 201, 212, 213
Sternhagen, Francis 67, 127
Stevens, Warren 143
Stevenson, Robert Louis 3, 9, 11, 16, 18, 22–24, 29, 32, 42, 44, 87, 89, 90–94, 104, 105, 106, 117, 118, 211
Stewart, James 48–51
Stewart, Patrick 136
Stoker, Bram 14
A Stolen Life 61
Stowe, Madeleine 181, 182
The Strange Case of Dr. Jekyll and Mr. Hyde 9, 22, 42, 87, 117
The Strange Case of Mr. Pelham 59, 63
Strange Days 185
Strange Impersonation 30, 33–34, 63, 212
Strangers on a Train (film) 9, 30, 42, 46–47, 57, 59, 211, 212
Strangers on a Train (novel) 4, 47
Strindberg, August 5
The Student of Prague (1913) 16, 56, 71, 84–86, 88, 96, 99, 101, 129, 132, 133, 211, 212, 213
The Student of Prague (1926) 86
The Student of Prague (1935) 86–87, 88
Sullivan, Thomas Russell 89
Sunset Boulevard 66, 67, 74
superheroes 136, 185, 187, 195, 196
Superman 9, 36, 126
Surrogates 8, 199–201, 213
The Surrogates 200
Suspicion 42
Sutherland, Donald 168–169
Svengali 96
Sybil 127
syphilis 6, 21, 22

T-Men 38
Talbot, Gloria 151–152
Talbot, Lyle 34
Tales of Hoffmann 14
Tales of Power 7
Tartovsky, Andrei 160, 161, 162, 211, 212
Taylor, Kent 153, 154
Taylor, Samuel W. 41, 51
Tchaikovsky 14
Telepathy 8, 71, 166
The Tempest 151
The Tenant 9, 121–122, 123, 134, 211
Terminator 2 179, 180, 189, 199
The Thing (1982) 27, 170–171, 173
The Thing (2011) 27, 171–173
The Thing (from Another World) 27, 143, 170, 171
The Thing with Two Heads 104
Thinnes, Roy 158–160
The 13th Floor 185
The 39 Steps 42, 52
Thomas, Damien 115, 116
Tilly, Meg 177, 178

The Time Machine 135
Time Travel 135, 174–177, 179, 180, 181, 182, 202, 204, 207, 208, 210, 213
Timecop 179–180, 191, 204, 208, 213
Titanic 77
To Catch a Thief 48
"Toby Dammit" 112
Topor, Roland 122
Total Recall 189
Tower of London 96
Tracy, Spencer 24, 94–95
Transformers 194
Travers, Alfred 35
Travolta, John 76–77
The Trial 81
Tron 173
Tryon, Sir George 7
Tryon, Tom 29, 67, 68, 118, 119, 151–152
Turing Test 141
Turner, Lana 94
12 Monkeys 180–183, 211, 213
The Twilight Zone 42, 59
Twin Dragons 75–76
twins 8–9, 10
Twins of Evil 9, 99, 107, 114–116, 134, 212
The Two Faces of Dr. Jekyll 104–106, 117
2001: A Space Odyssey 160

Udvarnoky, Chris 118–119
Udvarnoky, Martin 118–119
UFA Studios 42, 138
Uhls, Jim 79
Ulmer, Edward G. 40, 91, 97
The Unborn 131–132, 134, 213
"The Uncanny" (Freud) 4
Universal Studios 32, 60, 91. 95, 96, 99, 101, 104, 107, 171, 180

Vadim, Roger 112, 113, 114
Vampire 84
The Vampire Lovers 109
Van Damme, Jean-Claude 179–180
Van Devere, Trish 123, 124
Van Eyssen, John 142, 143
Van Heijningen, Matthijis 172
Vardogers 3
Vathek 14
Veidt, Conrad 86–87
Venditi, Robert 200
The Verdict 147
Vertigo 30, 48–51, 53, 56, 59, 64, 65, 66, 96, 114, 120, 169, 211, 212
Videodrome 104
The Vij 107
Virtuosity 185
Vivet, Louis 24

Wachowski, Andy 183, 185
Wachowski, Larry 183, 185
Wagner, Fritz Arno 88
Walbrook, Anton 87
Walker, Robert 46–47
Walpole, Horace 14
Wangenheim, Gustav von 88
Walsh, Raoul 71

Warner, H.B. 34
Warner Bros. Studios 39, 178
Warning Shadows 87–88, 96, 134, 212, 213
Wasikowska, Mia 80
Waxworks 86
Weaver, Sigourney 198
Weaving, Hugo 183, 184
Wegener, Paul 84–85
Welles, Orson 81, 112
Wells, H.G. 135
Westmore, Wally 93
Weyher, Ruth 88
Whatever Happened to Baby Jane? 60
Wheeler, Lyle 43
White Heat 71
Whitelaw, Billie 71, 72
Whitman, Ernest 31
Whittaker, Forest 177–178
Who Goes There? 26–27, 28, 135, 170
Wilcox, Fred MacLeod 151, 212
Wilde, Oscar 3, 11, 24, 68, 89, 99
Wilder, Billy 29, 41, 66, 74, 211
Wilson, Thomas F. 174, 175
"William Wilson" (film) 113–114
"William Wilson" (Poe Story) 20–21, 25, 42, 84, 101, 114
Williams, Robin 5
Willis, Bruce 180–182, 199–201, 202–204
Windsor, Marie 153, 154
Winstead, Mary Elizabeth 172
Winston, Stan 171
Winters, Shelley 121, 122
Wirth, Billy 177
Wise, Robert 96, 123
The Wizard of Oz 94
Woman in the Window 39
The Woman in White 39–41
Woo, John 76, 211
World War I 86, 136
World War II 35, 68, 79, 101
Worthington, Sam 197–199
Wraith 3
The Wrestler 70
Wright, Theresa 45–46
The Wrong Man 9, 30, 37, 47–49, 59, 211, 212
Wynter, Dana 146–147
Wynter, Sarah 188, 190

Xenomorphs 27, 144, 145, 170, 171
Ximenez, Fr. Francisco 13

Y2K Bug 185
York, Michael 67
Young, Gig 39–40
Yurei: The Japanese Ghost 132
Yustman, Odette 131–132

Zada, Jason 113
Zalewska, Halina 107, 108
Zemeckis, Robert 174, 177
Zimmern, Terri 103, 104
Zsigmond, Vilmos 66
Zucco, George 97–99

www.ingramcontent.com/pod-product-compliance
Lightning Source LLC
Chambersburg PA
CBHW081553300426
44116CB00015B/2866